The Anglo-American Establishment

The
Anglo-American
Establishment

FROM RHODES TO CLIVEDEN

Carroll Quigley

Books In Focus

Manufactured in the United States of America

Books in Focus, Inc.
P.O. Box 3481
Grand Central Station
New York, N.Y. 10163

Library of Congress Cataloging in Publication Data

Quigley, Carroll.
    The Anglo-American establishment.

    Includes index.
    1. Great Britain—Foreign relations—20th century.
2. Commonwealth of Nations.
3. Rhodes, Cecil John, 1853-1902.
4. Milner, Alfred Milner, Viscount, 1854-1925.
5. Secret societies—England. I. Title.
DA566.7.Q5   325'.32'06041   80-70620
ISBN 0-916728-50-1   AACR2

Contents

Preface

THE RHODES SCHOLARSHIPS, established by the terms of Cecil Rhodes's seventh will, are known to everyone. What is not so widely known is that Rhodes in five previous wills left his fortune to form a secret society, which was to devote itself to the preservation and expansion of the British Empire. And what does not seem to be known to anyone is that this secret society was created by Rhodes and his principal trustee, Lord Milner, and continues to exist to this day. To be sure, this secret society is not a childish thing like the Ku Klux Klan, and it does not have any secret robes, secret handclasps, or secret passwords. It does not need any of these, since its members know each other intimately. It probably has no oaths of secrecy nor any formal procedure of initiation. It does, however, exist and holds secret meetings, over which the senior member present presides. At various times since 1891, these meetings have been presided over by Rhodes, Lord Milner, Lord Selborne, Sir Patrick Duncan, Field Marshal Jan Smuts, Lord Lothian, and Lord Brand. They have been held in all the British Dominions, starting in South Africa about 1903; in various places in London, chiefly 175 Piccadilly; at various colleges at Oxford, chiefly All Souls; and at many English country houses such as Tring Park, Blickling Hall, Cliveden, and others.

This society has been known at various times as Milner's Kindergarten, as the Round Table Group, as the Rhodes crowd, as *The Times* crowd, as the All Souls group, and as the Cliveden set. All of these terms are unsatisfactory, for one reason or another, and I have chosen to call it the Milner Group. Those persons who have used the other terms, or heard them used, have not generally been aware that all these various terms referred to the same Group.

It is not easy for an outsider to write the history of a secret group of this kind, but, since no insider is going to do it, an outsider must attempt it. It should be done, for this Group is, as I shall show, one of the most important historical facts of the twentieth century. Indeed, the

Group is of such significance that evidence of its existence is not hard to find, if one knows where to look. This evidence I have sought to point out without overly burdening this volume with footnotes and bibliographical references. While such evidences of scholarship are kept at a minimum, I believe I have given the source of every fact which I mention. Some of these facts came to me from sources which I am not permitted to name, and I have mentioned them only where I can produce documentary evidence available to everyone. Nevertheless, it would have been very difficult to write this book if I had not received a certain amount of assistance of a personal nature from persons close to the Group. For obvious reasons, I cannot reveal the names of such persons, so I have not made reference to any information derived from them unless it was information readily available from other sources.

Naturally, it is not possible for an outsider to write about a secret group without falling into errors. There are undoubtedly errors in what follows. I have tried to keep these at a minimum by keeping the interpretation at a minimum and allowing the facts to speak for themselves. This will serve as an excuse for the somewhat excessive use of quotations. I feel that there is no doubt at all about my general interpretation. I also feel that there are few misstatements of fact, except in one most difficult matter. This difficulty arises from the problem of knowing just who is and who is not a member of the Group. Since membership may not be a formal matter but based rather on frequent social association, and since the frequency of such association varies from time to time and from person to person, it is not always easy to say who is in the Group and who is not. I have tried to solve this difficulty by dividing the Group into two concentric circles: an inner core of intimate associates, who unquestionably knew that they were members of a group devoted to a common purpose; and an outer circle of a larger number, on whom the inner circle acted by personal persuasion, patronage distribution, and social pressure. It is probable that most members of the outer circle were not conscious that they were being used by a secret society. More likely they knew it, but, English fashion, felt it discreet to ask no questions. The ability of Englishmen of this class and background to leave the obvious unstated, except perhaps in obituaries, is puzzling and sometimes irritating to an outsider. In general, I have undoubtedly made mistakes in my lists of members, but the mistakes, such as they are, are to be found rather in my attribution of any particular person to the outer circle instead of the inner core, rather than in my connecting him to the Group at all. In general, I have attributed no one to the inner core for whom I do not have evidence, convincing to me, that he attended the secret meetings of the Group. As a result, several persons whom I place in the outer circle, such as Lord Halifax, should probably be placed in the inner core.

I should say a few words about my general attitude toward this subject. I approached the subject as a historian. This attitude I have kept. I have tried to describe or to analyze, not to praise or to condemn. I hope that in the book itself this attitude is maintained. Of course I have an attitude, and it would be only fair to state it here. In general, I agree with the goals and aims of the Milner Group. I feel that the British way of life and the British Commonwealth of Nations are among the great achievements of all history. I feel that the destruction of either of them would be a terrible disaster to mankind. I feel that the withdrawal of Ireland, of Burma, of India, or of Palestine from the Commonwealth is regrettable and attributable to the fact that the persons in control of these areas failed to absorb the British way of life while they were parts of the Commonwealth. I suppose, in the long view, my attitude would not be far different from that of the members of the Milner Group. But, agreeing with the Group on goals, I cannot agree with them on methods. To be sure, I realize that some of their methods were based on nothing but good intentions and high ideals — higher ideals than mine, perhaps. But their lack of perspective in critical moments, their failure to use intelligence and common sense, their tendency to fall back on standardized social reactions and verbal cliches in a crisis, their tendency to place power and influence into hands chosen by friendship rather than merit, their oblivion to the consequences of their actions, their ignorance of the point of view of persons in other countries or of persons in other classes in their own country — these things, it seems to me, have brought many of the things which they and I hold dear close to disaster. In this Group were persons like Esher, Grey, Milner, Hankey, and Zimmern, who must command the admiration and affection of all who know of them. On the other hand, in this Group were persons whose lives have been a disaster to our way of life. Unfortunately, in the long run, both in the Group and in the world, the influence of the latter kind has been stronger than the influence of the former.

This has been my personal attitude. Little of it, I hope, has penetrated to the pages which follow. I have been told that the story I relate here would be better left untold, since it would provide ammunition for the enemies of what I admire. I do not share this view. The last thing I should wish is that anything I write could be used by the Anglophobes and isolationists of the *Chicago Tribune*. But I feel that the truth has a right to be told, and, once told, can be an injury to no men of good will. Only by a knowledge of the errors of the past is it possible to correct the tactics of the future.

1949   C.Q.

The Anglo-American Establishment

1

Introduction

ONE WINTRY AFTERNOON in February 1891, three men were engaged in earnest conversation in London. From that conversation were to flow consequences of the greatest importance to the British Empire and to the world as a whole. For these men were organizing a secret society that was, for more than fifty years, to be one of the most important forces in the formulation and execution of British imperial and foreign policy.

The three men who were thus engaged were already well known in England. The leader was Cecil Rhodes, fabulously wealthy empire-builder and the most important person in South Africa. The second was William T. Stead, the most famous, and probably also the most sensational, journalist of the day. The third was Reginald Baliol Brett, later known as Lord Esher, friend and confidant of Queen Victoria, and later to be the most influential adviser of King Edward VII and King George V.

The details of this important conversation will be examined later. At present we need only point out that the three drew up a plan of organization for their secret society and a list of original members. The plan of organization provided for an inner circle, to be known as "The Society of the Elect," and an outer circle, to be known as "The Association of Helpers." Within The Society of the Elect, the real power was to be exercised by the leader, and a "Junta of Three." The leader was to be Rhodes, and the Junta was to be Stead, Brett, and Alfred Milner. In accordance with this decision, Milner was added to the society by Stead shortly after the meeting we have described.[1]

The creation of this secret society was not a matter of a moment. As we shall see, Rhodes had been planning for this event for more than seventeen years. Stead had been introduced to the plan on 4 April 1889, and Brett had been told of it on 3 February 1890. Nor was the society thus founded an ephemeral thing, for, in modified form, it exists to this day. From 1891 to 1902, it was known to only a score of persons. During this period, Rhodes was leader, and Stead was the most influential member. From 1902 to 1925, Milner was leader, while Philip Kerr (Lord Lothian) and Lionel Curtis were probably the most important members. From 1925 to 1940, Kerr was leader, and since his death in 1940 this role has probably been played by Robert Henry Brand (now Lord Brand).

During this period of almost sixty years, this society has been called by various names. During the first decade or so it was called "the secret society of Cecil Rhodes" or "the dream of Cecil Rhodes." In the second and third decades of its existence it was known as "Milner's Kindergarten" (1901-1910) and as "the Round Table Group" (1910-1920). Since 1920 it has been called by various names, depending on which phase of its activities was being examined. It has been called "*The Times* crowd," "the Rhodes crowd," the "Chatham House crowd," the "All Souls group," and the "Cliveden set." All of these terms were more or less inadequate, because they focused attention on only part of the society or on only one of its activities. The Milner Kindergarten and the Round Table Group, for example, were two different names for The Association of Helpers and were thus only part of the society, since the real center of the organization, The Society of the Elect, continued to exist and recruited new members from the outer circle as seemed necessary. Since 1920, this Group has been increasingly dominated by the associates of Viscount Astor. In the 1930s, the misnamed "Cliveden set" was close to the center of the society, but it would be entirely unfair to believe that the connotations of superficiality and conspiracy popularly associated with the expression "Cliveden set" are a just description of the Milner Group as a whole. In fact, Viscount Astor was, relatively speaking, a late addition to the society, and the society should rather be pictured as utilizing the Astor money to further their own ideals rather than as being used for any purpose by the master of Cliveden.

Even the expression "Rhodes secret society," which would be perfectly accurate in reference to the period 1891-1899, would hardly be accurate for the period after 1899. The organization was so modified and so expanded by Milner after the eclipse of Stead in 1899, and especially after the death of Rhodes in 1902, that it took on quite a different organization and character, although it continued to pursue the same goals. To avoid this difficulty, we shall generally call the organization the "Rhodes secret society" before 1901 and "the Milner Group" after this date, but it must be understood that both terms refer to the same organization.

This organization has been able to conceal its existence quite successfully, and many of its most influential members, satisfied to possess the reality rather than the appearance of power, are unknown even to close students of British history. This is the more surprising when we learn that one of the chief methods by which this Group works has been through propaganda. It plotted the Jameson Raid of 1895; it caused the Boer War of 1899-1902; it set up and controls the Rhodes Trust; it created the Union of South Africa in 1906-1910; it established the South African periodical *The State* in 1908; it founded the British Empire periodical *The Round Table* in 1910, and this remains the mouthpiece of the Group; it has been the most powerful single influence in All Souls, Balliol, and New Colleges at Oxford for more than a generation; it has controlled *The Times* for more than fifty years, with the exception of the three years 1919-1922; it publicized the idea of and the name "British Commonwealth of Nations" in the period 1908-1918; it was the chief influence in Lloyd George's war administration in 1917-1919 and dominated the British delegation to the Peace Conference of 1919; it had a great deal to do with the formation and management of the League of Nations and of the system of mandates; it founded the Royal Institute of International Affairs in 1919 and still controls it; it was one of the chief influences on British policy toward Ireland, Palestine, and India in the period 1917-1945; it was a very important influence on the policy of appeasement of Germany during the years 1920-1940; and it controlled and still controls, to a very considerable extent, the sources and the writing of the history of British Imperial and foreign policy since the Boer War.

It would be expected that a Group which could number among its achievements such accomplishments as these would be a familiar subject for discussion among students of history and public affairs. In this case, the expectation is not realized, partly because of the deliberate policy of secrecy which this Group has adopted, partly because the Group itself is not closely integrated but rather appears as a series of overlapping circles or rings partly concealed by being hidden behind formally organized groups of no obvious political significance.

This Group, held together, as it is, by the tenuous links of friendship, personal association, and common ideals is so indefinite in its outlines (especially in recent years) that it is not always possible to say who is a member and who is not. Indeed, there is no sharp line of demarcation between those who are members and those who are not, since "membership" is possessed in varying degrees, and the degree changes at different times. Sir Alfred Zimmern, for example, while always close to the Group, was in its inner circle only for a brief period in 1910-1922, thereafter slowly drifting away into the outer orbits of the Group. Lord Halifax, on the other hand, while close to it from 1903, did not really become a member until after 1920. Viscount Astor, also close to the Group from its first beginnings (and much closer than Halifax), moved rapidly to the center of the Group after 1916, and especially after 1922, and in later years became increasingly a decisive voice in the Group.

Although the membership of the Milner Group has slowly shifted with the passing years, the Group still reflects the characteristics of its chief leader and, through him, the ideological orientation of Balliol in the 1870s. Although the Group did not actually come into existence until 1891, its history covers a much longer period, since its origins go back to about 1873. This history can be divided into four periods, of which the first, from 1873 to 1891, could be called the preparatory period and centers about the figures of W. T. Stead and Alfred Milner. The second period, from 1891 to 1901, could be called the Rhodes period, although Stead was the chief figure for most of it. The third period, from 1901 to 1922, could be called the New College period and centers about Alfred Milner. The fourth period, from about 1922 to the present, could be called the All Souls period and centers about Lord Lothian, Lord Brand, and Lionel Curtis. During these four periods, the Group grew steadily in power and influence, until about 1939. It was badly split on the policy of appeasement after 16 March 1939, and received a rude jolt from the General Election of 1945. Until 1939, however, the expansion in power of the Group was fairly consistent. This growth was based on the possession by its members of ability, social connections, and wealth. It is not possible to distinguish the relationship of these three qualities — a not uncommon situation in England.

Milner was able to dominate this Group because he became the focus or rather the intersection point of three influences. These we shall call "the Toynbee group," "the Cecil Bloc," and the "Rhodes secret society." The Toynbee group was a group of political intellectuals formed at Balliol about 1873 and dominated by Arnold Toynbee and Milner himself. It was really the group of Milner's personal friends. The Cecil Bloc was a nexus of political and social power formed by Lord Salisbury and extending from the great sphere of politics into the fields of education and publicity. In the field of education, its influence was chiefly visible at Eton and Harrow and at All Souls College, Oxford. In the field of publicity, its influence was chiefly visible in *The Quarterly Review* and *The Times*. The "Rhodes secret society" was a group of imperial federalists, formed in the period after 1889 and using the economic resources of South Africa to extend and perpetuate the British Empire.

It is doubtful if Milner could have formed his Group without assistance from all three of these sources. The Toynbee group gave him the ideology and the personal loyalties which he needed; the Cecil Bloc gave him the political influence without which his ideas could easily have died in the seed; and the Rhodes secret society gave him the economic resources which made it possible for him to create his own group independent of the Cecil Bloc. By 1902, when the leadership of the Cecil Bloc had fallen from the masterful grasp of Lord Salisbury into the rather indifferent hands of Arthur Balfour, and Rhodes had died, leaving Milner as the chief controller of his vast estate, the Milner Group was already established and had a most hopeful future. The long period of Liberal government which began in 1906 cast a temporary cloud over that future, but by 1916 the Milner Group had made its entrance into the citadel of political power and for the next twenty-three years steadily extended its influence until, by 1938, it was the most potent political force in Britain.

The original members of the Milner Group came from well-to-do, upper-class, frequently titled families. At Oxford they demonstrated intellectual ability and laid the basis for the Group. In later years they added to their titles and financial resources, obtaining these partly by inheritance and partly by ability to tap new sources of titles and money. At first their family fortunes may have been adequate to their ambitions, but in time these were supplemented by access to the funds in the foundation of All Souls, the Rhodes Trust and the Beit Trust, the fortune of Sir Abe Bailey, the Astor fortune, certain powerful British banks (of which the chief was Lazard Brothers and Company), and, in recent years, the Nuffield money.

Although the outlines of the Milner Group existed long before 1891, the Group did not take full form until after that date. Earlier, Milner and Stead had become part of a group of neo-imperialists who justified the British Empire's existence on moral rather than on economic or political grounds and who sought to make this justification a reality by advocating self-government and federation within the Empire. This group formed at Oxford in the early 1870s and was extended in the early 1880s. At Balliol it included Milner, Arnold Toynbee, Thomas Raleigh, Michael Glazebrook, Philip Lyttelton Gell, and George R. Parkin. Toynbee was Milner's closest friend. After his early death in 1883, Milner was active in establishing Toynbee Hall, a settlement house in London, in his memory. Milner was chairman of the governing board of this establishment from 1911 to his death in 1925. In 1931 plaques to both Toynbee and Milner were unveiled there by members of the Milner Group. In 1894 Milner delivered a eulogy of his dead friend at Toynbee Hall, and published it the next year as *Arnold Toynbee: A Reminiscence*. He also wrote the sketch of Toynbee in the *Dictionary of National Biography*. The connection is important because it undoubtedly gave Toynbee's nephew, Arnold J. Toynbee, his entree into government service in 1915 and into the Royal Institute of International Affairs after the war.

George R. Parkin (later Sir George, 1846-1922) was a Canadian who spent only one year in England before 1889. But during that year (1873-1874) he was a member of Milner's circle at Balliol and became known as a fanatical supporter of imperial federation. As a result of this, he became a charter member of the Canadian branch of the Imperial Federation League in 1885 and was sent, four years later, to New Zealand and Australia by the League to try to build up imperial sentiment. On his return, he toured around England, giving speeches to the same purpose. This brought him into close contact with the Cecil Bloc, especially George E. Buckle of *The Times*, G. W. Prothero, J. R. Seeley, Lord Rosebery, Sir Thomas (later Lord) Brassey, and Milner. For Buckle, and in support of the Canadian Pacific Railway, he made a survey of the resources and problems of Canada in 1892. This was published by Macmillan under the title *The Great Dominion* the following year. On a subsidy from Brassey and Rosebery he wrote and published his best-known book, *Imperial Federation*, in 1892. This kind of work as a propagandist for the Cecil Bloc did not provide a very adequate living, so on 24 April 1893 Milner offered to form a group of imperialists who would finance this work of Parkin's on a more stable basis. Accordingly, Parkin, Milner, and Brassey, on 1 June 1893, signed a contract by which Parkin was to be paid £450 a year for three years. During this period he was to propagandize as he saw fit for imperial solidarity. As a result of this agreement, Parkin began a steady correspondence with Milner, which continued for the rest of his life.

When the Imperial Federation League dissolved in 1894, Parkin became one of a group of propagandists known as the "Seeley lecturers" after Professor J. R. Seeley of Cambridge University, a famous imperialist. Parkin still found his income insufficient, however, although it was being supplemented from various sources, chiefly *The Times*. In 1894 he went to the Colonial Conference at Ottawa as special correspondent of *The Times*. The following year, when he was offered the position of Principal of Upper Canada College, Toronto, he consulted with Buckle and Moberly Bell, the editors of *The Times*, hoping to get a full-time position on *The Times*. There was none vacant, so he accepted the academic post in Toronto, combining with it the position of Canadian correspondent of *The Times*. This relationship with *The Times* continued even after he became organizing secretary of the Rhodes Trust in 1902. In 1908, for example, he was *The Times*'s correspondent at the Quebec tercentenary celebration. Later, in behalf of *The Times* and with the permission of Marconi, he sent the first press dispatch ever transmitted across the Atlantic Ocean by radio.

In 1902, Parkin became the first secretary of the Rhodes Trust, and he assisted Milner in the next twenty years in setting up the methods by which the Rhodes Scholars would be chosen. To this day, more than a quarter-century after his death, his influence is still potent in the

Milner Group in Canada. His son-in-law, Vincent Massey, and his namesake, George Parkin de T. Glazebrook, are the leaders of the Milner Group in the Dominion.[2]

Another member of this Balliol group of 1875 was Thomas Raleigh (later Sir Thomas, 1850-1922), close friend of Parkin and Milner, Fellow of All Souls (1876-1922), later registrar of the Privy Council (1896-1899), legal member of the Council of the Viceroy of India (1899-1904), and member of the Council of India in London (1909-1913). Raleigh's friendship with Milner was not based only on association at Balliol, for he had lived in Milner's house in Tubingen, Germany, when they were both studying there before 1868.

Another student, who stayed only briefly at Balliol but remained as Milner's intimate friend for the rest of his life, was Philip Lyttelton Gell (1852-1926). Gell was a close friend of Milner's mother's family and had been with Milner at King's College, London, before they both came up to Balliol. In fact, it is extremely likely that it was because of Gell, two years his senior, that Milner transferred to Balliol from London. Gell was made first chairman of Toynbee Hall by Milner when it was opened in 1884, and held that post for twelve years. He was still chairman of it when Milner delivered his eulogy of Toynbee there in 1894. In 1899 Milner made Gell a director of the British South Africa Company, a position he held for twenty-six years (three of them as president).

Another intimate friend, with whom Milner spent most of his college vacations, was Michael Glazebrook (1853-1926). Glazebrook was the heir of Toynbee in the religious field, as Milner was in the political field. He became Headmaster of Clifton College (1891-1905) and Canon of Ely (1905-1926) and frequently got into conflict with his ecclesiastical superiors because of his liberal views. This occurred in its most acute form after his publication of *The Faith of a Modern Churchman* in 1918. His younger brother, Arthur James Glazebrook, was the founder and chief leader of the Canadian branch of the Milner Group until succeeded by Massey about 1935.

While Milner was at Balliol, Cecil Rhodes was at Oriel, George E. Buckle was at New College, and H. E. Egerton was at Corpus. It is not clear if Milner knew these young men at the time, but all three played roles in the Milner Group later. Among his contemporaries at Balliol itself, we should list nine names, six of whom were later Fellows of All Souls: H. H. Asquith, St. John Brodrick, Charles Firth, W. P. Ker, Charles Lucas, Robert Mowbray, Rowland E. Prothero, A. L. Smith, and Charles A. Whitmore. Six of these later received titles from a grateful government, and all of them enter into any history of the Milner Group.

In Milner's own little circle at Balliol, the dominant position was held by Toynbee. In spite of his early death in 1883, Toynbee's ideas and outlook continue to influence the Milner Group to the present day. As Milner said in 1894, "There are many men now active in public life, and some whose best work is probably yet to come, who are simply working out ideas inspired by him." As to Toynbee's influence on Milner himself, the latter, speaking of his first meeting with Toynbee in 1873, said twenty-one years later, "I feel at once under his spell and have always remained under it." No one who is ignorant of the existence of the Milner Group can possibly see the truth of these quotations, and, as a result, the thousands of persons who have read these statements in the introduction to Toynbee's famous *Lectures on the Industrial Revolution* have been vaguely puzzled by Milner's insistence on the importance of a man who died at such an early age and so long ago. Most readers have merely dismissed the statements as sentimentality inspired by personal attachment, although it should be clear that Alfred Milner was about the last person in the world to display sentimentality or even sentiment.

Among the ideas of Toynbee which influenced the Milner Group we should mention three: (a) a conviction that the history of the British Empire represents the unfolding of a great moral idea — the idea of freedom — and that the unity of the Empire could best be preserved by the cement of this idea; (b) a conviction that the first call on the attention of any man should be a sense of duty and obligation to serve the state; and (c) a feeling of the necessity to do social service work (especially educational work) among the working classes of English society.[3] These ideas were accepted by most of the men whose names we have already mentioned and became dominant principles of the Milner Group later. Toynbee can also be regarded as the founder of the method used by the Group later, especially in the Round Table Groups and in the Royal Institute of International Affairs. As described by Benjamin Jowett, Master of Balliol, in his preface to the 1884 edition of Toynbee's *Lectures on the Industrial Revolution*, this method was as follows: "He would gather his friends around him; they would form an organization; they would work on quietly for a time, some at Oxford, some in London; they would prepare themselves in different parts of the subject until they were ready to strike in public." In a prefatory note to this same edition, Toynbee's widow wrote: "The whole has been revised by the friend who shared my husband's entire intellectual life, Mr. Alfred Milner, without whose help the volume would have been far more imperfect than it is, but whose friendship was too close and tender to allow now of a word of thanks." After Milner published his *Reminiscence of Arnold Toynbee*, it was reprinted in subsequent editions of the *Industrial Revolution* as a memoir, replacing Jowett's.

After leaving Oxford in 1877, Milner studied law for several years but continued to remain in close contact with his friends, through a club organized by Toynbee. This group, which met at the Temple in London as well as at Oxford, worked closely with the famous social reformer and curate of St. Jude's, Whitechapel, Samuel A. Barnett. The group lectured to working-class audiences in Whitechapel, Milner giving a course of speeches on "The State and the Duties of Rulers" in 1880 and another on "Socialism" in 1882. The latter series was published in the *National Review* in 1931 by Lady Milner.

In this group of Toynbee's was Albert Grey (later Earl Grey, 1851-1917), who became an ardent advocate of imperial federation. Later a loyal supporter of Milner's, as we shall see, he remained a member of the Milner Group until his death. Another member of the group, Ernest Iwan-Muller, had been at King's College, London, with Milner and Gell, and at New College while Milner was at Balliol. A close friend of Milner's, he became a journalist, was with Milner in South Africa during the Boer War, and wrote a valuable work on this experience called *Lord Milner in South Africa* (1903). Milner reciprocated by writing his sketch in the *Dictionary of National Biography* when he died in 1910.

At the end of 1881 Milner determined to abandon the law and devote himself to work of more social benefit. On 16 December he wrote in his diary: "One cannot have everything. I am a poor man and must choose between public usefulness and private happiness. I choose the former, or rather, I choose to strive for it."[4]

The opportunity to carry out this purpose came to him through his social work with Barnett, for it was by this connection that he met George J. (later Lord) Goschen, Member of Parliament and director of the Bank of England, who in the space of three years (1880-1883) refused the posts of Viceroy of India, Secretary of State for War, and Speaker of the House of Commons. Goschen became, as we shall see, one of the instruments by which Milner obtained political influence. For one year (1884-1885) Milner served as Goschen's private secretary, leaving the post only because he stood for Parliament himself in 1885.

It was probably as a result of Goschen's influence that Milner entered journalism, beginning to write for the *Pall Mall Gazette* in 1881. On this paper he established a number of personal relationships of later significance. At the time, the editor was John Morley, with William T. Stead as assistant. Stead was assistant editor in 1880-1883, and editor in 1883-1890. In the last year, he founded *The Review of Reviews*. An ardent imperialist, at the same time that he was a violent reformer in domestic matters, he was "one of the strongest champions in England of Cecil Rhodes." He introduced Albert Grey to Rhodes and, as a result, Grey became one of the original directors of the British South Africa Company when it was established by royal charter in

1889. Grey became administrator of Rhodesia when Dr. Jameson was forced to resign from that post in 1896 as an aftermath of his famous raid into the Transvaal. He was Governor-General of Canada in 1904-1911 and unveiled the Rhodes Memorial in South Africa in 1912. A Liberal member of the House of Commons from 1880 to 1886, he was defeated as a Unionist in the latter year. In 1894 he entered the House of Lords as the fourth Earl Grey, having inherited the title and 17,600 acres from an uncle. Throughout this period he was close to Milner and later was very useful in providing practical experience for various members of the Milner Group. His son, the future fifth Earl Grey, married the daughter of the second Earl of Selborne, a member of the Milner Group.

During the period in which Milner was working with the *Pall Mall Gazette* he became associated with three persons of some importance later. One of these was Edward T. Cook (later Sir Edward, 1857-1919), who became a member of the Toynbee-Milner circle in 1879 while still an undergraduate at New College. Milner had become a Fellow of New College in 1878 and held the appointment until he was elected Chancellor of the University in 1925. With Edward Cook he began a practice which he was to repeat many times in his life later. That is, as Fellow of New College, he became familiar with undergraduates whom he later placed in positions of opportunity and responsibility to test their abilities. Cook was made secretary of the London Society for the Extension of University Teaching (1882) and invited to contribute to the *Pall Mall Gazette*. He succeeded Milner as assistant editor to Stead in 1885 and succeeded Stead as editor in 1890. He resigned as editor in 1892, when Waldorf Astor bought the *Gazette*, and founded the new *Westminister Gazette*, of which he was editor for three years (1893-1896). Subsequently editor of the *Daily News* for five years (1896-1901), he lost this post because of the proprietors' objections to his unqualified support of Rhodes, Milner, and the Boer War. During the rest of his life (1901-1919) he was leader-writer for the *Daily Chronicle*, edited Ruskin's works in thirty-eight volumes, wrote the standard biography of Ruskin and a life of John Delane, the great editor of *The Times*.

Also associated with Milner in this period was Edmund Garrett (1865-1907), who was Stead's and Cook's assistant on the *Pall Mall Gazette* for several years (1887-1892) and went with Cook to the *Westminister Gazette* (1893-1895). In 1889 he was sent by Stead to South Africa for his health and became a great friend of Cecil Rhodes. He wrote a series of articles for the *Gazette*, which were published in book form in 1891 as *In Afrikanderland and the Land of Ophir*. He returned to South Africa in 1895 as editor of the *Cape Times*, the most important English-language paper in South Africa. Both as editor

(1895-1900) and later as a member of the Cape Parliament (1898-1902), he strongly supported Rhodes and Milner and warmly advocated a union of all South Africa. His health broke down completely in 1900, but he wrote a character analysis of Rhodes for the *Contemporary Review* (June 1902) and a chapter called "Rhodes and Milner" for *The Empire and the Century* (1905). Edward Cook wrote a full biography of Garrett in 1909, while Milner wrote Garrett's sketch in the *Dictionary of National Biography*, pointing out "as his chief title to remembrance" his advocacy "of a United South Africa absolutely autonomous in its own affairs but remaining part of the British Empire."

During the period in which he was assistant editor of the *Gazette*, Milner had as roommate Henry Birchenough (later Sir Henry, 1853-1937). Birchenough went into the silk-manufacturing business, but his chief opportunities for fame came from his contacts with Milner. In 1903 he was made special British Trade Commissioner to South Africa, in 1906 a member of the Royal Commission on Shipping Rings (a controversial South African subject), in 1905 a director of the British South Africa Company (president in 1925), and in 1920 a trustee of the Beit Fund. During the First World War, he was a member of various governmental committees concerned with subjects in which Milner was especially interested. He was chairman of the Board of Trade's Committee on Textiles after the war; chairman of the Royal Commission of Paper; chairman of the Committee on Cotton-Growing in the Empire; and chairman of the Advisory Council to the Ministry of Reconstruction.

In 1885, as a result of his contact with such famous Liberals as Goschen, Morley, and Stead, and at the direct invitation of Michael Glazebrook, Milner stood for Parliament but was defeated. In the following year he supported the Unionists in the critical election on Home Rule for Ireland and acted as head of the "Literature Committee" of the new party. Goschen made him his private secretary when he became Chancellor of the Exchequer in Lord Salisbury's government in 1887. The two men were similar in many ways: both had been educated in Germany, and both had mathematical minds. It was Goschen's influence which gave Milner the opportunity to form the Milner Group, because it was Goschen who introduced him to the Cecil Bloc. While Milner was Goschen's private secretary, his parliamentary private secretary was Sir Robert Mowbray, an older contemporary of Milner's at Balliol and a Fellow of All Souls for forty-six years (1873-1919).

As a result of Goschen's influence, Milner was appointed successively Under Secretary of Finance in Egypt (1887-1892), chairman of the Board of Inland Revenue (1892-1897), and High Commissioner to

South Africa (1897-1905). With the last position he combined several other posts, notably Governor of the Cape of Good Hope (1897-1901) and Governor of the Transvaal and the Orange River Colony (1901-1905). But Goschen's influence on Milner was greater than this, both in specific matters and in general. Specifically, as Chancellor of Oxford University in succession to Lord Salisbury (1903-1907) and as an intimate friend of the Warden of All Souls, Sir William Anson, Goschen became one of the instruments by which the Milner Group merged with All Souls. But more important than this, Goschen introduced Milner, in the period 1886-1905, into that extraordinary circle which rotated about the Cecil family.

2

The Cecil Bloc

THE MILNER GROUP could never have been built up by Milner's own efforts. He had no political power or even influence. All that he had was ability and ideas. The same thing is true about many of the other members of the Milner Group, at least at the time that they joined the Group. The power that was utilized by Milner and his Group was really the power of the Cecil family and its allied families such as the Lyttelton (Viscounts Cobham), Wyndham (Barons Leconfield), Grosvenor (Dukes of Westminster), Balfour, Wemyss, Palmer (Earls of Selborne and Viscounts Wolmer), Cavendish (Dukes of Devonshire and Marquesses of Hartington), and Gathorne-Hardy (Earls of Cranbrook). The Milner Group was originally a major fief within the great nexus of power, influence, and privilege controlled by the Cecil family. It is not possible to describe here the ramifications of the Cecil influence. It has been all-pervasive in British life since 1886. This Cecil Bloc was built up by Robert Arthur Talbot Gascoyne-Cecil, Viscount Cranborne and third Marquess of Salisbury (1830-1903). The methods used by this man were merely copied by the Milner Group. These methods can be summed up under three headings: (a) a triple-front penetration in politics, education, and journalism; (b) the recruitment of men of ability (chiefly from All Souls) and the linking of these men to the Cecil Bloc by matrimonial alliances and by gratitude for titles and positions of power; and (c) the influencing of public policy by placing members of the Cecil Bloc in positions of power shielded as much as possible from public attention.

The triple-front penetration can be seen in Lord Salisbury's own life. He was not only Prime Minister for a longer period than anyone else in recent history (fourteen years between 1885 and 1902) but also a Fellow of All Souls (from 1853) and Chancellor of Oxford University (1869-1903), and had a paramount influence on *The Quarterly Review* for many years. He practiced a shameless nepotism, concealed to some extent by the shifting of names because of acquisition of titles and female marital connections, and redeemed by the fact that ability as well as family connection was required from appointees.

Lord Salisbury's practice of nepotism was aided by the fact that he had two brothers and two sisters and had five sons and three daughters of his own. One of his sisters was the mother of Arthur J. Balfour and Gerald W. Balfour. Of his own daughters, one married the Second Earl of Selborne and had a son, Lord Wolmer, and a daughter, Lady Mabel Laura Palmer. The daughter married the son of Earl Grey, while the son married the daughter of Viscount Ridley. The son, known as Lord Wolmer until 1942 and Lord Selborne since that date, was an M.P. for thirty years (1910-1940), a figure in various Conservative governments since 1916, and Minister of Economic Warfare in 1942-1945.

Of Lord Salisbury's five sons, the oldest (now fourth Marquess of Salisbury), was in almost every Conservative government from 1900 to 1929. He had four children, of whom two married into the Cavendish family. Of these, a daughter, Lady Mary Cecil, married in 1917 the Marquess of Hartington, later tenth Duke of Devonshire; the older son, Viscount Cranborne, married Lady Elizabeth Cavendish, niece of the ninth Duke of Devonshire. The younger son, Lord David Cecil, a well-known writer of biographical works, was for years a Fellow of Wadham and for the last decade has been a Fellow of New College. The other daughter, Lady Beatrice Cecil, married W. G. A. Ormsby-Gore (now Lord Harlech), who became a member of the Milner Group. It should perhaps be mentioned that Viscount Cranborne was in the House of Commons from 1929 to 1941 and has been in the House of Lords since. He was Under Secretary for Foreign Affairs in 1935-1938, resigned in protest at the Munich agreement, but returned to office in 1940 as Paymaster General (1940), Secretary of State for Dominion Affairs (1940-1942), and Colonial Secretary (1942). He was later Lord Privy Seal (1942-1943), Secretary for Dominion Affairs again (1943-1945), and Leader of the Conservative Party in the House of Lords (1942-1945).

Lord Salisbury's second son, Lord William Cecil (1863-   ), was Rural Dean of Hertford (1904-1916) and Bishop of Exeter (1916-1936), as well as chaplain to King Edward VII.

Lord Salisbury's third son, Lord Robert Cecil (Viscount Cecil of Chelwood since 1923), was an M.P. from 1906 to 1923 as well as Parliamentary Under Secretary for Foreign Affairs (1915-1916), Assistant Secretary in the same department (1918), Minister of Blockade (1916-1918), Lord Privy Seal (1923-1924), and Chancellor of the Duchy of Lancaster (1924-1927). He was one of the original drafters of the Covenant of the League of Nations and was the Englishman most closely associated in the public mind with the work of the League. For this work he received the Nobel Prize in 1937.

Lord Salisbury's fourth son, Lord Edward Cecil (1867-1918), was the one most closely associated with Milner, and, in 1921, his widow married Milner. While Lord Edward was besieged with Rhodes in Mafeking in 1900, Lady Cecil lived in close contact with Milner and his Kindergarten. After the war, Lord Edward was Agent-General of the Sudan (1903-1905), Under Secretary of Finance in Egypt (1905-1912), and financial adviser to the Egyptian government (1912-1918). He was in complete control of the Egyptian government during the interval between Kitchener's departure and the arrival of Sir Henry McMahon as High Commissioner, and was the real power in McMahon's administration (1914-1916). In 1894 he had married Violet Maxse, daughter of Admiral Frederick Maxse and sister of General Sir Ivor Maxse. Sir Ivor, a good friend of Milner's, was the husband of Mary Caroline Wyndham, daughter of Baron Leconfield and niece of Lord Rosebery.

Lord Edward Cecil had a son and a daughter. The daughter, Helen Mary Cecil, married Captain Alexander Hardinge in the same year (1921) in which she became Milner's stepdaughter. Her husband was the heir of Baron Hardinge of Penshurst and a cousin of Sir Arthur Hardinge. Both Hardinges were proteges of Lord Salisbury, as we shall see.

The fifth son of Lord Salisbury was Lord Hugh Cecil (Baron Quickswood since 1941). He was a Member of Parliament for Greenwich (1895-1906) and for Oxford University (1910-1937). He is now a Fellow of New College, after having been a Fellow of Hertford for over fifty years.

The degree to which Lord Salisbury practiced nepotism can be seen by a look at his third government (1895-1902) or its successor, Balfour's first government (1902-1905). The Balfour government was nothing but a continuation of Salisbury's government, since, as we have seen, Balfour was Salisbury's nephew and chief assistant and was made premier in 1902 by his uncle. Salisbury was Prime Minister and Foreign Secretary; Balfour was First Lord of the Treasury and Party Leader in Commons (1895-1902); his brother, Gerald Balfour, was Chief Secretary for Ireland (1895-1900) and President of the Board of Trade (1900-1905); their cousin-in-law Lord Selborne was Under Secretary for the Colonies (1895-1900) and First Lord of the Admiralty (1905-1910). Arthur Balfour's most intimate friend, and the man who would have been his brother-in-law except for his sister's premature death in 1875 (an event which kept Balfour a bachelor for the rest of his life), Alfred Lyttelton, was chairman of a mission to the Transvaal in 1900 and Colonial Secretary (1903-1906). His older brother, Neville, was Assistant Military Secretary in the War Office (1897-1898),

Commander-in-Chief in South Africa under Milner (1902-1904), and Chief of the General Staff (1904-1908). Another intimate friend of Balfour's, George Wyndham, was Parliamentary Under Secretary for War (1898-1900) and Chief Secretary for Ireland (1900-1905). St. John Brodrick (later Lord Midleton), a classmate of Milner's, brother-in-law of P. L. Gell and son-in-law of the Earl of Wemyss, was Under Secretary for War (1895-1898), Under Secretary for Foreign Affairs (1898-1900), Secretary of State for War (1900-1903), and Secretary of State for India (1903-1905). James Cecil, Viscount Cranborne, Lord Salisbury's heir, was Under Secretary for Foreign Affairs (1900-1903) and Lord Privy Seal (1903-1905). Evelyn Cecil (Sir Evelyn since 1922), nephew of Lord Salisbury, was private secretary to his uncle (1895-1902). Walter Long (later Lord Long), a creation of Salisbury's, was President of the Board of Agriculture (1895-1900), President of the Local Government Board (1900-1905), and Chief Secretary for Ireland (1905-1906). George N. Curzon, (later Lord Curzon) a Fellow of All Souls, ex-secretary and protege of Lord Salisbury, was Under Secretary for Foreign Affairs (1895-1898) and Viceroy of India (1899-1905).

In addition to these personal appointees of Lord Salisbury, this government had the leaders of the Unionist Party, which had split off from the Liberal Party in the fight over Home Rule in 1886. These included the eighth Duke of Devonshire and his nephew, the Marquess of Hartington (the Cavendish family), the latter's father-in-law (Lord Lansdowne), Goschen, and Joseph Chamberlain. The Duke of Devonshire was Lord President of the Council (1895-1903); his nephew and heir was Treasurer of H.M. Household (1900-1903) and Financial Secretary to the Treasury (1903-1905). The latter's father-in-law, Lord Lansdowne, was Secretary for War (1895-1900) and Foreign Secretary (1900-1905); Goschen was First Lord of the Admiralty (1895-1900) and rewarded with a viscounty (1900). Joseph Chamberlain was Secretary for the Colonies (1895-1903).

Most of these persons were related by numerous family and marital connections which have not yet been mentioned. We should point out some of these connections, since they form the background of the Milner Group.

George W. Lyttelton, fourth Baron Lyttelton, married a sister of Mrs. William E. Gladstone and had eight sons. Of these, Neville and Alfred have been mentioned; Spencer was secretary to his uncle, W. E. Gladstone, for three extended periods between 1871 and 1894, and was an intimate friend of Arthur Balfour (world tour together in 1875); Edward was Headmaster of Haileybury (1890-1905) and of Eton (1905-1916); Arthur was chaplain to the Queen (1896-1898) and Bishop of Southampton (1898-1903). Charles, the oldest son, fifth Baron Lyttelton and eighth Viscount Cobham (1842-1922), married

Mary Cavendish and had four sons and three daughters. The oldest son, now ninth Viscount Cobham, was private secretary to Lord Selborne in South Africa (1905-1908) and Parliamentary Under Secretary of War (1939-1940). His brother George was assistant master at Eton. His sister Frances married the nephew of Lady Chelmsford.

The youngest son of the fourth Baron Lyttelton, Alfred, whom we have already mentioned, married twice. His first wife was Laura Tennant, whose sister Margot married Herbert Asquith and whose brother Baron Glenconner married Pamela Wyndham. Pamela married, for a second husband, Viscount Grey of Fallodon. For his second wife, Alfred Lyttelton married Edith Balfour. She survived him by many years and was later deputy director of the women's branch of the Ministry of Agriculture (1917-1919), a substitute delegate to the Assembly of the League of Nations for five sessions (1923-1931), and a member of the council of the Royal Institute of International Affairs. Her son, Captain Oliver Lyttelton, has been an M.P. since 1940, was managing director of the British Metals Corporation, Controller of Non-ferrous Metals (1939-1940), President of the Board of Trade (1940-1941, 1945), a member of the War Cabinet (1941-1945), and Minister of Production (1942-1945).

Almost as ramified as the Lyttelton clan were the Wyndhams, descendants of the first Baron Leconfield. The Baron had three sons. Of these, the oldest married Constance Primrose, sister of Lord Rosebery, daughter of Lord Dalmeny and his wife, Dorothy Grosvenor (later Lady Brassey), and granddaughter of Lord Henry Grosvenor and his wife, Dora Wemyss. They had four children. Of these, one, Hugh A. Wyndham, married Maud Lyttelton and was a member of Milner's Kindergarten. His sister Mary married General Sir Ivor Maxse and was thus the sister-in-law of Lady Edward Cecil (later Lady Milner). Another son of Baron Leconfield, Percy Scawen Wyndham, was the father of Pamela (Lady Glenconner and later Lady Grey), of George Wyndham (already mentioned), who married Countess Grosvenor, and of Mary Wyndham, who married the eleventh Earl of Wemyss. It should perhaps be mentioned that Countess Grosvenor's daughter Lettice Grosvenor married the seventh Earl of Beauchamp, brother-in-law of Samuel Hoare. Countess Grosvenor (Mrs. George Wyndham) had two nephews who must be mentioned. One, Lawrence John Lumley Dundas (Earl of Ronaldshay and Marquess of Zetland), was sent as military aide to Curzon, Viceroy of India, in 1900. He was an M.P. (1907-1916), a member of the Royal Commission on Public Services in India (1912-1914), Governor of Bengal (1917-1922), a member of the Indian Round Table Conference of 1930-1931 and of the Parliamentary Joint Select Committee on India in 1933. He was Secretary of State for India (1935-1940) and for Burma (1937-1940), as well as the official biographer of Lord Curzon and Lord Cromer.

The other nephew of Countess Grosvenor, Laurence Roger Lumley (Earl of Scarbrough since 1945), a cousin of the Marquess of Zetland, was an M.P. as soon as he graduated from Magdalen (1922-1929, 1931-1937), and later Governor of Bombay (1937-1943) and Parliamentary Under Secretary of State for India and Burma (1945).

Countess Grosvenor's sister-in-law Mary Wyndham (who married the Earl of Wemyss) had three children. The younger son, Guy Charteris, married a Tennant of the same family as the first Mrs. Alfred Lyttelton, the second Mrs. Herbert Asquith, and Baron Glenconner. His sister, Cynthia Charteris, married Herbert Asquith's son Herbert. In an earlier generation, Francis Charteris, tenth Earl of Wemyss, married Anne Anson, while his sister Lady Hilda Charteris married St. John Brodrick, eighth Viscount Midleton of first Earl Midleton. Lord Midleton's sister Edith married Philip Lyttelton Gell.

This complicated interrelationship of family connections by no means exhausts the links between the families that made up the Cecil Bloc as it existed in the period 1886-1900, when Milner was brought into it by Goschen. Nor would any picture of this Bloc be complete without some mention of the persons without family connections who were brought into the Bloc by Lord Salisbury. Most of these persons were recruited from All Souls and, like Arthur Balfour, Lord Robert Cecil, Baron Quickswood, Sir Evelyn Cecil, and others, frequently served an apprenticeship in a secretarial capacity to Lord Salisbury. Many of these persons later married into the Cecil Bloc. In recruiting his proteges from All Souls, Salisbury created a precedent that was followed later by the Milner Group, although the latter went much further than the former in the degree of its influence on All Souls.

All Souls is the most peculiar of Oxford Colleges. It has no undergraduates, and its postgraduate members are not generally in pursuit of a higher degree. Essentially, it consists of a substantial endowment originally set up in 1437 by Henry Chichele, sometime Fellow of New College and later Archbishop of Canterbury, from revenues of suppressed priories. From this foundation incomes were established originally for a warden, forty fellows, and two chaplains. This has been modified at various times, until at present twenty-one fellowships worth £300 a year for seven years are filled from candidates who have passed a qualifying examination. This group usually join within a year or two of receiving the bachelor's degree. In addition, there are eleven fellowships without emolument, to be held by the incumbents of various professorial chairs at Oxford. These include the Chichele Chairs of International Law, of Modern History, of Economic History, of Social and Political Theory, and of the History of War; the Drummond Chair of Political Economy; the Gladstone Chair of Government; the Regius Chair of Civil Law; the Vinerian Chair of English Law; the Marshal Foch Professorship of French Literature; and the Chair of Social Anthropology. There are ten Distinguished Persons fellowships without emolument, to be held for seven years by persons who have attained fame in law, humanities, science, or public affairs. These are usually held by past Fellows. There are a varying number of research fellowships and teaching fellowships, good for five to seven years, with annual emoluments of £300 to £600. There are also twelve seven-year fellowships with annual emoluments of £50 for past Fellows. And lastly, there are six fellowships to be held by incumbents of certain college or university offices.

The total number of Fellows at any one time is generally no more than fifty and frequently considerably fewer. Until 1910 there were usually fewer than thirty-five, but the number has slowly increased in the twentieth century, until by 1947 there were fifty-one. In the whole period of the twentieth century from 1900 to 1947, there was a total of 149 Fellows. This number, although small, was illustrious and influential. It includes such names as Lord Acton, Leopold Amery, Sir William Anson, Sir Harold Butler, G. N. Clark, G. D. H. Cole, H. W. C. Davis, A. V. Dicey, Geoffrey Faber, Keith Feiling, Lord Chelmsford, Sir Maurice Gwyer, Lord Halifax, W. K. Hancock, Sir Arthur Hardinge, Sir William Holdsworth, T. E. Lawrence, C. A. Macartney, Friedrich Max Muller, Viscount Morley of Blackburn, Sir Charles Oman, A. F. Pollard, Sir Charles Grant Robertson, Sir James Arthur Salter, Viscount Simon, Sir Donald Somervell, Sir Arthur Ramsay Steel-Maitland, Sir Ernest Swinton, K. C. Wheare, E. L. Woodward, Francis de Zulueta, etc. In addition, there were to be numbered among those who were fellows before 1900 such illustrious persons as Lord Curzon, Lord Ernle, Sir Robert Herbert, Sir Edmund Monson, Lord Phillimore, Viscount Ridley, and Lord Salisbury. Most of these persons were elected to fellowships in All Souls at the age of twenty-two or twenty-three years, at a time when their great exploits were yet in the future. There is some question whether this ability of the Fellows of All Souls to elect as their younger colleagues men with brilliant futures is to be explained by their ability to discern greatness at an early age or by the fact that election to the fellowship opens the door to achievement in public affairs. There is some reason to believe that the second of these two alternatives is of greater weight. As the biographer of Viscount Halifax has put it, "It is safe to assert that the Fellow of All Souls is a man marked out for a position of authority in public life, and there is no surprise if he reaches the summit of power, but only disappointment if he falls short of the opportunities that are set out before him."[1]

One Fellow of All Souls has confessed in a published work that his career was based on his membership in this college. The Right Reverend Herbert Hensley Henson, who rose from humble origins to become Bishop of Durham, wrote in his memoirs: "My election to a fellowship, against all probability, and certainly against all expectation, had decisive influence on my subsequent career. It brought me within the knowledge of the late Lord Salisbury, who subsequently recommended me to the Crown for appointment to a Canonry of Westminister. . . . It is to All Souls College that all the 'success' [!] of my career is mainly due."[2]

It would appear that the College of All Souls is largely influenced not by the illustrious persons whose names we have listed above (since they are generally busy elsewhere) but by another group within the college. This appears when we realize that the Fellows whose fellowships are renewed for one appointment after another are not generally the ones with famous names. The realization is increased when we see that these persons with the power to obtain renewing appointments are members of a shadowy group with common undergraduate associations, close personal relationships, similar interests and ideas, and surprisingly similar biographical experience. It is this shadowy group which includes the All Souls members of the Milner Group.

In the nineteenth century, Lord Salisbury made little effort to influence All Souls, although it was a period when influence (especially in elections to fellowships) was more important than later. He contented himself with recruiting proteges from the college and apparently left the wielding of influence to others, especially to Sir William Anson. In the twentieth century, the Milner Group has recruited from and influenced All Souls. This influence has not extended to the elections to the twenty-one competitive fellowships. There, merit has unquestionably been the decisive factor. But it has been exercised in regard to the seventeen ex-officio fellowships, the ten Distinguished Persons fellowships, and the twelve reelective fellowships. And it has also been important in contributing to the general direction and policy of the college.

This does not mean that the Milner Group is identical with All Souls, but merely that it is the chief, if not the controlling, influence in it, especially in recent years. Many members of the Milner Group are not members of All Souls, and many members of All Souls are not members of the Milner Group.

The fact that All Souls is influenced by some outside power has been recognized by others, but no one so far as I know has succeeded in identifying this influence. The erratic Christopher Hobhouse, in his recent book on Oxford, has come closer than most when he wrote: "The senior common room at All Souls is distinguished above all others by the great brains which meet there and by the singular unfruitfulness of their collaboration. . . . But it is not these who make the running. Rather is it the Editor of *The Times* and his circle of associates — men whom the public voice has called to no office and entrusted with no responsibility. These individuals elect to consider themselves the powers behind the scenes. The duty of purveying honest news is elevated in their eyes into the prerogative of dictating opinion. It is at All Souls that they meet to decide just how little they will let their readers know; and their newspaper has been called the *All Souls Parish Magazine*."[3] The inaccuracy and bitterness of this statement is caused by the scorn which a devotee of the humanities feels toward the practitioners of the social sciences, but the writer was shrewd enough to see that an outside group dominates All Souls. He was also able to see the link between All Souls and *The Times*, although quite mistaken in his conclusion that the latter controls the former. As we shall see, the Milner Group dominates both.

In the present chapter we are concerned only with the relationship between the Cecil Bloc and All Souls and shall reserve our consideration of the relationships between the Milner Group and the college to a later chapter. The former relationship can be observed in the following list of names, a list which is by no means complete:

NAME	COLLEGE	FELLOW OF ALL SOULS
C. A. Alington, 1872-	Trinity, Oxford 1891-1895	1896-1903
W. R. Anson, 1843-1914	Balliol 1862-1866	1867-1914; warden 1881-1914
G. N. Curzon, 1859-1925	Balliol 1878-1882	1883-1890
A. H. Hardinge, 1859-1933	Balliol 1878-1881	1881-
A. C. Headlam, 1862-	New College 1881-1885	1885-1897, 1924-
H. H. Henson, 1863-	Non-Collegiate 1881-1884	1884-1891, 1896-1903; 1939
C. G. Lang, 1864-1945	Balliol 1882-1886	1888-1928
F. W. Pember, 1862-	Balliol 1880-1884	1884- 1910- Warden, 1914-1932
W. G. F. Phillimore, 1845-1929	Christ Church 1863-1867	1867-
R. E. Prothero, 1852-1937	Balliol 1871-1875	1875-1891
E. Ridley, 1843-1928	Corpus Christi 1862-1866	1866-1882
M. W. Ridley, 1842-1904	Balliol 1861-1865	1865-1874
J. Simon, 1873-	Wadham 1892-1896	1897-
F. J. N. Thesiger, 1868-1933	Magdalen 1887-1891	1892-1899, 1929-1933

The Reverend Cyril A. Alington married Hester Lyttelton, daughter of the fourth Baron Lyttelton and sister of the famous eight brothers whom we have mentioned. He was Headmaster of Eton (1916-1933) in succession to his brother-in-law Edward Lyttelton, and at the same time chaplain to King George V (1921-1933). Since 1933 he has been Dean of Durham.

Sir William Anson can best be discussed later. He, Lord Goschen, and H. A. L. Fisher were the chief instruments by which the Milner Group entered into All Souls.

George Nathaniel Curzon (Lord Curzon after 1898, 1859-1925) studied at Eton and Balliol (1872-1882). At the latter he was intimate with the future Lords Midleton, Selborne, and Salisbury. On graduating, he went on a trip to the Near East with Edward Lyttelton. Elected a Fellow of All Souls in 1883, he became assistant private secretary to Lord Salisbury two years later. This set his future career. As Harold Nicolson says of him in the *Dictionary of National Biography*, "His activities centered from that moment on obedience to Lord Salisbury, an intense interest in foreign and colonial policy, and the enjoyment of the social amenities." A Member of Parliament from 1886 to 1898, he traveled widely, chiefly in Asia (1887-1894), financing his trips by writing for *The Times*. He was Under Secretary in the India Office (1891-1892), Under Secretary in the Foreign Office (1895-1898), and Viceroy of India (1899-1905) by Lord Salisbury's appointment. In the last-named post he had many controversies with the "Balfour-Brodrick combination" (as Nicolson calls it), and his career was more difficult thereafter, for, although he did achieve high office again, he failed to obtain the premiership, and the offices he did obtain always gave him the appearance rather than the reality of power. These offices included Lord Privy Seal (1915-1916, 1924-1925), Leader in Lords (1916-1924), Lord President of the Council (1916-1919), member of the Imperial War Cabinet (1916-1918), and Foreign Secretary (1919-1924). Throughout this later period, he was generally in opposition to what was being supported by the Cecil Bloc and the Milner Group, but his desire for high office led him to make constant compromises with his convictions.

Arthur Henry Hardinge (Sir Arthur after 1904) and his cousin, Charles Hardinge (Baron Hardinge of Penshurst after 1910), were both aided in their careers by Lord Salisbury. The former, a Fellow of All Souls in 1881 and an assistant secretary to Lord Salisbury four years later, rose to be Minister to Persia, Belgium, and Portugal (1900-1913) and Ambassador to Spain (1913-1919). The latter worked up in the diplomatic service to be First Secretary at the Embassy in St. Petersburg (1898-1903), then was Assistant Under Secretary and Permanent Under Secretary for Foreign Affairs (1903-1904, 1906-1910,

1916-1920), Ambassador at St. Petersburg (1904-1906), Viceroy of India (1910-1916), and Ambassador at Paris (1920-1922). Charles Hardinge, although almost unknown to many people, is one of the most significant figures in the formation of British foreign policy in the twentieth century. He was the close personal friend and most important adviser on foreign policy of King Edward VII and accompanied the King on all his foreign diplomatic tours. His post as Under Secretary was kept available for him during these trips and in later life during his service as Ambassador and Viceroy. He presents the only case in British history where an ex-Ambassador and ex-Viceroy was to be found in the position of Under Secretary. He was probably the most important single person in the formation of the Entente Cordiale in 1904 and was very influential in the formation of the understanding with Russia in 1907. His son, Captain Alexander Hardinge, married Milner's stepdaughter, Helen Mary Cecil, in 1921 and succeeded his father as Baron Hardinge of Penshurst in 1944. He was equerry and assistant private secretary to King George V (1920-1936) and private secretary and extra equerry to both Edward VIII and George VI (1936-1943). He had a son, George Edward Hardinge (born 1921), who married Janet Christian Goschen, daughter of Lieutenant Colonel F. C. C. Balfour, granddaughter of the second Viscount Goschen and of Lady Goschen, the former Lady Evelyn Gathorne-Hardy (fifth daughter of the first Earl of Cranbrook). Thus a grandchild of Milner was united with a great-grandchild of his old benefactor, Lord Goschen.[4]

Among the persons recruited from All Souls by Lord Salisbury were two future prelates of the Anglican Church. These were Cosmo Gordon Lang, Fellow for forty years, and Herbert Hensley Henson, Fellow for twenty-four years. Lang was Bishop of Stepney (1901-1908), Archbishop of York (1908-1928), and Archbishop of Canterbury (1928-1942). Henson was Canon of Westminister Abbey (1900-1912), Dean of Durham (1912-1918), and Bishop of Hereford and of Durham (1918-1939).

The Right Reverend Arthur Cayley Headlam was a Fellow of All Souls for about forty years and, in addition, was editor of the *Church Quarterly Review*, Regius Professor of Divinity, and Bishop of Gloucester. He is chiefly of interest to us because his younger brother, James W. Headlam-Morley (1863-1929), was a member of the Milner Group. James (Sir James in 1929) was put by the Group into the Department of Information (under John Buchan, 1917-1918), and the Foreign Office (under Milner and Curzon, 1918-1928), went to the Peace Conference in 1919, edited the first published volume of *British Documents on the Origin of the War* (1926), and was a mainstay of the Royal Institute of International Affairs, where his portrait still hangs.

His daughter, Agnes, was made Montague Burton Professor of International Relations at Oxford in 1948. This was a position strongly influenced by the Milner Group.

Francis W. Pember was used by Lord Salisbury from time to time as assistant legal adviser to the Foreign Office. He was Warden of All Souls in succession to Anson (1914-1932).

Walter Phillimore (Lord Phillimore after 1918) was admitted to All Souls with Anson in 1867. He was a lifelong friend and associate of the second Viscount Halifax (1839-1934). The latter devoted his life to the cause of church union and was for fifty-two years (1868-1919, 1934) president of the English Church Union. In this post he was succeeded in 1919 by Lord Phillimore, who had been serving as vice-president for many years and who was an intimate friend of the Halifax family. It was undoubtedly through Phillimore that the present Earl of Halifax, then simple Edward Wood, was elected to All Souls in 1903 and became an important member of the Milner Group. Phillimore was a specialist in ecclesiastical law, and it created a shock when Lord Salisbury made him a judge of the Queen's Bench in 1897, along with Edward Ridley, who had entered All Souls as a Fellow the year before Phillimore. The echoes of this shock can still be discerned in Lord Sankey's brief sketch of Phillimore in the *Dictionary of National Biography*. Phillimore became a Lord Justice of Appeal in 1913 and in 1918 drew up one of the two British drafts for the Covenant of the League of Nations. The other draft, known as the Cecil Draft, was attributed to Lord Robert Cecil but was largely the work of Alfred Zimmern, a member of the Milner Group.

Rowland Edmund Prothero (Lord Ernle after 1919) and his brother, George W. Prothero (Sir George after 1920), are two of the most important links between the Cecil Bloc and the Milner Group. They grew up on the Isle of Wight in close contact with Queen Victoria, who was a family friend. Through the connection, the elder Prothero was asked to tutor the Duke of Bedford in 1878, a position which led to his appointment in 1899 as agent-in-chief of the Duke. In the interval he was a Fellow of All Souls for sixteen years and engaged in literary work, writing unsigned articles for the *Edinburgh Review*, the *Church Quarterly Review* and *The Quarterly Review*. Of the last, possibly through the influence of Lord Salisbury, he became editor for five years (1894-1899), being succeeded in the position by his brother for twenty-three years (1899-1922).

As agent of the extensive agricultural holdings of the Duke of Bedford, Prothero became familar with agricultural problems and began to write on the subject. He ran for Parliament from Bedfordshire as a Unionist, on a platform advocating tariff reform, in 1907 and again in 1910, but in spite of his influential friends, he was not successful. He wrote of these efforts: "I was a stranger to the political world, without friends in the House of Commons. The only men prominent in public life whom I knew with any degree of real intimacy were Curzon and Milner."[5] In 1914, at Anson's death, he was elected to succeed him as one of Oxford's representatives in Parliament. Almost immediately he was named a member of Milner's Committee on Home Production of Food (1915), and the following year was on Lord Selborne's committee concerned with the same problem. At this point in his autobiography, Prothero wrote: "Milner and I were old friends. We had been undergraduates together at Balliol College. . . . The outside world thought him cold and reserved. . . . But between Milner and myself there was no barrier, mainly, I think, because we were both extremely shy men." The interim report of the Selborne Committee repeated the recommendations of the Milner Committee in December 1916. At the same time came the Cabinet crisis, and Prothero was named President of the Board of Agriculture with a seat in the new Cabinet. Several persons close to the Milner Group were put into the department, among them Sir Sothern Holland, Mrs. Alfred Lyttelton, Lady Evelyn Cecil, and Lord Goschen (son of Milner's old friend). Prothero retired from the cabinet and Parliament in 1919, was made a baron in the same year, and a Fellow of Balliol in 1922.

Sir George W. Prothero (1848-1922), brother of Lord Ernle, had been lecturer in history at his own college at Cambridge University and the first professor in the new Chair of Modern History at Edinburgh before he became editor of *The Quarterly Review* in 1899. He was editor of the *Cambridge Modern History* (1902-1912), Chichele Lecturer in History (1915), and director of the Historical Section of the Foreign Office and general editor of the *Peace Handbooks*, 155 volumes of studies preparatory to the Peace Conference (1917-1919). Besides his strictly historical works, he wrote a *Memoir of J.R. Seeley* and edited and published Seeley's posthumous *Growth of British Polity*. He also wrote the sketch of Lord Selborne in the *Dictionary of National Biography*. His own sketch in the same work was written by Algernon Cecil, nephew of Lord Salisbury, who had worked with Prothero in the Historical Section of the Foreign Office. The same writer also wrote the sketches of Arthur Balfour and Lord Salisbury in the same collective work. All three are very revealing sources for this present study.

G. W. Prothero's work on the literary remains of Seeley must have endeared him to the Milner Group, for Seeley was regarded as a precursor by the inner circle of the Group. For example, Lionel Curtis, in a letter to Philip Kerr (Lord Lothian) in November 1916, wrote: "Seeley's results were necessarily limited by his lack of any knowledge at first hand either of the Dominions or of India. With the Round

Table organization behind him Seeley by his own knowledge and insight might have gone further than us. If we have been able to go further than him it is not merely that we followed in his train, but also because we have so far based our study of the relations of these countries on a preliminary field-study of the countries concerned, conducted in close cooperation with people in those countries."[6]

Matthew White Ridley (Viscount Ridley after 1900) and his younger brother, Edward Ridley (Sir Edward after 1897), were both proteges of Lord Salisbury and married into the Cecil Bloc. Matthew was a Member of Parliament (1868-1885, 1886-1900) and held the offices of Under Secretary of the Home Department (1878-1880), Financial Secretary of the Treasury in Salisbury's first government (1885-1886), and Home Secretary in Salisbury's third government (1895-1900). He was made a Privy Councillor during Salisbury's second government. His daughter, Grace, married the future third Earl of Selborne in 1910, while his son married Rosamond Guest, sister of Lady Chelmsford and future sister-in-law of Frances Lyttelton (daughter of the eighth Viscount Cobham and the former Mary Cavendish).

Edward Ridley beat out Anson for the fellowship to All Souls in 1866, but in the following year both Anson and Phillimore were admitted. Ridley and Phillimore were appointed to the Queen's Bench of the High Court of Justice in 1897 by Lord Salisbury. The former held the post for twenty years (1897-1917).

John Simon (Viscount Simon since 1940) came into the Cecil Bloc and the Milner Group through All Souls. He received his first governmental task as junior counsel for Britain in the Alaska Boundary Arbitration of 1903. A Member of Parliament as a Liberal and National Liberal (except for a brief interval of four years) from the great electoral overturn of 1906 to his elevation to the upper house in 1940, he held governmental posts for a large portion of that period. He was Solicitor General (1910-1913), Attorney General (1913-1915), Home Secretary (1915-1916), Foreign Secretary (1931-1935), Home Secretary again (1935-1937), Chancellor of the Exchequer (1937-1940), and, finally, Lord Chancellor (1940-1945). He was also chairman of the Indian Statutory Commission (1927-1930).

Frederic John Napier Thesiger (Lord Chelmsford after 1905) was taken by Balfour from the London County Council in 1905 to be Governor of Queensland (1905-1909) and later Governor of New South Wales (1907-1913). In the latter post he established a contact with the inner circle of the Milner Group, which was useful to both parties later. He was Viceroy of India in 1916-1921 and First Lord of the Admiralty in the brief Labour government of 1924. He married Frances Guest in 1894 while still at All Souls and may have been the contact by which her sister married Matthew Ridley in 1899 and her brother married Frances Lyttelton in 1911.

The Cecil Bloc did not disappear with the death of Lord Salisbury in 1903 but was continued for a considerable period by Balfour. It did not, however, continue to grow but, on the contrary, became looser and less disciplined, for Balfour lacked the qualities of ambition and determination necessary to control or develop such a group. Accordingly, the Cecil Bloc, while still in existence as a political and social power, has largely been replaced by the Milner Group. This Group, which began as a dependent fief of the Cecil Bloc, has since 1916 become increasingly the active portion of the Bloc and in fact its real center. Milner possessed those qualities of determination and ambition which Balfour lacked, and was willing to sacrifice all personal happiness and social life to his political goals, something which was quite unacceptable to the pleasure-loving Balfour. Moreover, Milner was intelligent enough to see that it was not possible to continue a political group organized in the casual and familiar way in which it had been done by Lord Salisbury. Milner shifted the emphasis from family connection to ideological agreement. The former had become less useful with the rise of a class society based on economic conflicts and with the extension of democracy. Salisbury was fundamentally a conservative, while Milner was not. Where Salisbury sought to build up a bloc of friends and relatives to exercise the game of politics and to maintain the Old England that they all loved, Milner was not really a conservative at all. Milner had an idea — the idea he had obtained from Toynbee and that he found also in Rhodes and in all the members of his Group. This idea had two parts: that the extension and integration of the Empire and the development of social welfare were essential to the continued existence of the British way of life; and that this British way of life was an instrument which unfolded all the best and highest capabilities of mankind. Working with this ideology derived from Toynbee and Balliol, Milner used the power and the general strategic methods of the Cecil Bloc to build up his own Group. But, realizing that conditions had changed, he put much greater emphasis on propaganda activities and on ideological unity within the Group. These were both made necessary by the extension of political democracy and the rise of economic democracy as a practical political issue. These new developments had made it impossible to be satisfied with a group held together by no more than family and social connections and animated by no more far-sighted goal than the preservation of the existing social structure.

The Cecil Bloc did not resist this change by Milner of the aims and tactics of their older leader. The times made it clear to all that methods must be changed. However, it is possible that the split which appeared within the Conservative Party in England after 1923 followed roughly the lines between the Milner Group and the Cecil Bloc.

It should perhaps be pointed out that the Cecil Bloc was a social rather than a partisan group — at first, at least. Until 1890 or so it contained members of both political parties, including the leaders, Salisbury and Gladstone. The relationship between the two parties on the topmost level could be symbolized by the tragic romance between Salisbury's nephew and Gladstone's niece, ending in the death of the latter in 1875. After the split in the Liberal Party in 1886, it was the members of the Cecil Bloc who became Unionists — that is, the Lytteltons, the Wyndhams, the Cavendishes. As a result, the Cecil Bloc became increasingly a political force. Gladstone remained socially a member of it, and so did his protege, John Morley, but almost all the other members of the Bloc were Unionists or Conservatives. The chief exceptions were the four leaders of the Liberal Party after Gladstone, who were strong imperialists: Rosebery, Asquith, Edward Grey, and Haldane. These four supported the Boer War, grew increasingly anti-German, supported the World War in 1914, and were close to the Milner Group politically, intellectually, and socially.[7]

Socially, the Cecil Bloc could be divided into three generations. The first (including Salisbury, Gladstone, the seventh Duke of Devonshire, the eighth Viscount Midleton, Goschen, the fourth Baron Lyttelton, the first Earl of Cranbrook, the first Duke of Westminster, the first Baron Leconfield, the tenth Earl of Wemyss, etc.) was not as "social" (in the frivolous sense) as the second. This first generation was born in the first third of the nineteenth century, went to both Oxford and Cambridge in the period 1830-1855, and died in the period 1890-1915. The second generation was born in the second third of the nineteenth century, went almost exclusively to Oxford (chiefly Balliol) in the period 1860-1880, and died in the period 1920-1930. This second generation was much more social in a spectacularly frivolous sense, much more intellectual (in the sense that they read books and talked philosophy or social problems) and centered on a social group known at the time as "The Souls." The third generation of the Cecil Bloc, consisting of persons born in the last third of the nineteenth century, went to Oxford almost exclusively (New College or Balliol) in the period 1890-1905 and began to die off about 1940. This third generation of the Cecil Bloc was dominated and organized about the Milner Group. It was very serious-minded, very political, and very secretive.

The first two generations did not regard themselves as an organized group but rather as "Society." The Bloc was symbolized in the first two generations in two exclusive dining clubs called "The Club" and "Grillion's." The membership of the two was very similar, with about forty persons in each and a total of not over sixty in both together. Both organizations had illustrious pasts. The Club, founded in 1764, had as past members Joshua Reynolds (founder), Samuel Johnson, Edmund Burke, Oliver Goldsmith, James Boswell, Edward Gibbon, Charles Fox, David Garrick, Adam Smith, Richard B. Sheridan, George Canning, Humphry Davy, Walter Scott, Lord Liverpool, Henry Hallam, Lord Brougham, T. B. Macauley, Lord John Russell, George Grote, Dean Stanley, W. E. H. Lecky, Lord Kelvin, Matthew Arnold, T. H. Huxley, Bishop Wilberforce, Bishop Stubbs, Bishop Creighton, Gladstone, Lord Salisbury, Balfour, John Morley, Richard Jebb, Lord Goschen, Lord Acton, Lord Rosebery, Archbishop Lang, F. W. Pember (Warden of All Souls), Lord Asquith, Edward Grey, Lord Haldane, Hugh Cecil, John Simon, Charles Oman, Lord Tennyson, Rudyard Kipling, Gilbert Murray, H. A. L. Fisher, John Buchan, Maurice Hankey, the fourth Marquess of Salisbury, Lord Lansdowne, Bishop Henson, Halifax, Stanley Baldwin, Austen Chamberlain, Lord Carnock, and Lord Hewart. This list includes only members up to 1925. There were, as we have said, only forty members at any one time, and at meetings (dinner every fortnight while Parliament was in session) usually only about a dozen were present.

Grillion's was very similar to The Club. Founded in 1812, it had the same members and met under the same conditions, except weekly (dinner when Parliament was in session). The following list includes the names I can find of those who were members up to 1925: Gladstone, Salisbury, Lecky, Balfour, Asquith, Edward Grey, Haldane, Lord Bryce, Hugh Cecil, Robert Cecil, Curzon, Neville Lyttelton, Eustace Percy, John Simon, Geoffrey Dawson, Walter Raleigh, Balfour of Burleigh, and Gilbert Murray.[8]

The second generation of the Cecil Bloc was famous at the time that it was growing up (and political power was still in the hands of the first generation) as "The Souls," a term applied to them partly in derision and partly in envy but used by themselves later. This group, flitting about from one great country house to another or from one spectacular social event to another in the town houses of their elders, has been preserved for posterity in the autobiographical volumes of Margot Tennant Asquith and has been caricatured in the writings of Oscar Wilde. The frivolity of this group can be seen in Margot Tennant's statement that she obtained for Milner his appointment to the chairmanship of the Board of Inland Revenue in 1892 merely by writing to Balfour and asking for it after she had a too brief romantic interlude with Milner in Egypt. As a respected scholar of my acquaintance has said, this group did everything in a frivolous fashion, including entering the Boer War and the First World War.

One of the enduring creations of the Cecil Bloc is the Society for

Psychical Research, which holds a position in the history of the Cecil Bloc similar to that held by the Royal Institute of International Affairs in the Milner Group. The Society was founded in 1882 by the Balfour family and their in-laws, Lord Rayleigh and Professor Sidgwick. In the twentieth century it was dominated by those members of the Cecil Bloc who became most readily members of the Milner Group. Among these we might mention Gilbert Murray, who performed a notable series of experiments with his daughter, Mrs. Arnold J. Toynbee, in the years before 1914, and Dame Edith Lyttelton, herself a Balfour and widow of Arthur Balfour's closest friend, who was president of the Society in 1933-1934.

The third generation was quite different, partly because it was dominated by Milner, one of the few completely serious members of the second generation. This third generation was serious if not profound, studious if not broadly educated, and haunted consistently by the need to act quickly to avoid impending disaster. This fear of disaster they shared with Rhodes and Milner, but they still had the basic weakness of the second generation (except Milner and a few other adopted members of that Group), namely that they got everything too easily. Political power, wealth, and social position came to this third generation as a gift from the second, without the need to struggle for what they got or to analyze the foundations of their beliefs. As a result, while awake to the impending disaster, they were not able to avoid it, but instead tinkered and tampered until the whole system blew up in their faces.

This third generation, especially the Milner Group, which formed its core, differed from its two predecessors in its realization that it formed a group. The first generation had regarded itself as "England," the second regarded itself as "Society," but the third realized it was a secret group—or at least its inner circles did. From Milner and Rhodes they got this idea of a secret group of able and determined men, but they never found a name for it, contenting themselves with calling it "the Group," or "the Band," or even "Us."[9]

3

The Secret Society
of Cecil Rhodes[1]

WHEN MILNER went to South Africa in 1897, Rhodes and he were already old acquaintances of many years' standing. We have already indicated that they were contemporaries at Oxford, but, more than that, they were members of a secret society which had been founded in 1891. Moreover, Milner was, if not in 1897, at least by 1901, Rhodes's chosen successor in the leadership of that society.

The secret society of Cecil Rhodes is mentioned in the first five of his seven wills. In the fifth it was supplemented by the idea of an educational institution with scholarships, whose alumni would be bound together by common ideals — Rhodes's ideals. In the sixth and seventh wills the secret society was not mentioned, and the scholarships monopolized the estate. But Rhodes still had the same ideals and still believed that they could be carried out best by a secret society of men devoted to a common cause. The scholarships were merely a facade to conceal the secret society, or, more accurately, they were to be one of the instruments by which the members of the secret society could carry out his purpose. This purpose, as expressed in the first will (1877), was:

> The extension of British rule throughout the world, the perfecting of a system of emigration from the United Kingdom and of colonization by British subjects of all lands wherein the means of livelihood are attainable by energy, labour, and enterprise, . . . the ultimate recovery of the United States of America as an integral part of a British Empire, the consolidation of the whole Empire, the inauguration of a system of Colonial Representation in the Imperial Parliament which may tend to weld together the disjointed members of the Empire, and finally the foundation of so great a power as to hereafter render wars impossible and promote the best interests of humanity.

To achieve this purpose, Rhodes, in this first will, written while he was still an undergraduate of Oxford at the age of twenty-four, left all his wealth to the Secretary of State for the Colonies (Lord Carnarvon) and to the Attorney General of Griqualand West (Sidney Shippard), to be used to create a secret society patterned on the Jesuits. The reference to the Jesuits as the model for his secret society is found in a "Confession of Faith" which Rhodes had written two years earlier (1875) and which he enclosed in his will. Thirteen years later, in a letter to the trustee of his third will, Rhodes told how to form the secret society, saying, "In considering questions suggested take Constitution of the Jesuits if obtainable and insert 'English Empire' for 'Roman Catholic Religion.' "

In his "Confession of Faith" Rhodes outlined the types of persons who might be useful members of this secret society. As listed by the American Secretary to the Rhodes Trust, this list exactly describes the group formed by Milner in South Africa:

> Men of ability and enthusiasm who find no suitable way to serve their country under the current political system; able youth recruited from the schools and universities; men of wealth with no aim in life; younger sons with high thoughts and great aspirations but without opportunity; rich men whose careers are blighted by some great disappointment. All must be men of ability and character. . . . Rhodes envisages a group of the ablest and the best, bound together by common unselfish ideals of service to what seems to him the greatest cause in the world. There is no mention of material rewards. This is to be a kind of religious brotherhood like the Jesuits, "a church for the extension of the British Empire."

In each of his seven wills, Rhodes entrusted his bequest to a group of men to carry out his purpose. In the first will, as we have seen, the trustees were Lord Carnarvon and Sidney Shippard. In the second will (1882), the sole trustee was his friend N. E. Pickering. In the third will (1888), Pickering having died, the sole trustee was Lord Rothschild. In the fourth will (1891), W. T. Stead was added, while in the fifth (1892), Rhodes's solicitor, B. F. Hawksley, was added to the previous two. In the sixth (1893) and seventh (1899) wills, the personnel of the trustees shifted considerably, ending up, at Rhodes's death in 1902, with a board of seven trustees: Lord Milner, Lord Rosebery, Lord Grey, Alfred Beit, L. L. Michell, B. F. Hawksley, and Dr. Starr Jameson. This is the board to which the world looked to set up the Rhodes Scholarships.

Dr. Frank Aydelotte, the best-known American authority on Rhodes's wills, claims that Rhodes made no reference to the secret society in his last two wills because he had abandoned the idea. The first chapter of his recent book, *The American Rhodes Scholarships*, states and reiterates that between 1891 and 1893 Rhodes underwent a great change in his point of view and matured in his judgment to the point that in his sixth will "he abandons forever his youthful idea of a secret society." This is completely untrue, and there is no evidence to support such a statement.[2] On the contrary, all the evidence, both direct and circumstantial, indicates that Rhodes wanted the secret society from 1875 to his death in 1902. By Dr. Aydelotte's own admission, Rhodes wanted the society from 1877 to 1893, a period of sixteen years. Accepted practice in the use of historical evidence requires us to believe that Rhodes persisted in this idea for the remaining nine years of his life, unless there exists evidence to the contrary. There is no such evidence. On the other hand, there is direct evidence that he did not change his ideas. Two examples of this evidence can be mentioned here. On 5 February 1896, three years after his sixth will, Rhodes ended a long conversation with R. B. Brett (later Lord Esher) by saying, "Wish we could get our secret society." And in April 1900, a year after he wrote his seventh and last will, Rhodes was reprimanding Stead for his opposition to the Boer War, on the grounds that in this case he should have been willing to accept the judgment of the men on the spot who had made the war. Rhodes said to Stead, "That is the curse which will be fatal to our ideas — insubordination. Do not you think it is very disobedient of you? How can our Society be worked if each one sets himself up as the sole judge of what ought to be done? Just look at the position here. We three are in South Africa, all of us your boys . . . I myself, Milner, and Garrett, all of whom learned their politics from you. We are on the spot, and we are unanimous in declaring this war to be necessary. You have never been in South Africa, and yet, instead of deferring to the judgment of your own boys, you fling yourself into a violent opposition to the war."[3]

Dr. Aydelotte's assumption that the scholarships were an alternative to the secret society is quite untenable, for all the evidence indicates that the scholarships were but one of several instruments through which the society would work. In 1894 Stead discussed with Rhodes how the secret society would work and wrote about it after Rhodes's death as follows: "We also discussed together various projects for propaganda, the formation of libraries, the creation of lectureships, the dispatch of emissaries on missions of propaganda throughout the Empire, and the steps to be taken to pave the way for the foundation and the acquisition of a newspaper which was to be devoted to the service of the cause." This is an exact description of the way in which the society, that is the Milner Group, has functioned. Moreover, when Rhodes talked with Stead, in January 1895, about the scholarships at Oxford, he did not abandon the society but continued to speak of it as the real power behind the scholarships. It is perfectly clear that Rhodes omitted mentioning the secret society in his last two wills because he knew that by that time he was so famous that the one way to keep a society from being secret would be to mention it in his will. Obviously, if Rhodes wanted the secret society after 1893, he would have made no mention of it in his will but would have left his money in trust for a legitimate public purpose and arranged for the creation of the secret society by a private understanding with his trustees. This is clearly what happened, because the secret society was established, and Milner used Rhodes's money to finance it, just as Rhodes had intended.[4]

The creation of the secret society was the essential core of Rhodes's plans at all times. Stead, even after Rhodes's death, did not doubt that the attempt would be made to continue the society. In his book on Rhodes's wills he wrote in one place: "Mr. Rhodes was more than the founder of a dynasty. He aspired to be the creator of one of those vast semi-religious, quasi-political associations which, like the Society of Jesus, have played so large a part in the history of the world. To be more strictly accurate, he wished to found an Order as the instrument of the will of the Dynasty, and while he lived he dreamed of being both its Caesar and its Loyola. It was this far-reaching, world-wide aspiration of the man which rendered, to those who knew him, so absurdly inane the speculations of his critics as to his real motives." Sixty pages later Stead wrote: "The question that now arises is whether in the English-speaking world there are to be found men of faith adequate to furnish forth materials for the Society of which Mr. Rhodes dreamed."

This idea of a society throughout the world working for federal union fascinated Milner as it had fascinated Rhodes. We have already mentioned the agreement which he signed with George Parkin in 1893, to propagandize for this purpose. Eight years later, in a letter to Parkin from South Africa, Milner wrote at length on the subject of imperial union and ended: "Good-bye for today. Keep up the touch. I wish we had some like-minded persons in New Zealand and Australia, who were personal friends. More power to your elbow."[5] Moreover, there were several occasions after 1902 when Milner referred to his desire to see "a powerful body of men" working "outside the existing political parties" for imperial unity. He referred to this desire in his letter to Congdon in 1904 and referred to it again in his "farewell speech" to the Kindergarten in 1905. There is also a piece of negative evidence which seems to me to be of considerable significance. In 1912 Parkin wrote a book called *The Rhodes Scholarships*, in which he devoted several pages to Rhodes's wills. Although he said something about each will and gave the date of each will, he said nothing about the secret society. Now this secret society, which is found in five out of the seven wills, is so astonishing that Parkin's failure to mention it must be deliberate. He would have no reason to pass it by in silence unless the society had been formed. If the existing Rhodes Trust were a more mature alternative for the secret society rather than a screen for it, there would be no reason to pass it by, but, on the contrary, an urgent need to mention it as a matter of great intrinsic interest and as an example of how Rhodes's ideas matured.

As a matter of fact, Rhodes's ideas did not mature. The one fact which appears absolutely clearly in every biography of Rhodes is the fact that from 1875 to 1902 his ideas neither developed nor matured. Parkin, who clearly knew of the secret society, even if he did not mention it, says in regard to Rhodes's last will: "It is essential to remember that this final will is consistent with those which had preceded it, that it was no late atonement for errors, as some have supposed, but was the realization of life-long dreams persistently pursued."

Leaving aside all hypothesis, the facts are clear: Rhodes wanted to create a worldwide secret group devoted to English ideals and to the Empire as the embodiment of these ideals, and such a group was created. It was created in the period after 1890 by Rhodes, Stead, and, above all, by Milner.

The idea of a secret international group of propagandists for federal imperialism was by no means new to Milner when he became Rhodes Trustee in 1901, since he had been brought into Rhodes's secret society as the sixth member in 1891. This was done by his old superior, W. T. Stead. Stead, as we have indicated, was the chief Rhodes confidant in England and very close to Milner. Although Stead did not meet Rhodes until 1889, Rhodes regarded himself as a disciple of Stead's much earlier and eagerly embraced the idea of imperial federation based on Home Rule. It was in pursuit of this idea that Rhodes contributed £10,000 to Parnell in 1888. Although Rhodes accepted Stead's ideas, he did not decide that Stead was the man he wanted to be his lieutenant in the secret society until Stead was sent to prison in 1885 for his articles on organized vice in the *Pall Mall Gazette*. This courageous episode convinced Rhodes to such a degree that he tried to see Stead in prison but was turned away. After Stead was released, Rhodes did not find the opportunity to meet him until 4 April 1889. The excitement of that day for Stead can best be shown by quoting portions of the letter which he wrote to Mrs. Stead immediately after the conference. It said:

Mr. Rhodes is my man! I have just had three hours talk with him. He is full of a far more gorgeous idea in connection with the paper than even I have had. I cannot tell you his scheme because it is too secret. But it involves millions. He had no idea that it would cost £250,000 to start a paper. But he offered me down as a free gift £20,000 to buy a share in the *P.M. Gazette* as a beginning. Next year he would do more. He expects to own before he dies 4 or 5 millions, all of which he will leave to carry out the scheme of which the paper is an integral part. He is giving £500,000 to make a railway to Matabeleland, and so has not available, just at this moment, the money necessary for starting the morning paper. His ideas are federation, expansion, and consolidation of the Empire. . . . He took to me. Told me some things he has told no other man—save Lord Rothschild—and pressed me to take the £20,000, not to have any return, to give no receipt, to simply take it and use it to give me a freer hand on the *P.M.G.* It seems all like a fairy dream. . . . He said he had taken his ideas from the *P.M.G.*, that the paper permeated South Africa, that he met it everywhere. . . . How good God is to me. . . . Remember all the above about R. is very private.

The day following this sensational conversation Stead lost a libel action to the amount of £2000 damages. Rhodes at once sent a check to cover it and said: "You must keep my confidence secret. The idea is right, but until sure of the lines would be ruined in too many hands. Your subsidiary press idea can be discussed without risk, but the inner circle behind would never be many, perhaps three or four."[6]

About the same time, Rhodes revealed to Stead his plans to establish the British South Africa Company and asked him who in England could best help him get the necessary charter. Stead recommended Albert Grey, the future Earl Grey, who had been an intimate friend of Stead's since 1873 and had been a member of the Milner-Toynbee group in 1880-1884. As a result, Grey became one of the original directors of the British South Africa Company and took the first steps which eventually brought him into the select circle of Rhodes's secret society.

This society took another step forward during Rhodes's visit to England in February 1890. The evidence for this is to be found in the *Journals* of Lord Esher (at that time R. B. Brett), who had obviously been let in on the plan by Stead. Under date of 3 February 1890, we read in these *Journals*: "Cecil Rhodes arrived last night from South Africa. I was at Stead's today when he called. I left them together. Tonight I saw Stead again. Rhodes had talked for three hours of all his great schemes. . . . Rhodes is a splendid enthusiast. But he looks upon men as 'machines.' This is not very penetrating." Twelve days after this, on 15 February, at Lord Rothschild's country house, Brett wrote in his journal: "Came here last night. Cecil Rhodes, Arthur Balfour, Harcourts, Albert Grey, Alfred Lyttelton. A long talk with Rhodes today. He has vast ideas. Imperial notions. He seems disinterested. But he is very *ruse* and, I suspect, quite unscrupulous as to the means he employs."[7]

The secret society, after so much preliminary talk, took form in 1891, the same year in which Rhodes drew up his fourth will and made Stead as well as Lord Rothschild the trustee of his fortune. It is perfectly clear from the evidence that he expected Rothschild to handle the financial investments associated with the trust, while Stead was to have full charge of the methods by which the funds were used. About the same time, in February 1891, Stead and Rhodes had another long discussion about the secret society. First they discussed their goals and agreed that, if necessary in order to achieve Anglo-American unity, Britain should join the United States. Then they discussed the organization of the secret society and divided it into two circles: an inner circle, "The Society of the Elect", and an outer circle to include "The Association of Helpers" and *The Review of Reviews* (Stead's magazine, founded 1890). Rhodes said that he had already revealed the plan for "The Society of the Elect" to Rothschild and "little Johnston." By "little Johnston" he meant Harry H. Johnston (Sir Harry after 1896), African explorer and administrator, who had laid the basis for the British claims to Nyasaland, Kenya, and Uganda. Johnston was, according to Sir Frederick Whyte, the biographer of Stead, virtually unknown in England before Stead published his portrait as the frontispiece to the first issue of *The Review of Reviews* in 1890.[8] This was undoubtedly done on behalf of Rhodes. Continuing their discussion of the membership of "The Society of the Elect," Stead asked permission to bring in Milner and Brett. Rhodes agreed, so they telegraphed at once to Brett, who arrived in two hours. They then drew up the following "ideal arrangement" for the society:

1. GENERAL OF THE SOCIETY: RHODES
2. JUNTA OF THREE: Stead
   Brett
   Milner
3. CIRCLE OF INITIATES: Cardinal Manning
   General Booth
   Bramwell Booth
   "Little" Johnston
   Albert Grey
   Arthur Balfour
4. THE ASSOCIATION OF HELPERS
5. A COLLEGE, under Professor Seeley, to be established "to train people in the English-speaking idea."

Within the next few weeks Stead had another talk with Rhodes and a talk with Milner, who was "filled with admiration" for the scheme, according to Stead's notes as published by Sir Frederick Whyte.

The "ideal arrangement" for the secret society, as drawn up in 1891, never came into effect in all its details. The organization as drawn on paper reflected the romantic and melodramatic ideas of Cecil Rhodes and Stead, and doubtless they envisioned formal initiations, oaths, secret signs of recognition, etc. Once Milner and Brett were made initiates, the atmosphere changed. To them secret signs or oaths were so much claptrap and neither necessary nor desirable, for the initiates knew each other intimately and had implicit trust in each other without the necessity of signs or oaths. Thus the melodrama envisioned by Rhodes was watered down without in any way reducing the seriousness with which the initiates determined to use their own personal influence and Rhodes's wealth and power to achieve the consolidation of the British Empire, which they shared as an ideal with Rhodes.

With the elimination of signs, oaths, and formal initiations, the criteria for membership in "The Society of the Elect" became knowledge of the secret society and readiness to cooperate with the other initiates toward their common goal. The distinction between the initiates and The Association of Helpers rested on the fact that while members of both circles were willing to cooperate with one another in order to achieve their common goal, the initiates knew of the secret society, while the "helpers" probably did not. This distinction rapidly became of little significance, for the members of The Association of Helpers would have been very stupid if they had not realized that they were members of a secret group working in cooperation with other members of the same group. Moreover, the Circle of Initiates became in time of less importance because as time passed the members of this select circle died, were alienated, or became less immediately concerned with the project. As a result, the secret society came to be represented almost completely by The Association of Helpers — that is, by the group with which Milner was most directly concerned. And within this Association of Helpers there appeared in time gradations of intimacy, the more select ones participating in numerous areas of the society's activity and the more peripheral associated with fewer and less vital areas. Nevertheless, it is clear that "The Society of the Elect" continued to exist, and it undoubtedly recruited additional members now and then from The Association of Helpers. It is a very difficult task to decide who is and who is not a member of the society as a whole, and it is even more difficult to decide if a particular member is an initiate or a helper. Accordingly, the last distinction will not usually be made in this study. Before we abandon it completely, however, an effort should be made to name the initiates, in the earlier period at least.

Of the persons so far named, we can be certain that six were initiates. These were Rhodes, Lord Rothschild, Johnston, Stead, Brett, and Milner. Of these, Rothschild was largely indifferent and participated in the work of the group only casually. Of the others, Johnston received from £10,000 to £17,000 a year from Rhodes for several years after 1889, during which period he was trying to eliminate the influence of slave-traders and the Portuguese from Nyasaland. About 1894 he became alienated from Rhodes because of Johnston's refusal to cooperate with him in an attack on the Portuguese in Manikaland. As a result Johnston ceased to be an active member of the society. Lord Grey's efforts to heal the breach were only nominally successful.[9]

Stead was also eliminated in an informal fashion in the period 1899-1904, at first by Rhodes's removing him from his trusteeship and later by Milner's refusal to use him, confide in him, or even see him, although continuing to protest his personal affection for him. Since Milner was the real leader of the society after 1902, this had the effect of eliminating Stead from the society.[10]

Of the others mentioned, there is no evidence that Cardinal Manning or the Booths were ever informed of the scheme. All three were friends of Stead and would hardly be acceptable to the rising power of Milner. Cardinal Manning died in 1892. As for "General" Booth and his son, they were busily engaged in directing the Salvation Army from 1878 to 1929 and played no discernible role in the history of the Group.

Of the others who were mentioned, Brett, Grey, and Balfour can safely be regarded as members of the society, Brett because of the documentary evidence and the other two because of their lifelong cooperation with and assistance to Milner and the other members of the Group.

Brett, who succeeded his father as Viscount Esher in 1899, is one of the most influential and one of the least-known men in British politics in the last two generations. His importance could be judged better by the positions he refused than by those he held during his long life (1852-1930). Educated at Eton and Cambridge, he was a lifelong and intimate friend of Arthur Balfour, Albert Grey, Lord Rosebery, and Alfred Lyttelton. He was private secretary to the Marquess of Hartington (Duke of Devonshire) in 1878-1885 and a Liberal M.P. in 1880-1885. In the last year he was defeated in an attempt to capture the seat for Plymouth, and retired from public life to his country house near Windsor at the advanced age of thirty-three years. That he emerged from this retirement a decade later may well be attributed to his membership in the Rhodes secret society. He met Stead while still in public life and by virtue of his confidential position with the future Duke of Devonshire was able to relay to Stead much valuable information. These messages were sent over the signature "XIII."

This assistance was so highly esteemed by Stead that he regarded Brett as an important part of the *Pall Mall Gazette* organization. Writing in 1902 of Milner and Brett, Stead spoke of them, without mentioning their names, as "two friends, now members of the Upper House, who were thoroughly in sympathy with the gospel according to the *Pall Mall Gazette* and who had been as my right and left hands during my editorship of the paper." In return Stead informed Brett of Rhodes's secret schemes as early as February 1890 and brought him into the society when it was organized the following year.

The official positions held by Brett in the period after 1895 were secretary of the Office of Works (1895-1902), Lieutenant Governor and Governor of Windsor Castle (1901-1930), member of the Royal Commission on the South African War (1902-1903), permanent member of the Committee of Imperial Defence (1905-1930), chairman and later president of the London County Territorial Force Association (1909-1921), and chief British member of the Temporary Mixed Commission on Disarmament of the League of Nations (1922-1923). Although some of these posts, especially the one on the Committee of Imperial Defence, play an important role in the history of the Milner Group, none of them gives any indication of the significant position which Esher held in British political life. The same thing could be said of the positions which he refused, although they, if accepted, would have made him one of the greatest names in recent British history. Among the positions which he refused we might mention the following: Permanent Under Secretary in the Colonial Office (1899), Governor of Cape Colony (1900), Permanent Under Secretary in the War Office (1900), Secretary of State for War (1903), Director of *The Times* (1908), Viceroy of India (1908), and an earldom (date unknown). Esher's reasons for refusing these positions were twofold: he wanted to work behind the scenes rather than in the public view, and his work in secret was so important and so influential that any public post would have meant a reduction in his power. When he refused the exalted position of viceroy in 1908, he wrote frankly that, with his opportunity of influencing vital decisions at the center, India for him "would be (it sounds vain, but it isn't) parochial."[11] This opportunity for influencing decisions at the center came from his relationship to the monarchy. For at least twenty-five years (from 1895 to after 1920) Esher was probably the most important adviser on political matters to Queen Victoria, King Edward VII, and King George V. This position arose originally from his personal friendship with Victoria, established in the period 1885-1887, and was solidified later when, as secretary to the Office of Works and Lieutenant Governor of Windsor Castle, he was in charge of the physical properties of all the royal residences. These opportunities were not neglected. He organized the Diamond Jubilee of 1897, the royal funeral of 1901, and the coronation of the same year. In the latter case he proved to be indispensable, for in the sixty-four years without a coronation the precedents had been forgotten. In this way Esher reached a point where he was the chief unofficial representative of the King and the "liaison between King and ministers." As an example of the former role, we might mention that in 1908, when a purchaser known only as "X" acquired control of *The Times*, Esher visited Lord Northcliffe on behalf of "a very high quarter" to seek assurance that the policy of the paper would not be changed. Northcliffe, who was "X," hastened to give the necessary assurances, according to the official *History of The Times*. Northcliffe and the historian of *The Times* regarded Esher on this occasion as the emissary of King Edward, but we, who know of his relationship with the Rhodes secret society, are justified in asking if he were not equally the agent of the Milner Group, since it was as vital to the Group as to the King that the policy of *The Times* remain unchanged. As we shall see in a later chapter, when Northcliffe did adopt a policy contrary to that of the Group, in the period 1917-1919, the Group broke with him personally and within three years bought his controlling interest in the paper.

Certain other persons were probably taken into "The Society of the Elect" in the next few years. Hawksley, Rhodes's lawyer, was one. He obviously knew about the secret society, since he drew up the wills in which it was mentioned. This, combined with the fact that he was an intimate confidant of Rhodes in all the activities of the society and was made a trustee of the last three wills (1892), makes it probable that he should be regarded as an initiate.

Likewise it is almost certain that Milner brought in Sir Thomas Brassey (later Lord Brassey), the wealthy naval enthusiast whose name is preserved in *Brassey's Naval Annual.* Brassey was treasurer and most active figure in the Imperial Federation League during its ten years' existence. In 1889, as we have mentioned, he hired George Parkin to go to Australia on behalf of the League to make speeches in support of imperial federation. We have already indicated that Milner in 1893 approached Parkin in behalf of a mysterious and unnamed group of wealthy imperialists, and, some time later, Milner and Brassey signed a contract with Parkin to pay him £450 a year for three years to propagandize for imperial federation. Since this project was first broached to Parkin by Milner alone and since the Imperial Federation League was, by 1893, in process of dissolution, I think we have the right to assume that the unnamed group for which Milner was acting was the Rhodes secret society. If so, Brassey must have been introduced to the scheme sometime between 1891 and 1893. This last interpretation is substantiated by the numerous and confidential letters which passed between Milner and Brassey in the years which followed. Some of these will be mentioned later. It is worth mentioning here that Brassey was appointed Governor of Victoria in 1895 and played an important role in the creation of the Commonwealth of Australia in 1900.

The propaganda work which Parkin did in the period 1893-1895 in fulfillment of this agreement was part of a movement that was known at the time as "Seeley's lecturers." This movement was probably all that ensued from the fifth portion of the "ideal arrangement"—that is, from the projected college under Professor Seeley.

Another person who was brought into the secret society was Edmund Garrett, the intimate friend of Stead, Milner, and Rhodes, who was later used by Milner as a go-between for communications with the other two. Garrett had been sent to South Africa originally by Stead while he was still on the *Pall Mall Gazette* in 1889. He went there for a second time in 1895 as editor of the *Cape Times*, the most influential English-language newspaper in South Africa. This position he undoubtedly obtained from Stead and Rhodes. Sir Frederick Whyte, in his biography of Stead, says that Rhodes was the chief proprietor of the paper. Sir Edward Cook, however, the biographer of Garrett and a man who was very close to the Rhodes secret society, says that the owners of the *Cape Times* were Frederick York St. Leger and Dr. Rutherfoord Harris. This is a distinction without much difference, since Dr. Harris, as we shall see, was nothing more than an agent of Rhodes.

In South Africa, Garrett was on most intimate personal relationships with Rhodes. Even when the latter was Prime Minister of Cape Colony, Garrett used to communicate with him by tossing pebbles at his bedroom window in the middle of the night. Such a relationship naturally gave Garrett a prestige in South Africa which he could never have obtained by his own position or abilities. When High Commissioner Hercules Robinson drew up a proclamation after the Jameson Raid, he showed it to Garrett before it was issued and cut out a paragraph at the latter's insistence.

Garrett was also on intimate terms with Milner during his period as High Commissioner after 1897. In fact, when Rhodes spoke of political issues in South Africa, he frequently spoke of "I myself, Milner, and Garrett." We have already quoted an occasion on which he used this expression to Stead in 1900. Milner's relationship with Garrett can be gathered from a letter which he wrote to Garrett in 1899, after Garrett had to leave South Africa to go to a sanatorium in Germany: "It is no use protesting against the decrees of fate, nor do I want to say too much on what Rhodes calls 'the personal.' But this really was a great blow to me, and I have never quite got over your breakdown and departure, never quite felt the same man since, either politically or privately. . . . Dear Friend, I miss you fearfully, always shall miss you. So does this young country."[12]

I think we are justified in assuming that a man as intimate as this with Rhodes and Milner, who was used in such confidential and important ways by both of them, who knew of the plans for the Johannesburg revolt and the Jameson Raid before they occurred, and who knew of the Rhodes secret society, was an initiate. That Garrett knew of the Jameson plot beforehand is recorded by Sir Edward Cook in his biography. That Garrett knew of the secret society is recorded by Garrett himself in an article which he published in the *Contemporary Review* after Rhodes's death in 1902. The words in which Garrett made this last revelation are of some significance. He spoke of "that idea of a sort of Jesuit-like Secret Society for the Promotion of the Empire, which for long he hugged and which—minus, perhaps, the secrecy and the Jesuitry—I know to have had a good deal of fascination for others among our contemporaries not reckoned visionaries by the world."

We have said that Garrett was used by Milner as an intermediary with both Rhodes and Stead. The need for such an intermediary with Rhodes arose from Milner's feeling that it was politically necessary to conceal the intimacy of their relationship. As Rhodes told Stead, speaking of Milner, on 10 April 1900, "I have seen very little of him. He said to me, 'The less you and I are seen together the better.' Hence, I never invited him to Groote Schuur."[13]

Garrett was also used by Milner as an intermediary with Stead after the latter became alienated from the initiates because of his opposition to the Boer War. One example of this is of some significance. In 1902 Milner made a trip to England without seeing Stead. On 12 April of that year, Garrett, who had seen Milner, wrote the following letter to Stead: "I love the inner man, Stead, in spite of all differences, and should love him if he damned me and my policy and acts ten times more. So does Milner—in the inner court—we agreed when he was over—only there are temporary limitations and avoidances. . . . He told me why he thought on the whole he'd better not see you this time. I quite understood, though I'm not sure whether you would, but I'm sure you would have liked the way in which, without any prompting at all, he spoke of his personal feelings for you being unaffected by all this. Someday let us hope, all this tyranny will be overpast, and we shall be able to agree again, you and Milner, Cook and I." It is possible that the necessity for Milner to overrule his personal feelings and the mention of "the inner court" may be oblique references to the secret society. In any case, the letter shows the way in which Stead was quietly pushed aside in that society by its new leader.

Another prominent political figure who may have been an initiate in the period before 1902 is Lord Rosebery. Like his father-in-law, Lord Rothschild, who was an initiate, Rosebery was probably not a very active member of The Society of the Elect, although for quite different reasons. Lord Rothschild held aloof because to him the whole project was incomprehensible and unbusinesslike; Lord Rosebery held aloof because of his own diffident personality and his bad physical health. However, he cooperated with the members of the society and was on such close personal relationships with them that he probably knew of the secret society. Brett was one of his most intimate associates and introduced him to Milner in 1885. As for Rhodes, Rosebery's official biographer, the Marquess of Crewe, says that he "both liked and admired Cecil Rhodes who was often his guest." He made Rhodes a Privy Councillor, and Rhodes made him a trustee of his will. These things, and the fact that the initiates generally assumed that Rosebery would grant their requests, give certain grounds for believing that he was a member of their society.[14] If he was, he played little role in it after 1900.

Two other men, both fabulously wealthy South Africans, may be regarded as members of the society and probably initiates. These were Abe Bailey and Alfred Beit.

Abe Bailey (later Sir Abe, 1864-1940) was the largest landowner in Rhodesia, a large Transvaal mine-owner, and one of the chief, if not the chief, financial supporters of the Milner Group in the period up to 1925. These financial contributions still continue, although since 1925 they have undoubtedly been eclipsed by those of Lord Astor. Bailey was an associate of Rhodes and Alfred Beit, the two most powerful figures in South Africa, and like them was a close friend of Milner. He named his son, born in 1900, John Milner Bailey. Like Rhodes and Beit, he was willing that his money be used by Milner because he sympathized with his aims. As his obituary in *The Times* expressed it, "In politics he modeled himself deliberately on Rhodes as his ideal of a good South African and a devoted Imperialist. . . . He had much the same admiration of Milner and remained to the end a close friend of 'Milner's young men.' " This last phrase refers to Milner's Kindergarten or The Association of Helpers, which will be described in detail later.

Abe Bailey was one of the chief plotters in the Jameson Raid in 1895. He took over Rhodes's seat in the Cape Parliament in 1902-1907 and was Chief Whip in the Progressive Party, of which Dr. Jameson was leader. When the Transvaal obtained self-government in 1907, he went there and was Whip of the same party in the Legislative Assembly at Pretoria. After the achievement of the Union of South Africa, in the creation of which, as we shall see, he played a vital role, he was a member of the Union Parliament and a loyal supporter of Botha and Smuts from 1915 to 1924. After his defeat in 1924, he divided his time between South Africa and London. In England, as *The Times* said at his death, he "took a close interest behind the scenes in politics." This "close interest" was made possible by his membership in the innermost circle of the Milner Group, as we shall see.

Certain others of Rhodes's chief associates cooperated with Milner in his designs after Rhodes's death and might well be regarded as members of Rhodes's society and of the Milner Group. Of these we might mention Alfred Beit, Dr. Starr Jameson and his assistant R. S. Holland, J. Rochfort Maguire, and Lewis Loyd Michell.

Alfred Beit (1853-1906) was the business genius who handled all Rhodes's business affairs and incidentally had most to do with making the Rhodes fortune. He was a Rhodes Trustee and left much of his own fortune for public and educational purposes similar to those endowed by Rhodes. This will be discussed later. His biography was written by George Seymour Fort, a protege of Abe Bailey, who acted as Bailey's agent on the boards of directors of many corporations, a fact revealed by Fort himself in a letter to *The Times*, 13 August 1940.

Leander Starr Jameson (later Sir Starr, 1853-1917) was Rhodes's doctor, roommate, and closest friend, and had more to do with the opening up of Rhodesia than any other single man. His famous raid into the Transvaal with Rhodesian police in 1895 was one of the chief events leading up to the Boer War. After Rhodes's death, Jameson was leader of his party in Cape Colony and served as Premier in 1904-1908. A member of the National Convention of 1908-1909, he was also director of the British South Africa Company and a Rhodes Trustee. He was a great admirer of Milner and, even before the death of Rhodes, had given evidence of a desire to shift his allegiance from Rhodes to Milner. In 1898 he wrote to his brother: "Rhodes had done absolutely nothing but go backwards. . . . I hate it all and hate the people more than ever; would clear out by the next boat, but have not pluck enough to acknowledge myself beaten. . . . Milner is the only really healthy personality in the whole crowd."[15] This feeling may have been only a temporary reaction, resulting from the way in which Rhodes received news of the Jameson Raid, but it is likely that more basic issues were concerned, since more than two years had elapsed between the raid and these statements. At any rate, Milner and Jameson were able to cooperate loyally thereafter. Jameson's biographical sketch in *The Dictionary of National Biography* was written by Dougal Malcolm of Milner's Kindergarten.

Reginald Sothern Holland (now Sir Sothern) was private secretary to Dr. Jameson in 1904 and later for three years permanent head of the Prime Minister's Department (1905-1908). He was secretary to the South African Shipping Freights Conference (1905-1906) with Birchenough and succeeded Birchenough as His Majesty's Trade Commissioner to South Africa (1908-1913). During the war he was in charge of supply of munitions, at first in the War Office and later (1915) in the Ministry of Munitions. He was also on various commissions in which Milner was interested, such as the Royal Commission on Paper Supplies (with Birchenough), and ended the war as Controller of the Cultivation Division of the Food Production Department (which was seeking to carry out recommendations made by the Milner and Selborne Committee on Food Production). He became a Rhodes Trustee in 1932.

Lewis Loyd Michell (later Sir Lewis, 1842-1928) was Rhodes's banker in South Africa and after his death took over many of his interests. A Minister without Portfolio in Jameson's Cabinet in the Cape Colony (1904-1905), he was also a director of the British South Africa

Company and a Rhodes Trustee. He published a two-volume *Life of Rhodes* in 1910.

J. Rochfort Maguire (1855-1925), Fellow of All Souls, was an exact contemporary of Milner's at Oxford (1873-1877) and Rhodes's most intimate friend in college. He worked for Rhodes for the rest of his life. He obtained the original mining concession (which became the basis of the British South Africa Company) from Lobengula in 1883, was Rhodes's representative in the House of Commons for five years (1890-1895),[16] and his personal representative in Rhodesia or London during Rhodes's absences from either place. Director of the British South Africa Company for twenty-seven years (1898-1925), he was president for the last two. His sketch in the *Dictionary of National Biography* was written by Dougal Malcolm.

Of these six men whom Milner inherited from Rhodes, only one was young enough to become an active member of the Milner Group. This was Sothern Holland, born 1876, who did become a member, although perhaps not of the inner circle. The other five were Milner's own age, with established positions and power of their own. They all knew Milner well and cooperated with him. Even if they were initiates, they played no vital role in the history of the Milner Group after 1905.

As we have indicated, the character of the secret society and its personnel were changed after 1902. This was the result of the activities of Lord Milner. The death of Rhodes and the elimination of Stead gave the organization a much less melodramatic form while making it a much more potent political instrument. Moreover, as a result of the personal ascendancy of Milner, the membership of the organization was drastically changed. Of the initiates or probable initiates whom we have mentioned, Rothschild, Johnston, Hawksley, Rosebery, Jameson, Michell, and Maguire played little or no role in the society after 1902. Beit died in 1906, and Garrett the following year. Of the others, Grey, Brassey, Esher, and Balfour continued in active cooperation with the members of the Group. The real circle of initiates in the twentieth century, however, would appear to include the following names: Milner, Abe Bailey, George Parkin, Lord Selborne, Jan Smuts, A. J. Glazebrook, R. H. Brand (Lord Brand), Philip Kerr (Lord Lothian), Lionel Curtis, Geoffrey Dawson, H. A. L. Fisher, Edward Grigg, Leopold Amery, and Lord Astor. Since 1925, when Milner died, others have undoubtedly been added. This circle, with certain additional names, we shall call the "inner core" or the "inner circle" of the Milner Group. The history of these men's activities and the evidence which entitles us to attribute them to the circle of initiates will occupy most of the remainder of this volume.

The changes which Milner made in the Rhodes secret society were not important. There was no change in goals, and there was very little change in methods. In fact, both of these were modified more by Lord Lothian and his friends after Milner's death than they were by Milner after Rhodes's death.

Rhodes and Milner were aiming at the same goals, and had been for twenty-five years, in 1902. They differed slightly on how these goals could be obtained, a difference based on different personalities. To Rhodes it seemed that the ends could be won by amassing great wealth, to Milner it seemed that they could be won by quiet propaganda, hard work, and personal relationships (as he had learned from Toynbee). Neither rejected the other's methods, and each was willing to use the other and his methods to achieve their common dream as the occasion arose. With the death of Rhodes in 1902, Milner obtained control of Rhodes's money and was able to use it to lubricate the workings of his propaganda machine. This is exactly as Rhodes had wanted and had intended. Milner was Rhodes's heir, and both men knew it. Rhodes himself said before his death, "They tell me I can only live five years. I don't mean to die. I want to live. But if I go, there is one man — Sir Alfred Milner. Always trust Milner. You don't know yet what you have got in him." In 1898, in conversation with Stead, Rhodes said, "You will support Milner in any measure that he may take short of war. I make no such limitation. I support Milner absolutely without reserve. If he says peace, I say peace; if he says war, I say war. Whatever happens, I say ditto to Milner."[17]

The goals which Rhodes and Milner sought and the methods by which they hoped to achieve them were so similar by 1902 that the two are almost indistinguishable. Both sought to unite the world, and above all the English-speaking world, in a federal structure around Britain. Both felt that this goal could best be achieved by a secret band of men united to one another by devotion to the common cause and by personal loyalty to one another. Both felt that this band should pursue its goal by secret political and economic influence behind the scenes and by the control of journalistic, educational, and propaganda agencies. Milner's intention to work for this goal, and to use Rhodes's money and influence to do it, is clearly implied in all his actions (both before and after 1902), in his correspondence with Rhodes (some of it unpublished), and in letters to Parkin in September 1901 and to Lord Grey in May 1902.[18]

It is very likely that, long before Rhodes died, this plan was discussed in private conversations of which no record was kept. For example, three of the Rhodes Trustees under the last will — Grey, Milner, and Beit — with Lyttelton Gell had dinner at Beit's house and talked over important matters far into the night of 30 November 1898. It is quite clear that Rhodes talked over with his associates the ways in which his ideals would be carried out after his death. He lived constantly under the fear of death and regarded his whole life as a race in which he must achieve as much of his purpose as possible before he died. The biographer of Alfred Beit is quite confident that Rhodes discussed with Beit a plan by which Rhodes would omit from his will all mention of a project close to his heart — the Cape to Cairo Railway — leaving this project to be covered, as it was, by Beit's own will. There can be little doubt that Rhodes would have discussed a project even closer to his heart — the worldwide group of Anglo-Saxon sympathizers — with the trustees of his own will, and, above all, with the one most clearly devoted to his ideas, Milner.

4

Milner's Kindergarten,
1897-1910

THE APPOINTMENT as High Commissioner of South Africa was the turning point in Milner's life. It was obtained, apparently, through his membership in Rhodes's secret society, through the influence of Stead, Brett, and Rhodes. Stead, in his book on Rhodes's wills, claims the chief credit for the nomination, while Brett was with Milner at Windsor when he received the appointment and returned with him to London. Sir Harry Johnston, who had already been offered the appointment for himself by a Foreign Office official, felt that it was Rhodes's influence which gave it to Milner. In his autobiography he wrote: "At last the decision was made—Sir Alfred Milner. I suspect very much on the personal pleadings of Cecil Rhodes, who professed himself delighted with the choice. . . . The non-selection of myself for a work that would have greatly interested me, was a disappointment, and I felt it was due to Rhodes' enmity more than to any other cause."

As High Commissioner, Milner was subordinate to the Secretary of State for the Colonies, a post held at that time by Joseph Chamberlain, who was already acquainted with Milner. They had fought Home Rule together in the election of 1886 and had both been in Egypt in 1889. They already agreed on most of the important issues of the day, combining, like other members of the Milner Group, advocacy of social welfare and imperialism. Moreover, both were strong believers in union with Ireland and a new tariff policy based on imperial preference. When Chamberlain joined Lord Salisbury's government as Secretary of State for the Colonies (1895-1903), he was eager to accept the suggestion that Milner be sent to South Africa. As Colonial Secretary, Chamberlain did a number of things that won the complete support of Milner. Among these we might mention the new constitution for Jamaica (1899), the federation of the Malay States (1895), and the creation of the Commonwealth of Australia (1900). When Chamberlain resigned from the Colonial Office in 1903 on the issue of tariff reform, the post was offered by Balfour to Milner. The latter refused in order to complete the work he had started in South Africa. When he was ready to retire from his post, he recommended that his successor be either Alfred Lyttelton or Lord Selborne. The latter obtained the appointment and not only carried Milner's work to completion but did it with Milner's picked personnel. That personnel regarded Selborne as second leader to Milner in the Group.[1]

As High Commissioner, Milner built up a body of assistants known in history as "Milner's Kindergarten." The following list gives the chief members of the Kindergarten, their dates of birth and death (where possible), their undergraduate colleges (with dates), and the dates in which they were Fellows of All Souls.

NAME	DATES	COLLEGE	ALL SOULS
Patrick Duncan (later Sir Patrick	1870-1946	Balliol 1890-1894	Never
Philip Kerr (later Lord Lothian)	1882-1940	New 1897-1901	Never
Robert Henry Brand (later Lord Brand)	1878-1963	New 1897-1901	1901-
Lionel Curtis	1872-1955	New 1891-1905	1921-
Geoffrey Dawson (until 1917 Robinson)	1874-1944	Magdalen 1893-1897	1898-1905; 1915-1944
John Buchan (later Lord Tweedsmuir)	1875-1940	Brasenose 1895-1899	Never
Dougal Orme Malcolm (later Sir Dougal)	1877-1955	New 1895-1899	1899-1955
William Lionel Hichens	1874-1941	New 1894-1898	Never
Richard Feetham	1874-1965	New 1893-1898	Never
John Dove	1872-1934	New 1891-1895	Never
Basil Williams	1867-1950	New 1886-1891	1924-1925
Lord Basil Blackwood	1870-1917	Balliol 1891-	Never
Hugh A. Wyndham	1877-	New 1896-1900	Never
George V. Fiddes (later Sir George	1858-1925	Brasenose 1880-1884	Never
John Hanbury-Williams (later Sir John)	1859-1946	Wellington, N.Z.	Never
Main S. O. Walrond	1870-	Balliol	Never
Fabian Ware (later Sir Fabian)	1869-1949	Univ. of Paris	Never
William Flavelle Monypenny	1866-1912	Balliol 1888-1890	Never

To these eighteen names should be added five others who were present in South Africa between the Boer War and the creation of the Union and were members of the Milner Group but cannot be listed under the Kindergarten because they were not members of Milner's civil service.[2] These five are:

NAME	DATES	COLLEGE	ALL SOULS
Leopold Amery	1873-1955	Balliol 1892-1896	1897-1911, 1938-
Edward Grigg (later Lord Altrincham)	1879-1955	New 1898-1902	Never
H. A. L. Fisher	1865-1940	New 1884-1888	Never
Edward F. L. Wood (later Lord Irwin and Lord Halifax)	1881-1959	Christ Church 1899-1903	1903-1910
Basil K. Long	1878-1944	Brasenose 1897-1901	Never

Of these twenty-three names, eleven were from New College. Seven were members of All Souls, six as Fellows. These six had held their fellowships by 1947 an aggregate of one hundred and sixty-nine years, or an average of over twenty-eight years each. Of the twenty-three, nine were in the group which founded, edited, and wrote *The Round Table* in the period after 1910, five were in close personal contact with Lloyd George (two in succession as private secretaries) in the period 1916-1922, and seven were in the group which controlled and edited *The Times* after 1912.

Eleven of these twenty-three men, plus others whom we have mentioned, formed the central core of the Milner Group as it has existed from 1910 to the present. These others will be discussed in their proper place. At this point we should take a rapid glance at the biographies of some of the others.

Two members of the Kindergarten, Patrick Duncan and Richard Feetham, stayed in South Africa after the achievement of the Union in 1910. Both remained important members of the Milner Group and, as a result of this membership, rose to high positions in their adopted country. Patrick Duncan had been Milner's assistant on the Board of Internal Revenue from 1894 to 1897 and was taken with him to South Africa as private secretary. He was Treasurer of the Transvaal in 1901, Colonial Secretary of the Transvaal in 1903-1906, and Acting Lieutenant Governor in 1906. He remained in South Africa as a lieutenant to Jan Smuts, becoming an advocate of the Supreme Court there, a member of the South African Parliament, Minister of Interior, Public Health, and Education (1921-1924), Minister of Mines (1933-1936), and finally Governor-General of South Africa

(1936-1946). He frequently returned to England to confer with the Group (in September 1932, for example, at Lord Lothian's country house, Blickling).

Richard Feetham was made Deputy Town Clerk and later Town Clerk of Johannesburg (1902-1905). He was legal adviser to Lord Selborne, the High Commissioner, in 1907 and a member of the Legislative Council of the Transvaal later (1907-1910). He was chairman of the Committee on Decentralization of Powers in India in 1918-1919; a King's Counsel in Transvaal (1919-1923); a judge of the Supreme Court of South Africa (1923-1930); chairman of the Irish Boundary Commission (1924-1925); chairman of the Local Government Commission in Kenya Colony (of which Edward Grigg was Governor) in 1926; adviser to the Shanghai Municipal Council (1930-1931); chairman of the Transvaal Asiatic Land Tenure Commission (1930-1935); Vice-Chancellor of the University of Witwatersrand, Johannesburg (1938); and has been a judge of the Supreme Court of South Africa since 1939. Most of these positions, as we shall see, came to him as a member of the Milner Group.

Hugh A. Wyndham also remained in South Africa after 1910 and was a member of the Union Parliament for ten years (1910-1920). He had previously been secretary to Milner. In spite of the prominence of his family and his own position as heir presumptive to the third Baron Leconfield, it is difficult to obtain any adequate information about him. His biography in *Who's Who* does not mention his experiences in South Africa or his other connections with the Milner Group. This is obviously the result of a deliberate policy, since editions of *Who's Who* of thirty-five years ago do mention the South African connection. Wyndham wrote *Problems of Imperial Trusteeship* (1933); *Britain and the World;* and the chapter on "The Formation of the Union of South Africa, 1901-1910" in volume VIII of the *Cambridge History of the British Empire* (1936). He was, like all the members of the Milner Group, a member of the Royal Institute of International Affairs, wrote many book reviews for its *Journal*, and at the outbreak of war in 1939 became the usual presiding officer at its meetings (in the absence of Lord Astor). When publication of the *Journal* was resumed after the war, he became chairman of its editorial board, a position he still holds. Married to Maude Lyttelton, daughter of Viscount Cobham, he is also a brother-in-law of Sir Ivor Maxse (the brother of Lady Milner) and a nephew of Lord Rosebery.

Dougal Malcolm (Sir Dougal since 1938), a grandson of Lord Charles Wellesley, joined the Colonial Office in 1900 and served there under Chamberlain and Alfred Lyttelton for several years. In 1905 he went to South Africa as private secretary to Lord Selborne and remained there until Union was achieved. He was secretary to Lord

Grey, Governor-General of Canada, during the last year of his tenure (1910-1911); an official of the British Treasury for a year; and, in 1913, became a director of the British South Africa Company (president since 1938). He is also vice-president of the British North Borneo Company, of which his brother-in-law, General Sir Neill Malcolm, is president.[3] Sir Dougal wrote the biographies of Otto Beit, of Dr. Jameson, and of J. Rochford Maguire for the *Dictionary of National Biography*.

William Lionel Hichens (1874-1940), on graduating from New College, served briefly as a cyclist messenger in the Boer War and then joined the Egyptian Ministry of Finance (1900). After only nine months' service, he was shifted by Milner to South Africa to join the Kindergarten as Treasurer of Johannesburg. He at once went to England to float a loan, and on his return (in 1902) was made Colonial Treasurer of the Transvaal and Treasurer of the Intercolonial Council. Later he added to his responsibilities the role of Acting Commissioner of Railways. In 1907 he went to India as a member of the Royal Commission on Decentralization, following this with a stint as chairman of the Board of Inquiry into Public Service in Southern Rhodesia (1909). In 1910 he went into private business, becoming chairman of the board of a great steel firm, Cammell Laird and Company, but continued as a member of the Milner Group. In 1915, Lloyd George sent Hichens and Brand to organize the munitions industry of Canada. They set up the Imperial Munitions Board of Canada, on which Joseph Flavelle (Sir Joseph after 1917) was made chairman, Charles B. Gordon (Sir Charles after 1917) vice-chairman, and Brand a member. In later years Hichens was a prominent businessman, one of the great steel masters of England, director of the Commonwealth Trust Company (which sent John Dove to India in 1918), of the London Northwestern Railway and its successor, the London, Midlands and Scottish. He was a member of the Executive Committee of the Carnegie United Kingdom Trust for over twenty years (1919-1940), which may help to explain the extraordinary generosity of the Carnegie Foundation toward the Royal Institute of International Affairs (of which Hichens was a member). He was an enthusiastic supporter of adult education programs and spent years of effort on Birkbeck College, the graduate evening school of the University of London. He was chairman of the board of governors of this institution from 1927 until his death, by a German bomb, in December of 1940. From 1929 onwards, like most of the inner circle of the Milner Group, he lived close to Oxford (at North Aston). He married Hermione Lyttelton, daughter of Sir Neville Lyttelton, niece of Viscount Cobham, and cousin of the present Oliver Lyttelton.

George Vandeleur Fiddes (Sir George after 1912) had been private secretary to the Earl of Onslow, father of Lady Halifax, before he was secretary to Milner in South Africa (1897-1900). Later he was political secretary to the Commander-in-Chief in South Africa (1900), secretary to the Transvaal administration (1900-1902), Assistant Under Secretary of State for the Colonies (1909-1916), and Permanent Under Secretary for the Colonies (1916-1921).

John Hanbury-Williams (Sir John after 1908) had been in the regular army for nineteen years, chiefly as aide to various colonial administrators, when he was assigned to Milner as military secretary in 1897. After three years of that, he went to London as secretary to the Secretary of State for War (St. John Brodrick, 1900-1903), and to Canada as secretary and military secretary to the Governor-General, Earl Grey (1904-1909). Then he was brigadier general in charge of administration in Scotland (1909-1914) and on the General Staff (1914), Chief of the British Military Mission to Russia (1914-1917), in charge of the British Prisoners of War Department at The Hague (1917-1918) and in Switzerland (1918), and ended his career in a blaze of glory as a major general, marshal of the diplomatic corps (1920-1934), and extra equerry to three Kings of England (1934-1946).

John Buchan was not a member of the inner core of the Milner Group, but was close to it and was rewarded in 1935 by being raised to a barony as Lord Tweedsmuir and sent to Canada as Governor-General. He is important because he is (with Lionel Curtis) one of the few members of the inner circles of the Milner Group who have written about it in published work. In his autobiography, *Pilgrim's Way* (Boston, 1940), he gives a brief outline of the personnel of the Kindergarten and their subsequent achievements, and a brilliant analysis of Milner himself. He wrote:

He (Milner) had received — chiefly from Arnold Toynbee — an inspiration which centered all his interests on the service of the state. He had the instincts of a radical reformer joined to a close-textured intellect which reformers rarely possess. He had a vision of the Good Life spread in a wide commonalty; and when his imagination apprehended the Empire, his field of vision was marvellously enlarged. So at the outset of his career he dedicated himself to a cause, putting things like leisure, domestic happiness, and money-making behind him. In Bacon's phrase he espoused the State. On the intellectual side he found that which wholly satisfied him in the problems of administration, when he confronted them as Goschen's secretary, and in Egypt, and at Somerset House. He had a mind remarkable both for its scope and its mastery over details — the most powerful administrative intelligence, I think, which Britain has produced in our day. If I may compare him with others, he was as infallible as Cromer in detecting the center of gravity in a situation, as brilliant as Alfred Beit in bringing order out of tangled finances, and he had Curzon's power of keeping a big organization steadily at work. He was no fanatic — his intelligence was too supreme for that — but in the noblest sense of the word, he was an enthusiast. He narrowed his interests of set purpose, and this absorption meant a certain rigidity. He had cut himself off from some of the emollients of life. Consequently, the perfect administrator was a less perfect diplomatist. . . [Later, Buchan adds,] I was brought into close touch with a great character. Milner was the most selfless man I have ever known. He thought of his work and his cause, much of his colleagues, never of himself. He simply was not interested in what attracts common ambition. He could not be bribed, for there was nothing on the globe wherewith to bribe him; or deterred by personal criticism, for he cared not at all for fame; and it would have been as easy to bully the solar system, since he did not know the meaning of fear.

The effect Milner had on Buchan was shared by the other members of the Kindergarten and provided that spiritual bond which animated the Milner Group. This spirit, found in Toynbee, in Goschen, in Milner, and later in Lionel Curtis, was the motivating force of the Milner Group until after 1922. Indeed, much of what Buchan says here about Milner could be applied with slight change to Lionel Curtis, and Curtis, as we shall see, was the motivating force of the Milner Group from 1910 to 1922. After 1922, as the influence of Lord Lothian, Lord Astor, and Lord Brand increased and that of Milner declined, the spirit of the Group became somewhat tarnished but not completely lost.

Buchan went to Brasenose College, but, as he says himself, "I lived a good deal at Balliol and my closest friends were of that college." He mentions as his closest friends Hilaire Belloc, F. E. Smith (the future Lord Birkenhead), John Simon, Leo Amery, T. A. Nelson, Arthur Salter, Bron Lucas, Edward Wood (the future Lord Halifax), and Raymond Asquith. Of this list, five were future Fellows of All Souls, and four of these were important members of the Milner Group.

Buchan went to South Africa in 1901, on Milner's personal invitation, to be his private secretary, but stayed only two years. Placed in charge of resettlement of displaced Boers and agricultural reform (both close to Milner's heart), he left in 1903 to take an important position in the administration of Egypt. This appointment was mysteriously canceled after his return to England because, according to Buchan, he was too young for the task. It is more than likely that Milner, who had obtained the appointment for him, changed his mind because of Buchan's rapidly declining enthusiasm for imperial federation. This was a subject on which Milner and other members of his Group were adamant for many years. By 1915 most members of the Group began to believe that federation was impossible, and, as a compromise, took what we know now as the Commonwealth of Nations — that is, a group of nations joined together by common ideals and allegiances rather than by fixed political organization. Lionel Curtis remains to this day a fanatical believer in federation, and some of the decline in his influence after 1922 may be attributed to inability to obtain federation in the face of world — and above all Dominion — opposition. The present Commonwealth is in reality the compromises worked out when the details of the Milner Group clashed with the reality of political facts.

As a result of Buchan's failure to obtain the appointment of Egypt, he continued to practice law in London for three years, finally abandoning it to become a partner in the publishing firm of his old classmate Thomas A. Nelson (1906-1916). In 1907 he married Susan Grosvenor, whose family (Dukes of Westminister) was allied, as we have seen, to the Wyndhams, Cavendishes, Lytteltons, and Primroses (Earls of Rosebery and Lords Dalmeny). As a result of this family connection, Buchan wrote a memoir on Lord Rosebery for *Proceedings of the British Academy* in 1930 and a book on the Grosvenor twins, who were killed in the war.

During the war, Buchan was a correspondent for *The Times*, wrote *Nelson's History of the Great War* in twenty-four volumes (1915-1919), was the military intelligence in France (1916-1917), and finally was Director of Information for the War Office (1917-1918). During this period and later, he was a prolific writer of travel, historical, and adventure stories, becoming eventually, by such works as *Greenmantle, The Three Hostages*, and *The Thirty-nine Steps*, the most famous writer of adventure stories in Britain. His connection with South Africa gained him the post of official historian of the South African forces in France. He was a close friend of Lord Haldane and Lord Rosebery, both of whom can be regarded as members of the Milner Group. Of Haldane, Buchan wrote: "What chiefly attracted me to him was his loyalty to Milner. Milner thought him the ablest man in public life, abler even than Arthur Balfour, and alone of his former Liberal allies Haldane stood by him on every count." Haldane, with Rosebery, Asquith, and Edward Grey, had formed the Liberal League to support liberal imperialism, with which Milner was closely associated.

Buchan was representative of the Scottish universities in the House of Commons for eight years (1927-1935), Lord High Commissioner for the Church of Scotland in 1933-1934, president of the Scottish Historical Society (1929-1933), and Chancellor of Edinburgh University, before he obtained his last post, Governor-General of Canada (1935-1940).

Basil Williams graduated from New College in 1891 and almost immediately became clerk in the House of Commons, holding this post for nine years before he went soldiering in the Boer War. He became Secretary of the Transvaal Education Department, wrote Volume IV of *The Times History of the South African War*, and was *The Times* special correspondent at the South African Convention of 1908-1919, which made the Union. A major on the General Staff in 1918-1909, he was later Ford Lecturer at Oxford (in 1921), Professor of History at

McGill (1921-1925), and Professor of History at Edinburgh (1925-1937). He wrote the very revealing article on Milner in the *Dictionary of National Biography* and numerous other works, including *Cecil Rhodes* (1921), *The British Empire* (for the Home University Library, 1928), Volume XI of the Oxford History of England (*The Whig Supremacy, 1714-1760*), *Botha, Smuts, and South Africa* (1946), and edited *The Makers of the Nineteenth Century* (1915-1928).

Lord Basil Blackwood, son and heir of Lord Dufferin, went to Balliol in 1891 but never graduated, being an adventurer of the first order. Taken to South Africa by Milner, he was employed in the Judge Advocate's Department for a year (1900-1901), then was Assistant Colonial Secretary of Orange River Colony for six years (1901-1907). He became Colonial Secretary of Barbados in 1907 and Assistant Secretary of the Land Development Commission in England in 1910. He would have been an important member of the Milner Group but was killed in France in 1917.

Of the major members of the Kindergarten, Robert H. Brand (since 1946 Baron Brand) stands close to the top. His father was second Viscount Brand, twenty-fourth Baron Dacre (created 1307), son of a Speaker of the House of Commons (1872-1884), while his mother was Susan Cavendish, daughter of Lord George Cavendish, and niece of the seventh Duke of Devonshire. His father, as Governor of New South Wales in 1895-1899, was one of the original instigators of the federation of the Australian Colonies, which came into effect in 1900. His older brother, the third Viscount Hampden, was a lord-in-waiting to the King (1924-1936), while another brother, Admiral Sir Hubert Brand, was extra equerry to the King (1922) and principal naval aide to the King (1931-1932). His nephew, Freeman Freeman-Thomas (Baron Willingdon after 1910; Marquess of Willingdon after 1936), in 1892 married the daughter of Lord Brassey, and became Governor-General of Canada (1926-1931) and Viceroy of India (1931-1936).

Brand, who has been a Fellow of All Souls since 1901, is chiefly responsible for the Astor influence in the Milner Group. He went to South Africa in 1902 and was made secretary of the Intercolonial Council of the Transvaal and Orange River Colony and secretary of the Railway Committee of the Central South African Railways, with Philip Kerr (the future Lord Lothian) as assistant secretary on both organizations. He was secretary to the Transvaal Delegation at the South African National Convention (1908-1909) and at once wrote a deliberately naive work published by Oxford University Press in 1909 with the title *The Union of South Africa*. In this work there is no mention of the Kindergarten, and where it is necessary to speak of its work, this is done as if it were performed by persons unknown to the writer. He says, for example (page 40): "The Transvaal Delegation alone was assisted throughout the convention by a staff of legal advisers and experts," and thus dismisses the Kindergarten's essential work. His own work is passed over in silence, and at the front of the volume is placed a quotation in Dutch from President Sir John Brand of the Orange River Colony, possibly to mislead the ordinary reader into believing that there was a family connection between the South African politician and the author of the book.

Brand's role in the Milner Group after 1910 is too great to be covered adequately here. Suffice it to say that he was regarded as the economist of the Round Table Group and became a partner and managing director of Lazard Brothers and Company, a director of Lloyd's Bank, and a director of *The Times*, retiring from these positions in 1944 and 1945. During the First World War, he was a member of the Imperial Munitions Board of Canada (1915-1918) and deputy chairman of the British Mission in Washington (1917-1918). While in Washington, he married Nancy Astor's sister, daughter of Chiswell Dabney Langhorne of Viginia. It was this connection which gave him his entree to Cliveden in the period when that name became notorious.

Brand was one of the important figures in international finance in the period after 1918. At the Paris Peace Conference of 1919 he was financial adviser to Lord Robert Cecil, chairman of the Supreme Economic Council. He was later vice-president of the Brussels Conference (1920) and financial representative for South Africa at the Genoa Conference (1922). He was a member of the committee of experts on stabilization of the German mark in 1923, the committee which paved the way for the Dawes Plan. After an extended period in private business, he was head of the British Food Mission to Washington (1941-1944), chairman of the British Supply Council in North America (1942-1945, 1946), and His Majesty's Treasury Representative in Washington (1944-1946). In this last capacity he had much to do with negotiating the enormous American loan to Britain for postwar reconstruction. During the years 1942-1944, Brand put in his own place as managing director of Lazard Brothers his nephew, Thomas Henry Brand, son of Viscount Hampden, and, when Brand left Lazard in 1944, he brought the same nephew to Washington as chief executive officer on the British side of the Combined Production and Resources Board, and later (1945) as chairman of the official Committee on Supplies for Liberated Areas. In all of his activities Brand has remained one of the most central figures in the core of the Milner Group.

Just as important as Brand was his intimate friend Philip Kerr (later Lord Lothian), whom we have already seen as Brand's assistant in South Africa. Kerr, grandson, through his mother, of the fourteenth Duke of Norfolk, originally went to South Africa as private secretary to a friend of his father's, Sir Arthur Lawley, Lieutenant Governor of the Transvaal (1902). Kerr was Brand's assistant on the Intercolonial Council and on the Committee of the Central South African Railways (1905-1908). Later, as secretary to the Transvaal Indigency Commission (1907-1908), he wrote a report on the position of poor white laborers in a colored country which was so valuable that it was republished by the Union government twenty years later.

From 1908 on, Kerr was, as we shall see, one of the chief organizers of publicity in favor of the South African Union. He was secretary to the Round Table Group in London and editor of *The Round Table* from 1910 to1916, leaving the post to become secretary to Lloyd George (1916-1922), manager of the *Daily Chronicle* (1921), and secretary to the Rhodes Trust (1925-1939). He obtained several governmental offices after the death of his cousin, the tenth Marquess of Lothian, in 1930, gave him a title, 28,000 acres of land, and a seat in the House of Lords. He was Chancellor to the Duchy of Lancaster (1931), Parliamentary Under Secretary to the India Office (1931-1932), a member of the first and second Round Table Conferences on India, and chairman of the Indian Franchise Committee, before he finished his life as Ambassador to the United States (1939-1940). In 1923 he and Lionel Curtis published a book called *The Prevention of War*, consisting of lectures which they had previously given at Williams College. After his death, Curtis edited a collection of *American Speeches of Lord Lothian*, with an introduction by Lord Halifax and a biographical sketch by Edward Grigg (reprinted from *The Round Table*). This was published, as might be expected, by Chatham House.

On his death, Lord Lothian left his ancestral estate, Newbattle Abbey in Midlothian, as a residential college for adult education in Scotland, and left his Tudor country house, Blickling (frequent assembly place of the Milner Group), as a national monument. He never married and gave up his Roman Catholic faith for Christian Science in the course of an almost fatal illness in 1914.

Geoffrey Dawson (1874-1944), who changed his name from Robinson in 1917, was also one of the innermost members of the Milner Group. A member of the Colonial Office under Chamberlain (1898-1901), he became for five years private secretary to Milner in South Africa (1901-1905) and then was made South African correspondent of *The Times* and editor of the *Johannesburg Star* in the critical period of the formation of the Union (1905-1910). Always a member of the Round Table Group and the Milner Group, Dawson added to these the offices of editor of *The Times* (1912-1919, 1922-1941) and secretary to the Rhodes Trustees (1921-1922). During the period in which Dawson was not editor of *The Times*, he was well provided for by the

Milner Group, being made estates bursar of All Souls, a director of Consolidated Gold Fields, Ltd., and of Trust Houses, Ltd. (both Rhodes concerns), as well as being secretary to the Rhodes Trust. He married in 1919 the daughter of Sir Arthur Lawley (later sixth Baron Wenlock), Kerr's old chief in the Transvaal. Sir Arthur, who had started his career as private secretary to his uncle, the Duke of Westminster, in 1892, ended it as Governor of Madras (1906-1911).

Dawson was probably as close to Milner personally as any member of the Kindergarten, although Amery must be regarded as Milner's political heir. *The Times'* obituary of Dawson says: "To none was Milner's heart more wholly given than to Dawson; the sympathy between the older and the younger man was almost that of father and son, and it lasted unchanged until Milner's death." As editor of *The Times*, Dawson was one of the most influential figures in England. He used that influence in the directions decided by the Group. This was to be seen, in later years, in the tremendous role which he played in the affairs of India and, above all, in the appeasement policy. In 1929 he visited his "long-standing friend" Lord Halifax, then Viceroy of India, and subsequently wrote most of *The Times* editorials on India in the fight which preceded the Government of India Act of 1935. In 1937 he wrote *The Times* articles which inaugurated the last stage of appeasement, and personally guided *The Times* support of that policy. After his retirement from the chair of editor of *The Times* in 1941, he served for the last three years of his life as editor of *The Round Table*.

William Flavelle Monypenny was assistant editor of *The Times* (1894-1899) before he went to South Africa to become editor of the *Johannesburg Star*. He left this position at the outbreak of the Boer War, since the publication of a pro-British paper was not possible during the hostilities. After a short period as a lieutenant in the Imperial Light Horse (1899-1900), Monypenny was made Director of Civil Supplies under Milner (1900-1902) and then resumed his post as editor of the *Star*. In 1903 he resigned in protest against Milner's policy of importing Chinese laborers and walked across Africa from the Cape to Egypt. Resuming his position on *The Times* (1903-1908), he became a director of the firm for the last four years of his life (1908-1912). About this time Lord Rowton, who had been Disraeli's private secretary, left his papers to *The Times* to be used for a *Life* of Disraeli. The task was begun by Monypenny, but he finished only the first two volumes of the six-volume work. The last four volumes were written by George E. Buckle, editor of *The Times* (1884-1912), Fellow of All Souls (1877-1885), and a contemporary of Milner's at Oxford (1872-1876).

It is perhaps worth noting that when Monypenny resigned from the *Johannesburg Star* he was replaced as editor by William Basil Worsfold, who held the post for two years, being replaced, as we have

said, by Geoffrey Dawson. In the years 1906-1913 Worsfold published
a three-volume study of Milner's accomplishments in South Africa.
This contains the most valuable account in existence of the work of the
Kindergarten.[4]

Fabian Ware (Sir Fabian since 1922), who had been a reporter on
The Morning Post (1899-1901), was Assistant Director and Director of
Education in the Transvaal (1901-1905) and Director of Education in
the Orange River Colony (1903), as well as a member of the Transvaal
Legislative Council (1903-1905). He was editor of *The Morning Post* in
1905-1911 and then became special commissioner to the board of the
Rio Tinto Company, on which Milner was director. During the First
World War he rose to the rank of major general. Since then he has been
permanent vice-chairman of the Imperial War Graves Commission. A
book which he wrote in 1937, *The Immortal Heritage, The Work of
the Imperial War Graves Commission*, was made the occasion of an
article on this subject in *The Round Table*. Sir Fabian was a member of
the Imperial Committee on Economic Consultation and Cooperation
in 1933 and was a director-general in the War Office in 1939-1944.

Main Swete Osmond Walrond was in the Ministry of Finance in
Egypt (1894-1897) before he became Milner's private secretary for the
whole period of his High Commissionership (1897-1905). He was then
appointed District Commissioner in Cyprus but did not take the post.
In 1917-1919 he was in the Arab Bureau in Cairo under the High Commissioner and acted as an unofficial, but important, adviser to Milner's
mission to Egypt in 1919-1921. This mission led to Egyptian independence from Britain.

Lionel Curtis is one of the most important members of the Milner
Group, or, as a member of the Group expressed it to me, he is the *fons
et origo*. It may sound extravagant as a statement, but a powerful
defense could be made of the claim that what Curtis thinks should be
done to the British Empire is what happens a generation later. I shall
give here only two recent examples of this. In 1911 Curtis decided that
the name of His Majesty's Dominions must be changed from "British
Empire" to "Commonwealth of Nations." This was done officially in
1948. Again, about 1911 Curtis decided that India must be given complete self-government as rapidly as conditions permitted. This was carried out in 1947. As we shall see, these are not merely coincidental
events, for Curtis, working behind the scenes, has been one of the chief
architects of the present Commonwealth. It is not easy to discern the
places where he has passed, and no adequate biographical sketch can
be put on paper here. Indeed, much of the rest of this volume will be a
contribution to the biography of Lionel Curtis. Burning with an un-
quenchable ardor, which some might call fanatical, he has devoted his
life to his dominant idea, that the finer things of life—liberty,

democracy, toleration, etc. — could be preserved only within an in-tegrated world political system, and that this political system could be constructed about Great Britain, but only if Britain adopted toward her Dominions, her colonies, and the rest of the world a policy of generosity, of trust, and of developing freedom. Curtis was both a fanatic and an idealist. But he was not merely "a man in a hurry." He had a fairly clear picture of what he wanted. He did not believe that complete and immediate freedom and democracy could be given to the various parts of the imperial system, but felt that they could only be ex-tended to these parts in accordance with their ability to develop to a level where they were capable of exercising such privileges. When that level was achieved and those privileges were extended, he felt that they would not be used to disrupt the integrated world system of which he dreamed, but to integrate it more fully and in a sounder fashion — a fashion based on common outlook and common patterns of thought rather than on the dangerous unity of political subjection, censorship, or any kind of duress. To Curtis, as to H. G. Wells, man's fate de-pended on a race between education and disaster. This was similar to the feeling which animated Rhodes when he established the Rhodes Scholarships, although Curtis has a much broader and less nationalistic point of view than Rhodes. Moreover, Curtis believed that people could be educated for freedom and responsibility by giving them always a little more freedom, a little more democracy, and a little more responsibility than they were quite ready to handle. This is a basically Christian attitude — the belief that if men are trusted they will prove trustworthy — but it was an attitude on which Curtis was prepared to risk the existence of the British Empire. It is not yet clear whether Cur-tis is the creator of the Commonwealth of Nations or merely the destroyer of the British Empire. The answer will be found in the behavior of India in the next few years. The Milner Group knew this. That is why India, since 1913, has been the chief object of their atten-tions.

These ideas of Curtis are clearly stated in his numerous published works. The following quotations are taken from *The Problem of the Commonwealth* drawn up by the Round Table Group and published under Curtis's name in 1916:

> Responsible government can only be realized for any body of citizens in so far as they are fit for the exercise of political power. In the Dependencies the great majority of the citizens are not as yet capable of governing them-selves and for them the path to freedom is primarily a problem of educa-tion. . . . The Commonwealth is a typical section of human society in-cluding every race and level of civilization organized in one state. In this world commonwealth the function of government is reserved to the European minority, for the unanswerable reason that for the present this

portion of its citizens is alone capable of the task—civilized states are obliged to assume control of backward communities to protect them from exploitation by private adventurers from Europe. . . . The Commonwealth cannot, like despotisms, rest content with establishing order within and between the communities it includes. It must by its nature prepare these communities first to maintain order within themselves. The rule of law must be rooted in the habits and wills of the peoples themselves. . . . The peoples of India and Egypt, no less than those of the British Isles and Dominions, must be gradually schooled to the management of their national affairs. . . . It is not enough that free communities should submit their relations to the rule of law. Until all those people control that law the principle by which the commonwealth exists is unfulfilled. The task of preparing for freedom the races which cannot as yet govern themselves is the supreme duty of those races who can. It is the spiritual end for which the Commonwealth exists, and material order is nothing except a means to it. . . . In India the rule of law is firmly established. Its maintenance is a trust which rests on the government of the Commonwealth until such time as there are Indians enough able to discharge it. India may contain leaders qualified not only to make but also to administer laws, but she will not be ripe for self-government until she contains an electorate qualified to recognize those leaders and place them in office. . . . For England the change is indeed a great one. Can she face it? Can she bear to lose her life, as she knows it, to find it in a Commonwealth, wide as the world itself, a life greater and nobler than before? Will she fail at this second and last crisis of her fate, as she failed at the first, like Athens and Prussia, forsaking freedom for power, thinking the shadow more real than the light, and esteeming the muckrake more than the crown?

Four years later, in 1920, Curtis wrote: "The whole effect of the war has been to bring movements long gathering to a sudden head . . . companionship in arms has fanned . . . long smouldering resentment against the prescription that Europeans are destined to dominate the rest of the world. In every part of Asia and Africa it is bursting into flames. . . . Personally, I regard this challenge to the long unquestioned claim of the white man to dominate the world as inevitable and wholesome especially to ourselves."[5]

Unfortunately for the world, Curtis, and the Milner Group generally, had one grave weakness that may prove fatal. Skilled as they were in political and personal relations, endowed with fortune, education, and family connections, they were all fantastically ignorant of economics—even those, like Brand or Hichens, who were regarded within the Group as its experts on this subject. Brand was a financier, while Hichens was a businessman—in both cases occupations that guarantee nothing in the way of economic knowledge or understanding.

Curtis was registered as an undergraduate at New College for fourteen years (1891-1905) because he was too busy to take time to get his degree. This is undoubtedly also the reason he was admitted to All Souls so belatedly, since an ordinary fellowship requires as a qualification the possession either of a university prize or of a first-class honours degree. By the time Curtis took his degree he had fought in the Boer War, been Town Clerk of Johannesburg, and been assistant secretary for local government in the Transvaal. In 1906 he resigned his official positions to organize "Closer Union Groups" agitating for a federation of South Africa. When this work was well started, he became a member of the Transvaal Legislative Council and wrote the Transvaal draft of a projected constitution for such a federation. In 1910-1912, and at various times subsequently, he traveled about the world, organizing Round Table Groups in the Dominions and India. In 1912 he was chosen Beit Lecturer in Colonial History at Oxford, but gave it up in 1913 to turn his attention for almost six years to the preparatory work for the Government of India Act of 1919. He was secretary to the Irish Conference of 1921 (arranged by General Smuts) and was adviser on Irish affairs to the Colonial Office for the next three years. In 1919 he was one of the chief — if not the chief, — founders of the Royal Institute of International Affairs, and during the 1920s divided his attention between this and the League of Nations — in neither case, however, in a fashion to attract public attention. Undoubtedly his influence within the Milner Group declined after 1922, the perponderance falling into the hands of Lothian, Brand, and Dawson. The failure to achieve federation within the Empire was undoubtedly a blow to his personal feeling and possibly to his prestige within the Group. Nonetheless, his influence remained great, and still is. In the 1920s he moved to Kidlington, near Oxford, and thus was available for the Group conferences held at All Souls. His chief published works include *The Problem of the Commonwealth* (1915), *The Commonwealth of Nations* (1916), *Dyarchy* (1920), *The Prevention of War* (1924), the *Capital Question of China* (1932), *The Commonwealth of God* (1932-1938), and *The Protectorates of South Africa* (1935).

John Dove (1872-1934) was sent to Milner in 1903 by Sir William Anson, Warden of All Souls. He was assistant Town Clerk and later Clerk of Johannesburg (1903-1907) and then chairman of the Transvaal Land Settlement Board (1907-1909). After a trip to Australia and India with Lionel Curtis, for the purpose of organizing Round Table Groups, he returned to London in 1911 and lived with Brand and Kerr in Cumberland Mansions. He went to South Africa with Earl Grey in 1912 to unveil the Rhodes Memorial, and served in the First World War with military intelligence in France. In 1918 he became a kind of traveling representative of financial houses, probably as a result of his relationship with Brand. He began this with an extended trip to

India for the Commonwealth Trust Company in 1918 and in the next fifteen years made almost annual trips to Europe. Editor of *The Round Table* from 1921 to his death in 1934, he displayed an idealistic streak similar to that found in Curtis but without the same driving spirit behind it. After his death, Brand published a volume of his letters (1938). These are chiefly descriptive of foreign scenes, the majority written to Brand himself.

Leopold Amery was not a member of the Kindergarten but knew all the members well and was in South Africa, during their period of service, as chief correspondent of *The Times* for the Boer War and the editor of *The Times History of the South African War* (which appeared in seven volumes in the decade 1900-1909). Amery, who was a Fellow of All Souls for fourteen years early in the century and has been one again since 1938, is one of the inner core of the Milner Group. He started his career as private secretary to Leonard H. Courtney, Unionist Member of Parliament and Deputy Speaker in Lord Salisbury's second government. Through this connection, Amery was added to *The Times* editorial staff (1899-1909) and would have become editor but for his decision to go into politics. In this he was not, at first, successful, losing three contests as a Unionist and tariff reformer in the high tide of Liberal supremacy (1906-1910). When victory came in 1911, it was a good one, for Amery held the same seat (for Birmingham) for thirty-four years. During that time he held more important government posts than can be mentioned here. These included the following: assistant secretary of the War Cabinet and Imperial War Council (1917); secretary to the Secretary of State for War (Milner, 1917-1918); Parliamentary Under Secretary for Colonies (1919-1921); Parliamentary and Financial Secretary to the Admiralty (1921-1922); First Lord of the Admiralty (1922-1924); Secretary of State for Colonies (1924-1929) and for Dominion Affairs (1925-1929); Secretary of State for India and Burma (1940-1945). Amery wrote dozens of volumes, chiefly on the Empire and imperial trade relations. In 1910 he married the sister of a fellow Member of Parliament, Florence Greenwood. The colleague, Hamar Greenwood (Baron Greenwood since 1929 and Viscount Greenwood since 1937), was a Liberal M.P. for sixteen years (1906-1922) and a Conservative M.P. for five (1924-1929), a change in which Amery undoubtedly played an important role. Lord Greenwood was secretary of the Overseas Trade Department (1919-1920) and Chief Secretary for Ireland (1920-1922). In recent years he has been chairman of the board of directors of one of England's greatest steel firms (Dorman, Long, and Company), treasurer of the Conservative Party, and president of the British Iron and Steel Federation (1938-1939).

Amery can be regarded as Milner's political heir. From the beginning of his own political career in 1906 to the death of Milner in 1925, he was more closely associated with Milner's active political life than any other person. In 1906, when Amery made his first effort to be elected to Parliament, Milner worked actively in support of his candidacy. It is probable that this, in spite of Milner's personal prestige, lost more votes than it gained, for Milner made no effort to conceal his own highly unorthodox ideas. On 17 December 1906, for example, he spoke at Wolverhampton as follows: "Not only am I an Imperialist of the deepest dye — and Imperialism, you know, is out of fashion — but I actually believe in universal military training. . . . I am a Tariff Reformer and one of a somewhat pronounced type. . . . I am unable to join in the hue and cry against Socialism. That there is an odious form of Socialism I admit, a Socialism which attacks wealth simply because it is wealth, and lives on the cultivation of class hatred. But that is not the whole story; most assuredly not. There is a nobler Socialism, which so far from springing from envy, hatred, and uncharitableness, is born of genuine sympathy and a lofty and wise conception of what is meant by national life." These sentiments may not have won Amery many votes, but they were largely shared by him, and his associations with Milner became steadily more intimate. In his last years of public office, Milner was generally assisted by Amery (1917-1921), and when he died it was Amery who arranged the public memorial service and controlled the distribution of tickets.

Edward William Mackay Grigg (Sir Edward after 1920, Lord Altrincham since 1945) is one of the most important members of the Milner Group. On graduating from New College, he joined the staff of *The Times* and remained with it for ten years (1903-1913), except for an interval during which he went to South Africa. In 1913 he became joint editor of *The Round Table*, but eventually left to fight the war in the Grenadier Guards. In 1919, he went with the Prince of Wales on a tour of Canada, Australia, and New Zealand. After replacing Kerr for a year or so as secretary to Lloyd George (1921-1922), he was a Member of Parliament in 1922-1925 and again in 1933-1945. He has also been Governor of Kenya Colony (1925-1931), parliamentary secretary to the Ministry of Information (1939-1940), Joint Parliamentary Under Secretary of State for War (1940-1942), and Minister Resident in the Middle East (1944-1945). He also found time to write many books, such as *The Greatest Experiment in History* (1924); *Three Parties or Two?* (1931), *The Faith of an Englishman* (1931), *Britain Looks at Germany* (1938), *The British Commonwealth* (1943), and *British Foreign Policy* (1944).

Another visitor to South Africa during the period of the Kindergarten was H. A. L. Fisher. Fisher, a famous historian in his own right, can be regarded as one of the founders of the Kindergarten and was a member of the Milner Group from at least 1899. The chief recruiting for the Kindergarten, beyond that done by Milner himself, was done by Fisher and his close friend Sir William Anson. The relationships between these two, Goschen, and Milner were quite close (except that Milner and Anson were by no means close), and this quartet had a great deal to do with the formation of the Milner Group and with giving it a powerful hold on New College and All Souls. Fisher graduated from New College in 1888 and at once became fellow and tutor in the same college. These positions were held, with interruptions, until 1912, when Fisher left Oxford to become Vice-Chancellor of Sheffield University. He returned to New College as Warden for the last fifteen years of his life (1925-1940). Fisher originally expected to tutor in philosophy, but his appointment required him to teach history. His knowledge in this field was scanty, so it was amplified by vacation reading with A. L. Smith (the future Master of Balliol, an older contemporary of Milner's at Balliol, and a member of the Milner Group). Smith, in addition to teaching Fisher history, also taught him how to skate and to ride a bicycle and worked with him on the literary remains of Fisher's brother-in-law, Frederic W. Maitland, the great historian of the English law. As a result of this last activity, Fisher produced in 1911 a three-volume set of Maitland's *Collected Works*, and a biographical sketch of Maitland (1910), while Smith in 1908 published two lectures and a bibliography on Maitland. Smith's own biographical sketch in the *Dictionary of National Biography* was written by another member of the Milner Group, Kenneth Norman Bell (Fellow of All Souls, 1907-1914; Beit Lecturer in Colonial History, 1924-1927; and member of the family that controlled the publishing house of G. Bell and Sons). His son, Arthur Lionel Foster Smith, was a Fellow of All Souls under Anson (1904-1908) and later organized and supervised the educational system of Mesopotamia (1920-1931).

H. A. L. Fisher held many important posts in his career, partly because of membership in the Milner Group. In 1908, while the Kindergarten, which he had helped to assemble, was still in South Africa, he went there on an extended lecture tour; in 1911-1912 he was Chichele Lecturer in Foreign History; in 1912-1915 he was an important member of the Royal Commission on Public Services in India; in 1916-1926 he was a member of the House of Commons, the first half of the period as a Cabinet member (President of the Board of Education, 1916-1922). He was a delegate to the Assembly of the League of Nations for three years (1920-1922), governor of the British Broadcasting Corporation for four (1935-1939), and a Rhodes Trustee for about fifteen (1925-1940).[6]

Fisher's bibliography forms an extensive list of published works. Besides his *Unfinished Biography* (1940) and his famous three-volume

History of Europe (1935-1936), it contains many writings on subjects close to the Milner Group. His Creighton Lecture in 1911 on *Political Unions* examines the nature of federalism and other unions and fits in well with the discussions going on at the time within Round Table Groups on this subject — discussions in which Fisher played an important part. In the section of this lecture dealing with the Union of South Africa, Fisher was almost as deliberately evasive as Brand had been in his book on the Union, which appeared two years earlier. He mentions the preliminary work of the Kindergarten toward union (work in which he had taken a part himself during his visit to South Africa in 1908) as the work of anonymous persons, but does state that the resulting constitution for a united South Africa was largely the work of the Transvaal delegation (which, as we shall see, was one controlled by the Kindergarten).

Other writings of Fisher's resulting from his work with the Milner Group are his "Imperial Administration" in *Studies in History and Politics* (1920); his *An International Experiment*, dealing with the League of Nations (1921); *The Common Weal*, dealing with the duties of citizenship (1924); and *Our New Religion* (1929), dealing with Christian Science. In connection with this last book, it might be mentioned that Christian Science became the religion of the Milner Group after Milner's death. Among others, Nancy Astor and Lord Lothian were ardent supporters of the new belief. Christian Science was part of the atmosphere of Cliveden.

Fisher's relationship with Milner was quite close and appeared chiefly in their possession of fellowships in New College, obtained by the older man in 1878 and by the younger ten years later. In 1901, when the Kindergarten was formed, the two had been Fellows together for thirteen years, and in 1925, when Milner died and Fisher became Warden, they had been Fellows together for thirty-seven years.

There was also a more personal relationship, created in 1899, when Fisher married Lettice Ilbert. Her father, Sir Courtenay Ilbert (1841-1924), was a lifelong friend of Anson and an old friend of Milner. Sir Courtenay, as law member of the Viceroy of India's Council in 1883, had tried in vain to remove from the Indian code "every judicial disqualification based merely upon race distinctions." Under Lord Dufferin (Lord Basil Blackwood's father), he set up the general system of law and procedure for Burma (1885), and in 1898 he issued what became the basic codification of Indian law. He was clerk of the House of Commons from 1902 to 1921. Mrs. H. A. L. Fisher, one of Sir Courtenay's five daughters, recalls in *The Milner Papers* how Alfred Milner use to romp with the girls when they were children.

Fisher was a very valuable member of the Milner Group because he, along with Lord Goschen, became the chief means by which the Group secured access to the College of All Souls. This access was secured by the friendship of these two men with Sir William Anson. Anson himself was a member of the Cecil Bloc rather than the Milner Group. His personal relations with Milner were not very close, and, indeed, there is some doubt as to his actual feeling toward Milner. The only comment about Milner in the published portions of Anson's journal is a rather acid remark regarding the lack of eloquence in a Milner speech in the House of Lords against the Parliament Act of 1911.[7] Nor did Anson see eye to eye with Milner, or indeed with most members of the Milner Group, since he was much too conservative. He was, to be sure, a Liberal Unionist, as most important members of the Group were. He was also an imperialist and interested in social welfare, but he did not have the high disregard for systems of economics that is so characteristic of all members of the Group before 1917. Anson had an ingrained respect for the economic status quo, and the old Liberal's suspicion of the intervention by public authority in the economic field. These tendencies had been strengthened by years of tender attention to the extensive landed wealth possessed by All Souls. Nonetheless, Anson became one of the chief architects of the Milner Group and is undoubtedly the chief factor in the Group's domination of All Souls since Anson's death. During his wardenship (1881-1914), Anson was the most influential figure in All Souls, not merely in its social and intellectual life but also in the management of its fortune and the selection of its members. In the ordinary expectation of affairs, the former task was generally left in the hands of the estates bursar, and the latter was shared with the other Fellows. Anson, however, took the dominant role in both matters, to such a degree in fact that Bishop Henson (himself a member of All Souls since 1884), in his *Memoir* of Anson, says that the Warden was always able to have his candidate emerge with the prized fellowship.

In seeking to bestow fellowships at All Souls on those individuals whom we now regard as the chief members of the Milner Group, Anson was not conscious that he was dealing with a group at all. The candidates who were offering themselves from New College in the period 1897-1907 were of such high ability that they were able to obtain the election on their own merits. The fact that they came strongly recommended by Fisher served to clinch the matter. They thus did not enter All Souls as members of the Milner Group—at least not in Anson's lifetime. After 1914 this was probably done (as in the case of Lionel Curtis in 1921, Basil Williams in 1924, or Reginald Coupland in 1920), but not before. Rather, likely young men who went to New College in the period on either side of the Boer War were marked out by Fisher and Anson, elected to All Souls, and sent into Milner's Kindergarten on the basis of merit rather than connections.

Another young man who came to visit in South Africa in 1904 and 1905 was Edward Frederick Lindley Wood, already a Fellow of All Souls and a future member of the Milner Group. Better known to the world today as the first Earl of Halifax, he was the son of the second Viscount Halifax and in every way well qualified to become a member of the Milner Group. Lord Halifax is a great-grandson of Lord Grey of the great Reform Bill of 1832, and a grandson of Lord Grey's secretary and son-in-law, Charles Wood (1800-1885), who helped put the Reform Bill through. The same grandfather became, in 1859-1866, the first Secretary of State for the new India, putting through reforms for that great empire which were the basis for the later reforms of the Milner Group in the twentieth century. Lord Halifax is also a grand-nephew of Lord Durham, whose famous report became the basis for the federation of Canada in 1867.

As Edward Wood, the future Lord Halifax undoubtedly found his path into the select company of All Souls smoothed by his own father's close friendship with Phillimore and with the future Archbishop Lang, who had been a Fellow for fifteen years when Wood was elected in 1903.

As a newly elected Fellow, Wood went on a world tour, which took him to South Africa twice (in 1904 and 1905). Each time, he was accompanied by his father, Viscount Halifax, who dined with Milner and was deeply impressed. The Viscount subsequently became Milner's chief defender in the House of Lords. In 1906, for example, when Milner was under severe criticism in the Commons for importing Chinese laborers into South Africa, Lord Halifax introduced and carried in the Upper House a resolution of appreciation for Milner's work.

Edward Wood's subsequent career is one of the most illustrious of contemporary Englishmen. A Member of Parliament for fifteen years (1910-1925), he held posts as Parliamentary Under Secretary for the Colonies (1921-1922), President of the Board of Education (in succession to H. A. L. Fisher, 1922-1924), and Minister of Agriculture, before he went to India (as Baron Irwin) to be Viceroy. In this post, as we shall see, he furthered the plans of the Milner Group for the great subcontinent (1926-1931), before returning to more brilliant achievements as president of the Board of Education (1932-1935), Secretary of State for War (1935), Lord Privy Seal (1935-1937), Lord President of the Council (1937-1938), Secretary of State for Foreign Affairs (1938-1940), and, finally, Ambassador to Washington (as successor to Lord Lothian, 1941-1946). In Washington, as we shall see, he filled the embassy with members of All Souls College.

There can be little doubt that Lord Halifax owed much of his rise in public affairs to his membership in the Milner Group. His authorized biographer, Alan Campbell Johnson, writes in connection with one appointment of Halifax's: "It is widely believed that the influence of Geoffrey Dawson and other members of *The Times* editorial staff discovered him as an ideal Viceroy and whispered his name at the proper time both to the proper authorities in George V's entourage and at 10 Downing Street." In connection with his appointment as Foreign Secretary, Johnson says:

> Lothian, Geoffrey Dawson, and Brand, who used to congregate at Cliveden House as the Astors' guests and earned the title of a "set," to which, in spite of imaginative left-wing propaganda, they never aspired, urged Chamberlain at the decisive moment to have the courage of his convictions and place Halifax, even though he was a Peer, in the office to which his experience and record so richly entitled him. They argued forcibly that to have a Foreign Secretary safely removed from the heat of the House of Commons battle was just what was required to meet the delicate international situation.

Another member of this South African group who was not technically a member of the Kindergarten (because not a member of the civil service) was Basil Kellett Long. He went from Brasenose to Cape Town to study law in 1902 and was called to the bar three years later. In 1908 he was elected to the Cape Parliament, and a year later succeeded Kerr as editor of the Kindergarten's propagandist journal, *The State* (1909-1912). He was a member of the first Parliament of a united South Africa for three years (1910-1913) and then succeeded Amery as head of the Dominions Department of *The Times*. In 1921 he left this post and the position of foreign editor (held jointly with it in 1920-1921) to return to South Africa as editor of the *Cape Times* (1921-1935). He was one of the most important figures in the South African Institute of International Affairs after its belated foundation. With the outbreak of war in 1939, he was put in charge of liaison work between the South African branch and the parent institute in London.

The work of the Kindergarten in South Africa is not so well known as might be expected. Indeed, until very recently the role played by this group, because of its own deliberate policy of secrecy, has been largely concealed. The only good narration of their work is to be found in Worsfold's *The Reconstruction of the New Colonies under Lord Milner*, but Worsfold, writing so early, could not foresee the continued existence of the Kindergarten as a greater and more influential group. Lionel Curtis's own account of what the Group did, in his *Letter to the People of India* (1917), is very brief and virtually unknown in the United States or even in England. The more recent standard accounts, such as that in Volume VIII of the *Cambridge History of the British Empire* (1936), give even less than Worsfold. This will not appear surprising when we point out that the chapter in this tome dealing with

"The Formation of the Union, 1901-1910" is written by Hugh A. Wyndham, a member of the Kindergarten. It is one of the marvels of modern British scholarship how the Milner Group has been able to keep control of the writing of history concerned with those fields in which it has been most active.

Only in very recent years has the role played by the Kindergarten as part of a larger group been appreciated, and now only by a very few writers, such as the biographer of Lord Halifax, already mentioned, and M. S. Green. The latter, a high school teacher in Pretoria, South Africa, in his brief work on *The Making of the Union of South Africa* (1946) gives an account of the Kindergarten which clearly shows his realization that this was only the early stages of a greater group that exercised its influence through *The Round Table, The Times*, the Royal Institute of International Affairs, and the College of All Souls.

The work of union in South Africa was only part of the much greater task of imperial union. This was always the ultimate goal of Cecil Rhodes, of Milner, and of the Kindergarten. Milner wrote in his diary on 25 January 1904: "My work has been constantly directed to a great and distant end—the establishment in South Africa of a great and civilized and progressive community, one from Cape Town to the Zambesi—independent in the management of its own affairs, but still remaining, from its own firm desire, a member of the great community of free nations gathered together under the British flag. That has been the object of all my efforts. It is my object still."[8] In his great farewell speech of March 1905, Milner called upon his hearers, and especially the Kindergarten, to remain loyal to this ultimate goal. He said:

> What I pray for hardest is, that those with whom I have worked in a great struggle and who may attach some weight to my words should remain faithful, faithful above all in the period of reaction, to the great idea of Imperial Unity. Shall we ever live to see its fulfillment? Whether we do or not, whether we succeed or fail, I shall always be steadfast in that faith, though I should prefer to work quietly and in the background, in the formation of opinion rather than in the exercise of power. . . . When we who call ourselves Imperialists talk of the British Empire, we think of a group of states, all independent in their local concerns, but all united for the defense of their own common interests and the development of a common civilization; united, not in an alliance—for alliances can be made and unmade, and are never more than nominally lasting—but in a permanent organic union. Of such a union the dominions as they exist today, are, we fully admit, only the raw material. Our ideal is still distant but we deny that it is either visionary or unattainable. . . . The road is long, the obstacles are many, the goal may not be reached in my lifetime—perhaps not in that of any man in this room. You cannot hasten the slow growth of a great idea like that by any forcing process. But what you can do is to keep it steadily in view, to lose no opportunity to work for it, to resist like

grim death any policy which leads away from it. I know that the service of that idea requires the rarest combination of qualities, a combination of ceaseless effort with infinite patience. But then think on the other hand of the greatness of the reward; the immense privilege of being allowed to contribute in any way to the fulfillment of one of the noblest conceptions which has ever dawned on the political imagination of mankind.

For the first couple of years in South Africa the Kindergarten worked to build up the administrative, judicial, educational, and economic systems of South Africa. By 1905 they were already working for the Union. The first steps were the Intercolonial Council, which linked the Transvaal and Orange River Colony; the Central South African Railway amalgamation; and the customs union. As we have seen, the Kindergarten controlled the first two of these completely; in addition, they controlled the administration of Transvaal completely. This was important, because the gold and diamond mines made this colony the decisive economic power in South Africa, and control of this power gave the Kindergarten the leverage with which to compel the other states to join a union.

In 1906, Curtis, Dawson, Hichens, Brand, and Kerr, with the support of Feetham and Malcolm, went to Lord Selborne and asked his permission to work for the Union. They prevailed upon Dr. Starr Jameson, at that time Premier of Cape Colony, to write to Selborne in support of the project. When permission was obtained, Curtis resigned from his post in Johannesburg and, with Kerr's assistance, formed "Closer Union Societies" as propaganda bodies throughout South Africa. Dawson, as editor, controlled the *Johannesburg Star*. *The Times* of London was controlled completely, as far as news from South Africa was concerned, with Monypenny, Amery, Basil Williams, and Grigg in strategic spots — the last as head of the imperial department of the paper. Fabian Ware published articles by various members of the Milner Group in his *Morning Post*. In South Africa, £5000 was obtained from Abe Bailey to found a monthly paper to further the cause of union. This paper, *The State*, was edited by Philip Kerr and B. K. Long and became the predecessor of *The Round Table*, also edited by Kerr and financed by Bailey. Bailey was not only the chief financial support of the Kindergarten's activities for closer union in South Africa, but also the first financial contributor to *The Round Table* in 1910, and to the Royal Institute of International Affairs in 1919. He contributed to both during his life, and at his death in 1940 gave *The Round Table* £1000 a year for an indefinite period. He had given the Royal Institute £5000 a year in perpetuity in 1928. Like his close associates Rhodes and Beit, he left part of his immense fortune in the form of a trust fund to further imperial interests. In Bailey's case, the fund amounted to £250,000.

As part of the project toward a Union of South Africa, Curtis in 1906 drew up a memorandum on the need for closer union of the South African territories, basing his arguments chiefly on the need for greater railway and customs unity. This, with the addition of a section written by Kerr on railway rates, and a few paragraphs by Selborne, was issued with the famous Selborne Federation Dispatch of 7 January 1907 and published as an Imperial Blue Book (Cmd. 3564 of 1907). It was republished, with an introduction by Basil Williams of the Kindergarten, by Oxford University Press in 1925. The Central Committee of the Closer Union Societies (which was nothing but the Kindergarten) wrote a complete and detailed account of the political institutions of the various areas concerned. This was called *The Government of South Africa* and was issued anonymously in five parts, and revised later in two quarto volumes. A copy was sent to every delegate to the National Convention in Durban in 1908, along with another anonymous work (edited by B. K. Long), called *The Framework of Union*. This latter work contained copies of the five chief federal constitutions of the world (United States, Canada, Germany, Switzerland, and Australia). Curtis was also the chief author of the draft of projected constitution presented by the Transvaal delegation to the National Convention. This draft, with modifications, became the Constitution of the Union of South Africa in 1910. The Transvaal delegation, alone of the various delegations, lived together in one house and had a body of expert advisers; both of these circumstances were due to the Kindergarten.

After the convention accepted the Union Constitution, it was necessary to have it accepted by the Imperial Parliament and the various states of South Africa. In both of these tasks the Kindergarten played an important role, in England through their control of *The Times* and *The Morning Post* as well as other sources of propaganda, and in South Africa by the economic pressure of the Transvaal. In Natal, the only state which submitted the question to a referendum, the Kindergarten put on an intensive propaganda drive, financed with money from the Transvaal. Of this struggle in Natal, Brand, with his usual secrecy on all matters dealing with the Kindergarten, merely says: "A referendum was therefore taken — contrary to general expectation, it revealed an overwhelming majority for union, a good testimony to the sound sense of the people of the colony."[9] Brand, as secretary to the Transvaal delegation to the Convention, knew more than this!

The same secrecy was maintained in regard to the whole convention. No record of its proceedings was kept, but, according to Worsfold, its resolutions were drafted by Brand and Duncan.

Throughout these activities, the Kindergarten received powerful support from a man who by this time was a member of the Milner

Group and later gained international fame, chiefly because of this membership. This was Jan C. Smuts.

Smuts had studied in England, at Cambridge University and the Middle Temple. By 1895 he was a lawyer in Cape Town. His lack of success in this profession doubtless had some influence in turning him into the devious opportunist he soon became, but throughout his opportunism he clung to that ideal which he shared with Rhodes and Milner—the ideal of a united South Africa. All his actions from this date onward—no matter how much they may seem, viewed superficially, to lead in another direction—were directed toward the end ultimately achieved: a United South Africa within the British Empire—and, to him almost equally important, a United South Africa in which he would be the dominant figure. Smuts and Milner differed chiefly on this last point, for if Milner was "selfless," this was almost the last word which could be applied to Smuts. Otherwise the two seemed very similar—similar in their desires for a united South Africa and later a united British Empire, and extraordinarily similar in their cold austerity, impersonal intellectualism, and driving discipline (applied to self even more than to others). In spite of their similar goals for the Empire, Smuts and Milner were not close friends. Perhaps such similar personalities could not be expected to find mutual agreement, but the divergence probably rests, rather, on the one characteristic in their personalities where they most obviously differed.

Smuts and Rhodes, on the other hand, got on together very well. As early as 1895, the unsuccessful Cape Town lawyer was sent by the great imperialist to Kimberley to speak in his defense. But after the Jameson Raid, Smuts became one of the most vociferous critics of Rhodes and the British. These attacks gave Smuts a reputation as an Anglophobe, which yielded considerable profits immediately. Going to the Transvaal (where he added to his fame by uncompromising support of President Kruger), he was raised, at the age of twenty-eight, to the post of State Attorney (1898). In this position, and later as Colonial Secretary, he adopted tactics which led steadily to war (forcing the Uitlanders to pay taxes while denying them the franchise, arresting Uitlander newspaper editors like Monypenny, etc.). At the Bloemfontein Conference of 1899 between Kruger and Milner, all of Smuts's advice to the former was in the direction of concessions to Milner, yet it was Smuts who drafted the ultimatum of 9 October, which led to the outbreak of war. During the war he was one of the most famous of Boer generals, yet, when negotiations for peace began, it was he who drew up the proposal to accept the British terms without delay. With the achievement of peace, Smuts refused Milner's invitation to serve in the Legislative Council of the Transvaal, devoting himself instead to violent and frequently unfair attacks on Milner and the Kindergarten, yet as soon as self-government was granted (in 1906) he became Colonial Secretary and Minister of Education and worked in the closest cooperation with the Kindergarten to obtain Milner's ideal of a united South Africa.

There is really nothing puzzling or paradoxical in these actions. From the beginning, Smuts wanted a brilliant career in a united South Africa within a united British Empire, within, if possible, a united world. No stage would be too big for this young actor's ambitions, and these ambitions were not, except for his own personal role, much different from those of Milner or Rhodes. But, as a very intelligent man, Smuts knew that he could play no role whatever in the world, or in the British Empire, unless he could first play a role in South Africa. And that required, in a democratic regime (which he disliked), that he appear pro-Boer rather than pro-British. Thus Smuts was pro-Boer on all prominent and nonessential matters but pro-British on all unobtrusive and essential matters (such as language, secession, defense, etc.).

At the National Convention of 1908-1909, it was Smuts who dominated the Transvaal delegation and succeeded in pushing through the projects prepared by the Kindergarten. From this emerged a personal connection that still exists, and from time onward, as a member of the Milner Group, Smuts, with undeniable ability, was able to play the role he had planned in the Empire and the world. He became the finest example of the Milner Group's contention that within a united Empire rested the best opportunities for freedom and self-development for all men.[10]

In the new government formed after the creation of the Union of South Africa, Smuts held three out of nine portfolios (Mines, Defense, and Interior). In 1912 he gave up two of these (Mines and Interior) in exchange for the portfolio of Finance, which he held until the outbreak of war. As Minister of Defense (1910-1920) and Prime Minister (1919-1924), he commanded the British forces in East Africa (1916-1917) and was the South African representative and one of the chief members of the Imperial War Cabinet (1917-1918). At the Peace Conference at Paris he was a plenipotentiary and played a very important role behind the scenes in cooperation with other members of the Milner Group. In 1921 he went on a secret mission to Ireland and arranged for an armistice and opened negotiations between Lloyd George and the Irish leaders. In the period following the war, his influence in South African politics declined, but he continued to play an important role within the Milner Group and in those matters (such as the Empire) in which the Group was most concerned. With the approach of the Second World War, he again came to prominence in political affairs. He was Minister of Justice until the war began (1933-1939) and then became Prime Minister, holding the Portfolios of

External Affairs and Defense (1939-1948). Throughout his political life, his chief lieutenant was Patrick Duncan, whom he inherited directly from Milner.

Smuts was not the only addition made to the Milner Group by the Kindergarten during its stay in South Africa. Among the others were two men who were imported by Milner from the Indian Civil Service to guide the efforts of the Kindergarten in forming the Transvaal Civil Service. These two were James S. Meston (later Lord Meston, 1865-1943) and William S. Marris (later Sir William, 1873-1945). Both had studied briefly at Oxford in preparation for the Indian Civil Service. Meston studied at Balliol (after graduating from Aberdeen University) at the time when Milner was still very close to the college (c. 1884), and when Toynbee, tutor to Indian Civil Service candidates at Balliol, had just died. It may have been in this fashion that Milner became acquainted with Meston and thus called him to South Africa in 1903. Until that time, Meston's career in the Indian Civil Service had been fairly routine, and after eighteen years of service he had reached the position of Financial Secretary to the United Provinces.

Marris, a younger colleague of Meston's in the Indian Civil Service, was a native of New Zealand and, after studying at Canterbury College in his own country, went to Christ Church, Oxford, to prepare for the Indian Civil Service. He passed the necessary examinations and was made an assistant magistrate in the United Provinces. From this post he went to South Africa to join the Kindergarten two years after Meston had.

Meston's position in South Africa was adviser to the Cape Colony and the Transvaal on civil service reform (1904-1906). He remained ever after a member of the Milner Group, being used especially for advice on Indian affairs. On his return from South Africa, he was made secretary to the Finance Department of the Government of India (1906-1912). Two years later he was made Finance Member of the Governor-General's Council, and, the following year, became a member of the Imperial Legislative Council. In 1912 he became for five years Lieutenant Governor of the United Provinces. During this period he worked very closely with Lionel Curtis on the projected reforms which ultimately became the Government of India Act of 1919. In 1917 Meston went to London as Indian representative to the Imperial War Cabinet and to the Imperial Conference of that year. On his return to India, he again was Finance Member of the Governor-General's Council until his retirement in 1919. He then returned to England and, as the newly created Baron Meston of Agra and Dunottar, continued to act as chief adviser on Indian affairs to the Milner Group. He was placed on the boards of directors of a score of corporations in which the Group had influence. On several of these he sat with other members of the Group. Among these we might mention the English Electric Company (with Hichens), the Galloway Water Power Company (with Brand), and the British Portland Cement Manufacturers Association (with the third Lord Selborne). From its foundation he was an important member of the Royal Institute of International Affairs, was chairman of its executive committee in 1919-1926, and was a member of the council for most of the period 1926-1943.

Marris, who replaced Meston in the Transvaal in 1906, was eight years his junior (born 1873) and, perhaps for this reason, was much closer to the member of the Kindergarten and became, if possible, an even more intimate member of the Milner Group. He became Civil Service Commissioner of the Transvaal and deputy chairman of the Committee on the Central South African Railways. He did not return to India for several years, going with Curtis instead on a world tour through Canada, Australia, and New Zealand, organizing the Round Table Groups (1911). It was he who persuaded Curtis, and through him the Milner Group, that India should be allowed to proceed more rapidly than had been intended on the path toward self-government.

Back in India in 1912, Marris became a member of the Durbar Executive Committee and, later, secretary to the Home Department of the Government of India. In 1916 he became Inspector General of Police for the United Provinces, and the following year Joint Secretary to the Government of India. During this period he helped Curtis with the projected reforms plans, and he was made responsible for carrying them out when the act was passed in 1919, being made Commissioner of Reforms and Home Secretary to the Government of India (1919-1921). At the same time he was knighted. After a brief period as Governor of Assam (1921-1922), he was Governor of the United Provinces (1922-1928) and a member of the Council of India (1928-1929). After his retirement from active participation in the affairs of India, he embarked upon a career in academic administration, which brought him additional honors. He was Principal of Armstrong College in 1929-1937, Vice-Chancellor and Pro-Vice-Chancellor of Durham University in 1929-1937, a Governor of the Royal Agricultural College at Cirencester in 1937-1945.

Marris's son, Adam D. Marris, born in the year his father went to the Transvaal, is today still a member of the Milner Group. After graduating from Winchester School and Trinity College, Oxford, he went to work with Lazard Brothers. There is no doubt that this position was obtained through his father's relationship with Brand, at that time manager of Lazard. Young Marris remained with the banking firm for ten years, but at the outbreak of war he joined the Ministry of Economic Warfare for a year. Then he joined the All Souls Group that was monopolizing the British Embassy in Washington, originally as

First Secretary and later as Counsellor to the Embassy (1940-1945). After the war he was British Foreign Office representative on the Emergency Economic Committee for Europe as secretary-general. In 1946 he returned to Lazard Brothers.

The older Marris brought into the Milner Group from the Indian Civil Service another member who has assumed increasing importance in recent years. This was Malcolm Hailey (since 1936 Lord Hailey). Hailey, a year older than Marris, took the Indian Civil Service examinations with Marris in 1895 and followed in his footsteps thereafter. Secretary to the Punjab government in 1907 and Deputy Secretary to the Government of India the following year, he was a member of the Delhi Durbar Committee in 1912 and Chief Commissioner in that city for the next eight years. In this post he was one of the advisers used by Curtis on Indian reforms (1916). After the war Hailey was a member of the Executive Council of the Viceroy in the Financial and Home Departments (1919-1924), Governor of Punjab (1924-1928), and Governor of the United Provinces (1928-1930, 1931-1934). During this last period he was one of the closest advisers to Baron Irwin (Lord Halifax) during his term as Viceroy (1926-1936). After Hailey left the Indian Service in 1934, he was used in many important capacities by the Milner Group, especially in matters concerned with Africa and the mandates. Since this use illustrates to perfection the skillful way in which the Milner Group has functioned in recent years, it might be presented here as a typical case.

We have seen that the Milner Group controlled the Rhodes money after Rhodes's death in 1902. In 1929 the Group invited General Smuts to give the Rhodes Lectures at Oxford. In these lectures, Smuts suggested that a detailed survey of Africa and its resources was badly needed. The Royal Institute of International Affairs took up this suggestion and appointed a committee, with Lord Lothian as chairman, to study the project. This committee secured the services of the retiring Governor of the United Provinces to head the survey. Thus Sir Malcolm Hailey became the director of the project and general editor of the famous *African Survey*, published in 1938 by the Royal Institute of International Affairs, with funds obtained from the Carnegie Corporation of New York. Thus the hand of the Milner Group appears in this work from its first conception to its final fruition, although the general public, ignorant of the existence of such a group, would never realize it.

Hailey was also made a member of the Council of the Royal Institute of International Affairs, a member of the Permanent Mandate Commission of the League of Nations (1935-1939), chairman of the School of Oriental and African Studies (1941-1945), chairman of International African Institute, president of the Royal Central Asian Society, chairman of the Colonial Research Committee, member of the Senate of the University of London, Visiting Fellow of Nuffield College at Oxford (1939-1947), head of an economic mission to the Belgian Congo (1941), Romanes Lecturer at Oxford (1941), etc., etc.

Along with all these important posts, Lord Hailey found time to write in those fields with which the Milner Group was most concerned. Among these works we might mention: *Britain and Her Dependencies*, *The Future of Colonial Peoples*, and *Great Britain, India, and the Colonial Dependencies in the Post-War World* (all three published in 1943).

The achievement of the Union of South Africa in 1910 did not mean the end of the Kindergarten. Instead, it set out to repeat on the imperial scene what it had just accomplished in South Africa. In this new project the inspiration was the same (Milner), the personnel was the same (the Kindergarten), the methods were the same (with the Round Table Groups replacing the "Closer Union Societies" and *The Round Table* replacing *The State*. But, as befitted a larger problem, additional personnel and additional funds were required. The additional personnel came largely from New College and All Souls; the additional funds came from Cecil Rhodes and his associates and All Souls. The older sources of funds (like Abe Bailey) and influence (like *The Times*) remained loyal to the Group and continued to assist in this second great battle of the Milner Group. As John Buchan wrote in his autobiography, "Loyalty to Milner and his creed was a strong cement which endured long after our South African service ended, since the Round Table coterie in England continued the Kindergarten." Or, if we may call another competent witness, Lord Oxford and Asquith, writing of Milner after his death, stated: "His personality was so impressive that he founded a school of able young men who during his lifetime and since have acknowledged him as their principal political leader. . . . He was an Expansionist, up to a point a Protectionist, with a strain in social and industrial matters of semi-Socialist sentiment."[11]

More convincing, perhaps, than either Buchan or Asquith is the word of the Group itself. *The Round Table*, in its issue of September 1935, celebrated its twenty-fifth anniversary by printing a brief history of the Group. This sketch, while by no means complete and without mentioning any names of members, provides irrefutable proof of the existence and importance of the Milner Group. It said, in part:

> By the end of 1913 The Round Table had two aspects. On the one hand, it published a quarterly review. . . . On the other hand, it represented a body of men united in support of the principle of freedom and enquiring jointly, through the method of group study, how it could be preserved and expanded in the conditions of the then existing world. In calling for preparation against the German danger (as it did from the very beginning)

The Round Table was not merely, or even chiefly, concerned with saving British skins. It was concerned with upholding against the despotic state what it began to call "the principle of the commonwealth." . . . The root principle of The Round Table remained freedom—"the government of men by themselves" and it demanded that within the Empire this principle should be persistently pursued and expressed in institutions. For that reason it denounced the post-war attempt to repress the Irish demand for national self-government by ruthless violence after a century of union had failed to win Irish consent, as a policy in conflict with British wealth; and it played its part in achieving the Irish Treaty, and the Dominion settlement. Within the limits of the practiceable it fought for the Commonwealth ideal in India. It was closely associated with the device of dyarchy, which seemed for the time being the most practical method of preventing the perpetuation of an irremovable executive confronting an irresponsible legislature and of giving Indians practical training in responsibility for government—the device embodied in the Montagu-Chelmsford Report and the Government of India Act. . . . The Round Table, while supportting the legal formulation of national freedom in the shape of Dominion autonomy, has never lost sight of its ultimate ideal of an organic and articulate Commonwealth. The purpose of devolution is not to drive liberty to the point of license but to prepare for the ultimate basis on which alone freedom can be preserved the reign of law over all. . . . Federal Union is the only security for the freedom both of the individual and of the nation. . . . The principle of anonymity has never been broken and it remains not only as a means of obtaining material from sources that would otherwise be closed, but also as a guarantee that both the opinions and the facts presented in the articles are scrutinized by more than one individual judgment. . . . Imperceptibly, the form of the review has changed to suit altered circumstances. . . . But the fundamentals remain unchanged. Groups in the four overseas Dominions still assemble their material and hammer out their views, metaphorically, "round the table." Some of their members have shared continuously in this work for a quarter of a century; and in England, too, the group of friends who came together in South Africa still help to guide the destinies and contribute to the pages of the review they founded, though the chances of life and death have taken some of their number, and others have beeb brought in to contribute new points of view and younger blood.

5

The Milner Group, Rhodes, and Oxford, 1901-1925

IT IS GENERALLY BELIEVED, and stated as a fact by many writers, that Milner hoped for some new political appointment after his return from Africa and was deprived of this by the election of 1906, which swept the Conservatives from office and brought in the Liberals. It is perfectly true that Milner was out of political life for ten years, but there is, so far as I know, no evidence that this was contrary to his own wish. In his farewell speech of March 1905, delivered long before the Liberal victory at the polls, Milner stated in reference "to the great idea of Imperial Unity": "I shall always be steadfast in that faith, though I should prefer to work quietly and in the background, in the formation of opinion rather than in the exercise of power." This is exactly what Milner did. Even after he returned to positions of power in 1915-1921, he worked as quietly as possible and attracted public attention at an absolute minimum. [1]

Milner had nothing to gain from public office after 1905, until the great crisis of 1915-1918 made it imperative for all able men to take a hand in active affairs. If he wanted to speak his own mind, he always had his seat in the House of Lords, and speaking engagements elsewhere were easy — indeed, too easy — to get. In South Africa his union program after 1905 was going forward at a rate that exceeded his most optimistic hopes. And nowhere else did it seem, in 1905, that he could, in actual administration, accomplish more than he could in quietly building up a combination propaganda and patronage machine at home. This machine was constructed about Rhodes and his associates, New College, and All Souls.

Milner was not of any political party himself and regarded party politics with disgust long before 1905. As his friend Edmund Garrett wrote in 1905: "Rhodes and Milner both number themselves of that great unformed party which is neither the ins nor the outs, which touches here the foreign politics of the one, here the home politics of the other; a party to which Imperialism and Carlyle's Condition of the

84

People Question are one and the same business of fitly rearing, housing, distributing, coordinating, and training for war and peace the people of this commonwealth; a party which seems to have no name, no official leader, no paper even, but which I believe, when it comes by a soul and a voice, will prove to include a majority of the British in Britain and a still greater majority of the British overseas."[2] There can be no doubt that these were Milner's sentiments. He hoped to give that unformed party "a soul and a voice," and he intended to do this apart from party politics. When he was offered the position of president of the imperial federalist organization he refused it, but wrote to the secretary, Mr. F. H. Congdon, as follows:

> Personally I have no political interest worth mentioning, except the maintenance of the Imperial connection, and I look upon the future with alarm. The party system at home and in the Colonies seems to me to work for the severance of ties, and that contrary to the desire of our people on both sides. It is a melancholy instance of the manner in which bad political arrangements, lauded to the skies from year's end to year's end as the best in the world, may not only injure the interests, but actually frustrate the desires of the people. I can see no remedy or protection, under the present circumstances, except a powerful body of men — and it would have to be very powerful — determined at all times and under all circumstances to vote and work, regardless of every other circumstance, against the man or party who played fast and loose with the cause of National Unity. You can be sure that for my own part I shall always do that. . . .[3]

Milner, in his distaste for party politics and for the parliamentary system, and in his emphasis on administration for social welfare, national unity, and imperial federation, was an early example of what James Burnham has called the "managerial revolution" — that is, the growth of a group of managers, behind the scenes and beyond the control of public opinion, who seek efficiently to obtain what they regard as good for the people. To a considerable extent this point of view became part of the ideology of the Milner Group, although not of its most articulate members, like Lionel Curtis, who continued to regard democracy as a good in itself.

Milner's own antipathy to democracy as practiced in the existing party and parliamentary system is obvious. Writing to his old friend Sir Clinton Dawkins, who had been, with Milner, a member of the Toynbee group in 1879-1884, he said in 1902: "Two things constantly strike me. One is the soundness of the British nation as a whole, contrasted with the rottenness of party politics." About the same time he wrote to another old Balliol associate, George Parkin: "I am strongly impressed by two things: *one* that the heart of the nation is sound, — and *secondly* that our constitution and methods are antiquated and bad, and the real sound feeling of the nation does not get a chance of making itself effective." Two years later he wrote to a friend of Rhodes, Sir Lewis Michell: "Representative government has its merits, no doubt, but the influence of representative assemblies, organized on the party system, upon administration — 'government' in the true sense of the word — is almost uniformly bad."[4]

With sentiments such as these, Milner laid down the duties of public office with relief and devoted himself, not to private affairs, but to the secret public matters associated with his "Association of Helpers." To support himself during this period, Milner acted as confidential adviser to certain international financiers in London's financial district. His entree to this lucrative occupation may have been obtained through Lord Esher, who had just retired from a similar well-remunerated collaboration with Sir Ernest Cassel.

Milner's most important work in this period was concerned with the administration of the Rhodes Trust and the contacts with Oxford University which arose out of this and from his own position as a Fellow of New College.

The Rhodes Trust was already in operation when Milner returned from Africa in 1905, with the actual management of the scholarships in the hands of George Parkin, who had been brought from his position as Principal of Upper Canada College by Milner. He held the post for eighteen years (1902-1920). The year following his appointment, an Oxford secretary to the trustees was appointed to handle the local work during Parkin's extended absences. This appointment went to Francis Wylie (Sir Francis since 1929), Fellow and tutor of Brasenose, who was named by the influence of Lord Rosebery, whose sons he had tutored.[5] The real control of the trust has rested with the Milner Group from 1902 to the present. Milner was the only really active trustee and he controlled the bureaucracy which handled the trust. As secretary to the trustees before 1929, we find, for example, George Parkin (1902-1920), Geoffrey Dawson (1921-1922), Edward Grigg (1922-1925), and Lord Lothian (1925-1940) — all of them clearly Milner's nominees. On the Board of Trustees itself, in the same period, we find Lord Rosebery, Lord Milner, Lord Grey, Dr. Jameson, Alfred Beit, Lewis Michell, B. F. Hawksley, Otto Beit, Rudyard Kipling, Leopold Amery, Stanley Baldwin, Geoffrey Dawson, H. A. L. Fisher, Sothern Holland, and Sir Edward Peacock. Peacock had been teacher of English and housemaster at Upper Canada College during the seven years in which Parkin was principal of that institution (1895-1902) and became an international financier as soon as Parkin became secretary of the Rhodes Trust. Apparently he did not represent the Rhodes Trust but rather the interests of that powerful and enigmatic figure Edward Rogers Wood of Toronto. Wood and Peacock were very close to the Canadian branch of the Milner Group, that is to say, to A. J. Glazebrook, Parkin, and the Massey family, but it is not clear that either represented the interests of the Milner Group. Peacock was associated at first with the Dominion Securities Corporation of London (1902-1915) and later with Baring Brothers as a specialist in utility enterprises in Mexico, Spain, and Brazil (1915-1924). He was made Receiver-General of the Duchy of Cornwall in 1929 and was knighted in 1934. He was a director of the Bank of England from 1921-1946, managing director of Baring Brothers from 1926, a director of Vickers-Armstrong from 1929, and in addition a director of many world-famous corporations, such as the Canadian Pacific Railway, the Hudson Bay Company, and the Sun Life Assurance Society. He was an expert at the Genoa Conference in 1922 and acted as the British Treasury's representative in Washington during the Second World War.

If we look at the list of Rhodes Trustees, we see that the Milner Group always had complete control. Omitting the five original trustees, we see that five of the new additions were from the Milner Group, three were from the Rhodes clique, and three represented the outside world. In the 1930s the Board was stabilized for a long period as Amery, Baldwin, Dawson, Fisher, Holland, and Peacock, with Lothian as secretary. Six of these seven were of the Milner Group, four from the inner core.

A somewhat similar situation existed in respect to the Beit Railway Fund. Although of German birth, Alfred Beit became a British subject and embraced completely the ideas on the future role of the British Empire shared by Rhodes and Milner. An intimate friend of these and of Lord Rosebery, he was especially concerned with the necessity to link the British possessions in Africa together by improved transportation (including the Cape to Cairo Railway). Accordingly, he left £1,200,000 as the Beit Railway Trust, to be used for transportation and other improvements in Africa. The year before his death (1906), he was persuaded by the Milner Group to establish a Beit Professorship and a Beit Lecturership in Colonial History at Oxford. The money provided yielded an income far in excess of the needs of these two chairs, and the surplus has been used for other "imperialist" purposes. In addition, Beit gave money to the Bodleian Library at Oxford for books on colonial history. In 1929, when Rhodes House was opened, these and other books on the subject were moved from the Bodleian to Rhodes House, and the Beit Professor was given an office and lecture hall in Rhodes House. There have been only two incumbents of the Beit Professorship since 1905: Hugh Edward Egerton in 1905-1920, and Reginald (Sir Reginald since 1944) Coupland since 1920. Egerton, a member of the Cecil Bloc and the Round Table Group, was a contemporary of Milner's at Oxford whose father was a member of the House of Commons and Under Secretary for Foreign Affairs. He was originally private secretary to his cousin Edward Stanhope, Colonial Secretary and Secretary of War in Lord Salisbury's first government. In 1886, Egerton became a member of the managing committee of the newly created Emigrants Information Office. He held this job for twenty years, during which time he came into the sphere of the Milner Group, partly because of the efforts of South Africa, and especially the British South Africa Company, to encourage emigration to their territories, but also because of his *Short History of British Colonial Policy*, published in 1897. On the basis of this contact and this book, he was given the new Beit Chair in 1905 and with it a fellowship at All Souls. In his professional work he constantly supported the aims of the Milner Group, including the publication of *Federations and Unions within the British Empire* (1911) and *British Colonial Policy in the Twentieth Century* (1922). His book *Canadian Constitutional Development*, along with Sir Charles Lucas's edition of Lord Durham's reports, was the chief source of information for the process by which Canada was federated used by the Milner Group. He wrote the biography of Joseph Chamberlain in the *Dictionary of National Biography*, while his own biography in the same collection was written by Reginald Coupland. He remained a Fellow of All Souls and a member of the Milner Group until his death in 1927, although he yielded his academic post to Reginald Coupland in 1920. Coupland, who was a member of the Milner Group from his undergraduate days at New College (1903-1907), and who became one of the inner circle of the Milner Group as early as 1914, will be discussed later. He has been, since 1917, one of the most important persons in Britain in the formation of British imperial policy.

The Beit Railway Trust and the Beit chairs at Oxford have been controlled by the Milner Group from the beginning, through the board of trustees of the former and through the board of electors of the latter. Both of these have interlocking membership with the Rhodes Trust and the College of All Souls. For example, the board of electors of the Beit chair in 1910 consisted of the Vice-Chancellor of Oxford, the Regius Professor of Modern History, the Chichele Professor of Modern History, the Secretary of State for Colonies, Viscount Milner, H. A. L. Fisher, and Leopold Amery. By controlling All Souls and the two professorships (both ex-officio fellowships of All Souls), the Milner Group could control five out of seven electors to the Beit professorship. In recent years the board of electors has consistently had a majority of members of All Souls and/or the Milner Group. In 1940, for example, the board had, besides three ex-officio members, two members of All Souls, a Rhodes Trustee, and H. A. L. Fisher.

The Beit Lectureship in Colonial History was similarly controlled. In

1910 its board of electors had seven members, four ex-officio (The Vice-Chancellor, the Regius Professor of History, the Chichele Professor of History, the Beit Professor) and three others (A. L. Smith, H. A. L. Fisher, and Leopold Amery). In 1930 the board consisted of the Vice-Chancellor, the Beit Professor, H. A. L. Fisher, F. M. Powicke, and three fellows of All Souls. As a result, the lectureship has generally been held by persons close to the Milner Group, as can be seen from the following list of incumbents:

> W. L. Grant, 1906-1910
> J. Munro, 1910-1912
> L. Curtis, 1912-1913
> R. Coupland, 1913-1918
> E. M. Wrong, 1919-1924
> K. N. Bell, 1924-1927
> W. P. Morrell, 1927-1930
> V. T. Harlow, 1930-1935
> K. C. Wheare, 1935-1940

Without attempting to identify all of these completely, it should be pointed out that four were Fellows of All Souls, while, of the others, one was the son-in-law of George Parkin, another was the son-in-law of A. L. Smith, and a third was librarian of Rhodes House and later acting editor of *The Round Table*.

During this period after 1905, the Milner Group was steadily strengthening its relationships with New College, All Souls, and to some extent with Balliol. Through Fisher and Milner there came into the Group two tutors and a scholar of New College. These were Alfred Zimmern, Robert S. Rait (1874-1936), and Reginald Coupland.

Alfred Zimmern (Sir Alfred since 1936) was an undergraduate at New College with Kerr, Grigg, Brand, Curtis, Malcolm, and Waldorf Astor (later Lord Astor) in 1898-1902. As lecturer, fellow, and tutor there in the period 1903-1909, he taught a number of future members of the Milner Group, of whom the chief was Reginald Coupland. His teaching and his book *The Greek Commonwealth* (1911) had a profound effect on the thinking of the inner circle of the Milner Group, as can be seen, for example, in the writings of Lionel Curtis. In the period up to 1921 he was close to this inner core and in fact can be considered as a member of it. After 1921 he disagreed with the policy of the inner core toward the League of Nations and Germany, since the core wanted to weaken the one and strengthen the other, an opinion exactly opposite to that of Zimmern. He remained, however, a member of the Group and was, indeed, its most able member and one of its most courageous members. Since his activities will be mentioned frequently in the course of this study, we need do no more than point out his various positions here. He was a staff inspector of the Board of Education in 1912-1915; the chief assistant to Lord Robert Cecil in the Political Intelligence Department of the Foreign Office in 1918-1919; Wilson Professor of International Politics at University College of Wales, Abersytwyth, in 1919-1921; Professor of Political Science at Cornell in 1922-1923; deputy director and chief administrator of the League of Nations Institute of Intellectual Cooperation in 1926-1930; Montague Burton Professor of International Relations at Oxford in 1930-1944; deputy director of the Research Department of the Foreign Office in 1943-1945; adviser to the Ministry of Education in 1945; director of the Geneva School of International Studies in 1925-1939; adviser and chief organizer of the United Nations Educational, Scientific, and Cultural Organization in 1946; and Visiting Professor at Trinity College, Hartford, Connecticut, from 1947.

Another Fellow of New College who joined the Milner Group was R. S. Rait (1874-1936). Of much less significance than Zimmern, he worked with the Group in the Trade Intelligence Department of the War Office in 1915-1918. He is the chief reason why the Milner Group, especially in the writings of Lionel Curtis, emphasized the union with Scotland as a model for the treatment of Ireland. A close friend of A. V. Dicey, Fellow of All Souls, he wrote with him *Thoughts on the Union between England and Scotland* (1920), and, with C. H. Firth, another Fellow of All Souls, he wrote *Acts and Ordonnances of the Interregnum, 1642-1660* (1911). He left New College in 1913 to become Professor of Scottish History at the University of Glasgow (1913-1929) and five years later was made Royal Historiographer of Scotland (1919-1929). Originally intimate with the inner circle of the Milner Group, he drifted away after 1913.

Reginald Coupland (Sir Reginald since 1944) came into the Milner Group's inner circle shortly before Rait moved out, and has been there ever since. A student of Zimmern's at New College in 1903-1907, he became a Fellow and lecturer in ancient history at Trinity College, Oxford, immediately upon graduation and stayed there for seven years. Since then his academic career has carried him to the following positions: Beit Lecturer in Colonial History (1913-1918), Beit Professor of Colonial History (since 1920), Fellow of All Souls (since 1920), and Fellow of Nuffield College (since 1939). He was also editor of *The Round Table* after Lord Lothian left (1917-1919) and again at the beginning of the Second World War (1939-1941). His most important activities, however, have been behind the scenes: as member of the Royal Commission on Superior Civil Services in India (1923), as adviser to the Burma Round Table Conference of 1931, as a member of the Peel Commission to Palestine (1936-1937), and as a member of Sir Stafford Cripps's Mission to India (1942). He is reputed to have been the chief author of the Peel Report of 1937, which recommended partition of Palestine and restriction of Jewish immigration into the area — two principles which remained at the basis of British policy until 1949. In fact, the pattern of partition contained in the Peel Report, which would have given Transjordan an outlet to the Mediterranean Sea across the southern portion of Palestine, was a subject of violent controversy in 1948.

Coupland has been a prolific writer. Besides his many historical works, he has written many books that reflect the chief subjects of discussion in the inmost circle of the Milner Group. Among these, we might mention *Freedom and Unity*, his lecture at Patna College, India, in 1924; *The American Revolution and the British Empire* (1930); *The Empire in These Days* (1935); *The Cripps Mission* (1942); and *Report on the Constitutional Problem in India* (3 parts, 1942-1943).

The Milner Group's relationships with All Souls were also strengthened after Milner returned to England in 1905, and especially after the Kindergarten returned to England in 1909-1911. The Milner Group's strength in All Souls, however, was apparently not sufficiently strong for them to elect a member of the Milner Group as Warden when Anson died in 1914, for his successor, Francis W. Pember, one-time assistant legal adviser to the Foreign Office, and a Fellow of All Souls since 1884, was of the Cecil Bloc rather than of the Milner Group. Pember did not, however, resist the penetration of the Milner Group into All Souls, and as a result both of his successors as Warden, W. G. S. Adams (1933-1945) and B. H. Sumner (1945-   ), were members of the Milner Group.

In general, the movement of persons was not from the Milner Group to All Souls but in the reverse direction. All Souls, in fact, became the chief recruiting agency for the Milner Group, as it had been before 1903 for the Cecil Bloc. The inner circle of this Group, because of its close contact with Oxford and with All Souls, was in a position to notice able young undergraduates at Oxford. These were admitted to All Souls and at once given opportunities in public life and in writing or teaching, to test their abilities and loyalty to the ideals of the Milner Group. If they passed both of these tests, they were gradually admitted to the Milner Group's great fiefs such as the Royal Institute of International Affairs, *The Times*, *The Round Table*, or, on the larger scene, to the ranks of the Foreign or Colonial Offices. So far as I know, none of these persons recruited through All Souls ever reached the inner circle of the Milner Group, at least before 1939. This inner circle continued to be largely monopolized by the group that had been in South Africa in the period before 1909. The only persons who were not in South Africa, yet reached the inner circle of the Milner Group, would appear to be Coupland, Lord Astor, Lady Astor, Arnold Toynbee, and H. V.

Hodson. There may be others, for it is difficult for an outsider to be sure in regard to such a secret matter.

Of the members of All Souls who got into at least the second circle of the Milner Group, we should mention the names of the following:

NAME	BIRTH DATE	COLLEGE		ALL SOULS FELLOW
W. G. S. Adams	1874	Balliol	1896-1900	1910- (Warden 1933-1945)
K. N. Bell	1884	Balliol	1903-1906	1907-1914
I. Berlin	1909	Corpus Christi	1928-1932	1932-1939
H. B. Butler	1883	Balliol	1902-1905	1905-1912
R. D'O. Butler		Balliol	1935-1938	1938-
F. Clarke		Balliol	1905-1908	1908-1915
P. E. Corbett	1892	Balliol	1919-1920	1920-1928
C. R. M. F. Cruttwell		Queen's	1906-1910	1911-1918
H. W. C. Davis	1874	Balliol	1891-1895	1895-1902
G. C. Faber	1889	Christ Church	1908-1913	1919-
J. G. Foster		New College	1922-1925	1924-
M. L. Gwyer	1878	Christ Church	1897-1901	1902-1916
W. K. Hancock	1898	Balliol	1922-1923	1924-1930, 1944-
C. R. S. Harris	1896	Corpus Christi	1918-1923	1921-1936
H. V. Hodson	1906	Balliol	1925-1928	1928-1935
C. A. Macartney	1896	Trinity College, Cambridge		1936-
R. M. Makins	1904	Christ Church	1922-1925	1925-1932
J. Morley	1838	Lincoln	1856-1859	1904-1911
C. J. Radcliffe	1899	New College	1919-1922	1922-1937
J. A. Salter	1881	Brasenose	1899-1904	1932-
D. B. Somervell	1889	Magdalen	1907-1911	1912-
A. H. D. R. Steel-Maitland	1876	Balliol	1896-1900	1900-1907
B. H. Sumner	1893	Balliol	1912-1916	1919-1926, Warden 1945-
L. F. R. Williams	1890	University	1909-1912	1914-1921
E. L. Woodward	1890	Corpus Christi	1908-1911	1911-1944

Of these twenty-five names, four were Fellows of Balliol during the periods in which they were not Fellows of All Souls (Bell, David, Sumner, and Woodward).

It is not necessary to say much about these various men at this time, but certain of them should be identified. The others will be mentioned later.

William George Stewart Adams was lecturer in Economics at Chicago and Manchester universities and Superintendent of Statistics and Intelligence in the Department of Agriculture before he was elected to All Souls in 1910. Then he was Gladstone Professor of Political Theory and Institutions (1912-1933), a member of the committee to advise the Irish Cabinet (1911), in the Ministry of Munitions (1915), Secretary to Lloyd George (1916-1919), editor of the War Cabinet Reports (1917-1918), and a member of the Committee on Civil Service Examinations (1918).

The Reverend Kenneth Norman Bell was lecturer in history at Toronto University during his fellowship in All Souls (1907-1914); a director of G. Bell and Sons, Publishers; a tutor and Fellow of Balliol (1919-1941); Beit Lecturer in Colonial History (1924-1927); and a member of the committee for supervision of the selection of candidates for the Colonial Administrative Service. He edited, with W. P. Morrell, *Select Documents in British Colonial History, 1830-1860* (1928).

Harold Beresford Butler (Sir Harold since 1946) was a civil servant, chiefly in the Home Office, and secretary to the British delegation to the International Conference on Aerial Navigation in Paris during his Fellowship at All Souls. He was subsequently in the Foreign Trade Department of the Foreign Office (1914-1917) and in the Ministry of Labour (1917-1919). On the Labour Commission of the Paris Peace Conference and at the International Labor Conference in Washington (1919), he later became deputy director (1920-1932) and director (1932-1938) of the International Labour Office of the League of Nations. Since 1939, he has been Warden of Nuffield College (1939-1943) and minister in charge of publicity in the British Embassy in Washington (1942-1946). He has written a number of books, including a history of the interwar period called *The Lost Peace* (1941).

H. W. C. Davis, the famous medieval historian, became a Fellow of All Souls immediately after graduating from Balliol in 1895, and was a Fellow of Balliol for nineteen years after that, resigning from the latter to become Professor of History at Manchester University (1921-1925). During this period he was a lecturer at New College (1897-1899), Chichele Lecturer in Foreign History (1913), editor of the Oxford Pamphlets on the war (1914-1915), one of the organizers of the War

Trade Intelligence Department of the Ministry of Blockade in the Foreign Office (1915), acting director of the Department of Overseas Trade under Sir Arthur Steel-Maitland (1917-1919), an expert at the Paris Peace Conference (1918-1919), and editor of the *Dictionary of National Biography* (1920-1928). In 1925 he returned from Manchester to Oxford as Regius Professor of Modern History in succession to Sir Charles Firth, became a Fellow of Oriel College, Curator of the Bodleian, and was named by the International Labour Office (that is, by Harold Butler) as the British representative on the Blanesburgh Committee on Factory Legislation in Europe. He edited the report of this committee. In addition to his very valuable studies in medieval history, Davis also wrote *The History of the Blockade* (1920) and sections of the famous *History of the Peace Conference*, edited by Harold Temperley (also a member of the Group).

Sir Maurice Linford Gwyer was a Fellow of All Souls for fourteen years after graduating from Christ Church (1902-1916). During this time he was admitted to the bar, practiced law, was lecturer in Private International Law at Oxford (1912-1915) and solicitor to the Insurance Commissioners (1902-1916). He was then legal adviser to the Ministry of Shipping (1917-1919) and to the Ministry of Health (1919-1926), then Procurator-General and Solicitor to the Treasury (1926-1933), First Parliamentary Counsel to the Treasury (1934-1937), and Chief Justice of India (1937-1943). He was first British delegate to The Hague Conference on Codification of International Law (1930) and a member of the Indian States Inquiry Committee (1932). He edited the later editions of Anson's *Law of Contract* and *Law and Custom of the Constitution*.

William Keith Hancock, of Australia and Balliol, was a member of All Souls from 1924. He was Professor of History at Adelaide in 1924-1933, Professor of Modern History at Birmingham in 1934-1944, and is now Chichele Professor of Economic History at Oxford. He wrote the three-volume work *Survey of British Commonwealth Affairs*, published by Chatham House in 1937-1942.

John Morley (Lord Morley of Blackburn) was a member of the Cecil Bloc rather than of the Milner Group, but in one respect, his insistence on the inadvisability of using force and coercion within the Empire, a difference which appeared most sharply in regard to Ireland, he was more akin to the Group than to the Bloc. He was a close friend of Lord Salisbury, Lord Esher, and Joseph Chamberlain and was also a friend of Milner's, since they worked together on the *Pall Mall Gazette* in 1882-1883. He had close personal and family connections with H. A. L. Fisher, the former going back to a vacation together in 1892 and the latter based on Morley's lifelong friendship with Fisher's uncle, Leslie Stephen. It was probably through Fisher's influence that Morley was elected a Fellow of All Souls in 1904. He had shown that his heart was in the right place, so far as the Milner Group was concerned, in 1894, when Gladstone retired from the leadership of the Liberal Party and Morley used his influence to give the vacant position to Lord Rosebery. Morley was Secretary of State for India in the period 1905-1910, putting through the famous Morley-Minto reforms in this period. In this he made use of a number of members of the Milner and All Souls groups. The bill itself was put through the House of Commons by a member of All Souls, Thomas R. Buchanan (1846-1911), who was shifted from Financial Secretary in the War Office under Haldane to Under Secretary in the India Office for the purpose (1908-1909).[6]

James Arthur Salter (Sir Arthur since 1922) was born in Oxford and lived there until he graduated from Brasenose in 1904. He went to work for the Shipping Department of the Admiralty in the same year and worked in this field for most of the next fourteen years. In 1917 he was Director of Ship Requisitioning and later secretary and chairman of the Allied Maritime Transport Executive. He was on the Supreme Economic Council in 1919 and became general secretary to the Reparations Commission for almost three years (1920-1922). He was Director of the Economic and Finance Section of the League of Nations in 1919-1922 and again in 1922-1931. In the early 1930s he went on several missions to India and China and served on various committees concerned with railroad matters. He was Gladstone Professor of Political Theory and Institutions in 1934-1944, Member of Parliament from Oxford University after 1937, Parliamentary Secretary to the Ministry of Shipping in 1939-1941, head of the British Merchant Shipping Mission in America in 1941-1943, Senior Deputy Director General of UNRRA in 1944, and Chancellor to the Duchy of Lancaster in 1945.

Donald B. Somervell (Sir Donald since 1933) has been a Fellow of All Souls since he graduated from Magdalen in 1911, although he took his degree in natural science. He entered Parliament as a Unionist in 1931 and almost at once began a governmental career. He was Solicitor General (1933-1936), Attorney General (1936-1945), and Home Secretary (1945), before becoming a Lord Justice of Appeal in 1946. His brother, D. C. Somervell, edited the one-volume edition of Toynbee's *A Study of History* for Chatham House.

Sir Arthur Ramsay Steel-Maitland was a Fellow of All Souls for the seven years following his graduation from Balliol in 1900. He was unsuccessful as a candidate for Parliament in 1906, but was elected as a Conservative from Birmingham four years later. He was Parliamentary Under Secretary for Colonies (1915-1917), Joint Parliamentary Under Secretary in the Foreign Office and Parliamentary Secretary to the Board of Trade in the capacity of head of the Department of Overseas

Trade (1917-1919), and Minister of Labour (1924-1929).

Benedict H. Sumner was a Fellow of All Souls for six years (1919-1928) and a Fellow of Balliol for twenty (1925-1944), before he became Warden of All Souls (1945). During the First World War, he was with Military Intelligence and afterwards with the British delegation at the Peace Conference. During the Second World War, he was attached to the Foreign Office (1939-1942). He is an authority on Russian affairs, and this probably played an important part in his selection as Warden of All Souls in 1945.

Laurence F. R. Williams went to Canada as lecturer in medieval history at Queen's University after leaving Balliol (1913-1914). Immediately on becoming a Fellow of All Souls in 1914, he went to India as Professor of Indian History at the University of Allahabad. In 1918 and in 1919 he was busy on constitutional reforms associated with the Government of India Act of 1919, working closely with Sir William Marris. He then became director of the Central Bureau of Information for six years (1920-1926) and secretary to the Chancellor of the Chamber of Princes for four (1926-1930). He was, in this period, also secretary to the Indian Delegation at the Imperial Conference of 1923, political secretary to the Maharaja of Patiala, substitute delegate to the Assembly of the League of Nations (1925), member of the Legislative Assembly (1924-1925), joint director of the Indian Princes' Special Organization (1929-1931), adviser to the Indian States delegation at the Round Table Conference of 1930-1931, and delegate to the Round Table Conference of 1932. In the 1930s he was Eastern Service director of the BBC (under H. A. L. Fisher), and in the early days of the Second World War was adviser on Middle East Affairs to the Ministry of Information. Since 1944 he has been in the editorial department of *The Times*. His written output is considerable, much of it having been published as official documents or parliamentary papers. Among these are the *Moral and Material Progress Reports of India* for 1917-1925, the official *Report on Lord Chelmsford's Administration*, and the official *History of the Tour of the Prince of Wales*. He also wrote *Lectures on the Handling of Historical Material* (1917), a *History of the Abbey of St. Alban* (1917), and a half dozen books and pamphlets on India.

Ernest Llewellyn Woodward, the last Fellow of All Souls whom we shall mention here, is of great significance. After studying at Oxford for seven years (1908-1915) he went into the British Expeditionary Force for three, and then was elected a Fellow of All Souls, an appointment he held until he became a Fellow of Balliol in the middle of the 1940s. He was also a tutor and lecturer at New College, a Rhodes Travelling Fellow (1931), and in 1944 succeeded Sir Alfred Zimmern as Montague Burton Professor of International Relations. When the decision was made after the Second World War to publish an extensive selection of *Documents on British Foreign Policy, 1919-1939*, Woodward was made general editor of the series and at once associated with himself Rohan D'Olier Butler, who has been a Fellow of All Souls since leaving Balliol in 1938.

Woodward was a member of the council of the Royal Institute of International Affairs in the middle 1930s, and domestic bursar of All Souls a little later. He has written a number of historical works, of which the best known are Volume XIII of the *Oxford History of England* ("The Age of Reform," 1938), *Three Studies in European Conservatism* (1929), and *Great Britain and the German Navy* (1935).

These twenty-five names give the chief members of All Souls, in the period before 1939, who became links with the Milner Group and who have not previously been discussed. In the same period the links with New College and Balliol were also strengthened. The process by which this was done for the former, through men like H. A. L. Fisher, has already been indicated. Somewhat similar but less intimate relationships were established with Balliol, especially after A. L. Smith became Master of that college in 1916. Smith, as we have indicated, was a contemporary and old friend of Milner at Balliol and shared his (and Toynbee's) ideas regarding the necessity of uplifting the working classes and preserving the Empire. His connections with Fisher and with All Souls were intimate. He was a close friend of Lord Brassey, whose marital relationships with the Rosebery and Brand families and with the Cecil Bloc have been mentioned already. Through A. L. Smith, Brassey reorganized the financial structure of the Balliol foundation in 1904. He was, as we have shown, a close collaborator of Milner in his secret plans, by intimate personal relationships before 1897 and by frequent correspondence after that date. There can be no doubt that A. L. Smith shared in this confidence. He was a collaborator with the Round Table Group after 1910, being especially useful, by his Oxford position, in providing an Oxford background for Milner Group propaganda among the working classes. This will be mentioned later. A. L. Smith's daughter Mary married a Fellow of All Souls, F. T. Barrington-Ward, whose older brother, R. M. Barrington-Ward, was assistant editor of *The Times* in 1927-1941 and succeeded Dawson as editor in 1941. Smith's son, A. L. F. Smith, was elected to All Souls in 1904, was director, and later adviser, of education to the Government of Iraq in 1920-1931, and was Rector of Edinburgh Academy from 1931 to 1945.

A. L. Smith remained as Master of Balliol from 1916 to his death in 1924. His biographical sketch in *The Dictionary of National Biography* was written by K. N. Bell of All Souls.

The influence of the Milner Group and the Cecil Bloc on Balliol in the twentieth century can be seen from the following list of persons who were Fellows or Honorary Fellows of Balliol:

Archbishop Lang	K. N. Bell
Lord Asquith	H. W. C. Davis
Lord Brassey	J. H. Hofmeyr
Lord Curzon	Vincent Massey
Lord Ernle	F. W. Pember
Lord Grey of Fallodon	A. L. Smith
Lord Lansdowne	B. H. Sumner
Lord Milner	A. J. Toynbee
Leopold Amery	E. L. Woodward

Of these eighteen names, nine were Fellows of All Souls, and seven were clearly of the Milner Group.

There was also a close relationship between the Milner Group and New College. The following list gives the names of eight members of the Milner Group who were also Fellows or Honorary Fellows of New College in the years 1900-1947:

Lord Lothian
Lord Milner
Isaiah Berlin
H. A. L. Fisher
Sir Samuel Hoare (Lord Templewood)
Gilbert Murray
W. G. A. Ormsby-Gore (Lord Harlech)
Sir Alfred Zimmern

If we wished to add names to the Cecil Bloc, we would add those of Lord David Cecil, Lord Quickswood (Lord Hugh Cecil), and Bishop A. C. Headlam.

It is clear from these lists that almost every important member of the Milner Group was a fellow of one of the three colleges — Balliol, New College, or All Souls. Indeed, these three formed a close relationship, the first two on the undergraduate level and the last in its own unique position. The three were largely dominated by the Milner Group, and they, in turn, largely dominated the intellectual life of Oxford in the fields of law, history, and public affairs. They came close to dominating the university itself in administrative matters. The relationships among the three can be demonstrated by the proportions of All Souls Fellows who came from these two colleges, in relation to the numbers which came from the other eighteen colleges at Oxford or from the outside world. Of the one hundred forty-nine Fellows at All Souls in the twentieth century, forty-eight came from Balliol and thirty from New College, in spite of the fact that Christ Church was larger than these and Trinity, Magdalen, Brasenose, St. John's, and University colleges were almost as large. Only thirty-two came from these other five large colleges, while at least fifteen were educated outside Oxford.

The power of the Cecil Bloc and the Milner Group in Oxford in the twentieth century can be seen by glancing at the list of Chancellors of the University during the century:[7]

> Lord Salisbury, 1869-1903
> Lord Goschen, 1903-1907
> Lord Curzon, 1907-1925
> Lord Milner, 1925-
> Lord George Cave, 1925-1928
> Lord Grey of Fallodon, 1928-1933
> Lord Halifax, 1933-

The influence of the Milner Group at Oxford was sufficient to enable it to get control of the *Dictionary of National Biography* after this work was given to the university in 1917. This control was exercised by H. W. C. Davis and his protege J. R. H. Weaver during the period before 1938. The former had been brought into the gifted circle because he was a Fellow of All Souls and later a Fellow of Balliol (1895-1921). In this connection he was naturally acquainted with Weaver (who was a Fellow of Trinity from 1913 to 1938) and brought him into the War Trade Intelligence Department when Davis organized this under Cecil-Milner auspices in 1915. Davis became editor of the *Dictionary of National Biography* under the same auspices in 1921 and soon asked Weaver to join him. They jointly produced the *Dictionary* supplement for 1912-1921. After Davis's death in 1928, Weaver became editor and brought out the supplement for 1922-1930.[8] He continued as editor until shortly before he was made President of Trinity College in 1938. Weaver wrote the sketch of Davis in the *Dictionary* and also a larger work called *Henry William Carless Davis, a Memoir and a Selection of His Historical Papers*, published in 1933.

This control of the *Dictionary of National Biography* will explain how the Milner Group controlled the writing of the biographies of its own members so completely in that valuable work. This fact will already have been observed in the present work. The only instance, apparently, where a member of the Milner Group or the Cecil Bloc did not have his biographical sketch written by another member of these groups is to be found in the case of Lord Phillimore, whose sketch was written by Lord Sankey, who was not a member of the groups in question. Phillimore is also the only member of these groups whose sketch is not wholeheartedly adulatory.

The influence of the Milner Group in academic circles is by no means exhausted by the brief examination just made of Oxford. At Oxford itself, the Group has been increasingly influential in Nuffield College, while outside of Oxford it apparently controls (or greatly influences) the Stevenson Professorship of International Relations at London; the Rhodes Professorship of Imperial History at London; Birkbeck College at London; the George V Professorship of History in Cape Town University; and the Wilson Professorship of International Politics at University College of Wales, Aberystwyth. Some of these are controlled completely, while others are influenced in varying degrees. In Canada the influence of the Group is substantial, if not decisive, at the University of Toronto and at Upper Canada College. At Toronto the Glazebrook-Massey influence is very considerable, while at present the Principal of Upper Canada College is W. L. Grant, son-in-law of George Parkin and former Beit Lecturer at Oxford. Vincent Massey is a governor of the institution.

6

"The Times"

BEYOND THE ACADEMIC FIELD, the Milner Group engaged in journalistic activities that sought to influence public opinion in directions which the Group desired. One of the earliest examples of this, and one of the few occasions on which the Group appeared as a group in the public eye, was in 1905, the year in which Milner returned from Africa. At that time the Group published a volume, *The Empire and the Century*, consisting of fifty articles on various aspects of the imperial problem. The majority of these articles were written by members of the Milner Group, in spite of the fact that so many of the most important members were still in Africa with Lord Selborne. The volume was issued under the general editorship of Charles S. Goldman, a friend of John Buchan and author of *With General French and the Cavalry in South Africa*. Among those who wrote articles were W. F. Monypenny, Bernard Holland, John Buchan, Henry Birchenough, R. B. Haldane, Bishop Lang, L. S. Amery, Evelyn Cecil, George Parkin, Edmund Garrett, Geoffrey Dawson, E. B. Sargant (one of the Kindergarten), Lionel Phillips, Valentine Chirol, and Sir Frederick and Lady Lugard.

This volume has many significant articles, several of which have already been mentioned. It was followed by a sequel volume, called *The Empire and the Future*, in 1916. The latter consisted of a series of lectures delivered at King's College, University of London, in 1915, under the sponsorship of the Royal Colonial Institute. The lectures were by members of the Milner Group who included A. L. Smith, H. A. L. Fisher, Philip Kerr, and George R. Parkin.[1] A somewhat similar series of lectures was given on the British Dominions at the University of Birmingham in 1910-1911 by such men as Alfred Lyttelton, Henry Birchenough, and William Hely-Hutchinson. These were published by Sir William Ashley in a volume called *The British Dominions*.

These efforts, however, were too weak, too public, and did not reach the proper persons. Accordingly, the real efforts of the Milner Group were directed into more fruitful and anonymous activities such as *The Times* and *The Round Table*.

The Milner Group did not own *The Times* before 1922, but clearly controlled it at least as far back as 1912. Even before this last date, members of the innermost circle of the Milner Group were swarming about the great newspaper. In fact, it would appear that *The Times* had been controlled by the Cecil Bloc since 1884 and was taken over by the Milner Group in the same way in which All Souls was taken over, quietly and without a struggle. The midwife of this process apparently was George E. Buckle (1854-1935), graduate of New College in 1876, member of All Souls since 1877, and editor of *The Times* from 1884 to 1912.[2] The chief members of the Milner Group who were associated with *The Times* have already been mentioned. Amery was connected with the paper from 1899 to 1909. During this period he edited and largely wrote the *Times History of the South African War*. Lord Esher was offered a directorship in 1908. Grigg was a staff writer in 1903-1905, and head of the Imperial Department in 1908-1913. B. K. Long was head of the Dominion Department in 1913-1921 and of the Foreign Department in 1920-1921. Monypenny was assistant editor both before and after the Boer War (1894-1899, 1903-1908) and on the board of directors after the paper was incorporated (1908-1912). Dawson was the paper's chief correspondent in South Africa in the Selborne period (1905-1910), while Basil Williams was the reporter covering the National Convention there (1908-1909). When it became clear in 1911 that Buckle must soon retire, Dawson was brought into the office in a rather vague capacity and, a year later, was made editor. The appointment was suggested and urged by Buckle.[3] Dawson held the position from 1912 to 1941, except for the three years 1919-1922. This interval is of some significance, for it revealed to the Milner Group that they could not continue to control *The Times* without ownership. The Cecil Bloc had controlled *The Times* from 1884 to 1912 without ownership, and the Milner Group had done the same in the period 1912-1919, but, in this last year, Dawson quarreled with Lord Northcliffe (who was chief proprietor from 1908-1922) and left the editor's chair. As soon as the Milner Group, through the Astors, acquired the chief proprietorship of the paper in 1922, Dawson was restored to his post and held it for the next twenty years. Undoubtedly the skillful stroke which acquired the ownership of *The Times* from the Harmsworth estate in 1922 was engineered by Brand. During the interval of three years during which Dawson was not editor, Northcliffe entrusted the position to one of *The Time's* famous foreign correspondents, H. W. Steed.

Dawson was succeeded as editor in 1944 by R. M. Barrington-Ward, whose brother was a Fellow of All Souls and son-in-law of A. L. Smith.

Laurence Rushbrook Williams, who functions in many capacities in Indian affairs after his fellowship in All Souls (1914-1921), also joined the editorial staff in 1944. Douglas Jay, who graduated from New College in 1930 and was a Fellow of All Souls in 1930-1937, was on the staff of *The Times* in 1929-1933 and of the *Economist* in 1933-1937. He became a Labour M.P. in 1946, after having performed the unheard-of feat of going directly from All Souls to the city desk of the Labour Party's *Daily Herald* (1937-1941). Another interesting figure on *The Times* staff in the more recent period was Charles R. S. Harris, who was a Fellow of All Souls for fifteen years (1921-1936), after graduating from Corpus Christi. He was leader-writer of *The Times* for ten years (1925-1935) and, during part of the same period, was on the staff of the *Economist* (1932-1935) and editor of *The Nineteenth Century and After* (1930-1935). He left all three positions in 1935 to go for four years to the Argentine to be general manager of the Buenos Aires Great Southern and Western Railways. During the Second World War he joined the Ministry of Economic Warfare for a year, the Foreign Office for two years, and the Finance Department of the War Office for a year (1942-1943). Then he was commissioned a lieutenant colonel with the military government in occupied Sicily, and ended up the war as a member of the Allied Control Commission in Italy. Harris's written works cover a range of subjects that would be regarded as extreme anywhere outside the Milner Group. A recognized authority on Duns Scotus, he wrote two volumes on this philosopher as well as the chapter on "Philosophy" in *The Legacy of the Middle Ages*, but in 1935 he wrote *Germany's Foreign Indebtedness* for the Royal Institute of International Affairs.

Harris's literary versatility, as well as the large number of members of All Souls who drifted over to the staff on *The Times*, unquestionably can be explained by the activities of Lord Brand. Brand not only brought these persons from All Souls to *The Times*, but also brought the Astors to *The Times*. Brand and Lord Astor were together at New College at the outbreak of the Boer War. They married sisters, daughters of Chiswell Dabney Langhorne of Virginia. Brand was apparently the one who brought Astor into the Milner Group in 1917, although there had been a movement in this direction considerably earlier. Astor was a Conservative M.P. from 1910 to 1919, leaving the Lower House to take his father's seat in the House of Lords. His place in Commons has been held since 1919 by his wife, Nancy Astor (1919-1945), and by his son Michael Langhorne Astor (1945-   ). In 1918 Astor became parliamentary secretary to Lloyd George; later he held the same position with the Ministry of Food (1918-1919) and the Ministry of Health (1919-1921). He was British delegate to the Assembly of the League of Nations in 1931, chairman of the League

Committee on Nutrition (1936-1937), and chairman of the council of the Royal Institute of International Affairs (since 1935). With help from various people, he wrote three books on agricultural problems: *Land and Life* (1932), *The Planning of Agriculture* (1933), and *British Agriculture* (1938). Both of his sons graduated from New College, and both have been Members of Parliament, the older in the period 1935-1945, and the younger since 1945. The older was secretary to Lord Lytton on the League of Nations Commission of Enquiry into the Manchurian Episode (1932) and was parliamentary private secretary to Sir Samuel Hoare when he was First Lord of the Admiralty and Home Secretary (1936-1939).

Lord Astor's chief importance in regard to *The Times* is that he and his brother became chief proprietors in 1922 by buying out the Harmsworth interest. As a result, the brother, Colonel John Jacob Astor, has been chairman of the board of The Times Publishing Company since 1922, and Brand was a director on the board for many years before 1944. Colonel Astor, who matriculated at New College in 1937, at the age of fifty-one, was military aide to the Viceroy of India (Lord Hardinge) in 1911-1914, was a Member of Parliament from 1922 to 1945, and is a director of both Hambros' and Barclay's Banks.

This connection between the Milner Group and *The Times* was of the greatest importance in the period up to 1945, especially in the period just before the Munich crisis. However, the chief center of gravity of the Milner Group was never in *The Times*. It is true that Lord Astor became one of the more important figures in the Milner Group after Milner's death in 1925, but the center of gravity of the Group as a whole was elsewhere: before 1920, in the Round Table Group; and after 1920, in All Souls. Lord Astor was of great importance in the later period, especially after 1930, but was of no significance in the earlier period — an indication of his relatively recent arrival in the Group.

The Times has recently published the first three volumes of a four-volume history of itself. Although no indication is given as to the authorship of these volumes, the acknowledgments show that the authors worked closely with All Souls and the Milner Group. For example, Harold Temperley and Keith Feiling read the proofs of the first two volumes, while E. L. Woodward read those of the third volume.

While members of the Milner Group thus went into *The Times* to control it, relatively few persons ever came into the Milner Group from *The Times*. The only two who readily come to mind are Sir Arthur Willert and Lady Lugard.[4]

Arthur Willert (Sir Arthur since 1919) entered Balliol in 1901 but did not take a degree until 1928. From 1906 to 1910 he was on the staff of

The Times in Paris, Berlin, and Washington, and was then chief *Times* correspondent in Washington for ten years (1910-1920). During this period he was also secretary to the British War Mission in Washington (1917-1918) and Washington representative of the Ministry of Information. This brought him to the attention of the Milner Group, probably through Brand, and in 1921 he joined the Foreign Office as head of the News Department. During the next fifteen years he was a member of the British delegations to the Washington Conference of 1922, to the London Economic Conference of 1924, to the London Naval Conference of 1930, to the World Disarmament Conference of 1932-1934, and to the League of Nations in 1929-1934. He retired from the Foreign Office in 1935, but returned to an active life for the duration of the Second World War as head of the southern region for the Ministry of Information (1939-1945). In 1937, in cooperation with H. V. Hodson (then editor of *The Round Table*) and B. K. Long (of the Kindergarten), he wrote a book called *The Empire in the World*. He had previously written *Aspects of British Foreign Policy* (1928) and *The Frontiers of England* (1935).

The second person to come into the Milner Group from *The Times* was Lady Lugard (the former Flora Shaw), who was probably a member of the Rhodes secret society on *The Times* and appears to have been passing from *The Times* to the Milner Group, when she was really passing from the society to the Milner Group. She and her husband are of great significance in the latter organization, although neither was a member of the innermost circle.

Frederick Lugard (Sir Frederick after 1901 and Lord Lugard after 1928) was a regular British army officer who served in Afghanistan, the Sudan, and Burma in 1879-1887. In 1888 he led a successful expedition against slave-traders on Lake Nyasa, and was subsequently employed by the British East African Company, the Royal Niger Company, and British West Charterland in leading expeditions into the interior of Africa (1889-1897). In 1897 he was appointed by the Salisbury government to be Her Majesty's Commissioner in the hinterland of Nigeria and Lagos and commandant of the West African Frontier Force, which he organized. Subsequently he was High Commissioner of Northern Nigeria (1900-1906) and Governor of Hong Kong (1907-1912), as well as Governor, and later Governor-General, of Nigeria (1912-1919). He wrote *Our East African Empire* (1893) and *The Dual Mandate in British Tropical Africa* (1922), and also numerous articles (including one on West Africa in *The Empire and the Century*). He was one of the chief assistants of Lord Lothian and Lord Hailey in planning the *African Survey* in 1934-1937, was British member of the Permanent Mandates Commission of the League of Nations from 1922 to 1936, was one of the more influential figures in the Royal Institute of International Affairs, and is generally regarded as the inventor of the British system of "indirect rule" in colonial areas.

Flora Shaw, who married Sir Frederick Lugard in 1902, when he was forty-four and she was fifty, was made head of the Colonial Department of *The Times* in 1890, at the suggestion of Sir Robert George Wyndham Herbert, the Permanent Under Secretary of the Colonial Office. Sir Robert, whose grandmother was a Wyndham and whose grandfather was Earl of Carnarvon, was a Fellow of All Souls from 1854 to 1905. He was thus elected the year following Lord Salisbury's election. He began his political career as private secretary to Gladstone and was Permanent Under Secretary for twenty-one years (1871-1892, 1900). He was subsequently Agent General for Tasmania (1893-1896), High Sheriff of London, chairman of the Tariff Commission, and adviser to the Sultan of Johore, all under the Salisbury-Balfour governments.

When Miss Shaw was recommended to *The Times* as head of the Colonial Department, she was already a close friend of Moberly Bell, manager of *The Times*, and was an agent and close friend of Stead and Cecil Rhodes. The story of how she came to work for *The Times*, as told in that paper's official history, is simplicity itself: Bell wanted someone to head the Colonial Department, so he wrote to Sir Robert Herbert and was given the name of Flora Shaw. Accordingly, Bell wrote, "as a complete stranger," to Miss Shaw and asked her "as an inexperienced writer for a specimen column." She wrote a sample article on Egyptian finance, which pleased Bell so greatly that she was given the position of head of the Colonial Department. That is the story as it appears in volume III of *The History of The Times*, published in 1947. Shortly afterward appeared the biography of Flora Shaw, written by the daughter of Moberly Bell and based on his private papers. The story that emerges from this volume is quite different. It goes somewhat as follows:

Flora Shaw, like most members of that part of the Cecil Bloc which shifted over to the Milner Group, was a disciple of John Ruskin and an ardent worker among the depressed masses of London's slums. Through Ruskin, she came to write for W. T. Stead of the *Pall Mall Gazette* in 1886, and three years later, through Stead, she met Cecil Rhodes. In the meantime, in 1888, she went to Egypt as correspondent of the *Pall Mall Gazette* and there became a close friend of Moberly Bell, *The Times* correspondent in that country. Bell had been employed in this capacity in Egypt since 1865 and had become a close friend of Evelyn Baring (Lord Cromer), the British agent in Egypt. He had also become an expert on Egyptian finance and published a pamphlet on that subject in 1887. Miss Shaw's friendship with the Bell family was so close that she was practically a member of it, and Bell's children knew her, then and later, as "Aunt Flora."

In 1890, when Bell was transferred to Printing House Square as manager of *The Times*, Baring tried to persuade *The Times* to name Miss Shaw as Egyptian correspondent in Bell's place. This was not done. Instead, Miss Shaw returned to London and was introduced by Bell to Buckle. When Buckle told Miss Shaw that he wanted a head for the Colonial Department of the paper, she suggested that he consult with Sir Robert Herbert. From that point on, the account in *The History of The Times* is accurate. But it is clear, to anyone who has the information just mentioned, that the recommendation by Sir Robert Herbert, the test article on Egyptian finance, and probably the article itself, had been arranged previously between Moberly Bell and "Aunt Flora."

None of these early relationships of Miss Shaw with Bell, Buckle, and Herbert are mentioned in *The History of The Times*, and apparently they are not to be found in the records at Printing House Square. They are, however, a significant indication of the methods of the Milner Group. It is not clear what was the purpose of this elaborate scheme. Miss Moberly Bell apparently believes that it was to deceive Buckle. It is much more likely that it was to deceive the chief owners of *The Times*, John Walter III and his son, Arthur F. Walter.

Miss Shaw, when she came to *The Times*, was an open champion of Lord Salisbury and an active supporter of a vigorous imperial policy, especially in South Africa. She was in the confidence of the Colonial Office and of Rhodes to a degree that cannot be exaggerated. She met Rhodes, on Stead's recommendation, in 1889, at a time when Stead was one of Rhodes's closest confidants. In 1892, Miss Shaw was sent to South Africa by Moberly Bell, with instructions to set up two lines of communication from that area to herself. One of these was to be known to *The Times* and would handle routine matters; the second was to be known only to herself and was to bring confidential material to her private address. The expenses of both of these avenues would be paid for by *The Times*, but the expenses of the secret avenue would not appear on the records at Printing House Square.[5]

From this date onward, Miss Shaw was in secret communication with Cecil Rhodes. This communication was so close that she was informed by Rhodes of the plot which led up to the Jameson Raid, months before the raid took place. She was notified by Rhodes of the approximate date on which the raid would occur, two weeks before it did occur. She even suggested on several occasions that the plans be executed more rapidly, and on one occasion suggested a specific date for the event.

In her news articles, Miss Shaw embraced the cause of the British in the Transvaal even to the extent of exaggerating and falsifying their hardships under Boer rule.[6] It was *The Times* that published as an exclusive feature the famous (and fraudulent) "women and children" letter, dated 20 December 1895, which pretended to be an appeal for help from the persecuted British in the Transvaal to Dr. Jameson's waiting forces, but which had really been concocted by Dr. Jameson himself on 20 November and sent to Miss Shaw a month later. This letter was published by *The Times* as soon as news of the Jameson' Raid was known, as a justification of the act. *The Times* continued to defend and justify the raid and Jameson. After this became a rather delicate policy — that is, after the raid failed and had to be disavowed — *The Times* was saved from the necessity of reversing itself by the "Kruger telegram" sent by the German Kaiser to congratulate the Boers on their successful suppression of the raiders. This "Kruger telegram" was played up by *The Times* with such vigor that Jameson was largely eclipsed and the incident assumed the dimensions of an international crisis. As the official *History of The Times* puts it, "*The Times* was carried so far by indignation against the outrageous interference of the Kaiser in the affairs of the British Empire that it was able to overlook the criminality of Jameson's act." A little later, the same account says, "On January 7, Rhodes' resignation from the Premiership was announced, while the Editor found it more convenient to devote his leading article to the familiar topic of German interference rather than to the consequences of the Raid."[7]

All of this was being done on direct instructions from Rhodes, and with the knowledge and approval of the management of *The Times*. In fact, Miss Shaw was the intermediary between Rhodes, *The Times*, and the Colonial Office (Joseph Chamberlain). Until the end of November 1895, her instructions from Rhodes came to her through his agent in London, Dr. Rutherfoord Harris, but, when the good Dr. Harris and Alfred Beit returned to South Africa in order to be on hand for the anticipated excitement, the former gave Miss Shaw the secret code of the British South Africa Company and the cable address TELE-MONES LONDON, so that communications from Rhodes to Miss Shaw could be sent directly. Dr. Harris had already informed Rhodes by a cable of 4 November 1895: IF YOU CAN TELEGRAPH COURSE YOU WISH TIMES TO ADOPT NOW WITH REGARD TO TRANSVAAL FLORA WILL ACT.

On 10 December 1895, Miss Shaw cabled Rhodes: CAN YOU ADVISE WHEN WILL YOU COMMENCE THE PLANS, WE WISH TO SEND AT EARLIEST OPPORTUNITY SEALED INSTRUCTIONS REPRESENTATIVE OF THE LOND TIMES EUROPEAN CAPITALS; IT IS MOST IMPORTANT USING THEIR INFLUENCE IN YOUR FAVOR. The use of the word "we" in this message disposes once and for all of Miss Shaw's later defense that all her acts were done on her own private responsibility and not in her capacity as a department head of *The Times.* In answer to this request, Rhodes replied the next day: WE DO THINK ABOUT NEW YEAR. This answer made *The Times's* manager "very depressed," so the next day (12 December) Miss Shaw sent the following cable to Rhodes: DELAY DANGEROUS SYMPATHY NOW COMPLETE BUT WILL DEPEND VERY MUCH UPON ACTION BEFORE EUROPEAN POWERS GIVEN TIME ENTER A PROTEST WHICH AS EUROPEAN SITUATION CONSIDERED SERIOUS MIGHT PARALYSE GOVERNMENT. Five days after this came another cable, which said in part: CHAMBERLAIN SOUND IN CASE OF INTERFERENCE EUROPEAN POWERS BUT HAVE SPECIAL REASON TO BELIEVE WISHES YOU MUST DO IT IMMEDIATELY. To these very incriminating messages might be added two of several wires from Rhodes to Miss Shaw. One of 30 December 1895, after Rhodes knew that the Jameson Raid had begun and after Miss Shaw had been so informed by secret code, stated: INFORM CHAMBERLAIN THAT I SHALL GET THROUGH ALL RIGHT IF HE SUPPORTS ME, BUT HE MUST NOT SEND CABLE LIKE HE SENT HIGH COMMISSIONER IN SOUTH AFRICA. TODAY THE CRUX IS, I WILL WIN AND SOUTH AFRICA WILL BELONG TO ENGLAND. And the following day, when the outcome of the raid was doubtful because of the failure of the English in the Transvaal to rise against the Boers — a failure resulting from the fact that they were not as ill-treated as Miss Shaw, through *The Times,* had been telling the world for months — Rhodes cabled: UNLESS YOU CAN MAKE CHAMBERLAIN INSTRUCT THE HIGH COMMISSIONER TO PROCEED AT ONCE TO JOHANNESBURG THE WHOLE POSITION IS LOST. HIGH COMMISSIONER WOULD RECEIVE SPLENDID RECEPTION AND STILL TURN POSITION TO ENGLAND ADVANTAGE BUT MUST BE INSTRUCTED BY CABLE IMMEDIATELY. THE INSTRUCTIONS MUST BE SPECIFIC AS HE IS WEAK AND WILL TAKE NO RESPONSIBILITY.[8] When we realize that the anticipated uprising of the English in the Transvaal had been financed and armed with munitions from the funds of the British South Africa Company, it is clear that we must wait until Hitler's coup in Austria in March 1938 to find a parallel to Rhodes's and Jameson's attempted coup in South Africa forty-two years earlier.

The Jameson Raid, if the full story could ever be told, would give the finest possible example of the machinations of Rhodes's secret society. Another example, almost as good, would be the completely untold story of how the society covered up these activities in the face of the investigation of the Parliamentary Select Committee. The dangers from this investigation were so great that even Lord Rothschild was pressed into service as a messenger. It was obvious from the beginning that the star witness before the committee would be Cecil Rhodes and that the chief danger would be the incrimination of Joseph Chamberlain, who clearly knew of the plot. Milner, Garrett, Stead, and Esher discussed possible defenses and reached no conclusion, since Stead wanted to admit that Chamberlain was implicated in plans for *a* raid but not plans for *the* raid. By this, Stead meant that Chamberlain and Rhodes had seen the possibility of an uprising in the Transvaal and, solely as a precautionary measure, had made the preparations for Jameson's force so that it would be available to go to Johannesburg to restore order. The others refused to accept this strategy and insisted on the advantages of a general and blanket denial. This difference of opinion probably arose from the fact that Stead did not know that the prospective rebels in Johannesburg were armed and financed by Rhodes, were led by Rhodes's brother and Abe Bailey, and had written the "women and children" message, in collaboration with Jameson, weeks before. These facts, if revealed to the committee, would make it impossible to distinguish between "the raid" and "a raid." The event of 31 December 1895, which the committee was investigating, was the former and not the latter merely because the plotters in Johannesburg failed to revolt on schedule. This is clear from Edward Cook's statement, in his biography of Garrett, that Garrett expected to receive news of a revolution in Johannesburg at any moment on 30 December 1895.[9]

The difficulty which the initiates in London had in preparing a defense for the Select Committee was complicated by the fact that they were not able to reach Rhodes, who was en route from South Africa with Garrett. As soon as the boat docked, Brett (Lord Esher) sent "Natty" Rothschild from London with a message from Chamberlain to Rhodes. When Rothschild returned, Brett called in Stead, and they discussed the projected defense. Stead had already seen Rhodes and given his advice.[10] The following day (5 February 1896), Brett saw Rhodes and found that he was prepared to confess everything. Brett tried to dissuade him. As he wrote in his *Journal*, "I pointed out to him that there was one consideration which appeared to have escaped him, that was the position of Mr. Chamberlain, the Secretary of State. Chamberlain was obviously anxious to help and it would not do to embarrass him or to tie his hands. It appeared to me to be prudent to endeavour to ascertain how Chamberlain would receive a confidence of this kind. I said I would try to find out. On leaving me he said, 'Wish we could get our secret society.' " Brett went to Chamberlain, who refused to receive Rhodes's confession, lest he have to order the law officers to take proceedings against Rhodes as against Jameson. Accordingly, the view of the majority, a general denial, was adopted and proved successful, thanks to the leniency of the members of the Select Committee. Brett recognized this leniency. He wrote to Stead on 19 February 1897: "I came up with Milner from Windsor this morning. He has a heavy job; and has to start *de novo*. The committee will leave few of the old gang on their legs. Alas. Rhodes was a pitiful object. Harcourt very sorry for him; too sorry to press his question home. *Why* did Rhodes try to shuffle after all we had told him?"[11]

It is clear that the Select Committee made no real effort to uncover the real relationships between the conspirators, *The Times*, and the Salisbury government. When witnesses refused to produce documents or to answer questions, the committee did not insist, and whole fields of inquiry were excluded from examination by the committee.

One of these fields, and probably the most important one, was the internal policies and administration of *The Times* itself. As a result, when Campbell-Bannerman, an opposition leader, asked if it were usual practice for *The Times* correspondents to be used to propagate certain policies in foreign countries as well as to obtain information, Miss Shaw answered that she had been excused from answering questions about the internal administration of *The Times*. We now know, as a result of the publication of the official *History of The Times*, that all Miss Shaw's acts were done in consultation with the manager, Moberly Bell.[12] The vital telegrams to Rhodes, signed by Miss Shaw, were really drafted by Bell. As *The History of The Times* puts it, "Bell had taken the risk of allowing Miss Shaw to commit *The Times* to the support of Rhodes in a conspiracy that was bound to lead to controversy at home, if it succeeded, and likely to lead to prosecution if it failed. The conspiracy had failed; the prosecution had resulted. Bell's only salvation lay in Miss Shaw's willingness to take personal responsibility for the telegrams and in her ability to convince the Committee accordingly." And, as the evidence of the same source shows, in order to convince the committee it was necessary for Miss Shaw to commit perjury, even though the representatives of both parties on the Committee of Enquiry (except Labouchere) were making every effort to conceal the real facts while still providing the public with a good show.

Before leaving the discussion of Miss Shaw and the Jameson Raid, it might be fitting to introduce testimony from a somewhat unreliable witness, Wilfrid Scawen Blunt, a member by breeding and education of this social group and a relative of the Wyndhams, but a psychopathic anti-imperialist who spent his life praising and imitating the Arabs and criticizing Britain's conduct in India, Egypt, and Ireland. In his diaries, under the date 25 April 1896, he says: "[George Wyndham] has been seeing much of Jameson, whom he likes, and of the gang that have been running the Transvaal business, about a dozen of them, with Buckle, *The Times* editor, and Miss Flora Shaw, who, he told me confidentially, is really the prime mover in the whole thing, and who takes the lead in all their private meetings, a very clever middle-aged woman."[13] A somewhat similar conclusion was reached by W. T. Stead in a pamphlet called *Joseph Chamberlain: Conspirator or Statesman*, which he published from the office of *The Review of Reviews* in 1900. Stead was convinced that Miss Shaw was the intermediary among Rhodes, *The Times*, and the Colonial Office. And

Stead was Rhodes's closest confidant in England.

As a result of this publicity, Miss Shaw's value to *The Times* was undoubtedly reduced, and she gave up her position after her marriage in 1902. In the meantime, however, she had been in correspondence with Milner as early as 1899, and in December 1901 made a trip to South Africa for *The Times*, during which she had long interviews with Milner, Monypenny, and the members of the Kindergarten. After her resignation, she continued to review books for *The Times Literary Supplement*, wrote an article on tropical dependencies for *The Empire and the Century*, wrote two chapters for Amery's *History of the South African War*, and wrote a biographical sketch of Cecil Rhodes for the eleventh edition of the *Encyclopedia Britannica*.

A third member of this same type was Valentine Chirol (Sir Valentine after 1912). Educated at the Sorbonne, he was a clerk in the Foreign Office for four years (1872-1876) and then traveled about the world, but chiefly in the Near East, for sixteen years (1876-1892). In 1892 he was made *The Times* correspondent in Berlin, and for the next four years filled the role of a second British ambassador, with free access to the Foreign Ministry in Berlin and functioning as a channel of unofficial communication between the government in London and that in Berlin. After 1895 he became increasingly anti-German, like all members of the Cecil Bloc and the Milner Group, and was chiefly responsible for the great storm whipped up over the "Kruger telegram." In this last connection he even went so far as to announce in *The Times* that the Germans were really using the Jameson episode as part of a long-range project to drive Britain out of South Africa and that the next step in that process was to be the dispatch in the immediate future of a German expeditionary force to Delagoa Bay in Portuguese Angola. As a result of this attitude, Chirol found the doors of the Foreign Ministry closed to him and, after another unfruitful year in Berlin, was brought to London to take charge of the Foreign Department of *The Times*. He held this post for fifteen years (1897-1912), during which he was one of the most influential figures in the formation of British foreign and imperial policy. The policy he supported was the policy that was carried out, and included support for the Boer War, the Anglo-Japanese Alliance, the Entente Cordiale, the agreement of 1907 with Russia, the Morley-Minto Reforms in India, and the increasing resistance to Germany. When he retired in 1912, he was knighted by Asquith for his important contributions to the Morley-Minto Reforms of 1909 and was made a member of the Royal Commission on Public Services in India (1912-1914). He remained in India during most of the First World War, and, indeed, made seventeen visits to that country in his life. In 1916 he was one of the five chief advisers to Lionel Curtis in the preparatory work for the Government of India Act of 1919 (the other four being Lord Chelmsford, Meston, Marris, and Hailey). Later Chirol wrote articles for *The Round Table* and was a member of the British delegation at the Paris Peace Conference.

Chirol was replaced as head of the Foreign Department during his long absences from London by Leopold Amery. It was expected that Amery would be Chirol's successor in the post, but Amery entered upon a political career in 1910, so the position was given briefly to Dudley Disraeli Braham. Braham, a former classmate of many of the Kindergarten at New College, was a foreign correspondent of *The Times* for ten years (1897-1907) and Chirol's assistant for five (1907-1912), before he became Chirol's successor in the Foreign Department and Grigg's successor in the Imperial Department, thus combining the two. He resigned from *The Times* in 1914 to become editor of the *Daily Telegraph* in Sydney, Australia, and was subsequently a very important figure in Australian newspaper life.

This account, by no means complete, shows clearly that the Milner Group controlled *The Times*, indirectly from 1912 if not earlier, and directly from 1922. The importance of this control should be obvious. *The Times*, although of a very limited circulation (only about 35,000 at the beginning of the century, 50,000 at the outbreak of the First World War, and 187,000 in 1936), was the most influential paper in England. The reason for this influence is not generally recognized, although the existence of the condition itself is widely known. The influence depended upon the close relationship between the paper and the Foreign Office. This relationship, as we are trying to show, was the result of the Milner Group's influence in both.

This influence was not exercised by acting directly on public opinion, since the Milner Group never intended to influence events by acting through any instruments of mass propaganda, but rather hoped to work on the opinions of the small group of "important people," who in turn could influence wider and wider circles of persons. This was the basis on which the Milner Group itself was constructed; it was the theory behind the Rhodes Scholarships; it was the theory behind *"The Round Table* and the Royal Institute of International Affairs; it was the theory behind the efforts to control All Souls, New College, and Balliol and, through these three, to control Oxford University; and it was the theory behind *The Times*. No effort was made to win a large circulation for *The Times*, for, in order to obtain such a circulation, it would have been necessary to make changes in the tone of the paper that would have reduced its influence with the elite, to which it had been so long directed. The theory of "the elite" was accepted by the Milner Group and by *The Times*, as it was by Rhodes. The historian of *The Times* recognizes this and, after describing the departure from

Printing House Square of Bell, Chirol, and Buckle, says, "It is a valid criticism of the 'Old Gang' that they had not realized that they were in the habit of valuing news according to the demands and interests of a governing class too narrowly defined for the twentieth century." It was on this issue that the "Old Gang" disputed with Northcliffe in the period 1908-1912 and that Dawson disputed with Northcliffe in 1919. Although the new owner protested to all who would listen, in 1908 and later, that he would not try to make *The Times* into a popular paper, he was, as *The History of The Times* shows, incapable of judging the merits of a newspaper by any other standard than the size of its circulation. After he was replaced as chief proprietor by Astor, and Dawson reoccupied the editor's chair, the old point of view was reestablished. *The Times* was to be a paper for the people who are influential, and not for the masses. *The Times* was influential, but the degree of its influence would never be realized by anyone who examined only the paper itself. The greater part of its influence arose from its position as one of several branches of a single group, the Milner Group. By the interaction of these various branches on one another, under the pretense that each branch was an autonomous power, the influence of each branch was increased through a process of mutual reinforcement. The unanimity among the various branches was believed by the outside world to be the result of the influence of a single Truth, while really it was the result of the existence of a single group. Thus, a statesman (a member of the Group) announces a policy. About the same time, the Royal Institute of International Affairs publishes a study on the subject, and an Oxford don, a Fellow of All Souls (and a member of the Group) also publishes a volume on the subject (probably through a publishing house, like G. Bell and Sons or Faber and Faber, allied to the Group). The statesman's policy is subjected to critical analysis and final approval in a "leader" in *The Times*, while the two books are reviewed (in a single review) in *The Times Literary Supplement*. Both the "leader" and the review are anonymous but are written by members of the Group. And finally, at about the same time, an anonymous article in *The Round Table* strongly advocates the same policy. The cumulative effect of such tactics as this, even if each tactical move influences only a small number of important people, is bound to be great. If necessary, the strategy can be carried further, by arranging for the secretary to the Rhodes Trustees to go to America for a series of "informal discussions" with former Rhodes Scholars, while a prominent retired statesman (possibly a former Viceroy of India) is persuaded to say a few words at the unveiling of a plaque in All Souls or New College in honor of some deceased Warden. By a curious coincidence, both the "informal discussions" in America and the unveiling speech at Oxford touch on the same topical subject.

An analogous procedure in reverse could be used for policies or books which the Group did not approve. A cutting editorial or an unfriendly book review, followed by a suffocating blanket of silence and neglect, was the best that such an offering could expect from the instruments of the Milner Group. This is not easy to demonstrate because of the policy of anonymity followed by writers and reviewers in *The Times, The Round Table,* and *The Times Literary Supplement,* but enough cases have been found to justify this statement. When J. A. Farrer's book *England under Edward VII* was published in 1922 and maintained that the British press, especially *The Times,* was responsible for bad Anglo-German feeling before 1909, *The Times Literary Supplement* gave it to J. W. Headlam-Morley to review. And when Baron von Eckardstein, who was in the German Embassy in London at the time of the Boer War, published his memoirs in 1920, the same journal gave the book to Chirol to review, even though Chirol was an interested party and was dealt with in a critical fashion in several passages in the book itself. Both of these reviews were anonymous.

There is no effort here to contend that the Milner Group ever falsified or even concealed evidence (although this charge could be made against *The Times*). Rather it propagated its point of view by interpretation and selection of evidence. In this fashion it directed policy in ways that were sometimes disastrous. The Group as a whole was made up of intelligent men who believed sincerely, and usually intensely, in what they advocated, and who knew that their writings were intended for a small minority as intelligent as themselves. In such conditions there could be no value in distorting or concealing evidence. To do so would discredit the instruments they controlled. By giving the facts as they stood, and as completely as could be done in consistency with the interpretation desired, a picture could be construed that would remain convincing for a long time.

This is what was done by *The Times.* Even today, the official historian of *The Times* is unable to see that the policy of that paper was anti-German from 1895 to 1914 and as such contributed to the worsening of Anglo-German relations and thus to the First World War. This charge has been made by German and American students, some of them of the greatest diligence and integrity, such as Professors Sidney B. Fay, William L. Langer, Oron J. Hale, and others. The recent *History of The Times* devotes considerable space and obviously spent long hours of research in refuting these charges, and fails to see that it has not succeeded. With the usual honesty and industry of the Milner Group, the historian gives the evidence that will convict him, without seeing that his interpretation will not hold water. He confesses that the various correspondents of *The Times* in Berlin played up all anti-English actions and statements and played down all pro-English ones;

that they quoted obscure and locally discredited papers in order to do this; that all *The Times* foreign correspondents in Berlin, Paris, Vienna, and elsewhere were anti-German, and that these were the ones who were kept on the staff and promoted to better positions; that the one member of the staff who was recognized as being fair to Germany (and who was unquestionably the most able man in the whole *Times* organization), Donald Mackenzie Wallace, was removed as head of the Foreign Department and shunted off to be editor of the supplementary volumes of the *Encyclopedia Britannica* (which was controlled by *The Times*); and that *The Times* frequently printed untrue or distorted information on Germany. All of this is admitted and excused as the work of honest, if hasty, journalists, and the crowning proof that *The Times* was not guilty as charged is implied to be the fact that the Germans did ultimately get into a war with Britain, thus proving at one stroke that they were a bad lot and that the attitude of *The Times* staff toward them was justified by the event.

It did not occur to the historian of *The Times* that there exists another explanation of Anglo-German relations, namely that in 1895 there were two Germanies — the one admiring Britain and the other hating Britain — and that Britain, by her cold-blooded and calculated assault on the Boers in 1895 and 1899, gave the second (and worse) Germany the opportunity to criticize and attack Britain and gave it the arguments with which to justify a German effort to build up naval defenses. *The Times*, by quoting these attacks and actions representative of the real attitude and actual intentions of all Germans, misled the British people and abandoned the good Germans to a hopeless minority position, where to be progressive, peaceful, or Anglophile was to be a traitor to Germany itself. Chirol's alienation of Baron von Eckardstein (one of the "good" Germans, married to an English lady), in a conversation in February 1900,[14] shows exactly how *The Times* attitude was contributing to consolidate and alienate the Germans by the mere fact of insisting that they were consolidated and alienated — and doing this to a man who loved England and hated the reactionary elements in Germany more than Chirol ever did.

7

"The Round Table"

THE SECOND important propaganda effort of the Milner Group in the period after 1909 was *The Round Table*. This was part of an effort by the circle of the Milner Group to accomplish for the whole Empire what they had just done for South Africa. The leaders were Philip Kerr in London, as secretary of the London group, and Lionel Curtis throughout the world, as organizing secretary for the whole movement, but most of the members of the Kindergarten cooperated in the project. The plan of procedure was the same as that which had worked so successfully in South Africa — that is, to form local groups of influential men to agitate for imperial federation and to keep in touch with these groups by correspondence and by the circulation of a periodical. As in South Africa, the original cost of the periodical was paid by Abe Bailey. This journal, issued quarterly, was called *The Round Table*, and the same name was applied to the local groups.

Of these local groups, the most important by far was the one in London. In this, Kerr and Brand were the chief figures. The other local groups, also called Round Tables, were set up by Lionel Curtis and others in South Africa, in Canada, in New Zealand, in Australia, and, in a rather rudimentary fashion and somewhat later, in India.

The reasons for doing this were described by Curtis himself in 1917 in *A Letter to the People of India*, as follows: "We feared that South Africa might abstain from a future war with Germany, on the grounds that they had not participated in the decision to make war. . . . Confronted by this dilemma at the very moment of attaining Dominion self-government, we thought it would be wise to ask people in the oldest and most experienced of all Dominions what they thought of the matter. So in 1909, Mr. Kerr and I went to Canada and persuaded Mr. Marris, who was then on leave, to accompany us."[1]

On this trip the three young men covered a good portion of the Dominion. One day, during a walk through the forests on the Pacific slopes of the Canadian Rockies, Marris convinced Curtis that "self-

117

government, . . . however far distant, was the only intelligble goal of British policy in India. . . . The existence of political unrest in India, far from being a reason for pessimism, was the surest sign that the British, with all their manifest failings, had not shirked their primary duty of extending Western education to India and so preparing Indians to govern themselves." "I have since looked back on this walk," wrote Curtis, "as one of the milestones of my own education. So far I had thought of self-government as a Western institution, which was and would always remain peculiar to the peoples of Europe. . . . It was from that moment that I first began to think of 'the Government of each by each and of all by all' not merely as a principle of Western life, but rather of all human life, as the goal to which all human societies must tend. It was from that moment that I began to think of the British Commonwealth as the greatest instrument ever devised for enabling that principle to be realized, not merely for the children of Europe, but for all races and kindreds and peoples and tongues. And it is for that reason that I have ceased to speak of the British Empire and called the book in which I published my views *The Commonwealth of Nations.*"

Because of Curtis's position and future influence, this walk in Canada was important not only in his personal life but also in the future history of the British Empire. It needs only to be pointed out that India received complete self-government in 1947 and the British Commonwealth changed its name officially to Commonwealth of Nations in 1948. There can be no doubt that both of these events resulted in no small degree from the influence of Lionel Curtis and the Milner Group, in which he was a major figure.

Curtis and his friends stayed in Canada for four months. Then Curtis returned to South Africa for the closing session of the Transvaal Legislative Council, of which he was a member. He there drafted a memorandum on the whole question of imperial relations, and, on the day that the Union of South Africa came into existence, he sailed to New Zealand to set up study groups to examine the question. These groups became the Round Table Groups of New Zealand.[2]

The memorandum was printed with blank sheets for written comments opposite the text. Each student was to note his criticisms on these blank pages. Then they were to meet in their study groups to discuss these comments, in the hope of being able to draw up joint reports, or at least majority and minority reports, on their conclusions. These reports were to be sent to Curtis, who was to compile a comprehensive report on the whole imperial problem. This comprehensive report would then be submitted to the groups in the same fashion and the resulting comments used as a basis for a final report.

Five study groups of this type were set up in New Zealand, and then five more in Australia.[3] The decision was made to do the same thing in

Canada and in England, and this was done by Curtis, Kerr, and apparently Dove during 1910. On the trip to Canada, the missionaries carried with them a letter from Milner to his old friend Arthur J. Glazebrook, with whom he had remained in close contact throughout the years since Glazebrook went to Canada for an English bank in 1893. *The Round Table* in 1941, writing of Glazebrook, said, "His great political hero was his friend Lord Milner, with whom he kept up a regular correspondence." As a result of this letter from Milner, Glazebrook undertook the task of founding Round Table Groups in Canada and did this so well that he was for twenty years or more the real head of the network of Milner Group units in the Dominion. He regularly wrote the Canadian articles in *The Round Table* magazine. When he died, in 1940, *The Round Table* obituary spoke of him as "one of the most devoted and loyal friends that *The Round Table* has ever known. Indeed he could fairly claim to be one of its founding fathers." In the 1930s he relinquished his central position in the Canadian branch of the Milner Group to Vincent Massey, son-in-law of George Parkin. Glazebrook's admiration for Parkin was so great that he named his son George Parkin de Twenebrokes Glazebrook.[4] At the present time Vincent Massey and G. P. de T. Glazebrook are apparently the heads of the Milner Group organization in Canada, having inherited the position from the latter's father. Both are graduates of Balliol, Massey in 1913 and Glazebrook in 1924. Massey, a member of a very wealthy Canadian family, was lecturer in modern history at Toronto University in 1913-1915, and then served, during the war effort, as a staff officer in Canada, as associate secretary of the Canadian Cabinet's War Committee, and as secretary and director of the Government Repatriation Committee. Later he was Minister without Portfolio in the Canadian Cabinet (1924), a member of the Canadian delegation to the Imperial Conference of 1926, and first Canadian Minister to the United States (1926-1930). He was president of the National Liberal Federation of Canada in 1932-1935, Canadian High Commissioner in London in 1935-1946, and Canadian delegate to the Assembly of the League of Nations in 1936. He has been for a long time governor of the University of Toronto and of Upper Canada College (Parkin's old school). He remains to this day one of the strongest supporters of Oxford University and of a policy of close Canadian cooperation with the United Kingdom.

G. P. de T. Glazebrook, son of Milner's old friend Arthur J. Glazebrook and namesake of Milner's closest collaborator in the Rhodes Trust, was born in 1900 and studied at Upper Canada College, the University of Toronto, and Balliol. Since 1924 he has been teaching history at Toronto University, but since 1942 has been on leave to the Dominion government, engaged in strategic intelligence work with the

Department of External Affairs. Since 1948 he has been on loan from the Department of External Affairs to the Department of Defense, where he is acting as head of the new Joint Services Intelligence. This highly secret agency appears to be the Canadian equivalent to the American Central Intelligence Agency. Glazebrook has written a number of historical works, including a *History of Transportation in Canada* (1938), *Canadian External Affairs, a Historical Study to 1914* (1942), and *Canada at the Peace Conference* (1942).

It was, as we have said, George Parkin Glazebrook's father who, acting in cooperation with Curtis, Kerr, and Marris and on instructions from Milner, set up the Round Table organization in Canada in 1911. About a dozen units were established in various cities.

It was during the effort to extend the Round Table organization to Australia that Curtis first met Lord Chelmsford. He was later Viceroy of India (in 1916-1921), and there can be little doubt that the Milner Group was influential in this appointment, for Curtis discussed the plans which eventually became the Government of India Act of 1919 with him before he went to India and consulted with him in India on the same subject in 1916.[5]

From 1911 to 1913, Curtis remained in England, devoting himself to the reports coming in from the Round Table Groups on imperial organization, while Kerr devoted himself to the publication of *The Round Table* itself. This was an extraordinary magazine. The first issue appeared with the date 15 November 1910. It had no names in the whole issue, either of the officers or of the contributors of the five articles. The opening statement of policy was unsigned, and the only address to which communications could be sent was "The Secretary, 175 Piccadilly, London, W." This anonymity has been maintained ever since, and has been defended by the journal itself in advertisements, on the grounds that anonymity gives the contributors greater independence and freedom. The real reasons, however, were much more practical than this and included the fact that the writers were virtually unknown and were so few in numbers, at first at least, as to make the project appear ridiculous had the articles been signed. For example, Philip Kerr, during his editorship, always wrote the leading article in every issue. In later years the anonymity was necessary because of the political prominence of some of the contributors. In general, the policy of the journal has been such that it has continued to conceal the identity of its writers until their deaths. Even then, they have never been connected with any specific article, except in the case of one article (the first one in the first issue) by Lord Lothian. This article was reprinted in *The Round Table* after the author's death in 1940.

The Round Table was essentially the propaganda vehicle of a handful of people and could not have carried signed articles either originally, when they were too few, or later, when they were too famous. It was never intended to be either a popular magazine or self-supporting, but rather was aimed at influencing those in a position to influence public opinion. As Curtis wrote in 1920, "A large quarterly like *The Round Table* is not intended so much for the average reader, as for those who write for the average reader. It is meant to be a storehouse of information of all kinds upon which publicists can draw. Its articles must be taken on their merits and as representing nothing beyond the minds and information of the individual writer of each."[6]

It is perhaps worth mentioning that the first article of the first issue, called "Anglo-German Rivalry," was very anti-German and forms an interesting bit of evidence when taken in connection with Curtis's statement that the problem of the Empire was raised in 1909 by the problem of what role South Africa would play in a future war with Germany. The Group, in the period before 1914, were clearly anti-German. This must be emphasized because of the mistaken idea which circulated after 1930 that the Cliveden group, especially men like Lord Lothian, were pro-German. They were neither anti-German in 1910 nor pro-German in 1938, but pro-Empire all the time, changing there their attitudes on other problems as these problems affected the Empire. And it should be realized that their love for the Empire was not mere jingoism or flag-waving (things at which Kerr mocked within the Group)[7] but was based on the sincere belief that freedom, civilization, and human decency could best be advanced through the instrumentality of the British Empire.

In view of the specific and practical purpose of *The Round Table*—to federate the Empire in order to ensure that the Dominions would join with the United Kingdom in a future war with Germany—the paper could not help being a propagandist organ, propagandist on a high level, it is true, but nonetheless a journal of opinion rather than a journal of information. Every general article in the paper (excluding the reports from representatives in the Dominions) was really an editorial—an unsigned editorial speaking for the group as a whole. By the 1920s these articles were declaring, in true editorial style, that *"The Round Table* does not approve of" something or other, or, "It seems to *The Round Table* that" something else.

Later the members of the Group denied that the Group were concerned with the propagation of any single point of view. Instead, they insisted that the purpose of the Group was to bring together persons of various points of view for purposes of self-education. This is not quite accurate. The Group did not contain persons of various points of view but rather persons of unusual unaminity of opinion, especially in regard to goals. There was a somewhat greater divergence in regard to methods, and the circulating of memoranda within the Group to evoke various comments was for the purpose of reaching some agreement on methods only — the goals being already given. In this, meetings of the Group were rather like the meetings of the British Cabinet, although any normal Cabinet would contain a greater variety of opinion than did the usual meetings of the Group. In general, an expression of opinion by any one member of the Group sounded like an echo of any of the others. Their systems of values were identical; the position of the British Commonwealth at the apex of that system was almost axiomatic; the important role played by moral and ideological influences in the Commonwealth and in the value system was accepted by all; the necessity of strengthening the bonds of the Commonwealth in view of the approaching crisis of the civilization of the West was accepted by all; so also was the need for closer union with the United States. There was considerable divergence of opinion regarding the practicality of imperial federation in the immediate future; there was some divergence of ideas regarding the rate at which self-government should be extended to the various parts of the Empire (especially India). There was a slight difference of emphasis on the importance of relations between the Commonwealth and the United States. But none of these differences of opinion was fundamental or important. The most basic divergence within the Group during the first twenty years or so was to be found in the field of economic ideas — a field in which the Group as a whole was extremely weak, and also extremely conservative. This divergence existed, however, solely because of the extremely unorthodox character of Lord Milner's ideas. Milner's ideas (as expressed, for example, in his book *Questions of the Hour*, published in 1923) would have been progressive, even unorthodox, in 1935. They were naturally ahead of the times in 1923, and they were certainly far ahead of the ideas of the Group as a whole, for its economic ideas would have been old-fashioned in 1905. These ideas of the Group (until 1931, at least) were those of late-nineteenth-century international banking and financial capitalism. The key to all economics and prosperity was considered to rest in banking and finance. With "sound money," a balanced budget, and the international gold standard, it was expected that prosperity and rising standards of living would follow automatically. These ideas were propagated through *The Round Table*, in the period after 1912, in a series of articles written by Brand and subsequently republished under his name, with the title *War and National Finance* (1921). They are directly antithetical to the ideas of Milner as revealed in his book published two years later. Milner insisted that financial questions must be subordinated to economic questions and economic questions to political questions. As a result, if a deflationary policy, initiated for financial reasons, has deleterious economic or political effects, it must be abandoned. Milner regarded the financial policy advocated by Brand in 1919 and followed by the British government for the next twelve years as a disaster, since it led to unemployment, depression, and ruination of the export trade. Instead, Milner wanted to isolate the British economy from the world economy by tariffs and other barriers and encourage the economic development of the United Kingdom by a system of government spending, self-regulated capital and labor, social welfare, etc. This program, which was based on "monopoly capitalism" or even "national socialism" rather than "financial capitalism," as Brand's was, was embraced by most of the Milner Group after September 1931, when the ending of the gold standard in Britain proved once and for all that Brand's financial program of 1919 was a complete disaster and quite unworkable. As a result, in the years after 1931 the businessmen of the Milner Group embarked on a policy of government encouragement of self-regulated monopoly capitalism. This was relatively easy for many members of the Group because of the distrust of economic individualism which they had inherited from Toynbee and Milner. In April 1932, when P. Horsfall, manager of Lazard Brothers Bank (a colleague of Brand), asked John Dove to write a defense of individualism in *The Round Table*, Dove suggested that he write it himself, but, in reporting the incident to Brand, he clearly indicated that the Group regarded individualism as obsolete.[8]

This difference of opinion between Milner and Brand on economic questions is not of great importance. The important matter is that Brand's opinion prevailed within the Group from 1919 to 1931, while Milner's has grown in importance from 1931 to the present. The importance of this can be seen in the fact that the financial and economic policy followed by the British government from 1919 to 1945 runs exactly parallel to the policy of the Milner Group. This is no accident but is the result, as we shall see, of the dominant position held by the Milner Group in the councils of the Conservative-Unionist party since the First World War.

During the first decade or so of its existence, *The Round Table* continued to be edited and written by the inner circle of the Milner Group, chiefly by Lothian, Brand, Hichens, Grigg, Dawson, Fisher, and Dove. Curtis was too busy with the other activities of the Group to devote much time to the magazine and had little to do with it until after the war. By that time a number of others had been added to the Group, chiefly as writers of occasional articles. Most of these were members or future members of All Souls; they include Coupland, Zimmern, Arnold Toynbee, Arthur Salter, Sir Maurice Hankey, and others. The same Group that originally started the project in 1910 still controls it today, with the normal changes caused by death or old age. The vacancies resulting from these causes have been filled by new recruits from All Souls. It would appear that Coupland and Brand are the most influential figures today. The following list gives the editors of *The Round Table* from 1910 to the recent past:

Philip Kerr, 1910-1917
  (assisted by E. Grigg, 1913-1915)
Reginald Coupland, 1917-1919
Lionel Curtis, 1919-1921
John Dove, 1921-1934
Henry V. Hodson, 1934-1939
Vincent Todd Harlow, (acting editor) 1938
Reginald Coupland, 1939-1941
Geoffrey Dawson, 1941-1944

Of these names, all but two are already familiar. H. V. Hodson, a recent recruit to the Milner Group, was taken from All Souls. Born in 1906, he was at Balliol for three years (1925-1928) and on graduation obtained a fellowship to All Souls, which he held for the regular term (1928-1935). This fellowship opened to him the opportunities which he had the ability to exploit. On the staff of the Economic Advisory Council from 1930 to 1931 and an important member of the Royal Institute of International Affairs, he was assistant editor of *The Round Table* for three years (1931-1934) and became editor when Dove died in 1934. At the same time he wrote for Toynbee the economic sections of the *Survey of International Affairs* from 1929 on, publishing these in a modified form as a separate volume, with the title *Slump and Recovery, 1929-1937*, in 1938. With the outbreak of the Second World War in 1939, he left *The Round Table* editorship and went to the Ministry of Information (which was controlled completely by the Milner Group) as director of the Empire Division. After two years in this post he was given the more critical position of Reforms Commissioner in the Government of India for two years (1941-1942) and then was made assistant secretary and later head of the non-munitions division of the Ministry of Production. This position was held until the war ended, three years later. He then returned to private life as assistant editor of *The Sunday Times*. In addition to the writings already mentioned, he published *The Economics of a Changing World* (1933) and *The Empire in the World* (1937), and edited *The British Commonwealth and the Future* (1939).

Vincent T. Harlow, born in 1898, was in the Royal Field Artillery in 1917-1919 and then went to Brasenose, where he took his degree in 1923. He was lecturer in Modern History at University College, Southampton, in 1923-1927, and then came into the magic circle of the Milner Group. He was keeper of Rhodes House Library in 1928-1938, Beit Lecturer in Imperial History in 1930-1935, and has been Rhodes

Professor of Imperial History at the University of London since 1938. He was a member of the Imperial Committee of the Royal Institute of International Affairs and, during the war, was head of the Empire Information Service at the Ministry of Information. He lives near Oxford, apparently in order to keep in contact with the Group.

In the decade 1910-1920, the inner circle of the Milner Group was busy with two other important activities in addition to *The Round Table* magazine. These were studies of the problem of imperial federation and of the problem of extending self-government to India. Both of these were in charge of Lionel Curtis and continued with little interruption from the war itself. *The Round Table*, which was in charge of Kerr, never interrupted its publication, but from 1915 onward it became a secondary issue to winning the war and making the peace. The problem of imperial federation will be discussed here and in Chapter 8, the war and the peace in Chapter 7, and the problem of India in Chapter 10.

During the period 1911-1913, as we have said, Curtis was busy in England with the reports from the Round Table Groups in the Dominions in reply to his printed memorandum. At the end of 1911 and again in 1913, he printed these reports in two substantial volumes, without the names of the contributors. These volumes were never published, but a thousand copies of each were distributed to the various groups. On the basis of these reports, Curtis drafted a joint report, which was printed and circulated as each section was completed. It soon became clear that there was no real agreement within the groups and that imperial federation was not popular in the Dominions. This was a bitter pill to the Group, especially to Curtis, but he continued to work for several years more. In 1912, Milner and Kerr went to Canada and made speeches to Round Table Groups and their associates. The following year Curtis went to Canada to discuss the status of the inquiry on imperial organization with the various Round Table Groups there and summed up the results in a speech in Toronto in October 1913.[9] He decided to draw up four reports as follows: (a) the existing situation; (b) a system involving complete independence for the Dominions; (c) a plan to secure unity of foreign relations by each Dominion's following a policy independent from but parallel to that of Britain itself; (d) a plan to reduce the United Kingdom to a Dominion and create a new imperial government over all the Dominions. Since the last was what Curtis wanted, he decided to write that report himself and allow supporters of each of the other three to write theirs. A thousand copies of this speech were circulated among the groups throughout the world.

When the war broke out in 1914, the reports were not finished, so it was decided to print the four sections already sent out, with a concluding chapter. A thousand copies of this, with the title *Project of a Commonwealth*, were distributed among the groups. Then a popular volume on the subject, with the title *The Problem of the Commonwealth* and Curtis's name as editor, was published (May 1916). Two months later, the earlier work (*Project*) was published under the title *The Commonwealth of Nations*, again with Curtis named as editor. Thus appeared for the first time in public the name which the British Empire was to assume thirty-two years later. In the September 1916 issue of *The Round Table*, Kerr published a statement on the relationship of the two published volumes to the Round Table Groups. Because of the paper shortage in England, Curtis in 1916 went to Canada and Australia to arrange for the separate publication of *The Problem of the Commonwealth* in those countries. At the same time he set up new Round Table Groups in Australia and New Zealand. Then he went to India to begin serious work on Indian reform. From this emerged the Government of India Act of 1919, as we shall see later.

By this time Curtis and the others had come to realize that any formal federation of the Empire was impossible. As Curtis wrote in 1917 (in his *Letter to the People of India*): "The people of the Dominions rightly aspire to control their own foreign affairs and yet retain their status as British citizens. On the other hand, they detest the idea of paying taxes to any Imperial Parliament, even to one upon which their own representatives sit. The inquiry convinced me that, unless they sent members and paid taxes to an Imperial Parliament, they could not control their foreign affairs and also remain British subjects. But I do not think that doctrine is more distasteful to them than the idea of having anything to do with the Government of India."

Reluctantly Curtis and the others postponed the idea of a federated Empire and fell back on the idea of trying to hold the Empire together by the intangible bonds of common culture and common outlook. This had originally (in Rhodes and Milner) been a supplement to the project of a federation. It now became the chief issue, and the idea of federation fell into a secondary place. At the same time, the idea of federation was swallowed up in a larger scheme for organizing the whole world within a League of Nations. This idea had also been held by Rhodes and Milner, but in quite a different form. To the older men, the world was to be united around the British Empire as a nucleus. To Curtis, the Empire was to be absorbed into a world organization. This second idea was fundamentally mystical. Curtis believed: "Die and ye shall be born again." He sincerely felt that if the British Empire died in the proper way (by spreading liberty, brotherhood, and justice), it would be born again in a higher level of existence — as a world community, or, as he called it, a "Commonwealth of Nations." It is not yet clear whether the resurrection envisaged by Curtis and his associates will occur, or whether they merely assisted at the crucifixion of the British Empire. The conduct of the new India in the next few decades will decide this question.

The idea for federation of the Empire was not original with the Round Table Group, although their writings would indicate that they sometimes thought so. The federation which they envisaged had been worked out in detail by persons close to the Cecil Bloc and was accepted by Milner and Rhodes as their own chief goal in life.

The original impetus for imperial federation arose within the Liberal Party as a reaction against the Little England doctrines that were triumphant in England before 1868. The original movement came from men like John Stuart Mill (whose arguments in support of the Empire are just like Curtis's) and Earl Grey (who was Colonial Secretary under Russell in 1846-1852).[10]

This movement resulted in the founding of the Royal Colonial Society (now Royal Empire Society) in 1868 and, as a kind of subsidiary of this, the Imperial Federation League in 1884. Many Unionist members of the Cecil Bloc, such as Brassey and Goschen, were in these organizations. In 1875 F. P. Labilliere, a moving power in both organizations, read a paper before the older one on "The Permanent Unity of the Empire" and suggested a solution of the imperial problem by creating a superimposed imperial legislative body and a central executive over the whole Empire, including the United Kingdom. Seven years later, in "The Political Organization of the Empire," he divided authority between this new federal authority and the Dominions by dividing the business of government into imperial questions, local questions, and questions concerning both levels. He then enumerated the matters that would be allotted to each division, on a basis very similar to that later advocated by Curtis. Another speaker, George Bourinot, in 1880, dealt with "The Natural Development of Canada" in a fashion that sounds exactly like Curtis.[11]

These ideas and projects were embraced by Milner as his chief purpose in life until, like Curtis, he came to realize their impracticality.[12] Milner's ideas can be found in his speeches and letters, especially in two letters of 1901 to Brassey and Parkin. Brassey had started a campaign for imperial federation accompanied by devolution (that is, granting local issues to local bodies even within the United Kingdom) and the creation of an imperial parliament to include representatives of the colonies. This imperial parliament would deal with imperial questions, while local parliaments would deal with local questions. In pursuit of this project, Brassey published a pamphlet, in December 1900, called *A Policy on Which All Liberals May Unite* and sent to Milner an invitation to join him. Milner accepted in February 1901, saying:

There are probably no two men who are more fully agreed in their general view of Imperial policy [than we]. . . . It is clear to me that we require separate organs to deal with local home business and with Imperial business. The attempt to conduct both through one so-called Imperial Parliament is breaking down. . . . Granted that we must have separate Parliaments for Imperial and Local business, I have been coming by a different road, and for somewhat different reasons, to the conclusion which you also are heading for, viz: that it would be better not to create a new body *over* the so-called Imperial Parliament, but . . . to create new bodies, or a new body *under* it for the local business of Great Britain and Ireland, leaving it to deal with the wider questions of Foreign Policy, the Defence of the Empire, and the relations of the several parts. In that case, of course, the colonies would have to be represented in the Imperial Parliament, which would thus become really Imperial. One great difficulty, no doubt, is that, if this body were to be really effective as an instrument of Imperial Policy, it would require to be reduced in numbers. . . . The reduction in numbers of British members might no doubt be facilitated by the creation of local legislatures. . . . The time is ripe to make a beginning. . . . I wish Rosebery, who could carry through such a policy if any man could, was less pessimistic.

The idea of devolving the local business of the imperial parliament upon local legislative bodies for Scotland, England, Wales, and Ireland was advocated in a book by Lord Esher called *After the War* and in a book called *The Great Opportunity* by Edward Wood (the future Lord Halifax). These books, in their main theme, were nothing more than a restatement of this aspect of the imperial federation project. They were accompanied, on 4 June 1919, by a motion introduced in the House of Commons by Wood, and carried by a vote of 187 to 34, that "the time has come for the creation of subordinate legislatures within the United Kingdom." Nothing came of this motion, just as nothing came of the federation plans.

Milner's ideas on the latter subject were restated in a letter to Parkin on 18 September 1901:

The existing Parliaments, whether British or Colonial, are too small, and so are the statesmen they produce (except in accidental cases like Chamberlain), for such big issues. Until we get a real Imperial Council, not merely a Consultative, but first a Constitutional, and then an Executive Council with control of all our *world business*, we shall get nothing. Look at the way in which the splendid opportunities for federal defence which this war afforded, have been thrown away. I believe it will come about, but at present I do not see the man to do it. Both you and I could help him enormously, almost decisively indeed, for I have, and doubtless you have, an amount of illustration and argument to bring to bear on the subject, *drawn from practical experience*, which would logically smash the opposition. Our difficulty in the old days was that we were advocating a grand, but, as it seemed, an impractical idea. I should advocate the same thing today as an urgent practical necessity.[13]

The failure of imperial federation in the period 1910-1917 forced Parkin and Milner to fall back on ideological unity as achieved through the Rhodes Scholarships, just as the same event forced Curtis and others to fall back on the same goal as achieved through the Royal Institute of International Affairs. All parties did this with reluctance. As Dove wrote to Brand in 1923, "This later thing [the RIIA] is all right—it may help us to reach that unity of direction in foreign policy we are looking for, if it becomes a haunt of visitors from the Dominions; but Lionel's first love has still to be won, and if, as often happens, accomplishment lessens appetite, and he turns again to his earlier and greater work, we shall all be the gainers."[14]

This shift from institutional to ideological bonds for uniting the Empire makes it necessary that we should have a clear idea of the outlook of *The Round Table* and the whole Milner Group. This outlook was well stated in an article in Volume III of that journal, from the pen of an unidentified writer. This article, entitled "The Ethics of Empire," is deserving of close attention. It emphasized that the arguments for the Empire and the bonds which bind it together must be moral and not based on considerations of material advantage or even of defense. This emphasis on moral considerations, rather than economic or strategic, is typical of the Group as a whole and is found in Milner and even in Rhodes. Professional politicians, bureaucrats, utilitarians, and materialist social reformers are criticized for their failure to "appeal convincingly as an ideal of moral welfare to the ardour and imagination of a democratic people." They are also criticized for failure to see that this is the basis on which the Empire was reared.

> The development of the British Empire teaches how moral conviction and devotion to duty have inspired the building of the structure. Opponents of Imperialism are wont to suggest that the story will not bear inspection, that it is largely a record of self-aggrandizement and greed. Such a charge betrays ignorance of its history. . . . The men who have laboured most enduringly at the fabric of Empire were not getters of wealth and plunderers of spoil. It was due to their strength of character and moral purpose that British rule in India and Egypt has become the embodiment of order and justice. . . . Duty is an ı bstract term, but the facts it signifies are the most concrete and real in our experience. The essential thing is to grasp its meaning as a motive power in men's lives. [This was probably from Kerr, but could have been Toynbee or Milner speaking. The writer continued:] The end of the State is to make men, and its strength is measured not in terms of defensive armaments or economic prosperity but by the moral personality of its citizens. . . . The function of the State is positive and ethical, to secure for its individual members that they shall not merely live

but live well. Social reformers are prone to insist too strongly on an ideal of material comfort for the people. . . . A life of satisfaction depends not on higher wages or lower prices or on leisure for recreation, but on work that calls into play the higher capacities of man's nature. . . . The cry of the masses should be not for wages or comforts or even liberty, but for opportunities for enterprise and responsibility. A policy for closer union in the Empire is full of significance in relation to this demand. . . . There is but one way of promise. It is that the peoples of the Empire shall realize their national unity and draw from that ideal an inspiration to common endeavour in the fulfillment of the moral obligations which their membership of the Empire entails. The recognition of common Imperial interests is bound to broaden both their basis of public action and their whole view of life. Public life is ennobled by great causes and by these alone. . . . Political corruption, place-hunting, and party intrigue have their natural home in small communities where attention is concentrated upon local interests. Great public causes call into being the intellectual and moral potentialities of people. . . . The phrases "national character," "national will," and "national personality" are no empty catchwords. Everyone knows that *esprit de corps* is not a fiction but a reality; that the spirit animating a college or a regiment is something that cannot be measured in terms of the private contributions of the individual members. . . . The people of the Empire are face to face with a unique and an historic opportunity! It is their mission to base the policy of a Great Empire on the foundations of freedom and law. . . . It remains for them to crown the structure by the institution of a political union that shall give solidarity to the Empire as a whole. Duty and the logic of facts alike point this goal of their endeavour.

In this article can be found, at least implicitly, all the basic ideas of the Milner Group: their suspicion of party politics; their emphasis on moral qualities and the cement of common outlook for linking people together; their conviction that the British Empire is the supreme moral achievement of man, but an achievement yet incomplete and still unfolding; their idea that the highest moral goals are the development of personality through devotion to duty and service under freedom and law; their neglect, even scorn, for economic considerations; and their feeling for the urgent need to pursuade others to accept their point of view in order to allow the Empire to achieve the destiny for which they yearn.

The Milner Group is a standing refutation of the Marxist or Leninist interpretations of history or of imperialism. Its members were motivated only slightly by materialistic incentives, and their imperialism was motivated not at all by the desire to preserve or extend capitalism. On the contrary their economic ideology, in the early stages at least, was more socialistic than Manchester in its orientation. To be sure, it was an undemocratic kind of socialism, which was willing to make many sacrifices to the well-being of the masses of the people but reluctant to share with these masses political power that might allow them to seek their own well-being. This socialistic leaning was more evident in the earlier (or Balliol) period than in the later (or New College) period, and disappeared almost completely when Lothian and Brand replaced Esher, Grey, and Milner at the center of the Group. Esher regarded the destruction of the middle class as inevitable and felt that the future belonged to the workers and an administrative state. He dedicated his book *After the War* (1919) to Robert Smillie, President of the Miners' Federation, and wrote him a long letter on 5 May 1919. On 12 September of the same year, he wrote to his son, the present Viscount Esher: "There are things that cannot be confiscated by the Smillies and Sidney Webbs. These seem to me the real objectives." Even earlier, Arnold Toynbee was a socialist of sorts and highly critical of the current ideology of liberal capitalism as proclaimed by the high priests of the Manchester School. Milner gave six lectures on socialism in Whitechapel in 1882 (published in 1931 in *The National Review*). Both Toynbee and Milner worked intermittently at social service of a mildly socialistic kind, an effort that resulted in the founding of Toynbee Hall as a settlement house in 1884. As chairman of the board of Internal Revenue in 1892-1897, Milner drew up Sir William Harcourt's budget, which inaugurated the inheritance tax. In South Africa he was never moved by capitalistic motives, placing a heavy profits tax on the output of the Rand mines to finance social improvements, and considering with objective calm the question of nationalizing the railroads or even the mines. Both Toynbee and Milner were early suspicious of the virtues of free trade — not, however, because tariffs could provide high profits for industrial concerns but because tariffs and imperial preference could link the Empire more closely into economic unity. In his later years, Milner became increasingly radical, a development that did not fit any too well with the conservative financial outlook of Brand, or even Hichens. As revealed in his book *Questions of the Hour* (1923), Milner was a combination of technocrat and guild socialist and objected vigorously to the orthodox financial policy of deflation, balanced budget, gold standard, and free international exchange advocated by the Group after 1918. This orthodox policy, inspired by Brand and accepted by *The Round Table* after 1918, was regarded by Milner as an invitation to depression, unemployment, and the dissipation of Britain's material and moral resources. On this point there can be no doubt that Milner was correct. Not himself a trained economist, Milner, nevertheless, saw that the real problems were of a technical and material nature and that Britain's ability to produce goods should be limited only by the real supply of knowledge, labor, energy, and materials and not by the artificial limitations of a de-

liberately restricted supply of money and credit. This point of view of
Milner's was not accepted by the Group until after 1931, and not as
completely as by Milner even then. The point of view of the Group, at
least in the period 1918-1931, was the point of view of the international
bankers with whom Brand, Hichens, and others were so closely connected. This point of view, which believed that Britain's prewar financial supremacy could be restored merely by reestablishing the prewar
financial system, with the pound sterling at its prewar parity, failed
completely to see the changed conditions that made all efforts to restore
the prewar system impossible. The Group's point of view is clearly
revealed in *The Round Table* articles of the period. In the issue of
December 1918, Brand advocated the financial policy which the
British government followed, with such disastrous results, for the next
thirteen years. He wrote:

> That nation will recover quickest after the war which corrects soonest any
> depreciation in currency, reduces by production and saving its inflated
> credit, brings down its level of prices, and restores the free import and
> export of gold. . . . With all our wealth of financial knowledge and exper-
> ience behind us it should be easy for us to steer the right path—though it
> will not be always a pleasant one—amongst the dangers of the future.
> Every consideration leads to the view that the restoration of the gold stan-
> dard—whether or not it can be achieved quickly—should be our aim.
> Only by that means can we be secure that our level of prices shall be as
> low as or lower than prices in other countries, and on that condition
> depends the recovery of our export trade and the prevention of excessive
> imports. Only by that means can we provide against and abolish the
> depreciation of our currency which, though the [existing] prohibition
> against dealings in gold prevents our measuring it, almost certainly exists,
> and safeguard ourself against excessive grants of credit.

He then outlined a detailed program to contract credit, curtail
government spending, raise taxes, curtail imports, increase exports,
etc.[15] Hichens, who, as an industrialist rather than a banker, was not
nearly so conservative in financial matters as Brand, suggested that the
huge public debt of 1919 be met by a capital levy, but, when Brand's
policies were adopted by the government, Hichens went along with
them and sought a way out for his own business by reducing costs by
"rationalization of production."

These differences of opinion on economic matters within the Group
did not disrupt the Group, because it was founded on political rather
than economic ideas and its roots were to be found in ancient Athens
rather than in modern Manchester. The Balliol generation, from
Jowett and Nettleship, and the New College generation, from
Zimmern, obtained an idealistic picture of classical Greece which left
them nostalgic for the fifth century of Hellenism and drove them to

seek to reestablish that ancient fellowship of intellect and patriotism in modern Britain. The funeral oration of Pericles became their political covenant with destiny. Duty to the state and loyalty to one's fellow citizens became the chief values of life. But, realizing that the jewel of Hellenism was destroyed by its inability to organize any political unit larger than a single city, the Milner Group saw the necessity of political organization in order to insure the continued existence of freedom and higher ethical values and hoped to be able to preserve the values of their day by organizing the whole world around the British Empire.

Curtis puts this quite clearly in *The Commonwealth of Nations* (1916), where he says:

> States, whether autocracies or commonwealths, ultimately rest on duty, not on self-interest or force. . . . The quickening principle of a state is a sense of devotion, an adequate recognition somewhere in the minds of its subjects that their own interests are subordinate to those of the state. The bond which unites them and constitutes them collectively as a state is, to use the words of Lincoln, in the nature of *dedication*. Its validity, like that of the marriage tie, is at root not contractual but sacramental. Its foundation is not self-interest, but rather some sense of obligation, however conceived, which is strong enough to over-master self-interest.

History for this Group, and especially for Curtis, presented itself as an age-long struggle between the principles of autocracy and the principles of commonwealth, between the forces of darkness and the forces of light, between Asiatic theocracy and European freedom. This view of history, founded on the work of Zimmern, E. A. Freeman, Lord Bryce, and A. V. Dicey, felt that the distinguishing mark between the two hosts could be found in their views of law—the forces of light regarding law as manmade and mutable, but yet above all men, while the forces of darkness regarded law as divine and eternal, yet subordinate to the king. The one permitted diversity, growth, and freedom, while the other engendered monotony, stultification, and slavery. The struggle between the two had gone on for thousands of years, spawning such offspring as the Persian Wars, the Punic Wars, and the struggles of Britain with the forces of Philip II, of Louis XIV, of Napoleon, and of Wilhelm II. Thus, to this Group, Britain stood as the defender of all that was fine or civilized in the modern world, just as Athens had stood for the same values in the ancient world.[17] Britain's mission, under this interpretation, was to carry freedom and light (that is, the principles of commonwealth) against the forces of theocracy and darkness (that is, autocracy) in Asia—and even in Central Europe. For this Group regarded the failure of France or Germany to utilize the English idea of "supremacy of law" (as described by Dicey in his *The Law of the Constitution*, 1885) as proof that these countries were still immersed, at least partially, in the darkness of theocratic law. The slow spread of English political institutions to Europe as well as Asia in the period before the First World War was regarded by the Group as proof both of their superiority and of the possibility of progress. In Asia and Africa, at least, England's civilizing mission was to be carried out by force, if necessary, for "the function of force is to give moral ideas time to take root." Asia thus could be compelled to accept civilization, a procedure justifiable to the Group on the grounds that Asians are obviously better off under European rule than under the rule of fellow Asians and, if consulted, would clearly prefer British rule to that of any other European power. To be sure, the blessings to be extended to the less fortunate peoples of the world did not include democracy. To Milner, to Curtis, and apparently to most members of the Group, democracy was not an unmixed good, or even a good, and far inferior to rule by the best, or, as Curtis says, by those who "have some intellectual capacity for judging the public interest, and, what is no less important, some moral capacity for treating it as paramount to their own."

This disdain for unrestricted democracy was quite in accordance with the ideas revealed by Milner's activities in South Africa and with the Greek ideals absorbed at Balliol or New College. However, the restrictions on democracy accepted by the Milner Group were of a temporary character, based on the lack of education and background of those who were excluded from political participation. It was not a question of blood or birth, for these men were not racists.

This last point is important because of the widespread misconception that these people were racially intolerant. They never were; certainly those of the inner circle never were. On the contrary, they were ardent advocates of a policy of education and uplift of all groups, so that ultimately all groups could share in political life and in the rich benefits of the British way of life. To be sure, the members of the Group did not advocate the immediate extension of democracy and self-government to all peoples within the Empire, but these restrictions were based not on color of skin or birth but upon cultural outlook and educational background. Even Rhodes, who is widely regarded as a racist because his scholarships were restricted to candidates from the Nordic countries, was not a racist. He restricted his scholarships to these countries because he felt that they had a background sufficiently homogeneous to allow the hope that educational interchange could link them together to form the core of the worldwide system which he hoped would ultimately come into existence. Beyond this, Rhodes insisted that there must be no restrictions placed on the scholarships on a basis of race, religion, skin color, or national origin.[18] In his own life, Rhodes cared nothing about these things. Some of his closest friends were Jews (like Beit), and in three of his wills he left Lord Rothschild as his trustee, in one as his sole trustee. Milner and the other members felt similarly. Lionel Curtis, in his writings, makes perfectly clear both his conviction that character is acquired by training rather than innate ability and his insistence on tolerance in personal contact between members of different races. In his *The Commonwealth of Nations* (1916) he says: "English success in planting North America and the comparative failure of their rivals must, in fact, be traced to the respective merits not of breed but of institutions"; and again: "The energy and intelligence which had saved Hellas [in the Persian Wars] was the product of her free institutions." In another work he protests against English mistreatment of natives in India and states emphatically that it must be ended. He says: "The conduct on the part of Europeans . . . is more than anything else the root cause of Indian unrest . . . I am strongly of opinion that governors should be vested with powers to investigate judicially cases where Europeans are alleged to have outraged Indian feelings. Wherever a case of wanton and unprovoked insult such as those I have cited is proved, government should have the power to order the culprit to leave the country. . . . A few deportations would soon effect a definite change for the better."[19] That Dove felt similarly is clear from his letters to Brand.

Without a belief in racism, it was perfectly possible for this Group to believe, as they did, in the ultimate extension of freedom and self-government to all parts of the Empire. To be sure, they believed that this was a path to be followed slowly, but their reluctance was measured by the inability of "backward" peoples to understand the principles of a commonwealth, not by reluctance to extend to them either democracy or self-government.

Curtis defined the distinction between a commonwealth and a despotism in the following terms: "The rule of law as contrasted with the rule of an individual is the distinguishing mark of a commonwealth. In despotism government rests on the authority of the ruler or of the invisible and uncontrollable power behind him. In a commonwealth rulers derive their authority from the law and the law from a public opinion which is competent to change it." Accordingly, "the institutions of a commonwealth cannot be successfully worked by peoples whose ideas are still those of a theocratic or patriarchal society. The premature extension of representative institutions throughout the Empire would be the shortest road to anarchy."[20] The people must first be trained to understand and practice the chief principles of commonwealth, namely the supremacy of law and the subjection of the motives of self-interest and material gain to the sense of duty to the interests of the community as a whole. Curtis felt that such an educational process was not only morally necessary on the part of Britain but was a practical necessity, since the British could not expect to keep 430 million persons in subjection forever but must rather hope to educate them up to a level where they could appreciate and cherish British ideals. In one book he says: "The idea that the principle of the commonwealth implies universal suffrage betrays an ignorance of its real nature. That principle simply means that government rests on the duty of the citizens to each other, and is to be vested in those who are capable of setting public interest before their own."[21] In another work he says: "As sure as day follows the night, the time will come when they [the Dominions] will have to assume the burden of the whole of their affairs. For men who are fit for it, self-government is a question not of privilege but rather of obligation. It is duty, not interest, which impels men to freedom, and duty, not interest, is the factor which turns the scale in human affairs." India is included in this evolutionary process, for Curtis wrote: " A despotic government might long have closed India to Western ideas. But a commonwealth is a living thing. It cannot suffer any part of itself to remain inert. To live it must move, and move in every limb. . . . Under British rule Western ideas will continue to penetrate and disturb Oriental society, and whether the new spirit ends in anarchy or leads to the establishment of a higher order depends upon how far the millions of India can be raised to a fuller and more rational conception of the ultimate foundations upon which the duty of obedience to government rests."

These ideas were not Curtis's own, although he was perhaps the most prolific, most eloquent, and most intense in his feelings. They were apparently shared by the whole inner circle of the Group. Dove, writing to Brand from India in 1919, is favorable to reform and says: "Lionel is right. You can't dam a world current. There is, I am convinced, 'purpose' under such things. All that we can do is to try to turn the flood into the best channel." In the same letter he said: "Unity will, in the end, have to be got in some other way. . . . Love—call it, if you like, by a longer name—is the only thing that can make our post-war world go round, and it has, I believe, something to say here too. The future of the Empire seems to me to depend on how far we are able to recognize this. Our trouble is that we start some way behind scratch. Indians must always find it hard to understand us." And the future Lord Lothian, ordering an article on India for The Round Table from a representative in India, wrote: "We want an article in The Round Table and I suggest to you that the main conclusion which the reader should draw from it should be that the responsibility rests upon him of seeing that the Indian demands are sympathetically handled without delay after the war."[22]

What this Group feared was that the British Empire would fail to profit from the lessons they had discerned in the Athenian empire or in the American Revolution. Zimmern had pointed out to them the sharp contrast between the high idealism of Pericles's funeral oration and the crass tyranny of the Athenian empire. They feared that the British Empire might fall into the same difficulty and destroy British idealism and British liberties by the tyranny necessary to hold on to a reluctant Empire. And any effort to hold an empire by tyranny they regarded as doomed to failure. Britain would be destroyed, as Athens was destroyed, by powers more tyrannical than herself. And, still drawing parallels with ancient Greece, the Group feared that all culture and civilization would go down to destruction because of our inability to construct some kind of political unit larger than the national state, just as Greek culture and civilization in the fourth century B.C. went down to destruction because of the Greeks' inability to construct some kind of political unit larger than the city-state. This was the fear that had animated Rhodes, and it was the same fear that was driving the Milner Group to transform the British Empire into a Commonwealth of Nations and then place that system within a League of Nations. In 1917, Curtis wrote in his *Letter to the People of India:* "The world is in throes which precede creation or death. Our whole race has outgrown the merely national state, and as surely as day follows night or night the day, will pass either to a Commonwealth of Nations or else an empire of slaves. And the issue of these agonies rests with us."

At the same time the example of the American Revolution showed the Group the dangers of trying to rule the Empire from London: to tax without representation could only lead to disruption. Yet it was no longer possible that 45 million in the United Kingdom could tax themselves for the defense of 435 million in the British Empire. What, then, was the solution? The Milner Group's efforts to answer this question led eventually, as we shall see in Chapter 8, to the present Commonwealth of Nations, but before we leave *The Round Table*, a few words should be said about Lord Milner's personal connection with the Round Table Group and the Group's other connections in the field of journalism and publicity.

Milner was the creator of the Round Table Group (since this is but another name for the Kindergarten) and remained in close personal contact with it for the rest of his life. In the sketch of Milner in the *Dictionary of National Biography*, written by Basil Williams of the Kindergarten, we read: "He was always ready to discuss national questions on a non-party basis, joining with former members of his South African 'Kindergarten' in their 'moot,' from which originated the political review, *The Round Table*, and in a more heterogeneous society, the 'Coefficients,' where he discussed social and imperial problems with such curiously assorted members as L. S. Amery, H. G. Wells, (Lord) Haldane, Sir Edward Grey, (Sir) Michael Sadler, Bernard Shaw, J. L. Garvin, William Pember Reeves, and W. A. S. Hewins." In the obituary of Hichens, as already indicated, we find in reference to the Round Table the sentence: "Often at its head sat the old masters of the Kindergarten, Lord Milner and his successor, Lord Selborne, close friends and allies of Hichens to the end." And in the obituary of Lord Milner in *The Round Table* for June 1925, we find the following significant passage:

> The founders and the editors of *The Round Table* mourn in a very special sense the death of Lord Milner. For with him they have lost not only a much beloved friend, but one whom they have always regarded as their leader. Most of them had the great good fortune to serve under him in South Africa during or after the South African war, and to learn at first-hand from him something of the great ideals which inspired him. From those days at the very beginning of this century right up to the present time, through the days of Crown Colony Government in the Transvaal and Orange Free State, of the making of the South African constitution, and through all the varied and momentous history of the British Empire in the succeeding fifteen years, they have had the advantage of Lord Milner's counsel and guidance, and they are grateful to think that, though at times he disagreed with them, he never ceased to regard himself as the leader to whom, above everyone else, they looked. It is of melancholy interest to recall that Lord Milner had undertaken to come on May 13, the very day of his death, to a meeting specially to discuss with them South African problems.

The Round Table was published during the Second World War from Rhodes House, Oxford, which is but one more indication of the way in which the various instruments of the Milner Group are able to co-operate with one another.

The Times and *The Round Table* are not the only publications which have been controlled by the Milner Group. At various times in the past, the Group has been very influential on the staffs of the *Quarterly Review*, *The Nineteenth Century and After*, *The Economist*, and the *Spectator*. Anyone familiar with these publications will realize that most of them, for most of the time, have been quite secretive as to the names of the members of their staffs or even as to the names of their editors. The extent of the Milner Group's influence and the periods during which it was active cannot be examined here.

The Milner Group was also very influential in an editorial fashion in regard to a series of excellent and moderately priced volumes known as The Home University Library. Any glance at the complete list of volumes in this series will reveal that a large number of the names are those of persons mentioned in this study. The influence of the Group on The Home University Library was chiefly exercised through H. A. L.

Fisher, a member of the inner circle of the Group, but the influence, apparently, has survived his death in 1940.

The Milner Group also attempted, at the beginning at least, to use Milner's old connections with adult education and working-class schools (a connection derived from Toynbee and Samuel Barnett) to propagate its imperial doctrines. As A. L. Smith, the Master of Balliol, put it in 1915, "We must educate our masters." In this connection, several members of the Round Table Group played an active role in the Oxford Summer School for Working Class Students in 1913. This was so successful (especially a lecture on the Empire by Curtis) that a two-week conference was held early in the summer of 1914, "addressed by members of the Round Table Group, and others, on Imperial and Foreign Problems" (to quote A. L. Smith again). As a result, a plan was drawn up on 30 July 1914 to present similar programs in the 110 tutorial classes existing in industrial centers. The outbreak of war prevented most of this program from being carried out. After the war ended, the propaganda work among the British working classes became less important, for various reasons, of which the chief were that working-class ears were increasingly monopolized by Labour Party speakers and that the Round Table Group were busy with other problems like the League of Nations, Ireland, and the United States.[23]

8

War and Peace, 1915-1920

THE MILNER GROUP was out of power for a decade from 1906 to 1915. We have already indicated our grounds for believing that this condition was not regarded with distaste, since its members were engaged in important activities of their own and approved of the conduct of foreign policy (their chief field of interest) by the Liberal Party under Asquith, Grey, and Haldane. During this period came the Union of South Africa, The Morley-Minto reforms, the naval race with Germany, the military conversations with France, the agreement of 1907 with Russia, the British attitude against Germany in the Agadir crisis (a crisis to whose creation *The Times* had contributed no little material) — in fact, a whole series of events in which the point of view of the Milner Group was carried out just as if they were in office. To be sure, in domestic matters such as the budget dispute and the ensuing House of Lords dispute, and in the question of Home Rule for Ireland, the Milner Group did not regard the Liberal achievements with complete satisfaction, but in none of these were the members of the Milner Group diehards (as members of the Cecil Bloc sometimes were).[1] But with the outbreak of war, the Milner Group and the Cecil Bloc wanted to come to power and wanted it badly, chiefly because control of the government in wartime would make it possible to direct events toward the postwar settlement which the Group envisaged. The Group also believed that the war could be used by them to fasten on Britain the illiberal economic regulation of which they had been dreaming since Chamberlain resigned in 1903 (at least).

The Group got to power in 1916 by a method which they repeated with the Labour Party in 1931. By a secret intrigue with a parvenu leader of the government, the Group offered to make him head of a new government if he would split his own party and become Prime Minister, supported by the Group and whatever members he could split off from his own party. The chief difference between 1916 and 1931 is that in the former year the minority that was being betrayed

140

was the Group's own social class—in fact, the Liberal Party members of the Cecil Bloc. Another difference is that in 1916 the plot worked—the Liberal Party was split and permanently destroyed—while in 1931 the plotters broke off only a fragment of the Labour Party and damaged it only temporarily (for fourteen years). This last difference, however, was not caused by any lack of skill in carrying out the intrigue but by the sociological differences between the Liberal Party and the Labour Party in the twentieth century. The latter was riding the wave of the future, while the former was merely one of two "teams" put on the field by the same school for an intramural game, and, as such, it was bound to fuse with its temporary antagonist as soon as the future produced an extramural challenger. This strange (to an outsider) point of view will explain why Asquith had no real animosity for Bonar Law or Balfour (who really betrayed him) but devoted the rest of his life to belittling the actions of Lloyd George. Asquith talked later about how he was deceived (and even lied to) in December 1915, but never made any personal attack on Bonar Law, who did the prevaricating (if any). The actions of Bonar Law were acceptable in the code of British politics, a code largely constructed on the playing fields of Eton and Harrow, but Lloyd George's actions, which were considerably less deliberate and cold-blooded, were quite unforgivable, coming as they did from a parvenu who had been built up to a high place in the Liberal Party because of his undeniable personal ability, but who, nonetheless, was an outsider who had never been near the playing fields of Eton.

In the coalition governments of May 1915 and December 1916, members of the Cecil Bloc took the more obvious positions (as befitted their seniority), while members of the Milner Group took the less conspicuous places, but by 1918 the latter group had the whole situation tied up in a neat package and held all the strings.

In the first coalition (May 1915), Lansdowne came into the Cabinet without portfolio, Curzon as Lord Privy Seal, Bonar Law at the Colonial Office, Austen Chamberlain at the India Office, Balfour at the Admiralty, Selborne as President of the Board of Agriculture, Walter Long as President of the Local Government Board, Sir Edward Carson as Attorney General, F. E. Smith as Solicitor General, Lord Robert Cecil as Under Secretary in the Foreign Office, and Arthur Steel-Maitland as Under Secretary in the Colonial Office. Of these eleven names, at least nine were members of the Cecil Bloc, and four were close to the Milner Group (Cecil, Balfour, Steel-Maitland, and Selborne).

In the second coalition government (December 1916), Milner was Minister without Portfolio; Curzon was Lord President of the Council; Bonar Law, Chancellor of the Exchequer; Sir Robert Finlay, Lord

Chancellor; the Earl of Crawford, Lord Privy Seal; Sir George Cave, Home Secretary; Arthur Balfour, Foreign Secretary; The Earl of Derby, War Secretary; Walter Long, Colonial Secretary; Austen Chamberlain, at the India Office; Sir Edward Carson, First Lord of the Admiralty; Henry E. Duke, Chief Secretary for Ireland; H. A. L. Fisher, President of the Board of Education; R. E. Prothero, President of the Board of Agriculture; Sir Albert Stanley, President of the Board of Trade; F. E. Smith, Attorney General; Robert Cecil, Minister of Blockade; Lord Hardinge, Under Secretary for Foreign Affairs; Steel-Maitland, Under Secretary for the Colonies; and Lord Wolmer (son of Lord Selborne), assistant director of the War Trade Department. Of these twenty names, eleven, at least, were members of the Cecil Bloc, and four or five were members of the Milner Group.

Milner himself became the second most important figure in the government (after Lloyd George), especially while he was Minister without Portfolio. He was chiefly interested in food policy, war trade regulations, and postwar settlements. He was chairman of a committee to increase home production of food (1915) and of a committee on post-war reconstruction (1916). From the former came the food-growing policy adopted in 1917, and from the latter came the Ministry of Health set up in 1919. In 1917 he went with Lloyd George to a meeting of the Allied War Council in Rome and from there on a mission to Russia. He went to France after the German victories in March 1918, and was the principal influence in the appointment of Foch as Supreme Commander in the west. In April he became Secretary of State for War, and, after the election of December 1918, became Colonial Secretary. He was one of the signers of the Treaty of Versailles. Of Milner's role at this time, John Buchan wrote in his memoirs: "In the Great War from 1916 to 1918, he was the executant of the War Cabinet who separated the sense from the nonsense in the deliberations of that body, and was responsible for its chief practical achievements. To him were largely due the fruitful things which emerged from the struggle, the new status of the Dominions, and the notable advances in British social policy." In all of these actions Milner remained as unobtrusive as possible. Throughout this period Milner's opinion of Lloyd George was on the highest level. Writing twenty years later in *The Commonwealth of God*, Lionel Curtis recorded two occasions in which Milner praised Lloyd George in the highest terms. On one of these he called him a greater war leader than Chatham.

At this period it was not always possible to distinguish between the Cecil Bloc and the Milner Group, but it is notable that the members of the former who were later clearly members of the latter were generally in the fields in which Milner was most interested. In general, Milner and his Group dominated Lloyd George during the period from 1917 to

1921. As Prime Minister, Lloyd George had three members of the Group as his secretaries (P. H. Kerr, 1916-1922; W. G. S. Adams, 1916-1919; E. W. M. Grigg, 1921-1922) and Waldorf Astor as his parliamentary secretary (1917-1918). The chief decisions were made by the War Cabinet and Imperial War Cabinet, whose membership merged and fluctuated but in 1917-1918 consisted of Lloyd George, Milner, Curzon, and Smuts—that is, two members of the Milner Group, one of the Cecil Bloc, with the Prime Minister himself. The secretary to these groups was Maurice Hankey (later a member of the Milner Group), and the editor of the published reports of the War Cabinet was W. G. S. Adams. Amery was assistant secretary, while Meston was a member of the Imperial War Cabinet in 1917. Frederick Liddell (Fellow of All Souls) was made First Parliamentary Counsel in 1917 and held the position for eleven years, following this post with a fifteen-year period of service as counsel to the Speaker (1928-1943).[2]

Within the various government departments a somewhat similar situation prevailed. The Foreign Office in its topmost ranks was held by the Cecil Bloc, with Balfour as Secretary of State (1916-1919), followed by Curzon (1919-1924). When Balfour went to the United States on a mission in 1917, he took along Ian Malcolm (brother-in-law of Dougal Malcolm). Malcolm was later Balfour's private secretary at the Peace Conference in 1919. In Washington, Balfour had as deputy chairman to the mission R. H. Brand. In London, as we have seen, Robert Cecil was Parliamentary Under Secretary and later Assistant Secretary. In the Political Intelligence Department, Alfred Zimmern was the chief figure. G. W. Prothero was director of the Historical Section and was, like Cecil and Zimmern, chiefly concerned with the future peace settlement. He was succeeded by J. W. Headlam-Morley, who held the post of historical adviser from 1920 to his death in 1928. All of these persons were members of the Cecil Bloc or Milner Group.

In the India Office we need mention only a few names, as this subject will receive a closer scrutiny later. Austen Chamberlain was Secretary of State in 1915-1917 and gave the original impetus toward the famous act of 1919. Sir Frederick Duke (a member of the Round Table Group, whom we shall mention later) was chief adviser to Chamberlain's successor, E. S. Montagu, and became Permanent Under Secretary in 1920. Sir Malcolm Seton (also a member of the Round Table Group from 1913 onward) was Assistant Under Secretary (1919-1924) and later Deputy Under Secretary.

In blockade and shipping, Robert Cecil was Minister of Blockade (1916-1918), while Reginald Sothern Holland organized the attack on German trade in the earlier period (1914). M. L. Gwyer was legal adviser to the Ministry of Shipping during the war and to the Ministry of Health after the war (1917-1926), while J. Arthur Salter (later a contributor to *The Round Table* and a Fellow of All Souls for almost twenty years) was director of ship requisitioning in 1917 and later secretary to the Allied Maritime Transport Council and chairman of the Allied Maritime Transport Executive (1918). After the war he was a member of the Supreme Economic Council and general secretary to the Reparations Commission (1919-1922).

A. H. D. R. Steel-Maitland was head of the War Trade Department in 1917-1919, while Lord Wolmer (son of Lord Selborne and grandson of Lord Salisbury) was assistant director in 1916-1918. Henry Birchenough was a member or chairman of several committees dealing with related matters. R. S. Rait was a member of the department from its creation in 1915 to the end of the war; H. W. C. Davis was a member in 1915 and a member of the newly created War Trade Advisory Committee thereafter. Harold Butler was secretary to the Foreign Trade Department of the Foreign Office (1916-1917). H. D. Henderson (who has been a Fellow of All Souls since 1934) was secretary of the Cotton Control Board (1917-1919).

The Board of Agriculture was dominated by members of the Cecil Bloc and Milner Group. Lord Selborne was President of the board in 1915-1916, and Prothero (Lord Ernle) in 1916-1919. Milner and Selborne were chairmen of the two important committees of the board in 1915 and 1916. These sought to establish as a war measure (and ultimately as a postwar measure also) government-guaranteed prices for agricultural products at so high a level that domestic production of adequate supplies would be insured. This had been advocated by Milner for many years but was not obtained on a permanent basis until after 1930, although used on a temporary basis in 1917-1919. The membership of these committees was largely made up of members of the Cecil Bloc. The second Viscount Goschen (son of Milner's old friend and grandfather-in-law of Milner's step-grandson) was Parliamentary Secretary to the Board; Lord Astor was chairman of a dependent committee on milk supplies; Sothern Holland was controller of the Cultivation Department within the Food Production Department of the board (1918); Mrs. Alfred Lyttelton was deputy director of the Women's Branch; Lady Alicia Cecil was assistant director of horticulture in the Food Production Department; and Edward Strutt (brother-in-law of Balfour), who had been a member of both the Milner and Selborne Committees, was technical adviser to Prothero during his term as President and was the draftsman of the Corn Production Act of 1917. He later acted as one of Milner's assistants in the effort to establish a tariff in 1923. His sketch in the *Dictionary of National Biography* was written by his nephew (and Balfour's nephew) Lord Rayleigh.

In the Colonial Office, Milner was Secretary of State in 1918-1921; George Fiddes (of the Milner Kindergarten) was Permanent Under

Secretary in 1916-1921; Steel-Maitland was Parliamentary Under Secretary in 1915-1917; while Amery was in the same position in 1919-1921.

In intelligence and public information, we find John Buchan as head of the Information Department of the War Office, with John Dove and B. H. Sumner (the present Warden of All Souls) in military intelligence. H. W. C. Davis was general editor of the Oxford Pamphlets justifying Britain's role in the war, while Algernon Cecil (nephew of Lord Salisbury) was in the intelligence division of the Admiralty and later in the historical section of the Foreign Office. J. W. Headlam-Morley was adviser on all historical matters at Wellington House (the propaganda department) in 1915-1918 and assistant director of political intelligence in the Department of Information in 1917-1918, ultimately being shifted to similar work in the Foreign Office in 1918.

In the War Office, Milner was Secretary of State in 1918, while Amery was assistant to the Secretary from 1917 until Milner took him to the Colonial Office a year or so later.

This enumeration, by no means complete, indicates the all-pervasive influence of this small clique in the later years of the war. This influence was not devoted exclusively to winning the war, and, as time went on, it was directed increasingly toward the postwar settlement. As a result, both groups tended more and more to concentrate in the Foreign Office. There G. W. Prothero, an old member of the Cecil Bloc, was put in charge of the preparations for the future peace conference. Depending chiefly on his own branch of the Foreign Office (the Historical Section), but also using men and materials from the War Trade Intelligence Department and the Intelligence Section of the Admiralty, he prepared a large number of reports on questions that might arise at the Peace Conference (1917-1919). In 1920, 155 volumes of these reports were published under the title *Peace Handbooks*. A glance at any complete list of these will show that a very large number of the "experts" who wrote them were from the Cecil Bloc and Milner Group. About the same time, Phillimore and Zimmern prepared drafts for the organization of the future League of Nations. Most of the group went en masse to the Peace Conference at Paris as expert advisers, and anyone familar with the history of the Peace Conference cannot fail to recognize names which we have mentioned frequently. At about this time, Lloyd George began to get out of hand as far as the Milner Group was concerned, and doubtless also as far as the Cecil Bloc was concerned. Some of this was caused by the weakness of Balfour, titular head of the latter group, but much more was caused by the fact that the Group could not control Lloyd George either in his electoral campaign in December 1918 or in his negotiations in the Council of Four from March to June 1919. Lloyd George was perfectly willing to use the abilities of the Milner Group in administration, but, when it came to an appeal to the electorate, as in the "khaki election," he had no respect for the Group's judgment or advice. Lloyd George realized that the electorate was hysterical with hatred of Germany, and was willing to appeal to that feeling if he could ride into office again on its impetus. The Milner Group, on the other hand, was eager to get rid of the Kaiser, the Prussian officers' corps, and even the Junker landlords, but, once Germany was defeated, their feeling of animosity against her (which had waxed strong since before 1896) vanished. By 1919 they began to think in terms of balance of power and of the need to reconstruct Germany against the dangers of "bolshevism" on one hand and of "French militarism" on the other, and they felt that if Germany were made democratic and treated in a friendly fashion she could be incorporated into the British world system as well as the Cape Boers had been. The intellectual climate of the Milner Group early in 1919 has been described by a man who was, at this time, close to the Group, Harold Nicolson, in his volume *Peacemaking, 1919.*

This point of view was never thoroughly thought out by the Group. It was apparently based on the belief that if Germany were treated in a conciliatory fashion she could be won from her aggressive attitudes and become a civilized member of the British world system. This may have been possible, but, if so, the plan was very badly executed, because the aggressive elements in Germany were not eliminated and the conciliatory elements were not encouraged in a concrete fashion. This failure, however, was partly caused by the pressure of public opinion, by the refusal of the French to accept this concept as an adequate goal of foreign policy, and by the failure to analyze the methods of the policy in a sound and adequate fashion. The first step toward this policy was made by Milner himself as early as October 1918, when he issued a warning not to denounce "the whole German nation as monsters of iniquity" or to carry out a policy of punishment and reprisal against them." The outburst of public indignation at this sentiment was so great that "the whole band of men who had learned under him in South Africa to appreciate his patriotism united to testify to him their affectionate respect." This quotation from one of the band, Basil Williams, refers to a testimonial given by the Group to their leader in 1918.

Another evidence of this feeling will be found in a volume of Alfred Zimmern's, published in 1922 under the title *Europe in Convalescence* and devoted to regretting Britain's postwar policies and especially the election of 1918. Strangely enough, Zimmern, although most articulate in this volume, was basically more anti-German than the other members of the Group and did not share their rather naive belief that the Germans could be redeemed merely by the victors tossing away the advantages of victory. Zimmern had a greater degree of sympathy for the French idea that the Germans should give more concrete examples of a reformed spirit before they were allowed to run freely in civilized society.[3] Halifax, on the other hand, was considerably more influenced by popular feeling in 1918 and years later. He shared the public hysteria against Germany in 1918 to a degree which he later wished to forget, just as in 1937 he shared the appeasement policy toward Germany to a degree he would now doubtless want to forget. Both of these men, however were not of the inner circle of the Milner Group. The sentiments of that inner circle, men like Kerr, Brand, and Dawson, can be found in the speeches of the first, *The Times* editorials of the last, and the articles of *The Round Table*. They can also be seen in the letters of John Dove. The latter, writing to Brand, 4 October 1923, stated: "It seems to me that the most disastrous affect of Poincare's policy would be the final collapse of democracy in Germany, the risk of which has been pointed out in *The Round Table*. The irony of the whole situation is that if the Junkers should capture the Reich again, the same old antagonisms will revive and we shall find ourselves, willy-nilly, lined up again with France to avert a danger which French action has again called into being. . . . Even if Smuts follows up his fine speech, the situation may have changed so much before the Imperial Conference is over that people who think like him and us may find themselves baffled. . . . I doubt if we shall again have as good a chance of getting a peaceful democracy set up in Germany."

9

The Creation of
the Commonwealth

THE EVOLUTION of the British Empire into the Commonwealth of
Nations is to a very great extent a result of the activities of the Milner
Group. To be sure, the ultimate goal of the Group was quite different
from the present system, since they wanted a federation of the Empire,
but this was a long-run goal, and en route they accepted the present
system as a temporary way station. However, the strength of colonial
and Dominion feeling, which made the ideal of federation admittedly
remote at all times, has succeeded in making this way-station a permanent terminal and thus had eliminated, apparently forever, the hope
for federation. With the exception of a few diehards (of whom Milner
and Curtis were the leaders), the Group has accepted the solution of
imperial cooperation and "parallelism" as an alternative to federation.
This was definitely stated in *The Round Table* of December 1920. In
that issue the Group adopted the path of cooperation as its future
policy and added: "Its [*The Round Table's*] promoters in this country
feel bound to state that all the experience of the war and of the peace
has not shaken in the least the fundamental conviction with which they
commenced the publication of this Review. . . . *The Round Table* has
never expressed an opinion as to the form which this constitutional
organization would take, nor as to the time when it should be undertaken. But it has never disguised its conviction that a cooperate system
would eventually break down." In September 1935, in a review of its
first twenty-five years, the journal stated: "Since the war, therefore,
though it has never abandoned its view that the only final basis for
freedom and enduring peace is the organic union of nations in a
commonwealth embracing the whole world or, in the first instance, a
lesser part of it, *The Round Table* has been a consistent supporter . . .
of the principles upon which the British Empire now rests, as set forth
in the Balfour Memorandum of 1926. . . . It has felt that only by trying
the cooperation method to the utmost and realizing its limitations in
practice would nations within or without the British Empire be

148

brought to face the necessity for organic union."

There apparently exists within the Milner Group a myth to the effect that they invented the expression "Commonwealth of Nations," that it was derived from Zimmern's book *The Greek Commonwealth* (published in 1911) and first appeared in public in the title of Curtis's book in 1916. This is not quite accurate, for the older imperialists of the Cecil Bloc had used the term "commonwealth" in reference to the British Empire on various occasions as early as 1884. In that year, in a speech at Adelaide, Australia, Lord Rosebery referred to the possibility of New Zealand seceding from the Empire and added: "God forbid. There is no need for any nation, however great, leaving the Empire, because the Empire is a Commonwealth of Nations."

If the Milner Group did not invent the term, they gave it a very definite and special meaning, based on Zimmern's book, and they popularized the use of the expression. According to Zimmern, the expression "commonwealth" referred to a community based on freedom and the rule of law, in distinction to a government based on authority or even arbitrary tyranny. The distinction was worked out in Zimmern's book in the contrast between Athens, as described in Pericles's funeral oration, and Sparta (or the actual conduct of the Athenian empire). As applied to the modern world, the contrast was between the British government, as described by Dicey, and the despotisms of Philip II, Wilhelm II, and Nicholas II. In this sense of the word, commonwealth was not originally an alternative to federation, as it later became, since it referred to the moral qualities of government, and these could exist within either a federated or a nonfederated Empire.

The expression "British Commonwealth of Nations" was, then, not invented by the Group but was given a very special meaning and was propagated in this sense until it finally became common usage. The first step in this direction was taken on 15 May 1917, when General Smuts, at a banquet in his honor in the Houses of Parliament, used the expression. This banquet was apparently arranged by the Milner Group, and Lord Milner sat at Smuts's right hand during the speech. The speech itself was printed and given the widest publicity, being disseminated throughout Great Britain, the Commonwealth, the United States, and the rest of the world. In retrospect, some persons have believed that Smuts was rejecting the meaning of the expression as used by the Milner Group, because he did reject the project for imperial federation in this speech. This, however, is a mistake, for, as we have said, the expression "commonwealth" at that time had a meaning which could include either federation or cooperation among the members of the British imperial system. The antithesis in meaning between federation and commonwealth is a later development which took place outside the Group. To this day, men like Curtis, Amery, and Grigg still use the term "commonwealth" as applied to a federated Empire, and they always define the word "commonwealth" as "a government of liberty under the law" and not as an arrangement of independent but cooperating states.

The development of the British Empire into the Commonwealth of Nations and the role which the Milner Group played in this development cannot be understood by anyone who feels that federation and commonwealth were mutually exclusive ideas.

In fact, there were not two ideas, but three, and they were not regarded by the Group as substitutes for each other but as supplements to each other. These three ideas were: (1) the creation of a common ideology and world outlook among the peoples of the United Kingdom, the Empire, and the United States; (2) the creation of instruments and practices of cooperation among these various communities in order that they might pursue parallel policies; and (3) the creation of a federation on an imperial, Anglo-American, or world basis. The Milner Group regarded these as supplementary to one another and worked vigorously for all of them, without believing that they were mutually exclusive alternatives. They always realized, even the most fanatical of them, that federation, even of the Empire only, was very remote. They always, in this connection, used such expressions as "not in our lifetime" or "not in the present century." They always insisted that the basic unity of any system must rest on common ideology, and they worked in this direction through the Rhodes Scholarships, the Round Table Groups, and the Institutes of International Affairs, even when they were most ardently seeking to create organized constitutional relationships. And in these constitutional relationships they worked equally energetically and simultaneously for imperial federation and for such instruments of cooperation as conferences of Prime Ministers of Dominions. The idea, which seems to have gained currency, that the Round Table Group was solely committed to federation and that the failure of this project marked the defeat and eclipse of the Group is erroneous. On the contrary, by the 1930s, the Round Table Group was working so strongly for a common ideology and for institutions of cooperation that many believers in federation regarded them as defeatist. For this reason, some believers in federation organized a new movement called the "World Commonwealth Movement." Evidence of this movement is an article by Lord Davies in *The Nineteenth Century and After* for January 1935, called "*Round Table* or World Commonwealth?" This new movement was critical of the foreign policy rather than the imperial policy of the Round Table Group, especially its policy of appeasement toward Germany and of weakening the League of Nations, and its belief that Britain could find security in isolation from the Continent and a balance-of-power policy supported by the United Kingdom, the Dominions, and the United States.

The effort of the Round Table Group to create a common ideology to unite the supporters of the British way of life appears in every aspect of their work. It was derived from Rhodes and Milner and found its most perfect manifestation in the Rhodes Scholarships. As a result of these and of the Milner Group's control of so much of Oxford, Oxford tended to become an international university. Here the Milner Group had to tread a narrow path between the necessity of training non-English (including Americans and Indians) in the English way of life and the possibility of submerging that way of life completely (at Oxford, at least) by admitting too many non-English to its cloistered halls. On the whole, this path was followed with considerable success, as will be realized by anyone who has had any experience with Rhodes Scholars. To be sure, the visitors from across the seas picked up the social customs of the English somewhat more readily than they did the English ideas of playing the game or the English ideas of politics, but, on the whole, the experiment of Rhodes, Milner, and Lothian cannot be called a failure. It was surely a greater success in the United States than it was in the Dominions or in India, for in the last, at least, the English idea of liberty was assimilated much more completely than the idea of loyalty to England.

The efforts of the Milner Group to encourage federation of the Empire have already been indicated. They failed and, indeed, were bound to fail, as most members of the Group soon realized. As early as 1903, John Buchan and Joseph Chamberlain had given up the attempt. By 1917, even Curtis had accepted the idea that federation was a very remote possibility, although in his case, at least, it remained as the beckoning will-o-the-wisp by which all lesser goals were measured and found vaguely dissatisfying.[1]

The third string to the bow — imperial cooperation — remained. It became in time the chief concern of the Group. The story of these efforts is a familiar one, and no attempt will be made here to repeat it. We are concerned only with the role played by the Milner Group in these efforts. In general this role was very large, if not decisive.

The proposals for imperial cooperation had as their basic principle the assumption that communities which had a common ideology could pursue parallel courses toward the same goal merely by consultation among their leaders. For a long time, the Milner Group did not see that the greater the degree of success obtained by this method, the more remote was the possibility that federation could ever be attained. It is very likely that the Group was misled in this by the fact that they were for many years extremely fortunate in keeping members of the Group in positions of power and influence in the Dominions. As long as men like Smuts, Botha (who did what Smuts wanted), Duncan, Feetham, or Long were in influential positions in South Africa; as long as men like Eggleston, Bavin, or Dudley Braham were influential in Australia; as long as men like Glazebrook, Massey, Joseph Flavelle, or Percy Corbett were influential in Canada — in a nutshell, as long as members of the Milner Group were influential throughout the Dominions, the technique of the parallel policy of cooperation would be the easiest way to reach a common goal. Unfortunately, this was not a method that could be expected to continue forever, and when the Milner Group grew older and weaker, it could not be expected that their newer recruits in England (like Hodson, Coupland, Astor, Woodward, Elton, and others) could continue to work on a parallel policy with the newer arrivals to power in the Dominions. When that unhappy day arrived, the Milner Group should have had institutionalized modes of procedure firmly established. They did not, not because they did not want them, but because their members in the Dominions could not have remained in influential positions if they had insisted on creating institutionalized links with Britain when the people of the Dominions obviously did not want such links.

The use of Colonial or Imperial Conferences as a method for establishing closer contact with the various parts of the Empire was originally established by the Cecil Bloc and taken over by the Milner Group. The first four such Conferences (in 1887, 1897, 1902, and 1907) were largely dominated by the former group, although they were not technically in power during the last one. The decisive changes made in the Colonial Conference system at the Conference of 1907 were worked out by a secret group, which consulted on the plans for eighteen months and presented them to the Royal Colonial Institute in April 1905. These plans were embodied in a dispatch from the Colonial Secretary, Alfred Lyttelton, and carried out at the Conference of 1907. As a result, it was established that the name of the meeting was to be changed to Imperial Conference; it was to be called into session every four years; it was to consist of Prime Ministers of the self-governing parts of the Empire; the Colonial Secretary was to be eliminated from the picture; and a new Dominion Department, under Sir Charles Lucas, was to be set up in the Colonial Office. As the future Lord Lothian wrote in *The Round Table* in 1911, the final result was to destroy the hopes for federation by recognizing the separate existence of the Dominions.[2]

At the Conference of 1907, at the suggestion of Haldane, there was created a Committee of Imperial Defence, and a plan was adopted to organize Dominion defense forces on similar patterns, so that they could be integrated in an emergency. The second of these proposals, which led to a complete reorganization of the armies of New Zealand,

Australia, and South Africa in 1909-1912, with very beneficial results in the crisis of 1914-1918, is not of immediate concern to us. The Committee of Imperial Defence and its secretarial staff were creations of Lord Esher, who had been chairman of a special committee to reform the War Office in 1903 and was permanent member of the Committee of Imperial Defence from 1905 to his death. As a result of his influence, the secretariat of this committee became a branch of the Milner Group and later became the secretariat of the Cabinet itself, when that body first obtained a secretariat in 1917.

From this secretarial staff the Milner Group obtained three recruits in the period after 1918. These were Maurice Hankey, Ernest Swinton, and W. G. A. Ormsby-Gore (now Lord Harlech). Hankey was assistant secretary of the Committee of Imperial Defence from 1908 to 1912 and was secretary from 1912 to 1938. Swinton was assistant secretary from 1917 to 1925. Both became members of the Milner Group, Hankey close to the inner circle, Swinton in one of the less central rings. Ormsby-Gore was an assistant secretary in 1917-1918 at the same time that he was private secretary to Lord Milner. All three of these men are of sufficient importance to justify a closer examination of their careers.

Maurice Pascal Alers Hankey (Sir Maurice after 1916, Baron Hankey since 1939), whose family was related by marriage to the Wyndhams, was born in 1877 and joined the Royal Marines when he graduated from Rugby in 1895. He retired from that service in 1918 as a lieutenant colonel and was raised to colonel on the retired list in 1929. He was attached for duty with the Naval Intelligence Department in 1902 and by this route reached the staff of the Committee of Imperial Defence six years later. In 1917, when it was decided to give the Cabinet a secretariat for the first time, and to create the Imperial War Cabinet by adding overseas representatives to the British War Cabinet (a change in which Milner played the chief role), the secretariat of the Committee of Imperial Defence became also the secretariat of the other two bodies. At the same time, as we have seen, the Prime Minister was given a secretariat consisting of two members of the Milner Group (Kerr and Adams). In this way Hankey became secretary and Swinton assistant secretary to the Cabinet, the former holding that post, along with the parallel post in the Committee of Imperial Defence, until 1938. It was undoubtedly through Hankey and the Milner Group that Swinton became Chichele Professor of Military History and a Fellow of All Souls in 1925. As for Hankey himself, he became one of the more significant figures in the Milner Group, close to the inner circle and one of the most important (although relatively little-known) figures in British history of recent times. He was clerk of the Privy Council in 1923-1938; he was secretary to the British delegation at the Peace Conference of 1919, at the Washington Conference of

1921, at the Genoa Conference of 1922, and at the London Reparations Conference of 1924. He was secretary general of the Hague Conference of 1929-1930, of the London Naval Conference of 1930, and of the Lausanne Conference of 1932. He was secretary general of the British Imperial Conferences of 1921, 1923, 1926, 1930, and 1937. He retired in 1938, but became a member of the Permanent Mandates Commission (succeeding Lord Hailey) in 1939. He was British government director of the Suez Canal Company in 1938-1939, Minister without Portfolio in 1939-1940, Chancellor of the Duchy of Lancaster in 1940-1941, Paymaster General in 1941-1942, chairman of the Scientific Advisory Committee and of the Engineering Advisory Committee in 1942-1943. At the present time he is a director of the Suez Canal Company (since 1945), chairman of the Technical Personnel Committee (since 1941), chairman of the Interdepartmental Committee on Further Education and Training and of the Committee on Higher Appointments in the Civil Service (since 1944), and chairman of the Colonial Products Research Committee (since 1942). Hankey, in 1903, married Adeline de Smidt, daughter of a well-known South African political figure. His oldest son, Robert, is now a First Secretary in the diplomatic service, while his daughter, Ursula, has been married since 1929 to John A. Benn, chairman of the board of Benn Brothers, publishers.

Hankey was Lord Esher's chief protégé in the Milner Group and in British public life. They were in constant communication with one another, and Esher gave Hankey a constant stream of advice about his conduct in his various official positions. The following scattered examples can be gleaned from the published *Journals and Letters of Reginald, Viscount Esher*. On 18 February 1919, Esher wrote Hankey, advising him not to accept the position as Secretary General of the League of Nations. On 7 December 1919, he gave him detailed advice on how to conduct himself as secretary to the Conference of Dominion Prime Ministers, telling him to work for "a League of Empire" based on cooperation and not on any "rigid constitutional plan," to try to get an Imperial General Staff, and to use the Defence Committee as such a staff in the meantime. In 1929, when Ramsay MacDonald tried to exclude Hankey from a secret Cabinet meeting, Esher went so far in support of his protégé as to write a letter of admonition to the Prime Minister. This letter, dated 21 July 1929, said: "What is this I see quoted from a London paper that you are excluding your Secretary from Cabinet meetings? It probably is untrue, for you are the last person in the world to take a retrograde step toward 'secrecy' whether in diplomacy or government. The evolution of our Cabinet system from 'Cabal' has been slow but sure. When the Secretary to the Cabinet became an established factor in conducting business, almost the last traces of Mumbo Jumbo, cherished from the days when Bolingbroke was a danger to public peace, disappeared."

Hankey was succeeded as secretary of the Cabinet in 1938 by Edward E. Bridges, who has been close to the Milner Group since he became a Fellow of All Souls in 1920. Bridges, son of the late Poet Laureate Robert Bridges, had the advantages of a good education at Eton and Magdalen. He was a Treasury civil servant from 1919, was knighted in 1939, and since 1945 has combined with his Cabinet position the exalted post of Permanent Secretary of the Treasury and head of His Majesty's Civil Service.

The Imperial Conference of 1911 has little concern with our story, although Asquith's opening speech could have been written in the office of *The Round Table*. Indeed, it is quoted with approval by Lionel Curtis in his *The Problem of the Commonwealth*, published five years later. Asquith pointed out that the Empire rested on three foundations: (a) the reign of law, in Dicey's sense, (b) local autonomy, and (c) trusteeship of the interests and fortunes of fellow subjects who have not yet attained "to the full stature of self-government." He then pointed out the two principles of *centralization* and *disintegration* which had applied to the Empire in the early Victorian period, and declared: "Neither of these theories commands the faintest support today, either at home or in any part of our self-governing Empire. . . . Whether in this United Kingdom or in any one of the great communities which you represent, we each of us are, and we each of us intend to remain, master in our own household. This is, here at home and throughout the Dominions, the lifeblood of our polity." Thus spoke Asquith, and even the ultra-federalist Curtis approved. He also approved when Asquith squelched Sir John Ward's suggestion for the creation of an Imperial Council, although doubtless from quite a different motivation.

At the Conference of 1911, as is well known, the overseas members were for the first time initiated into the mysteries of high policy, because of the menace of Germany. Except for this, which paid high dividends in 1914, the Conference was largely wasted motion.

The Conference of 1915 was not held, because of the war, but as soon as Milner came into the government in December 1915, *The Round Table*'s argument that the war should be used as a means for consolidating the Empire, rather than as an excuse for postponing consolidation, began to take effect. *The Round Table* during 1915 was agitating for an immediate Imperial Conference with Indian participation for the first time. As soon as Milner joined the Cabinet in December 1915, he sent out cables to the Dominions and to India, inviting them to come. It was Milner also who created the Imperial War Cabinet by adding Dominion members to the British War

Cabinet. These developments were foretold and approved by *The Round Table*. In its June 1917 issue it said, in the course of a long article on "New Developments in the Constitution of the Empire":

> At a date which cannot be far distant an Imperial Conference will assemble, the purpose of which will be to consider what further steps can be taken to transform the Empire of a State in which the main responsibilities and burdens of its common affairs are sustained and controlled by the United Kingdom into a commonwealth of equal nations conducting its foreign policy and common affairs by some method of continuous consultation and concerted action. . . . The decision today is against any federated reconstruction after the war. . . . It is evident, however, that the institution through which the improved Imperial system will chiefly work will be the newly constituted Imperial Cabinet. The Imperial Cabinet will be different in some important respects from the Imperial Conference. It will meet annually instead of once in four years. It will be concerned more particularly with foreign policy, which the Imperial Conference has never yet discussed. . . . Its proceedings will consequently be secret. . . . It will also consist of the most important British Ministers sitting in conclave with the Overseas Ministers instead of the Secretary of State for the Colonies alone as has been usually the case hitherto.

As is well known, the Imperial War Cabinet met fourteen times in 1917, met again in 1918, and assembled at Paris in 1918-1919 as the British Empire delegation to the Peace Conference. Parallel with it, the Imperial War Conference met in London in 1917, under the Colonial Secretary, to discuss nonwar problems. At the meetings of the former body it was decided to hold annual meetings in the future and to invite the Dominions to establish resident ministers in London to insure constant consultation. At a meeting in 1917 was drawn up the famous Imperial Resolution, which excluded federation as a solution of the imperial problem and recognized the complete equality of the Dominions and the United Kingdom under one King. These developments were not only acceptable to Milner but apparently were largely engineered by him. On 9 July 1919, he issued a formal statement containing the sentences, "The only possibility of a continuance of the British Empire is on a basis of absolute-out-and-out-equal partnership between the United Kingdom and the Dominions. I say that without any kind of reservation whatever."

When Milner died, in May 1925, *The Times* obituary had this to say about this portion of his life:

> With the special meeting of the War Cabinet attended by the Dominion Prime Ministers which, beginning on March 20, came to be distinguished as the Imperial War Cabinet . . . Milner was more closely concerned than any other British statesman. The conception of the Imperial War Cabinet and the actual proposal to bring the Dominion Premiers into the

United Kingdom Cabinet were his. And when, thanks to Mr. Lloyd George's ready acceptance of the proposal, Milner's conception was realized, it proved to be not only a solution of the problem of Imperial Administrative unity in its then transient but most urgent phase, but a permanent and far-reaching advance in the constitutional evolution of the Empire. It met again in 1918, and was continued as the British Empire Delegation in the peace negotiations at Versailles in 1919. Thus, at the moment of its greatest need, the Empire was furnished by Milner with a common Executive. For the Imperial War Cabinet could and did, take executive action, and its decisions bound the Empire at large.[3]

It was also Milner who insisted on and made the arrangements for the Imperial Conference of 1921, acting in his capacity as Colonial Secretary, although he was forced, by reason of poor health, to resign before the conference assembled. It was in this period as Colonial Secretary that Milner, assisted by Amery, set up the plans for the new "dyarchic" constitution for Malta, gave Egypt its full freedom, set Curtis to work on the Irish problem, and gave Canada permission to establish its own legation in the United States — the latter post filled only in 1926, and then by the son-in-law of Milner's closest collaborator in the Rhodes Trust.

The Imperial Conferences of 1921 and 1923 were largely in the control of the Cecil Bloc, at least so far as the United Kingdom delegation was concerned. Three of the five members of this delegation in 1921 were from this Bloc (Balfour, Curzon, and Austen Chamberlain), the other two being Lloyd George and Winston Churchill. Of the members of the other five delegations, only Smuts, from South Africa, is of significance to us. On the secretarial staff for the United Kingdom delegation, we might point out the presence of Hankey and Grigg.

In the Imperial Conference of 1923 we find a similar situation. Three of the four delegates from the United Kingdom were of the Cecil Bloc (Lord Salisbury, Curzon, and the Duke of Devonshire), the other being Prime Minister Baldwin. Smuts again led the South African delegation. The secretarial staff was headed by Hankey, while the separate Indian secretarial group was led by L. F. Rushbrook Williams. The latter, whom we have already mentioned, had been associated with the Milner Group since he was elected a Fellow of All Souls in 1914, had done special work in preparation of the Government of India Act of 1919, and worked under Marris in applying that act after it became law. His later career carried him to various parts of the Milner Group's extensive system, as can be seen from the fact that he was a delegate to the Assembly of the League of Nations in 1925, Foreign Minister of Patiala State in 1925-1931, a member of the Indian Round Table Conference in 1920-1932, a significant figure in the British Broadcasting Corporation and the Ministry of Information in delegation. There is nothing to indicate that Mr. Latham (later Sir John) was a member of the Milner Group, but in later years his son, Richard, clearly was. Sir John had apparently made his first contact with the Milner Group in 1919, when he, a Professor of Law at the University of Melbourne, was a member of the staff of the Australian delegation to the Paris Peace Conference and, while there, became an assistant secretary to the British delegation. In 1922, at the age of forty-five, he began a twelve-year term as an Australian M. P. During that brief period he was Attorney General in 1925-1929, Minister of Industry in 1928-1929, Leader of the Opposition in 1929-1931, Deputy Leader of the Majority in 1931-1932, and Deputy Prime Minister, Attorney General, and Minister for Industry in 1932-1934. In addition, he was British secretary to the Allied Commission on Czechoslovak Affairs in 1919, first president of the League of Nations Union, Australian delegate to the League of Nations in 1926 and 1932, Australian representative to the World Disarmament Conference in 1932, Chancellor of the University of Melbourne in 1939-1941; Australian Minister of Japan in 1940-1941, and vice-president of the the period 1932-1944, and is now a member of the editorial staff of *The Times.*

At these two conferences, various members of the Cecil Bloc and Milner Group were called in for consultation on matters within their competence. Of these persons, we might mention the names of H. A. L. Fisher, Sir Eyre Crowe, Sir Cecil Hurst, Robert Cecil, Leopold Amery, Samuel Hoare, and Sir Fabian Ware (of the Kindergarten).

The Imperial Conference of 1926 is generally recognized as one of the most important of the postwar period. The Cecil Bloc and Milner Group again had three out of five members of the United Kingdom delegation (Balfour, Austen Chamberlain, and Leopold Amery), with Baldwin and Churchill the other two. Hankey was, as usual, secretary of the conference. Of the other seven delegations, nothing is germane to our investigation except that Vincent Massey was an adviser to the Canadian, and John Greig Latham was a member of the Australian, Australian Red Cross in 1944. Since 1934, he has been Chief Justice of Australia. In this brilliant, if belated, career, Sir John came into contact with the Milner Group, and this undoubtedly assisted his son, Richard, in his more precocious career. Richard Latham was a Rhodes Scholar at Oxford until 1933 and a Fellow of All Souls from 1935. He wrote the supplementary legal chapter in W. K. Hancock's *Survey of British Commonwealth Affairs* and was one of the chief advisers of K. C. Wheare in his famous book, *The Statute of Westminister and Dominion Status* (1938). Unfortunately, Richard Latham died a few years later while still in his middle thirties. It is clear from Professor Wheare's book that Sir John Latham, although a member of the opposition at the time, was one of the chief figures in Australia's acceptance of the Statute of Westminster.

The new status of the Dominions, as enunciated in the *Report* of the conference and later known as the "Balfour Declaration," was accepted by the Milner Group both in *The Round Table* and in *The Times*. In the latter, on 22 November 1926, readers were informed that the "Declaration" merely described the Empire as it was, with nothing really new except the removal of a few anachronisms. It concluded: "In all its various clauses there is hardly a statement or a definition which does not coincide with familiar practice."

The Imperial Conference of 1930 was conducted by a Labour government and had no members of the Cecil Bloc or Milner Group among its chief delegates. Sir Maurice Hankey, however, was secretary of the conference, and among its chief advisers were Maurice Gwyer and H. D. Henderson. Both of these were members of All Souls and probably close to the Milner Group.

The Imperial Conference of 1937 was held during the period in which the Milner Group was at the peak of its power. Of the eight members of the United Kingdom delegation, five were from the Milner Group (Lord Halifax, Sir John Simon, Malcolm MacDonald, W. G. A. Ormsby-Gore, and Sir Samuel Hoare). The others were Baldwin, Neville Chamberlain, and J. Ramsay MacDonald. In addition, the chief of the Indian delegation was the Marquess of Zetland of the Cecil Bloc. Sir Maurice Hankey was secretary of the conference, and among the advisers were Sir Donald Somervell (of All Souls and the Milner Group), Vincent Massey, Sir Fabian Ware, and the Marquess of Hartington.

In addition to the Imperial Conferences, where the influence of the Milner Group was probably more extensive than appears from the membership of the delegations, the Group was influential in the administration of the Commonwealth, especially in the two periods of its greatest power, from 1924 to 1929 and from 1935 to 1939. An indication of this can be seen in the fact that the office of Colonial Secretary was held by the Group for seven out of ten years from 1919 to 1929 and for five out of nine years from 1931 to 1940, while the office of Dominion Secretary was held by a member of the Group for eight out of the fourteen years from its creation in 1925 to the outbreak of the war in 1939 (although the Labour Party was in power for two of those years). The Colonial Secretaries to whom we have reference were:

Lord Milner, 1919-1921
Leopold Amery, 1924-1929
Malcolm MacDonald, 1935
W. G. A. Ormsby-Gore, 1936-1938
Malcolm MacDonald, 1938-1940

The Dominion Secretaries to whom we have reference were:

Leopold Amery, 1925-1929
Malcolm MacDonald, 1935-1938, 1938-1939

The lesser positions within the Colonial Office were not remote from the Milner Group. The Permanent Under Secretary was Sir George Fiddes of the Kindergarten in 1916-1921. In addition, James Masterton-Smith, who had been Balfour's private secretary previously, was Permanent Under Secretary in succession to Fiddes in 1921-1925, and John Maffey, who had been Lord Chelmsford's secretary while the latter was Viceroy in 1916-1921, was Permanent Under Secretary from 1933 to 1937. The position of Parliamentary Under Secretary, which had been held by Lord Selborne in 1895-1900 and by Sir Arthur Steel-Maitland in 1915-1917, was held by Amery in 1919-1921, by Edward Wood (Lord Halifax) in 1921-1922, by Ormsby-Gore in 1922-1924, 1924-1929, and by Lord Dufferin (brother of Lord Blackwood of the Kindergarten) from 1937 to 1940.

Most of these persons (probably all except Masterton-Smith, Maffey, and Lord Dufferin) were members of the Milner Group. The most important, of course, was Leopold Amery, whom we have already shown as Milner's chief political prótegé. We have not yet indicated that Malcolm MacDonald was a member of the Milner Group, and must be satisfied at this point with saying that he was a member, or at least an instrument, of the Group, from 1931 or 1932 onward, without ever becoming a member of the inner circle. The evidence indicating this relationship will be discussed later.

At this point we should say a few words about W. G. A. Ormsby-Gore (Lord Harlech since 1938), who was a member of the Cecil Bloc by marriage and of the Milner Group by adoption. A graduate of Eton in 1930, he went to New College as a contemporary of Philip Kerr and Reginald Coupland. He took his degree in 1908 and was made a Fellow of New College in 1936. A Conservative member of Parliament from 1910 until he went to the Upper House in 1938, he spent the early years of the First World War in military intelligence, chiefly in Egypt. In 1913 he married Lady Beatrice Cecil, daughter of the fourth Marquess of Salisbury, and four years later became Parliamentary Private Secretary to Lord Milner as well as assistant secretary to the War Cabinet (associated in the latter post with Hankey, Kerr, W. G. S. Adams, and Amery of the Milner Group). Ormsby-Gore went on a mission to Palestine in 1918 and was with the British delegation at the Paris Peace Conference as an expert on the Middle East. He was Under Secretary for the Colonies with the Duke of Devonshire in 1922-1924 and with Leopold Amery in 1924-1929, becoming Colonial Secretary in his own right in 1936-1938. In the interval he was Postmaster

General in 1931 and First Commissioner of Works in 1931-1936. He was a member of the Permanent Mandates Commission (1921-1923) and of the Colonial Office Mission to the British West Indies (1921-1922), and was Chairman of the East African Parliamentary Commission in 1924. He was High Commissioner of South Africa and the three native protectorates in 1941-1944. He has been a director of the Midland Bank and of the Standard Bank of South Africa. He was also one of the founders of the Royal Institute of International Affairs, a member of Lord Lothian's committee on the African Survey, and a member of the council of the Institute.

The Milner Group also influenced Commonwealth affairs by publicity work of great quantity and good quality. This was done through the various periodicals controlled by the Group, such as *The Round Table, The Times, International Affairs* and others; by books published by the Royal Institute of International Affairs and individual members of the Group; by academic and university activities by men like Professor Coupland, Professor Zimmern, Professor Harlow, and others; by public and private discussion meetings sponsored by the Round Table Groups throughout the Commonwealth, by the Institute of International Affairs everywhere, by the Institute of Pacific Relations (IPR), by the Council on Foreign Relations, by the Williamstown Institute of Politics, by the Rhodes Scholarship group; and through the three unofficial conferences on British Commonwealth relations held by the Group since 1933. Some of these organizations and activities have already been mentioned. The last will be discussed here. The rest are to be described in Chapter 10.

The three unofficial conferences on British Commonwealth relations were held at Toronto in 1933, at Sydney in 1938, and at London in 1945. They were initiated and controlled by the Milner Group, acting through the various Institutes of International Affairs, in the hope that they would contribute to the closer union of the Commonwealth by inclining the opinion of prominent persons in the Dominions in that direction. The plan was originated by the British Empire members of the Institute of Pacific Relations at the Kyoto meeting in 1929. The members from Great Britain consisted of Lord Robert Cecil, Sir Herbert Samuel, Sir Donald Somervell, Sir John Power, P. J. Noel-Baker, G. M. Gathorne-Hardy, H. V. Hodson, H. W. Kerr, A. J. Toynbee, J. W. Wheeler-Bennett, and A. E. Zimmern. Of these, two were from the Cecil Bloc and five from the Milner Group. Discussion was continued at the Shanghai meeting of the Institute of Pacific Relations in 1931, and a committee under Robert Cecil drew up an agenda for the unofficial conference. This committee made the final arrangements at a meeting in Chatham House in July 1932 and published as a preliminary work a volume called *Consultation and*

Cooperation in the British Commonwealth.

The conference was held at the University of Toronto, 11-21 September 1933, with forty-three delegates and thirty-three secretaries, the traveling expenses being covered by a grant from the Carnegie Corporation. The United Kingdom delegation consisted of the eleven names mentioned above plus R. C. M. Arnold as private secretary to Lord Cecil and J. P. Maclay (the famous shipbuilder) as private secretary to Sir Herbert Samuel. The Australian delegation of six included Professor A. H. Charteris, Professor Ernest Scott, A. Smithies (a Rhodes Scholar of 1929), Alfred Stirling (an Oxford B.A.), W. J. V. Windeyer, and Richard Latham (a Rhodes Scholar of 1933). The Canadian delegation consisted of N. W. Rowell, Sir Robert Borden, Louis Cote, John W. Dafoe, Sir Robert Falconer, Sir Joseph Flavelle, W. Sanford Evans, Vincent Massey, René L. Morin, J. S. Woodsworth, W. M. Birks, Charles J. Burchell, Brooke Claxton, Percy E. Corbett, W. P. M. Kennedy, J. J. MacDonnell (Rhodes Trustee for Canada), and E. J. Tarr. The secretary to the delegation was George Parkin Glazebrook (Balliol 1924). Most of these names are significant, but we need only point out that at least four of them, including the secretary, were members of the Milner Group (Massey, Corbett, Flavelle, Glazebrook). The New Zealand delegation had three members, one of which was W. Downie Stewart, and the South African delegation had five members, including F. S. Malan and Professor Eric A. Walker. The secretariat to the whole conference was headed by I. S. Macadam of the Royal Institute of International Affairs. The secretary to the United Kingdom delegation was H. V. Hodson. Thus it would appear that the Milner Group had eight out of forty-three delegates, as well as the secretaries to the Canadian and United Kingdom delegations.

The conference was divided into four commissions, each of which had a chairman and a rapporteur. In addition, the first commission (on foreign policy) was subdivided into two subcommittees. The chairmen of the four commissions were Robert Cecil, Vincent Massey, F. S. Malan, and W. Downie Stewart. Thus the Milner Group had two out of four. The rapporteurs (including the two subcommittees) were A. L. Zimmern, H. V. Hodson, P. E. Corbett, E. A. Walker, P. J. Noel-Baker, D. B. Somervell, and A. H. Charteris. Thus the Milner Group had four out of seven and possibly more (as Walker may be a member of the Group).

The discussions at the conference were secret, the press was excluded, and in the published *Proceedings*, edited by A. J. Toynbee, all remarks were presented in indirect discourse and considerably curtailed, without identification of the speakers. The conference made a number of recommendations, including the following: (1) Dominion

High Commissioners in London should be given diplomatic status with direct access to the Foreign Office; (2) junior members of Dominion Foreign Offices should receive a period of training in the Foreign Office in London; (3) diplomatic representatives should be exchanged between Dominions; (4) Commonwealth tribunals should be set up to settle legal disputes between Dominions; (5) collective security and the League of Nations should be supported; (6) cooperation with the United States was advocated.

The second unofficial conference on British Commonwealth relations was held near Sydney, Australia, 3-17 September 1938. The expenses were met by grants from the Carnegie Corporation and the Rhodes Trustees. The decision to hold the second conference was made by the British members at the Yosemite meeting of the Institute of Pacific Relations in 1936. A committee under Viscount Samuel met at Chatham House in June 1937 and drew up the arrangements and the agenda. The selection of delegates was left to the various Institutes of International Affairs. From the United Kingdom went Lord Lothian (chairman), Lionel Curtis, W. K. Hancock, Hugh A. Wyndham, A. L. Zimmern, Norman Bentwich, Ernest Bevin, V. A. Cazalet, A. M. Fraser, Sir John Burnett-Stuart, Miss Grace Hadow, Sir Howard Kelly, Sir Frederick Minter, Sir John Pratt, and James Walker. At least five out of fifteen, including the chairman, were of the Milner Group. From Australia came thirty-one members, including T. R. Bavin (chairman of the delegation), K. H. Bailey (a Rhodes Scholar), and A. H. Charteris. From Canada came fifteen, including E. J. Tarr (chairman of the delegation) and P. E. Corbett. From India came four Indians. From Ireland came five persons. From New Zealand came fourteen, with W. Downie Stewart as chairman. From South Africa came six, including P. Van der Byl (chairman) and G. R. Hofmeyr (an old associate of the Milner Kindergarten in the Transvaal).

Of ninety delegates, nine were members of the Milner Group and three others may have been. This is a small proportion, but the conduct of the conference was well controlled. The chairmen of the three most important delegations were of the Milner Group (Eggleston, Downie Stewart, and Lothian); the chairman of the conference itself (Bavin) was. The secretary of the conference was Macadam, the recorder was Hodson, and the secretary to the press committee was Lionel Vincent Massey (grandson of George Parkin). The *Proceedings* of the conference were edited by Hodson, with an Introduction by Bavin, and published by the Royal Institute of International Affairs. Again, no indication was given of who said what.

The third unofficial conference on British Commonwealth relations was similar to the others, although the war emergency restricted its membership to persons who were already in London. As background material it prepared sixty-two books and papers, of which many are now published. Among these was *World War; Its Cause and Cure* by Lionel Curtis. The committee on arrangements and agenda, with Lord Astor as chairman, met in New York in January 1944. The delegations outside the United Kingdom were made up of persons doing war duty in London, with a liberal mixture of Dominion Rhodes Scholars. The chairmen of the various delegations included Professor K. H. Bailey from Australia, E. J. Tarr from Canada, Sir Sardar E. Singh from India, W. P. Morrell (whom we have already seen as a Beit Lecturer, a Rhodes Scholar, and a co-editor with the Reverend K. N. Bell of All Souls), Professor S. H. Frankel from South Africa, and Lord Hailey from the United Kingdom. There were also observers from Burma and Southern Rhodesia. Of the fifty-three delegates, sixteen were from the United Kingdom. Among these were Lord Hailey, Lionel Curtis, V. T. Harlow, Sir Frederick Whyte, A. G. B. Fisher, John Coatman, Miss Kathleen Courtney, Viscount Hinchingbrooke, A. Creech Jones, Sir Walter Layton, Sir Henry Price, Miss Heather Harvey, and others. Of the total of fifty-three members, no more than five or six were of the Milner Group. The opening speech to the conference was made by Lord Robert Cecil, and the *Proceedings* were published in the usual form under the editorship of Robert Frost, research secretary of the Royal Institute of International Affairs and author of the imperial sections of *The History of the Times*.

In all the various activities of the Milner Group in respect to Commonwealth affairs, it is possible to discern a dualistic attitude. This attitude reveals a wholehearted public acceptance of the existing constitutional and political relationships of Great Britain and the Dominions, combined with an intense secret yearning for some form of closer union. The realization that closer union was not politically feasible in a democratic age in which the majority of persons, especially in the Dominions, rejected any effort to bind the various parts of the Empire together explains this dualism. The members of the Group, as *The Round Table* pointed out in 1919, were not convinced of the effectiveness or workability of any program of Dominion relations based solely on cooperation without any institutional basis, but publicly, and in the next breath, the Group wholeheartedly embraced all the developments that destroyed one by one the legal and institutional links which bound the Dominions to the mother country. In one special field after another — in defense, economic cooperation, raw materials conservation, war graves, intellectual cooperation, health measures, etc., etc. — the Group eagerly welcomed efforts to create new institutional links between the self-governing portions of the Commonwealth. But all the time the Group recognized that these innovations were unable to satisfy the yearning that burned in the Group's collective heart. Only as the Second World War began to enter its second, and more hopeful, half, did the Group begin once again to raise its voice with suggestions for some more permanent organization of the constitutional side of Commonwealth relations. All of these suggestions were offered in a timid and tentative fashion, more or less publicly labeled as trial balloons and usually prefaced by an engaging statement that the suggestion was the result of the personal and highly imperfect ideas of the speaker himself. "Thinking aloud," as Smuts called it, became epidemic among the members of the Group. These idle thoughts could be, thus, easily repudiated if they fell on infertile or inhospitable ground, and even the individual whence these suggestions emanated could hardly be held responsible for "thinking aloud." All of these suggestions followed a similar pattern: (1) a reflection on the great crisis which the Commonwealth survived in 1940-1942; (2) an indication that this crisis required some reorganization of the Commonwealth in order to avoid its repetition; (3) a passage of high praise for the existing structure of the Commonwealth and an emphatic statement that the independence and autonomy of its various members is close to the speaker's heart and that nothing he suggests must be taken as implying any desire to infringe in the slightest degree on that independence; and (4) the suggestion itself emerges. The logical incompatibility of the four sections of the pattern is never mentioned and if pointed out by some critic would undoubtedly be excused on the grounds that the English are practical rather than logical — an excuse behind which many English, even outside the Milner Group, frequently find refuge.

We shall give three examples of the Milner Group's suggestions for Commonwealth reform in the second half of the recent war. They emanated from General Smuts, Lord Halifax, and Sir Edward Grigg. All of them were convinced that the British Commonwealth would be drastically weaker in the postwar world and would require internal reorganization in order to take its place as a balancing force between the two great powers, the United States and the Soviet Union. Smuts, in an article in the American weekly magazine *Life* for 28 December 1942, and in a speech before the United Kingdom branch of the Empire Parliamentary Association in London on 25 November 1943, was deliberately vague but hoped to use the close link between the United Kingdom and the dependent colonies as a means of bringing the self-governing Dominions closer to the United Kingdom by combining the Dominions with the colonies in regional blocs. This plan had definite advantages, although it had been rejected as impractical by Lionel Curtis in 1916. If regional blocs could be formed by dividing the British Commonwealth into four or five geographic groupings, with a Dominion in each region closely associated with the colonies in the same region, and if this could be done without weakening the link between the United Kingdom and the colonies, it would serve to strengthen the link between the United Kingdom and the Dominions. This latter goal was frankly admitted by Smuts. He also suggested that a federated Western Europe be included in the United Kingdom regional bloc.

Sir Edward Grigg's suggestion, made in his book *The British Commonwealth*, appeared also in 1943. It was very similar to Smuts's, even to the use of the same verbal expressions. For example, both spoke of the necessity for ending the "dual Empire," of which one part was following a centralizing course and the other a decentralizing course. This expression was derived from Lord Milner (and was attributed to this source by Sir Edward) and referred to the difference between the dependent and the self-governing portions of the Commonwealth. Sir Edward advocated creation of five regional blocs, with Western Europe, associated by means of a military alliance with the United Kingdom, in one. Without any sacrifice of sovereignty by anyone, he visualized the creation of a regional council ("like a miniature Imperial Conference") and a joint parliamentary assembly in three of these regions. The members of the council would be representatives of legislatures and not of governments; the assembly would consist of select members from the existing national parliaments in proper ratio; and each region would have a permanent secretariat to carry out agreed decisions. How this elaborate organization could be reconciled with the continuance of unrestricted national sovereignty was not indicated.

Lord Halifax's suggestion, made in a speech before the Toronto Board of Trade on 24 January 1944, was somewhat different, although he clearly had the same goal in view and the same mental picture of existing world conditions. He suggested that Britain could not maintain her position as a great power, in the sense in which the United States and Russia were great powers, on the basis of the strength of the United Kingdom alone. Accordingly, he advocated the creation of some method of coordination of foreign policy and measures of defense by which the Dominions could participate in both and a united front could be offered to other powers.

That these trial balloons of Smuts, Grigg, and Halifax were not their isolated personal reactions but were the results of a turmoil of thought within the Milner Group was evident from the simultaneous suggestions which appeared in *The Times* editorials during the first week in December 1943 and the issue of *The Round Table* for the same month. The *Winnipeg Free Press*, a paper which has frequently shown knowledge of the existence of the Milner Group, in editorials of 26 and 29 January 1944, pointed out this effusion of suggestions for a reconstruction of the Empire and said:

Added to the record of earlier statements, the Halifax speech affords conclusive evidence that there is a powerful movement on foot in the United Kingdom for a Commonwealth which will speak with a single voice. And it will be noted that Lord Halifax believes that this change in the structure of the Commonwealth will be the first consideration of the next Imperial Conference. . . . Running through all these speeches and articles is the clear note of fear. The spokesmen are obsessed by the thought of power as being the only force that counts. The world is to be governed by Leviathans. . . . It is tragic that the sincere and powerful group of public men in England, represented by Lord Halifax and Field Marshal Smuts, should react to the problem of maintaining peace in this way.

These suggestions were met by an uproar of protests that reached unnecessary heights of denunciation, especially in Canada. They were rejected in South Africa, repulsed by Mackenzie King and others in Canada, called "isolationist" by the CCF party, censured unanimously by the Quebec Assembly, and repudiated by Prime Minister Churchill. Except in New Zealand and Australia, where fear of Japan was having a profound effect on public opinion, and in the United Kingdom, where the Milner Group's influence was so extensive, the suggestions received a cold reception. In South Africa only *The Cape Times* was favorable, and in Canada *The Vancouver Province* led a small band of supporters. As a result, the Milner Group once again rejected any movement toward closer union. It continued to toy with Grigg's idea of regional blocs within the Commonwealth, but here it found an almost insoluble problem. If a regional bloc were to be created in Africa, the natives of the African colonial areas would be exposed to the untender mercies of the South African Boers, and it would be necessary to repudiate the promises of native welfare which the Group had supported in the Kenya White Paper of 1923, its resistance to Boer influence in the three native protectorates in South Africa, the implications in favor of native welfare in *The African Survey* of 1938, and the frequent pronouncements of *The Round Table* on the paramount importance of protecting native rights. Such a repudiation was highly unlikely, and indeed was specifically rejected by Grigg himself in his book.[4]

The Milner Group itself had been one of the chief, if not the chief, forces in Britain intensifying the decentralizing influences in the self-governing portions of the Empire. This influence was most significant in regard to India, Palestine, Ireland, and Egypt, each of which was separated from Great Britain by a process in which the Milner Group was a principal agent. The first of these is so significant that it will be discussed in a separate chapter, but a few words should be said about the other three here.

The Milner Group had relatively little to do with the affairs of

Palestine except in the early period (1915-1919), in the later period (the Peel Report of 1937), and in the fact that the British influence on the Permanent Mandates Commission was always exercised through a member of the Group.

The idea of establishing a mandate system for the territories taken from enemy powers as a result of the war undoubtedly arose from the Milner Group's inner circle. It was first suggested by George Louis Beer in a report submitted to the United States Government on 1 January 1918, and by Lionel Curtis in an article called "Windows of Freedom" in *The Round Table* for December 1918. Beer was a member of the Round Table Group from about 1912 and was, in fact, the first member who was not a British subject. That Beer was a member of the Group was revealed in the obituary published in *The Round Table* for September 1920. The Group's attention was first attracted to Beer by a series of Anglophile studies on the British Empire in the eighteenth century which he published in the period after 1893. A Germanophobe as well as an Anglophile, he intended by writing, if we are to believe *The Round Table*, "to counteract the falsehoods about British Colonial policy to be found in the manuals used in American primary schools." When the Round Table Group, about 1911, began to study the causes of the American Revolution, they wrote to Beer, and thus began a close and sympathetic relationship. He wrote the reports on the United States in *The Round Table* for many years, and his influence is clearly evident in Curtis's *The Commonwealth of Nations*. He gave a hint of the existence of the Milner Group in an article which he wrote for the *Political Science Quarterly* of June 1915 on Milner. He said: "He stands forth as the intellectual leader of the most progressive school of imperial thought throughout the Empire." Beer was one of the chief supporters of American intervention in the war against Germany in the period 1914-1917; he was the chief expert on colonial questions on Colonel House's "Inquiry," which was studying plans for the peace settlements; and he was the American expert on colonial questions at the Peace Conference in Paris. The Milner Group was able to have him named head of the Mandate Department of the League of Nations as soon as it was established. He was one of the originators of the Royal Institute of International Affairs in London and its American branch, The Council on Foreign Relations. With Lord Eustace Percy, he drew up the plan for the *History of the Peace Conference* which was carried out by Harold Temperley.

Curtis's suggestion for a mandates system was published in *The Round Table* after discussions with Kerr and other members of the inner circle. It was read by Smuts before it was printed and was used by the latter as the basis for his memorandum published in December 1918 with the title *The League of Nations: A Practical Suggestion*. This embodied a constitution for the League of Nations in twenty-one articles. The first nine of these dealt with the question of mandates. The mandates article of the final Covenant of the League (Article 22) was drafted by Smuts and Kerr (according to Temperley) and was introduced by Smuts to the League Commission of the Peace Conference. The mandates themselves were granted under conditions drawn up by Lord Milner. Since it was felt that this should be done on an international basis, the Milner drafts were not accepted at once but were submitted to an international committee of five members meeting in London. On this committee Milner was chairman and sole British member and succeeded in having his drafts accepted.[5]

The execution of the terms of the mandates were under the supervision of a Permanent Mandates Commission of nine members (later ten). The British member of this commission was always of the Milner Group, as can be seen from the following list:

> W. G. A. Ormsby-Gore, February 1921-July 1923
> Lord Lugard, July 1923-July 1936
> Lord Hailey, September 1936-March 1939
> Lord Hankey, May 1939-September 1939
> Lord Hailey, September 1939-

The origins and the supervision power of the mandates system were thus largely a result of the activities of the Milner Group. This applied to Palestine as well as the other mandates. Palestine, however, had a peculiar position among mandates because of the Balfour Declaration of 1917, which states that Britain would regard with favor the establishment of a national home for the Jews in Palestine. This declaration, which is always known as the Balfour Declaration, should rather be called "the Milner Declaration," since Milner was the actual draftsman and was, apparently, its chief supporter in the War Cabinet. This fact was not made public until 21 July 1937. At that time Ormsby-Gore, speaking for the government in Commons, said, "The draft as originally put up by Lord Balfour was not the final draft approved by the War Cabinet. The particular draft assented to by the War Cabinet and afterwards by the Allied Governments and by the United States . . . and finally embodied in the Mandate, happens to have been drafted by Lord Milner. The actual final draft had to be issued in the name of the Foreign Secretary, but the actual draftsman was Lord Milner." Milner had referred to this fact in a typically indirect and modest fashion in the House of Lords on 27 June 1923, when he said, "I was a party to the Balfour Declaration." In the War Cabinet, at the time, he received strong support from General Smuts.

Once the mandate was set up, also in terms drafted by Milner, the Milner Group took little actual part in the administration of Palestine.

None of the various high commissioners was a member of the Group, and none of the various commissions concerned with this problem possessed a member from the Group until the Peel Commission of 1936. Reginald Coupland was one of the six members of the Peel Commission and, according to unofficial information, was the chief author of its report. In spite of this lack of direct contact with the subject, the Milner Group exercised a certain amount of influence in regard to Palestine because of its general power in the councils of the Conservative Party and because Palestine was administered through the Colonial Office, where the Milner Group's influence was considerable.

The general attitude of the Milner Group was neither pro-Arab nor pro-Zionist, although tending, if at all, toward the latter rather than the former. The Group were never anti-Semitic, and not a shred of evidence in this direction has been found. In fact, they were very sympathetic to the Jews and to their legitimate aspirations to overcome their fate, but this feeling, it must be confessed, was rather general and remote, and they did not, in their personal lives, have much real contact with Jews or any real appreciation of the finer qualities of those people. Their feeling against anti-Semitism was, on the whole, remote and academic. On the other hand, as with most upper-class English, their feeling for the Arabs was somewhat more personal. Many members of the Group had been in Arab countries, found their personal relationships with the Arabs enjoyable, and were attracted to them. However, this attraction of the Arabs never inclined the Milner Group toward that pro-Arab romanticism that was to be found in people like W. S. Blunt or T. E. Lawrence. The reluctance of the Milner Group to push the Zionist cause in Palestine was based on more academic considerations, chiefly two in number: (1) the feeling that it would not be fair to allow the bustling minority of Zionists to come into Palestine and drive the Arabs either out or into an inferior economic and social position; and (2) the feeling that to do this would have the effect of alienating the Arabs from Western, and especially British, culture, and that this would be especially likely to occur if the Jews obtained control of the Mediterranean coast from Egypt to Syria. Strangely enough, there is little evidence that the Milner Group was activated by strategic or economic considerations at all. Thus the widely disseminated charges that Britain failed to support Zionism in Palestine because of anti-Semitism or strategic and economic considerations is not supported by any evidence found within the Milner Group. This may be true of other sections of British public opinion, and certainly is true of the British Labour Party, where the existence of anti-Semitism as an influence seems clearly established.

In Palestine, as in India and probably in Ireland, the policy of the Milner Group seems to have been motivated by good intentions which alienated the contending parties, encouraged extremism, and weakened British influence with both. In the long run, this policy was pro-Arab, just as in India it was pro-Moslem, and in both cases it served to encourage an uncompromising obstructionism which could have been avoided if Britain had merely applied the principles to which she stood committed.

The attitude of the Milner Group toward the Arabs and Jews can be seen from some quotations from members of the Group. At the Peace Conference of 1919, discussing the relative merits of the Jews and Arabs, Smuts said: "They haven't the Arabs' attractive manners. They do not warm the heart by graceful subjection. They make demands. They are a bitter, recalcitrant little people, and, like the Boers, impatient of leadership and ruinously quarrelsome among themselves. They see God in the shape of an Oriental potentate." A few years later, John Dove, in a letter to Brand, asked himself why there was so much pro-Arab feeling among the British, especially "the public school caste," and attributed it to the Arabs' good manners, derived from desert life, and their love for sports, especially riding and shooting, both close to the heart of the public-school boy. A little later, in another letter, also written from Palestine, Dove declared that the whole Arab world should be in one state and it must have Syria and Palestine for its front door, not be like South Africa, with Delagoa Bay in other hands. The Arab world, he explained, needs this western door because we are trying to westernize the Arabs, and without it they would be driven to the east and to India, which they hate. He concluded:

If the Arab belongs to the Mediterranean, as T. E. Lawrence insists, we should do nothing to stop him getting back to it. Why our own nostrum for the ills of mankind everywhere is Western Civilization, and, if it is a sound one, what would be the good of forcing a people who want direct contact with us to slink in and out of their country by a back door which, like the Persian Gulf, opens only on the East? It would certainly check development, if it did not actually warp it. I suggest then that partition should not be permanent, but this does not mean that a stage of friendly tutelage is necessarily a bad thing for the Arabs. On the contrary, advanced peoples can give so much to stimulate backward ones if they do it with judgment and sympathy. Above all, it must not be the kind of help which kills individuality. . . . Personally, I don't see the slightest harm in Jews coming to Palestine under reasonable conditions. They are the Arabs' cousins as much as the Phoenicians, and if Zionism brings capital and labour which will enable industries to start, it will add to the strength of the larger unit which some day is going to include Palestine. But they must be content to be part of such a potential unit. They need have no fear of absorption, for they have everything to gain from an Arab Federation. It would mean a far larger field for their activities.

The attitude of the Milner Group toward the specific problem of Zionism was expressed in explicit terms by Lord Milner himself in a speech in the House of Lords on 27 June 1923. After expressing his wholehearted agreement with the policy of the British government as revealed in its actions and in its statements, like the Balfour Declaration and the White Paper of 1922 (Cmd. 1700), he added:

> I am not speaking of the policy which is advocated by the extreme Zionists, which is a totally different thing. . . . I believe that we have only to go on steadily with the policy of the Balfour Declaration as we have ourselves interpeted it in order to see great material progress in Palestine and a gradual subsistence of the present [Arab] agitation, the force of which it would be foolish to deny, but which I believe to be largely due to artificial stimulus and, to a very great extent, to be excited from without. The symptoms of any real and general dissatisfaction among the mass of the Arab population with the conditions under which they live, I think it would be very difficult to discover. . . . There is plenty of room in that country for a considerable immigrant population without injuring in any way the resident Arab population, and, indeed, in many ways it would tend to their extreme benefit. . . . There are about 700,000 people in Palestine, and there is room for several millions. . . . I am and always have been a strong supporter of the pro-Arab policy which was first advocated in this country in the course of the war. I believe in the independence of the Arab countries, which they owe to us and which they can only maintain with our help. I look forward to an Arab Federation. . . . I am convinced that the Arab will make a great mistake . . . in claiming Palestine as a part of the Arab Federation in the same sense as are the other countries of the Near East which are mainly inhabited by Arabs.

He then went on to say that he felt that Palestine would require a permanent mandate and under that condition could become a National Home for the Jews, could take as many Jewish immigrants as the country could economically support, but "must never become a Jewish state."

This was the point of view of the Milner Group, and it remained the point of view of the British government until 1939. Like the Milner Group's point of view on other issues, it was essentially fair, compromising, and well-intentioned. It broke down in Palestine because of the obstructionism of the Arabs; the intention of the Zionists to have political control of their National Home, if they got one; the pressure on both Jews and Arabs from the world depression after 1929; and the need for a refuge from Hitler for European Jews after 1933. The Milner Group did not approve of the efforts of the Labour government in 1929-1931 to curtail Zionist rights in Palestine. They protested vigorously against the famous White Paper of 1930 (Cmd. 3692), which was regarded as anti-Zionist. Baldwin, Austen Chamberlain, and Leopold Amery protested against the document in a letter to *The*

Times on 30 October 1930. Smuts sent a telegram of protest to the Prime Minister, and Sir John Simon declared it a violation of the mandate in a letter to *The Times*. Seven years later, the report of the Peel Commission said that the White Paper "betrayed a marked insensitiveness to Jewish feelings." As a result of this pressure, Ramsay MacDonald wrote a letter to Dr. Weizmann, interpreting the document in a more moderate fashion.

As might be expected, in view of the position of Reginald Coupland on the Peel Commission, the report of that Commission met with a most enthusiastic reception from the Milner Group. This report was a scholarly study of conditions in Palestine, of a type usually found in any document with which the Milner Group had direct contact. For the first time in any government document, the aspirations of Jews and Arabs in Palestine were declared to be irreconcilable and the existing mandate unworkable. Accordingly, the report recommended the partition of Palestine into a Jewish state, an Arab state, and a neutral enclave containing the Holy Places. This suggestion was accepted by the British government in a White Paper (Cmd. 5513) issued through Ormsby-Gore. He also defended it before the Permanent Mandates Commission of the League of Nations. In the House of Lords it was defended by Lord Lugard, but recently retired as the British member of the Permanent Mandates Commission. It was also supported by Lord Dufferin and Archbishop Lang. In the House of Commons the motion to approve the government's policy as outlined in the White Paper Cmd. 5513 was introduced by Ormsby-Gore. The first speech in support of the motion, which was passed without a division, was from Leopold Amery.

Amery's speech in support of this motion is extremely interesting and is actually an evolution, under the pressure of hard facts, from the point of view described by Lord Milner in 1923. Amery said: "However much we may regret it, we have lost the situation in Palestine, as we lost it in Ireland, through a lack of wholehearted faith in ourselves and through the constitutional inability of the individual Briton, and indeed of the country as a whole, not to see the other fellow's point of view and to be influenced by it, even to the detriment of any consistent policy." According to Amery, the idea of partition occurred to the Peel Commission only after it had left Palestine and the report was already written. Thus the commission was unable to hear any direct evidence on this question or make any examination of how partition should be carried out in detail. He said:

> Of the 396 pages of the Report almost the whole of the first 368 pages, including the whole of chapters 7 to 19, represent an earlier Report of an entirely different character. That earlier Report envisaged the continuation of the Mandate in its present form. . . . Throughout all these chapters

to which I have referred, the whole text of the chapters deals with the assumption that the Mandate is continued, but here and there, at the end of some chapter, there is tacked on in a quite obviously added last paragraph, something to this effect: "All the rest of the chapter before is something that might have been considered if, as a matter of fact, we were not going to pursue an entirely different policy." These last paragraphs were obviously added by the Secretary, or whoever helped draft the Report, after the main great conclusion was reached at a very late stage.

Since the Milner Group supported partition in Palestine, as they had earlier in Ireland and as they did later in India, it is not too much to believe that Coupland added the additional paragraphs after the commission had returned to England and he had had an opportunity to discuss the matter with other members of the inner circle. In fact, Amery's remarks were probably based on knowledge rather than internal textual evidence and were aimed to get the motion accepted, with the understanding that it approved no more than the principle of partition, with the details to be examined by another commission later. This, in fact, is what was done.

Amery's speech is also interesting for its friendly reference to the Jews. He said that in the past the Arabs had obtained 100 percent of what they were promised, while the Jews had received "a raw deal," in spite of the fact that the Jews had a much greater need of the country and would make the best use of the land.

To carry out the policy of partition, the government appointed a new royal commission of four members in March 1938. Known as the Woodhead Commission, this body had no members of either the Milner Group or the Cecil Bloc on it, and its report (Cmd. 5854) rejected partition as impractical on the grounds that any acceptable method of partition into two states would give a Jewish state with an annual financial surplus and an Arab state with an annual financial deficit. This conclusion was accepted by the government in another White Paper (Cmd. 5893 of 1938). As an alternative, the government called a Round Table Conference of Jews and Arabs from Palestine along with representatives of the Arab states outside of Palestine. During all this, the Arabs had been growing increasingly violent; they refused to accept the Peel Report; they boycotted the Woodhead Commission; and they finally broke into open civil war. In such conditions, nothing was accomplished at the Round Table meetings at London in February-March 1939. The Arab delegation included leaders who had to be released from prison in order to come and who refused to sit in the same conference with the Jews. Compromise proposals presented by the government were rejected by both sides.

After the conference broke up, the government issued a new statement of policy (Cmd. 6019 of May 1939). It was a drastic reversal of previous statements and was obviously a turn in favor of the Arabs. It fixed Jewish immigration into Palestine at 75,000 for the whole of the next five years (including illegal immigration) and gave the Arabs a veto on any Jewish immigration after the five-year period was finished. As a matter of principle, it shifted the basis for Jewish immigration from the older criterion of the economic absorptive capacity of Palestine to the political absorptive capacity. This was really an invitation to the Arabs to intensify their agitation and constituted a vital blow at the Jews, since it was generally conceded that Jewish immigration increased the economic absorptive capacity for both Jews and Arabs.

The Milner Group were divided on this concrete policy. In general, they continued to believe that the proper solution to the Zionist problem could be found in a partitioned Palestine within a federation of Arab states. *The Round Table* offered this as its program in March 1939 and repeated it in June of the same year. But on the issue of an immediate and concrete policy, the Group was split. It is highly unlikely that this split originated with the issue of Zionism. It was, rather, a reflection of the more fundamental split within the Group, between those, like Amery and Salter, who abandoned the appeasement policy in March 1939 and those, like the Astors and Lothian, who continued to pursue it in a modified form.

The change in the policy of the government resulted in a full debate in the House of Commons. This debate, and the resulting division, revealed the split within the Milner Group. The policy of the White Paper was denounced by Amery as a betrayal of the Jews and of the mandate, as the final step in a scaling down of Jewish hopes that began in 1922, as a yielding of principle to Arab terrorists, as invalid without the approval of the League of Nations, and as unworkable because the Jews would and could resist it. The speeches for the government from Malcolm MacDonald and R. A. Butler were weak and vague. In the division, the government won approval of the White Paper by 268 to 179, with Major Astor, Nancy Astor, Hoare, Simon, Malcolm MacDonald, and Sir Donald Somervell in the majority and Amery, Noel-Baker, and Arthur Salter in the minority. On the same day, a similar motion in the House of Lords was approved without a division.

The government at once began to put the White Paper policy into effect, without waiting for the approval of the Permanent Mandates Commission. In July 1939 rumors began to circulate that this body had disapproved of the policy, and questions were asked in the House of Commons, but MacDonald evaded the issue, refused to give information which he possessed, and announced that the government would take the issue to the Council of the League. As the Council meeting was canceled by the outbreak of war, this could not be done, but within a week of the announcement the minutes of the Permanent Mandates Commission were released. They showed that the commission had, by unanimous vote, decided that the policy of the White Paper was contrary to the accepted interpretations of the mandate, and, by a vote of 4-3, that the White Paper was inconsistent with the mandate under any possible interpretation. In this last vote Hankey, at his first session of the commission, voted in the minority.

As a result of the release of this information, a considerable section of the House was disturbed by the government's high-handed actions and by the Colonial Secretary's evasive answers in July 1939. In March 1940, Noel-Baker introduced a motion of censure on this issue. The motion did not go to a division, but Amery once again objected to the new policy and to inviting representatives of the Arab states to the abortive Round Table Conference of 1939. He called the presence of agents of the Mufti at the Round Table "surrender."

By this time the Milner Group was badly shattered on other issues than Palestine. Within two months of this debate, it was reunited on the issue of all-out war against Germany, and Amery had resumed a seat in the Cabinet as Secretary of State for India. The Palestine issue declined in importance and did not revive to any extent until the Labour government of 1945 had taken office. From that time on the members of the Milner Group were united again on the issue, objecting to the Labour government's anti-Jewish policy and generally following the line Amery had laid down in 1939. In fact, it was Amery who did much of the talking in 1946-1949, but this is not strictly part of our story.

In Irish affairs, the Milner Group played a much more decisive role than in Palestine affairs, although only for the brief period from 1917 to 1925. Previous to 1917 and going back to 1887, Irish affairs had been one of the most immediate concerns of the Cecil Bloc. A nephew of Lord Salisbury was Chief Secretary for Ireland in 1887-1891, another nephew held the post in 1895-1900, and the private secretary and protege of the former held the post in 1900-1905. The Cecil Bloc had always been opposed to Home Rule for Ireland, and when, in 1912-1914, the Liberal government took steps to grant Home Rule, Sir Edward Carson took the lead in opposing these steps. Carson was a creation of the Cecil Bloc, a fact admitted by Balfour in 1929, when he told his niece, "I made Carson." Balfour found Carson a simple Dublin barrister in 1887, when he went to Ireland as Chief Secretary. He made Carson one of his chief prosecuting attorneys in 1887, an M.P. for Dublin University in 1892, and Solicitor General in his own government in 1900-1906. When the Home Rule Bill of 1914 was about to pass, Carson organized a private army, known as the Ulster Volunteers, armed them with guns smuggled in from Germany, and formed a plot to seize control of Belfast at a given signal from him. This signal, in the form of a code telegram, was written in 1914 and on its way to be dispatched by Carson when he received word from Asquith that war with Germany was inevitable. Accordingly, the revolt was canceled and the date on which the Home Rule Bill was to go into effect was postponed by special act of Parliament until six months after peace should be signed.

The information about the telegram of 1914 was revealed to Lionel Curtis by Carson in a personal conversation after war began. Curtis's attitude was quite different, and he thoroughly disapproved of Carson's plot. This difference is an indication of the difference in point of view in regard to Ireland between the Milner Group and the Cecil Bloc. The latter was willing to oppose Home Rule even to the point where it would condone illegal actions; the former, on the contrary, was in favor of Home Rule because it believed that Ireland would aid Britain's enemies in every crisis and leave the Commonwealth at the first opportunity unless it were given freedom to govern itself.

The Milner Group's attitude toward the Irish question was expressed by *The Round Table* in a retrospective article in the September 1935 issue in the following words:

> The root principle of *The Round Table* remained freedom — "the govern-ment of men by themselves" — and it demanded that within the Empire this principle should be persistently pursued and expressed in institutions. For that reason it denounced the post-war attempt to repress the Irish demand for national self-government by ruthless violence after a century of union had failed to win Irish consent, as a policy in conflict with British institutions and inconsistent with the principle of the British Commonwealth; and it played its part in achieving the Irish Treaty and the Dominion settlement.

The part which the Group played in the Irish settlement was con-siderably more than this brief passage might indicate, but it could not take effect until the group in Britain advocating repression and the group in Ireland advocating separation from the crown had brought each other to some realization of the advantages of compromise.

These advantages were pointed out by the Group, especially by Lionel Curtis, who began a two-year term as editor of *The Round Table* immediately after his great triumph in the Government of India Act of 1919. In the March 1920 issue, for example, he discussed and ap-proved a project, first announced by Lloyd George in December 1919, to separate northern and southern Ireland and give self-government to both as autonomous parts of Great Britain. This was really nothing but an application of the principle of devolution, whose attractiveness to the Milner Group has already been mentioned.

The Irish Settlement in the period 1920-1923 is very largely a Milner Group achievement. For most of this period Amery's brother-in-law, Hamar Greenwood (Viscount Greenwood since 1937), was Chief Secretary for Ireland. He was, indeed, the last person to hold this office before it was abolished at the end of 1922. Curtis was adviser on Irish affairs to the Colonial Office in 1921-1924, and Smuts and Feetham intervened in the affair at certain points.

A settlement of the Irish problem along lines similar to those advocated by *The Round Table* was enacted in the Government of Ireland Act of December 1920. Drafted by H. A. L. Fisher and piloted through Commons by him, it passed the critical second reading by a vote of 348-94. In the majority were Amery, Nancy Astor, Austen Chamberlain, H. A. L. Fisher, Hamar Greenwood, Samuel Hoare, G. R. Lane-Fox (brother-in-law of Lord Halifax), and E. F. L. Wood (Lord Halifax). In the minority were Lord Robert Cecil and Lord Wolmer (son of Lord Selborne). In the House of Lords the bill passed by 164-75. In the majority were Lords Curzon, Lytton, Onslow (brother-in-law of Lord Halifax), Goschen, Hampden (brother of Robert Brand), Hardinge, Milner, Desborough, Ernle, Meston, Monson, Phillimore, Riddell, and Wemyss. In the minority were Lords Linlithgow, Beauchamp (father-in-law of Samuel Hoare), Midleton, Bryce, Ampthill (brother-in-law of Samuel Hoare), and Leconfield (brother of Hugh Wyndham).

The act of 1920 never went into effect because the extremists on both sides were not yet satiated with blood. By June 1921 they were. The first movement in this direction, according to W. K. Hancock, "may be said to open as early as October 1920 when *The Times* published suggestions for a truce and negotiations between plenipotentiaries of both sides." The same authority lists ten voices as being raised in protest at British methods of repression. Three of these were of the Milner Group (*The Times, The Round Table*, and Sir John Simon). He quotes *The Round Table* as saying: "If the British Commonwealth can only be preserved by such means, it would become a negation of the principle for which it has stood."[6] Similar arguments were brought to bear on the Irish leaders by Jan Smuts.

Smuts left South Africa for England at the end of May 1921, to attend the Imperial Conference of that year, which was to open on a Monday. He arrived in England the preceding Saturday and went to Oxford to stay with friends of the Milner Group. In the evening he attended a Rhodes dinner, which means he saw more of the Group. The following day, he was called by the King to Windsor Castle and went immediately. The King told Smuts that he was going to make a speech at the opening of the new Ulster Parliament. He asked Smuts to write down suggestions for this speech. Smuts stayed the night at Windsor

Castle, drafted a speech, and gave it to the King's private secretary. The sequel can best be told in Smuts's own words as recorded in the second volume of S. G. Millin's biography: "The next day Lloyd George invited me to attend a committee meeting of the Cabinet, to give my opinion of the King's speech. And what should this King's speech turn out to be but a typewritten copy of the draft I had myself written the night before. I found them working on it. Nothing was said about my being the author. They innocently consulted me and I innocently answered them. But imagine the interesting position. Well, they toned the thing down a bit, they made a few minor alterations, but in substance the speech the King delivered next week in Belfast was the one I prepared."[7] Needless to say, this speech was conciliatory.

Shortly afterward, Tom Casement, brother of Sir Roger Casement, who had been executed by the British in 1916, opened negotiations between Smuts and the Irish leaders in Dublin. Tom Casement was an old friend of Smuts, for he had been British Consul at Delagoa Bay in 1914 and served with Smuts in East Africa in 1916-1917. As a result, Smuts went to Ireland in June 1921 under an alias and was taken to the hiding place of the rebels. He tried to persuade them that they would be much better off with Dominion status within the British Commonwealth than as a republic, offering as an example the insecure position of the Transvaal before 1895 in contrast with its happy condition after 1909. He said in conclusion, "Make no mistake about it, you have more privilege, more power, more peace, more security in such a sisterhood of equal nations than in a small, nervous republic having all the time to rely on goodwill, and perhaps the assistance, of foreigners. What sort of independence do you call that? By comparison with real independence it is a shadow. You sell the fact for the name." Smuts felt that his argument was having an effect on Arthur Griffith and some others, but de Valera remained suspicious, and Erskine Childers was "positively hostile." Nevertheless, the Irish decided to open negotiations with London, and Smuts promised to arrange an armistice. The armistice went into effect on 11 July 1921, and three days later the conference began.

The Irish Conference of 1921 was held in two sessions: a week in July and a series of meetings from 11 October to 6 December 1921. The secretary to the conference was Lionel Curtis, who resigned his editorship of *The Round Table* for the purpose and remained as chief adviser on Irish affairs to the Colonial Office for the next three years. As a result of the conference, the Irish moderates negotiated the Articles of Agreement of 6 December 1921. De Valera had refused to form part of the Irish delegation at the second session of the conference, and refused to accept Dominion status, although Smuts begged him to do so in a letter published in *The Times* on 15 August.

As a result of the Articles of Agreement of December 1921 and the Irish Free State Act of March 1922, Southern Ireland became an independent Dominion within the British Commonwealth. Its boundary with Northern Ireland was to be settled by a Boundary Commission of three members representing the three interested parties. On this commission, Richard Feetham of the Milner Group was the British member and also chairman.

The subsequent revolt of de Valera and the Irish Republicans against the Free State government, and the ultimate victory of their ideas, is not part of our story. It was a development which the Milner Group were powerless to prevent. They continued to believe that the Irish, like others, could be bound to Britain by invisible ties if all visible ones were destroyed. This extraordinary belief, admirable as it was, had its basis in a profoundly Christian outlook and, like appeasement of Hitler, self-government for India, or the Statute of Westminister, had its ultimate roots in the Sermon on the Mount. Unfortunately, such Christian tactics were acutely dangerous in a non-Christian world, and in this respect the Irish were only moderately different from Hitler.

The Milner Group's reward for their concessions to Ireland was not to be obtained in this world. This became clear during the Second World War, when the inability of the British to use Irish naval bases against German submarines had fatal consequences for many gallant British seamen. These bases had been retained for Britain as a result of the agreement of 1922 but were surrendered to the Irish on 25 April 1938, just when Hitler's threat to Britain was becoming acute. *The Round Table* of June 1938 welcomed this surrender, saying: "The defence of the Irish coast, as John Redmond vainly urged in 1914, should be primarily a matter for Irishmen."

As the official links between Eire and Britain were slowly severed, the Group made every effort to continue unofficial relationships such as those through the Irish Institute of International Affairs and the unofficial British Commonwealth relations conference, which had Irish members in 1938.

The relationships of Britain with Egypt were also affected by the activity of the Milner Group. The details need not detain us long. It is sufficient to state that the Egyptian Declaration of 1922 was the result of the personal negotiations of Lord Milner in Egypt in his capacity as Colonial Secretary. In this post his Permanent Under Secretary was Sir George Fiddes of the Kindergarten, his Parliamentary Under Secretary was Amery, and his chief adviser in Egypt was M. S. O. Walrond, also of the Kindergarten.

Without going into the very extensive influence which members of the Milner Group have had on other parts of the Commonwealth (especially tropical Africa), it must be clear that, however unsatisfactory Commonwealth relations may be to the Group now, they nevertheless were among the chief creators of the existing system. This will appear even more clearly when we examine their influence in the history of India.

10

The Royal Institute of
International Affairs

THE ROYAL INSTITUTE OF INTERNATIONAL AFFAIRS (RIIA) is nothing but the Milner Group "writ large." It was founded by the Group, has been consistently controlled by the Group, and to this day is the Milner Group in its widest aspect. It is the legitimate child of the Round Table organization, just as the latter was the legitimate child of the "Closer Union" movement organized in South Africa in 1907. All three of these organizations were formed by the same small group of persons, all three received their initial financial backing from Sir Abe Bailey, and all three used the same methods for working out and propagating their ideas (the so-called Round Table method of discussion groups plus a journal). This similarity is not an accident. The new organization was intended to be a wider aspect of the Milner Group, the plan being to influence the leaders of thought through *The Round Table* and to influence a wider group through the RIIA.

The real founder of the Institute was Lionel Curtis, although this fact was concealed for many years and he was presented to the public as merely one among a number of founders. In more recent years, however, the fact that Curtis was the real founder of the Institute has been publicly stated by members of the Institute and by the Institute itself on many occasions, and never denied. One example will suffice. In the *Annual Report* of the Institute for 1942-1943 we read the following sentence: "When the Institute was founded through the inspiration of Mr. Lionel Curtis during the Peace Conference of Paris in 1919, those associated with him in laying the foundations were a group of comparatively young men and women."

The Institute was organized at a joint conference of British and American experts at the Hotel Majestic on 30 May 1919. At the suggestion of Lord Robert Cecil, the chair was given to General Tasker Bliss of the American delegation. We have already indicated that the experts of the British delegation at the Peace Conference were almost exclusively from the Milner Group and Cecil Bloc. The American

182

group of experts, "the Inquiry," was manned almost as completely by persons from institutions (including universities) dominated by J. P. Morgan and Company. This was not an accident. Moreover, the Milner Group has always had very close relationships with the associates of J. P. Morgan and with the various branches of the Carnegie Trust. These relationships, which are merely examples of the closely knit ramifications of international financial capitalism, were probably based on the financial holdings controlled by the Milner Group through the Rhodes Trust. The term "international financier" can be applied with full justice to several members of the Milner Group inner circle, such as Brand, Hichens, and above all, Milner himself.

At the meeting at the Hotel Majestic, the British group included Lionel Curtis, Philip Kerr, Lord Robert Cecil, Lord Eustace Percy, Sir Eyre Crowe, Sir Cecil Hurst, J. W. Headlam-Morley, Geoffrey Dawson, Harold Temperley, and G. M. Gathorne-Hardy. It was decided to found a permanent organization for the study of international affairs and to begin by writing a history of the Peace Conference. A committee was set up to supervise the writing of this work. It had Lord Meston as chairman, Lionel Curtis as secretary, and was financed by a gift of £2000 from Thomas W. Lamont of J. P. Morgan and Company. This group picked Harold Temperley as editor of the work. It appeared in six large volumes in the years 1920-1924, under the auspices of the RIIA.

The British organization was set up by a committee of which Lord Robert Cecil was chairman, Lionel Curtis was honorary secretary and the following were members: Lord Eustace Percy, J. A. C. (later Sir John) Tilley, Philip Noel-Baker, Clement Jones, Harold Temperley, A. L. Smith (classmate of Milner and Master of Balliol), George W. Prothero, and Geoffrey Dawson. This group drew up a constitution and made a list of prospective members. Lionel Curtis and Gathorne-Hardy drew up the by-laws.

The above description is based on the official history of the RIIA published by the Institute itself in 1937 and written by Stephen King-Hall. It does not agree in its details (committees and names) with information from other sources, equally authoritative, such as the journal of the Institute or the preface to Temperley's *History of the Peace Conference*. The latter, for example, says that the members were chosen by a committee consisting of Lord Robert Cecil, Sir Valentine Chirol, and Sir Cecil Hurst. As a matter of fact, all of these differing accounts are correct, for the Institute was formed in such an informal fashion, as among friends, that membership on committees and lines of authority between committees were not very important. As an example, Mr. King-Hall says that he was invited to join the Institute in 1919 by Philip Kerr (Lord Lothian), although this name is not to be found on any membership committee. At any rate, one thing is clear: The Institute was formed by the Cecil Bloc and the Milner Group, acting together, and the real decisions were being made by members of the latter.

As organized, the Institute consisted of a council with a chairman and two honorary secretaries, and a small group of paid employees. Among these latter, A. J. Toynbee, nephew of Milner's old friend at Balliol, was the most important. There were about 300 members in 1920, 714 in 1922, 1707 in 1929, and 2414 in 1936. There have been three chairmen of the council: Lord Meston in 1920-1926, Major-General Sir Neill Malcolm in 1926-1935, and Lord Astor from 1935 to the present. All of these are members of the Milner Group, although General Malcolm is not yet familiar to us.

General Malcolm, from Eton and Sandhurst, married the sister of Dougal Malcolm of Milner's Kindergarten in 1907, when he was a captain in the British Army. By 1916 he was a lieutenant colonel and two years later a major general. He was with the British Military Mission in Berlin in 1919-1921 and General Officer Commanding in Malaya in 1921-1924, retiring in 1924. He was High Commissioner for German Refugees (a project in which the Milner Group was deeply involved) in 1936-1938 and has been associated with a number of industrial and commercial firms, including the British North Borneo Company, of which he is president and Dougal Malcolm is vice-president. It must not be assumed that General Malcolm won advancement in the world because of his connections with the Milner Group, for his older brother, Sir Ian Malcolm was an important member of the Cecil Bloc long before Sir Neill joined the Milner Group. Sir Ian, who went to Eton and New College, was assistant private secretary to Lord Salisbury in 1895-1900, was parliamentary private secretary to the Chief Secretary for Ireland (George Wyndham) in 1901-1903, and was private secretary to Balfour in the United States in 1917 and at the Peace Conference in 1919. He wrote the sketch of Walter Long of the Cecil Bloc (Lord Long of Wraxall) in the *Dictionary of National Biography*.

From the beginning, the two honorary secretaries of the Institute were Lionel Curtis and G. M. Gathorne-Hardy. These two, especially the latter, did much of the active work of running the organization. In 1926 the *Report of the Council* of the RIIA said: "It is not too much to say that the very existence of the Institute is due to those who have served as Honorary Officers." The burden of work was so great on Curtis and Gathorne-Hardy by 1926 that Sir Otto Beit, of the Rhodes Trust, Milner Group, and British South Africa Company, gave £1000 for 1926 and 1927 for secretarial assistance. F. B. Bourdillon assumed the task of providing this assistance in March 1926. He had been secretary to Feetham on the Irish Boundary Commission in 1924-1925 and a member of the British delegation to the Peace Conference in 1919. He has been in the Research Department of the Foreign Office since 1943.

The active governing body of the Institute is the council, originally called the executive committee. Under the more recent name, it generally had twenty-five to thirty members, of whom slightly less than half were usually of the Milner Group. In 1923, five members were elected, including Lord Meston, Headlam-Morley, and Mrs. Alfred Lyttelton. The following year, seven were elected, including Wilson Harris, Philip Kerr, and Sir Neill Malcolm. And so it went. In 1936, at least eleven out of twenty-six members of the council were of the Milner Group. These included Lord Astor (chairman), L. Curtis, G. M. Gathorne-Hardy, Lord Hailey, H. D. Henderson, Stephen King-Hall, Mrs. Alfred Lyttelton, Sir Neill Malcolm, Lord Meston, Sir Arthur Salter, J. W. Wheeler-Bennett, E. L. Woodward, and Sir Alfred Zimmern. Among the others were A. V. Alexander, Sir John Power, Sir Norman Angell, Clement Jones, Lord Lytton, Harold Nicolson, Lord Snell, and C. K. Webster. Others who were on the council at various times were E. H. Carr, Harold Butler, G. N. Clark, Geoffrey Crowther, H. V. Hodson, Hugh Wyndham, G. W. A. Ormsley-Gore, Walter Layton, Austen Chamberlain, Malcolm MacDonald (elected 1933), and many other members of the Group.

The chief activities of the RIIA were the holding of discussion meetings, the organization of study groups, the sponsoring of research, and the publication of information and materials based on these. At the first meeting, Sir Maurice Hankey read a paper on "Diplomacy by Conference," showing how the League of Nations grew out of the Imperial Conferences. This was published in *The Round Table.* No complete record exists of the meetings before the fall of 1921, but, beginning then, the principal speech at each meeting and résumés of the comments from the floor were published in the *Journal.* At the first of these recorded meetings, D. G. Hogarth spoke on "The Arab States," with Lord Chelmsford in the chair. Stanley Reed, Chirol, and Meston spoke from the floor. Two weeks later, H. A. L. Fisher spoke on "The Second Assembly of the League of Nations," with Lord Robert Cecil in the chair. Temperley and Wilson Harris also spoke. In November, Philip Kerr was the chief figure for two evenings on "Pacific Problems as They Would Be submitted to the Washington Conference." At the end of the same month, A. J. Toynbee spoke on "The Greco-Turkish Question," with Sir Arthur Evans in the chair, and early in December his father-in-law, Gilbert Murray, spoke on "Self-Determination," with Lord Sumner in the chair. In January 1922, Chaim Weizmann spoke on "Zionism"; in February, Chirol spoke on "Egypt"; in April,

Walter T. Layton spoke on "The Financial Achievement of the League of Nations," with Lord Robert Cecil in the chair. In June, Wilson Harris spoke on "The Genoa Conference," with Robert H. Brand in the chair. In October, Ormsby-Gore spoke on "Mandates," with Lord Lugard in the chair. Two weeks later, Sir Arthur Steel-Maitland spoke on "The League of Nations," with H. A. L. Fisher in the chair. In March 1923, Harold Butler spoke on the "International Labour Office," with G. N. Barnes in the chair. Two weeks later, Philip Kerr spoke on "The Political Situation in the United States," with Arthur Balfour in the chair. In October 1923, Edward F. L. Wood (Lord Halifax) spoke on "The League of Nations," with H. A. L. Fisher in the chair. In November 1924, E. R. Peacock (Parkin's protege) spoke on "Mexico," with Lord Eustace Percy in the chair. In October 1925, Leopold Amery spoke on "The League of Nations," with Robert Cecil as chairman, while in May 1926, H. A. L. Fisher spoke on the same subject, with Neill Malcolm as chairman. In November 1925, Paul Mantoux spoke on "The Procedure of the League," with Brand as chairman. In June 1923, Edward Grigg spoke on "Egypt," with D. G. Hogarth in the chair. In the season of 1933-1934 the speakers included Ormsby-Gore, Oliver Lyttelton, Edward Grigg, Donald Somervell, Toynbee, Zimmern, R. W. Seton-Watson, and Lord Lothian. In the season of 1938-1939 the list contains the names of Wilson Harris, C. A. Macartney, Toynbee, Lord Hailey, A. G. B. Fisher, Harold Butler, Curtis, Lord Lothian, Zimmern, Lionel Hichens, and Lord Halifax. These rather scattered observations will show how the meetings were peppered by members of the Milner Group. This does not mean that the Group monopolized the meetings, or even spoke at a majority of them. The meetings generally took place once a week from October to June of each year, and probably members of the Group spoke or presided at no more than a quarter of them. This, however, represents far more than their due proportion, for when the Institute had 2500, members the Milner Group amounted to no more than 100.

The proceedings of the meetings were generally printed in abbreviated form in the *Journal* of the Institute. Until January 1927, this periodical was available only to members, but since that date it has been open to public subscription. The first issue was as anonymous as the first issue of *The Round Table:* no list of editors, no address, and no signature to the opening editorial introducing the new journal. The articles, however, had the names of the speakers indicated. When it went on public sale in January 1927, the name of the Institute was added to the cover. In time it took the name *International Affairs*. The first editor, we learn from a later issue, was Gathorne-Hardy. In January 1932 an editorial board was placed in charge of the publication. It consisted of Meston, Gathorne-Hardy, and Zimmern. This same board remained in control until war forced suspension of publication at the end of 1939. When publication was resumed in 1944 in Canada, the editorial board consisted of Hugh Wyndham, Geoffrey Crowther, and H. A. R. Gibb. Wyndham is still chairman of the board, but since the war the membership of the board has changed somewhat. In 1948 it had six members, of whom three are employees of the Institute, one is the son-in-law of an employee, the fifth is Professor of Arabic at Oxford, and the last is the chairman, Hugh Wyndham. In 1949 Adam Marris was added.

In addition to the *History of the Peace Conference* and the journal *International Affairs*, the Institute publishes the annual *Survey of International Affairs*. This is written either by members of the Group or by employees of the Institute. The chief writers have been Toynbee; his second wife, V. M. Boulter; Robert J. Stopford, who appears to be one of R. H. Brand's men and who wrote the reparations section each year;[1] H. V. Hodson, who did the economic sections from 1930-1938; and A. G. B. Fisher, who has done the economic sections since Hodson. Until 1928 the *Survey* had an appendix of documents, but since that year these have been published in a separate volume, usually edited by J. W. Wheeler-Bennett. Mr. Wheeler-Bennett became a member of the Milner Group and the Institute by a process of amalgamation. In 1924 he had founded a document service, which he called Information Service on International Affairs, and in the years following 1924 he published a number of valuable digests of documents and other information on disarmament, security, the World Court, reparations, etc., as well as a periodical called the *Bulletin of International News*. In 1927 he became Honorary Information Secretary of the RIIA, and in 1930 the Institute bought out all his information services for £3500 and made them into the Information Department of the Institute, still in charge of Mr. Wheeler-Bennett. Since the annual *Documents on International Affairs* resumed publication in 1944, it has been in charge of Monica Curtis (who may be related to Lionel Curtis), while Mr. Wheeler-Bennett has been busy elsewhere. In 1938-1939 he was Visiting Professor of International Relations at the University of Virginia: in 1939-1944 he was in the United States in various propaganda positions with the British Library of Information and for two years as Head of the British Political Warfare Mission in New York. Since 1946, he has been engaged in editing, from the British side, an edition of about twenty volumes of the captured documents of the German Foreign Ministry. He has also lectured on international affairs at New College, a connection obviously made through the Milner Group.

The *Survey of International Affairs* has been financed since 1925 by an endowment of £20,000 given by Sir Daniel Stevenson for this purpose and also to provide a Research Chair of International History at the University of London. Arnold J. Toynbee has held both the professorship and the editorship since their establishment. He has also been remunerated by other grants from the Institute. When the first major volume of the *Survey,* covering the years 1920-1923, was published, a round-table discussion was held at Chatham House, 17 November 1925, to criticize it. Headlam-Morley was chairman, and the chief speakers were Curtis, Wyndham, Gathorne-Hardy, Gilbert Murray, and Toynbee himself.

Since the *Survey* did not cover British Commonwealth affairs, except in a general fashion, a project was established for a parallel *Survey of British Commonwealth Relations.* This was financed by a grant of money from the Carnegie Corporation of New York. The task was entrusted to W. K. Hancock, a member of All Souls since 1924 and Chichele Professor of Economic History residing at All Souls since 1944. He produced three substantial volumes of the *Survey* in 1940-1942, with a supplementary legal chapter in volume I by R. T. E. Latham of All Souls and the Milner Group.

The establishment of the Stevenson Chair of International History at London, controlled by the RIIA, gave the Group the idea of establishing similar endowed chairs in other subjects and in other places. In 1936, Sir Henry Price gave £20,000 to endow for seven years a Chair of International Economics at Chatham House. This was filled by Allan G. B. Fisher of Australia.

In 1947 another chair was established at Chatham House: the Abe Bailey Professorship of Commonwealth Relations. This was filled by Nicholas Mansergh, who had previously written a few articles on Irish affairs and has since published a small volume on Commonwealth affairs.

By the terms of the foundation, the Institute had a voice in the election of professors to the Wilson Chair of International Politics at the University College of Wales, Aberystwyth. As a result, this chair has been occupied by close associates of the Group from its foundation. The following list of incumbents is significant:

> A. E. Zimmern, 1919-1921
> C. K. Webster, 1922-1932
> J. D. Greene, 1932-1934
> J. F. Vranek, (Acting), 1934-1936
> E. H. Carr, 1936 to now

Three of these names are familiar. Of the others, Jiri Vranek was secretary to the International Institute of Intellectual Cooperation (to be discussed in a moment). Jerome Greene was an international banker close to the Milner Group. Originally Mr. Greene had been a close associate of J. D. Rockefeller, but in 1917 he shifted to the international banking firm Lee, Higginson, and Company of Boston. In 1918 he was American secretary to the Allied Maritime Transport Council in London (of which Arthur Salter was general secretary). He became a resident of Toynbee Hall and established a relationship with the Milner Group. In 1919 he was secretary to the Reparations Commission of the Peace Conference (a post in which his successor was Arthur Salter in 1920-1922). He was chairman of the Pacific Council of the Institute of Pacific Relations in 1929-1932. This last point will be discussed in a moment. Mr. Greene was a trustee and secretary of the Rockefeller Foundation in 1913-1917, and was a trustee of the Rockefeller Institute and of the Rockefeller General Education Board in 1912-1939.

The study groups of the RIIA are direct descendants of the round-table meetings of the Round Table Group. They have been defined by Stephen King-Hall as "unofficial Royal Commissions charged by the Council of Chatham House with the investigation of specific problems." These study groups are generally made up of persons who are not members of the Milner Group, and their reports are frequently published by the Institute. In 1932 the Rockefeller Foundation gave the Institute a grant of £8000 a year for five years to advance the study-group method of research. This was extended for five years more in 1937.

In 1923, Lionel Curtis got a Canadian, Colonel R. W. Leonard, so interested in the work of the Institute that he bought Lord Kinnaird's house at 10 St. James Square as a home for the Institute. Since William Pitt had once lived in the building, it was named "Chatham House," a designation which is now generally applied to the Institute itself. The only condition of the grant was that the Institute should raise an endowment to yield at least £10,000 a year for upkeep. Since the building had no adequate assembly hall, Sir John Power, the honorary treasurer, gave £10,000 to build one on the rear. The building itself was renovated and furnished under the care of Mrs. Alfred Lyttelton, who, like her late husband but unlike her son, Oliver, was a member of the Milner Group.

The assumption of the title to Chatham House brought up a major crisis within the Institute when a group led by Professor A. F. Pollard (Fellow of All Souls but not a member of the Milner Group) opposed the acceptance of the gift because of the financial commitment involved. Curtis put on an organized drive to mobilize the Group and put the opposition to flight. The episode is mentioned in a letter from John Dove to Brand, dated 9 October 1923.

This episode opens up the whole question of the financial resources available to the Institute and to the Milner Group in general. Unfortunately, we cannot examine the subject here, but it should be obvious that a group with such connections as the Milner Group would not find it difficult to finance the RIIA. In general, the funds came from the various endowments, banks, and industrial concerns with which the Milner Group had relationships. The original money in 1919, only £200, came from Abe Bailey. In later years he added to this, and in 1928 gave £5000 a year in perpetuity on the condition that the Institute never accept members who were not British subjects. When Sir Abe died in 1940, the annual *Report of the Council* said: "With the passing of Sir Bailey the Council and all the members of Chatham House mourn the loss of their most munificent Founder." Sir Abe had paid various other expenses during the years. For example, when the Institute in November 1935 gave a dinner to General Smuts, Sir Abe paid the cost. All of this was done as a disciple of Lord Milner, for whose principles of imperial policy Bailey always had complete devotion.

Among the other benefactors of the Institute, we might mention the following. In 1926 the Carnegie United Kingdom Trustees (Hichens and Dame Janet Courtney) gave £3000 for books; the Bank of England gave £600; J. D. Rockefeller gave £3000. In 1929 pledges were obtained from about a score of important banks and corporations, promising annual grants to the Institute. Most of these had one or more members of the Milner Group on their boards of directors. Included in the group were the Anglo-Iranian Oil Company; the Bank of England; Barclay's Bank; Baring Brothers; the British American Tobacco Company; the British South Africa Company; Central Mining and Investment Corporation; Erlangers, Ltd; the Ford Motor Company; Hambros' Bank; Imperial Chemical Industries; Lazard Brothers; Lever Brothers; Lloyd's; Lloyd's Bank; the Mercantile and General Insurance Company; the Midland Bank; Reuters; Rothschild and Sons; Stern Brothers; Vickers-Armstrong; the Westminster Bank; and Whitehall Securities Corporation.

Since 1939 the chief benefactors of the Institute have been the Astor family and Sir Henry Price. In 1942 the latter gave £50,000 to buy the house next door to Chatham House for an expansion of the library (of which E. L. Woodward was supervisor). In the same year Lord Astor, who had been giving £2000 a year since 1937, promised £3000 a year for seven years to form a Lord Lothian Memorial Fund to promote good relations between the United States and Britain. At the same time, each of Lord Astor's four sons promised £1000 a year for seven years to the general fund of the Institute.

Chatham House had close institutional relations with a number of other similar organizations, especially in the Dominions. It also has a parallel organization, which was regarded as a branch, in New York. This latter, the Council on Foreign Relations, was not founded by the American group that attended the meeting at the Hotel Majestic in

1919, but was taken over almost entirely by that group immediately after its founding in 1919. This group was made up of the experts on the American delegation to the Peace Conference who were most closely associated with J. P. Morgan and Company. The Morgan bank has never made any real effort to conceal its position in regard to the Council on Foreign Relations. The list of officers and board of directors are printed in every issue of *Foreign Affairs* and have always been loaded with partners, associates, and employees of J. P. Morgan and Company. According to Stephen King-Hall, the RIIA agreed to regard the Council on Foreign Relations as its American branch. The relationship between the two has always been very close. For example, the publications of one are available at reduced prices to the members of the other; they frequently sent gifts of books to each other (the Council, for example, giving the Institute a seventy-five-volume set of the *Foreign Relations of the United States* in 1933); and there is considerable personal contact between the officers of the two (Toynbee, for example, left the manuscript of Volumes 7-9 of *A Study of History* in the Council's vault during the recent war).

Chatham House established branch institutes in the various Dominions, but it was a slow process. In each case the Dominion Institute was formed about a core consisting of the Round Table Group's members in that Dominion. The earliest were set up in Canada and Australia in 1927. The problem was discussed in 1933 at the first unofficial British Commonwealth relations conference (Toronto), and the decision made to extend the system to New Zealand, South Africa, India, and Newfoundland. The last-named was established by Zimmern on a visit there the same year. The others were set up in 1934-1936.

As we have said, the members of the Dominion Institutes of International Affairs were the members of the Milner Group and their close associates. In Canada, for example, Robert L. Borden was the first president (1927-1931); N. W. Rowell was the second president; Sir Joseph Flavelle and Vincent Massey were vice-presidents; Glazebrook was honorary secretary; and Percy Corbett was one of the most important members. Of these, the first three were close associates of the Milner Group (especially of Brand) in the period of the First World War; the last four were members of the Group itself. When the Indian Institute was set up in 1936, it was done at the Viceroy's house at a meeting convened by Lord Willingdon (Brand's cousin). Robert Cecil sent a message, which was read by Stephen King-Hall. Sir Maurice Gwyer of All Souls became a member of the council. In South Africa, B. K. Long of the Kindergarten was one of the most important members. In the Australian Institute, Sir Thomas Bavin was president in 1934-1941, while F. W. Eggleston was one of its principal founders and vice-president for many years. In New Zealand, W. Downie Stewart was president of the Institute of International Affairs from 1935 on. Naturally, the Milner Group did not monopolize the membership or the official positions in these new institutes any more than they did in London, for this would have weakened the chief aim of the Group in setting them up, namely to extend their influence to wider areas.

Closely associated with the various Institutes of International Affairs were the various branches of the Institute of Pacific Relations. This was originally founded at Atlantic City in September 1924 as a private organization to study the problems of the Pacific Basin. It has representatives from eight countries with interests in the area. The representatives from the United Kingdom and the three British Dominions were closely associated with the Milner Group. Originally each country had its national unit, but by 1939, in the four British areas, the local Institute of Pacific Relations had merged with the local Institute of International Affairs. Even before this, the two Institutes in each country had practically interchangeable officers, dominated by the Milner Group. In the United States, the Institute of Pacific Relations never merged with the Council on Foreign Relations, but the influence of the associates of J. P. Morgan and other international bankers remained strong on both. The chief figure in the Institute of Pacific Relations of the United States was, for many years, Jerome D. Greene, Boston banker close to both Rockefeller and Morgan and for many years secretary to Harvard University.

The Institutes of Pacific Relations held joint meetings, similar to those of the unofficial conferences on British Commonwealth relations and with a similar group of delegates from the British member organizations. These meetings met every two years at first, beginning at Honolulu in 1925 and then assembling at Honolulu again (1927), at Kyoto (1929), at Shanghai (1931), at Banff (1933), and at Yosemite Park (1936). F. W. Eggleston, of Australia and the Milner Group, presided over most of the early meetings. Between meetings, the central organization, set up in 1927, was the Pacific Council, a self-perpetuating body. In 1930, at least five of its seven members were from the Milner Group, as can be seen from the following list:

THE PACIFIC COUNCIL, 1930
Jerome D. Greene of the United States
F. W. Eggleston of Australia
N. W. Rowell of Canada
D. Z. T. Yui of China
Lionel Curtis of the United Kingdom
I. Nitobe of Japan
Sir James Allen of New Zealand

The close relationships among all these organizations can be seen from a tour of inspection which Lionel Curtis and Ivison S. Macadam (secretary of Chatham House, in succession to F. B. Bourdillon, since 1929) made in 1938. They not only visited the Institutes of International Affairs of Australia, New Zealand, and Canada but attended the Princeton meeting of the Pacific Council of the IPR. Then they separated, Curtis going to New York to address the dinner of the Council on Foreign Relations and visit the Carnegie Foundation, while Macadam went to Washington to visit the Carnegie Endowment and the Brookings Institution.

Through the League of Nations, where the influence of the Milner Group was very great, the RIIA was able to extend its intellectual influence into countries outside the Commonwealth. This was done, for example, through the Intellectual Cooperation Organization of the League of Nations. This Organization consisted of two chief parts: (a) The International Committee on Intellectual Cooperation, an advisory body; and (b) The International Institute of Intellectual Cooperation, an executive organ of the Committee, with headquarters in Paris. The International Committee had about twenty members from various countries; Gilbert Murray was its chief founder and was chairman from 1928 to its disbandment in 1945. The International Institute was established by the French government and handed over to the League of Nations (1926). Its director was always a Frenchman, but its deputy director and guiding spirit was Alfred Zimmern from 1926 to 1930. It also had a board of directors of six persons; Gilbert Murray was one of these from 1926.

It is interesting to note that from 1931 to 1939 the Indian representative on the International Committee on Intellectual Cooperation was Sarvepalli Radhakrishnan. In 1931 he was George V Professor of Philospohy at Calcutta University. His subsequent career is interesting. He was knighted in 1931, became Spalding Professor of Eastern Religions and Ethics at Oxford in 1936, and became a Fellow of All Souls in 1944.

Beginning in 1928 at Berlin, Professor Zimmern organized annual round-table discussion meetings under the auspices of the International Institute of Intellectual Cooperation. These were called the International Studies Conferences and devoted themselves to an effort to obtain different national po nts of view on international problems. The members of the Studies Conferences were twenty-five organizations. Twenty of these were Coordinating Committees created for the purpose in twenty different countries. The other five were the following international organizations: The Academy of International Law at The Hague; The European Center of the Carnegie Endowment for International Peace; the Geneva School of International Studies; the Graduate Institute of International Studies at Geneva; the Institute of Pacific

Relations. In two of these five, the influence of the Milner Group and its close allies was preponderant. In addition, the influence of the Group was decisive in the Coordinating Committees within the British Commonwealth, especially in the British Coordinating Committee for International Studies. The members of this committee were named by four agencies, three of which were controlled by the Milner Group. They were: (1) the RIIA, (2) the London School of Economics and Political Science, (3) the Department of International Politics at University College of Wales, Aberystwyth, and (4) the Montague Burton Chair of International Relations at Oxford. We have already indicated that the Montague Burton Chair was largely controlled by the Milner Group, since the Group always had a preponderance on the board of electors to that chair. This was apparently not assured by the original structure of this board, and it was changed in the middle 1930s. After the change, the board had seven electors: (1) the Vice-Chancellor of Oxford, ex officio; (2) the Master of Balliol, ex officio; (3) Viscount Cecil of Chelwood; (4) Gilbert Murray, for life; (5) B. H. Sumner; (6) Sir Arthur Salter; and (7) Sir. J. Fischer Williams of New College. Thus, at least four of this board were members of the Group. In 1947 the electoral board to the Montague Burton Professorship consisted of R. M. Barrington-Ward (editor of *The Times*); Miss Agnes Headlam-Morley (daughter of Sir James Headlam-Morley of the Group); Sir Arthur Salter; R. C. K. Ensor; and one vacancy, to be filled by Balliol College. It was this board, apparently, that named Miss Headlam-Morley to the Montague Burton Professorship when E. L. Woodward resigned in 1947. As can be seen, the Milner Group influence was predominant, with only one member out of five (Ensor) clearly not of the Group.

The RIIA had the right to name three persons to the Coordinating Committee. Two of these were usually of the Milner Group. In 1933, for example, the three were Lord Meston, Clement Jones, and Toynbee.

The meetings of the International Studies Conferences were organized in a fashion identical with that used in other meetings controlled by the Milner Group — for example, in the unofficial conferences on British Commonwealth relations — and the proceedings were published by the Institute of Intellectual Cooperation in a similar way to those of the unofficial conferences just mentioned, except that the various speakers were identified by name. As examples of the work which the International Studies Conferences handled, we might mention that at the fourth and fifth sessions (Copenhagen in 1931 and Milan in 1932), they examined the problem of "The State and Economic Life"; at the seventh and eighth session (Paris in 1934 and London in 1935), they examined the problem of "Collective Security"; and at the ninth and tenth sessions (Madrid in 1936 and Paris 1937) they examined the problem of "University Teaching of International Relations."

In all of these conferences the Milner Group played a certain part. They could have monopolized the British delegations at these meetings if they had wished, but, with typical Milner Group modesty they made no effort to do so. Their influence appeared most clearly at the London meeting of 1935. Thirty-nine delegates from fourteen countries assembled at Chatham House to discuss the problem of collective security. Great Britain had ten delegates. They were Dr. Hugh Dalton, Professor H. Lauterpacht, Captain Liddell Hart, Lord Lytton, Professor A. D. McNair, Professor C. A. W. Manning, Dr. David Mitrany, Rear Admiral H. G. Thursfield, Arnold J. Toynbee, and Professor C. K. Webster. In addition, the Geneva School of International Studies sent two delegates: J. H. Richardson and A. E. Zimmern. The British delegation presented three memoranda to the conference. The first, a study of "Sanctions," was prepared by the RIIA and has been published since. The second, a study of "British Opinion on Collective Security," was prepared by the British Coordinating Committee. The third, a collection of "British Views on Collective Security," was prepared by the delegates. It had an introduction by Meston and nine articles, of which one was by G. M. Gathorne-Hardy and one by H. V. Hodson. Zimmern also presented a memorandum on behalf of the Geneva School. Opening speeches were made by Austen Chamberlain, Allen W. Dulles (of the Council on Foreign Relations), and Louis Eisenmann of the University of Paris. Closing speeches were made by Lord Meston, Allen Dulles, and Gilbert Murray. Meston acted as president of the conference, and Dulles as chairman of the study meetings. The proceedings were edited and published by a committee of two Frenchmen and A. J. Toynbee.

At the sessions on "Peaceful Change" in 1936-37, Australia presented one memorandum ("The Growth of Australian Population"). It was written by F. W. Eggleston and G. Packer. The United Kingdom presented fifteen memoranda. Eight of these were prepared by the RIIA, and seven by individuals. Of the seven individual works, two were written by members of All Souls who were also members of the Milner Group (C. A. Macartney and C. R. M. F. Cruttwell). The other five were written by experts who were not members of the Group (A. M. Carr-Saunders, A. B. Keith, D. Harwood, H. Lauterpacht, and R. Kuczynski).

In the middle 1930s the Milner Group began to take an interest in the problem of refugees and stateless persons, as a result of the persecutions of Hitler and the approaching closing of the Nansen Office of the League of Nations. Sir Neill Malcolm was made High Commissioner for German Refugees in 1936. The following year the RIIA began a research program in the problem. This resulted in a massive report, edited by Sir John Hope Simpson who was not a member of the Group and was notoriously unsympathetic to Zionism (1939). In 1938 Roger M. Makins was made secretary to the British delegation to the Evian Conference on Refugees. Mr. Makins' full career will be examined later. At this point it is merely necessary to note that he was educated at Winchester School and at Christ Church, Oxford, and was elected to a Fellowship at All Souls in 1925, when only twenty-one years old. After the Evian Conference (where the British, for strategic reasons, left all the responsible positions to the Americans), Mr. Makins was made secretary to the Intergovernmental Committee on Refugees. He was British Minister in Washington from 1945 to 1947 and is now Assistant Under Secretary in the Foreign Office.

Before leaving the subject of refugees, we might mention that the chief British agent for Czechoslovakian refugees in 1938-1939 was R. J. Stopford, an associate of the Milner Group already mentioned.

At the time of the Czechoslovak crisis in September 1938, the RIIA began to act in an unofficial fashion as an adviser to the Foreign Office. When war began a year later, this was made formal, and Chatham House became, for all practical purposes, the research section of the Foreign Office. A special organization was established in the Institute, in charge of A. J. Toynbee, with Lionel Curtis as his chief support acting "as the permanent representative of the chairman of the Council, Lord Astor." The organization consisted of the press-clipping collection, the information department, and much of the library. These were moved to Oxford and set up in Balliol, All Souls, and Rhodes House. The project was financed by the Treasury, All Souls, Balliol, and Chatham House jointly. Within a brief time, the organization became known as the Foreign Research and Press Service (FRPS). It answered all questions on international affairs from government departments, prepared a weekly summary of the foreign press, and prepared special research projects. When Anthony Eden was asked a question in the House of Commons on 23 July 1941, regarding the expense of this project, he said that the Foreign Office had given it £53,000 in the fiscal year 1940-1941.

During the winter of 1939-1940 the general meetings of the Institute were held in Rhodes House, Oxford, with Hugh Wyndham generally presiding. The periodical *International Affairs* suspended publication, but the *Bulletin of International News* continued, under the care of Hugh Latimer and A. J. Brown. The latter had been an undergraduate at Oxford in 1933-1936, was elected a Fellow of All Souls in 1938, and obtained a D.Phil. in 1939. The former may be Alfred Hugh Latimer, who was an undergraduate at Merton from 1938 to 1946 and was elected to the foundation of the same college in 1946.

As the work of the FRPS grew too heavy for Curtis to supervise alone, he was given a committee of four assistants. They were G. N. Clark, H. J. Paton, C. K. Webster, and A. E. Zimmern. About the same time, the London School of Economics established a quarterly journal devoted to the subject of postwar reconstruction. It was called *Agenda,* and G. N. Clark was editor. Clark had been a member of All Souls since 1912 and was Chichele Professor of Economic History from 1931 to 1943. Since 1943 he has been Regius Professor of Modern History at Cambridge. Not a member of the Milner Group, he is close to it and was a member of the council of Chatham House during the recent war.

At the end of 1942 the Foreign Secretary (Eden) wrote to Lord Astor that the government wished to take the FRPS over completely. This was done in April 1943. The existing Political Intelligence Department of the Foreign Office was merged with it to make the new Research Department of the Ministry. Of this new department Toynbee was director and Zimmern deputy director.

This brief sketch of the Royal Institute of International Affairs does not by any means indicate the very considerable influence which the organization exerts in English-speaking countries in the sphere to which it is devoted. The extent of that influence must be obvious. The purpose of this chapter has been something else: to show that the Milner Group controls the Institute. Once that is established, the picture changes. The influence of Chatham House appears in its true perspective, not as the influence of an autonomous body but as merely one of many instruments in the arsenal of another power. When the influence which the Institute wields is combined with that controlled by the Milner Group in other fields—in education, in administration, in newspapers and periodicals—a really terrifying picture begins to emerge. This picture is called terrifying not because the power of the Milner Group was used for evil ends. It was not. On the contrary, it was generally used with the best intentions in the world—even if those intentions were so idealistic as to be almost academic. The picture is terrifying because such power, whatever the goals at which it may be directed, is too much to be entrusted safely to any group. That it was too much to be safely entrusted to the Milner Group will appear quite clearly in Chapter 12. No country that values its safety should allow what the Milner Group accomplished in Britain—that is, that a small number of men should be able to wield such power in administration and politics, should be given almost complete control over the publication of the documents relating to their actions, should be able to exercise such influence over the avenues of information that create public opinion, and should be able to monopolize so completely the writing and the teaching of the history of their own period.

11

India, 1911-1945

INDIA WAS one of the primary concerns of both the Cecil Bloc and Milner Group. The latter probably devoted more time and attention to India than to any other subject. This situation reached its peak in 1919, and the Government of India Act of that year is very largely a Milner Group measure in conception, formation, and execution. The influence of the two groups is not readily apparent from the lists of Governors-general (Viceroys) and Secretaries of State for India in the twentieth century:

VICEROYS	SECRETARIES OF STATE
Lord Curzon, 1898-1905	Lord George Hamilton, 1895-1903
Lord Minto, 1905-1910	St. John Brodrick, 1903-1908
Lord Hardinge of Penshurst, 1910-1916	John Morley, 1908-1910
Lord Chelmsford, 1916-1921	Lord Crewe, 1910-1915
Lord Reading, 1921-1926	Austen Chamberlain, 1915-1917
Lord Irwin, 1926-1931	Edward Montagu, 1917-1922
Lord Willingdon, 1931-1936	Lord Peel, 1922-1924
Lord Linlithgow, 1936-1943	Lord Olivier, 1924
	Lord Birkenhead, 1924-1928
	Lord Peel, 1928-1929
	Wedgwood Benn, 1929-1931
	Samuel Hoare, 1931-1935
	Lord Zetland, 1935-1940
	Leopold Amery, 1940-1945

Of the Viceroys only one (Reading) is clearly of neither the Cecil Bloc nor the Milner Group; two were members of the Milner Group (Irwin and Willingdon); another was a member of both groups (Chelmsford); the rest were of the Cecil Bloc, although in two cases (Minto and Linlithgow) in a rather peripheral fashion. Three of the eight were members of All Souls. According to Lord Esher, the appointment of Lord Hardinge in 1910 was made at his suggestion, by John Morley. At the time, Esher's son, the present Viscount Esher, was acting as unpaid private secretary to Morley, a position he held for five years (1905-1910). From the same source we learn that the Viceroyship was offered to Selborne in 1903 and to Esher himself in 1908. The former failed of appointment because Curzon refused to retire, while the latter rejected the post as of too limited influence.

Of the thirteen Secretaries of State, two were Labour and two Liberals. One of these latter (Morley) was close to the Milner Group. Of the other nine, three were of the Cecil Bloc (St. John Brodrick, Austen Chamberlain, and Lord Zetland), two were of the Milner Group (Hoare and Amery), and four were of neither group.

The political and constitutional history of India in the twentieth century consists largely of a series of investigations by various committees and commissions, and a second, and shorter, series of legislative enactments. The influence of the Milner Group can be discerned in both of these, especially in regard to the former.

Of the important commissions that investigated Indian constitutional questions in the twentieth century, every one has had a member of the inner circle of the Milner Group. The following list gives the name of the commission, the dates of its existence, the number of British members (in distinction from Indian members), the names of representatives from the Cecil Bloc and Milner Group (with the latter italicized), and the command number of its report:

1. The Royal Commission on Decentralization in India, 1907-1909, five members, including *W. L. Hichens* (Cmd. 4360 of 1908).

2. The Royal Commission on Public Services in India, 1912-1915, nine members, including Baron Islington, the Earl of Ronaldshay (later Marquess of Zetland), Sir Valentine Chirol, and *H. A. L. Fisher*. The chairman of this commission, Lord Islington, was later father-in-law to Sir Edward Grigg (Lord Altrincham) (Cmd. 8382 of 1916).

3. The Government of India Constitutional Reform Committee on Franchise, 1919, four members, including *Malcolm Hailey*.

4. The Government of India Constitutional Reform Committee on Functions, 1919, four members, including *Richard Feetham* as chairman.

5. The Joint Select Committee on the Government of India Bill, 1919, fourteen members, including *Lord Selborne* (chairman), Lord Midleton (St. John Brodrick), Lord Islington, Sir Henry Craik (whose son was in Milner's Kindergarten), and *W. G. A. Ormsby-Gore* (now Lord Harlech) (Cmd. 97 of 1919).

6. The Committee on Home Administration of Indian Affairs, 1919, eight members, including *W. G. A. Ormsby-Gore* (Lord Harlech) (Cmd. 207 of 1919).

7. The Royal Commission on Superior Civil Services in India, 1923-1924, five members, including Lord Lee of Fareham as chairman and *Reginald Coupland* (Cmd. 2128 of 1924).

8. The Indian Statutory Commission, 1927-1930, seven members, with *Sir John Simon* as chairman (Cmd. 3568 and 3569 of 1930).

9. The Indian Franchise Committee, 1931-1932, eight members, including *Lord Lothian* as chairman and Lord Dufferin (whose brother, Lord Basil Blackwood, had been in Milner's Kindergarten) (Cmd. 4086 of 1932).

10. The three Indian Round Table Conferences of 1930-1932 contained a number of members of the Milner Group. The first session (November 1930-January 1931) had eighty-nine delegates, sixteen from Britain, sixteen from the Indian States, and fifty-seven from British India. Formed as they were by a Labour government, the first two sessions had eight Labour members among the sixteen from Britain. The other eight were Earl Peel, the Marquess of Zetland, Sir Samuel Hoare, Oliver Stanley, the Marquess of Reading, the Marquess of Lothian, Sir Robert Hamilton, and Isaac Foot. Of these eight, two were of the Milner Group (Hoare and Lothian) and two of the Cecil Bloc (Zetland and Stanley). The chief adviser to the Indian States Delegation was *L. F. Rushbrook Williams* of the Milner Group, who was named to his position by the Chamber of Princes Special Organization. Among the five officials called in for consultation by the conference, we find the name of *Malcolm Hailey* (Cmd. 3778).

The membership of delegations at the second session (September-December 1931) was practically the same, except that thirty-one additional members were added and *Rushbrook Williams* became a delegate as the representative of the Maharaja of Nawanagar (Cmd. 3997).

At the third session (November-December 1932) there were no Labour Party representatives. The British delegation was reduced to twelve. Four of these were of the Milner Group (*Hoare, Simon, Lothian,* and *Irwin,* now Halifax). *Rushbrook Williams* continued as a delegate of the Indian States (Cmd. 4238).

11. The Joint Select Committee on Indian Constitutional Reform, appointed in April 1933, had sixteen members from the House of Commons and an equal number of Lords. Among these were such members of the Milner Group as *Sir Samuel Hoare, Sir John Simon, Lord Lothian,* and *Lord Irwin* (Halifax). The Cecil Bloc was also well represented by Archbishop Lang of Canterbury, Austen Chamberlain, Lord Eustace Percy, Lord Salisbury, Lord Zetland, Lord Lytton, and Lord Hardinge of Penshurst.

12. The Cripps Mission, 1942, four members, including *Reginald Coupland,* who wrote an unofficial but authoritative book on the mission as soon as it returned to England (Cmd. 6350).

The chief legislative events in this period were five in number: the two Indian Councils Acts of 1892 and 1909, the two Government of India Acts of 1919 and 1935, and the achievement of self-government in 1947.

The Indian Councils Act of 1892 was put through the House of Commons by George Curzon, at that time Under Secretary in the India

Office as the protégé of Lord Salisbury, who had discovered him in All Souls nine years earlier. This act was important for two reasons: (1) it introduced a representative principle into the Indian government by empowering the Governor-General and Provincial Governors to seek nominations to the "unofficial" seats in their councils from particular Indian groups and associations; and (2) it accepted a "communal" basis for this representation by seeking these nominations separately from Hindus, Moslems, and others. From these two sources flowed ultimately self-government and partition, although it is perfectly evident that neither of these was anticipated or desired by the persons who supported the act.

The nominations for "unofficial" members of the councils provided in the Act of 1892 became elections in practice, because the Governor-General always accepted the suggested nominations as his nominees. This practice became law in the Act of 1909.

The Indian Councils Act of 1909 was passed under a Liberal government and was only remotely influenced by the Cecil Bloc or Milner Group. The Prime Minister, Asquith, was practically a member of the Cecil Bloc, being an intimate friend of Balfour and Rosebery. This relationship had been tightened when he married Margot Tennant, a member of "the Souls," in 1894. Margot Tennant's sister, Laura, had previously married Alfred Lyttelton, and both sisters had been intimate friends of Curzon and other members of "the Souls." Asquith had also been, as we have stated, a close associate of Milner's. Asquith, however, was never a member of the Milner Group. After 1890, and especially after 1915, he increasingly became a member of the Cecil Bloc. It was Balfour who persuaded Asquith to write his *Memories and Reflections* after he (Balfour) had discussed the matter with Margot Asquith over a tête-à-tête dinner. These dinners were a not infrequent occurrence on the evenings when Asquith himself dined at his club, Asquith usually stopping by later in the evening to get his wife and escort her home. Another indication of Asquith's feeling toward the Cecil Bloc can be found in his autobiography under the date 22 December 1919. On that occasion Asquith told Lady Hartington, daughter of Lord Salisbury, that he "had not expected to live to see the day when the best safeguard for true liberalism would be found in an unreformed House of Lords and the Cecil family."

In 1908-1909, however, the situation was somewhat different, and Asquith could hardly be called a member of the Cecil Bloc. In a somewhat similar situation, although much closer to the Milner Group (through H. A. L. Fisher and All Souls), was John Morley, the Secretary of State for India. Lord Minto, the Governor-General in India, was also a member of the Cecil Bloc in a peripheral fashion but held his appointment through a family claim on the Governor-Generalship rather than by favor of the Cecils.

The Act of 1909, however, while not a product of the groups with which we are concerned, was formed in the same social tradition, drawn up from the same intellectual and social outlook, and put into effect in the same fashion. It legalized the principle of election (rather than nomination) to Indian councils, enlarged their membership to provide majorities of nonofficials in the provincial councils, and gave them the power to discuss affairs and pass resolutions. The seats were allotted to communal groups, with the minorities (like Moslems and Sikhs) receiving more than their proportionate share and the Moslems having, in addition, a separate electorate for the incumbents of Moslem seats. This served to encourage extremism among the Moslems and, while a logical development of 1892, was a long step on the road to Pakistan. This Act of 1909 was, as we have mentioned, put through the House of Commons by Sir Thomas Buchanan, a Fellow of All Souls and an associate of the Cecil Bloc.

The Government of India Act of 1919 is outstanding in many ways. It is the most drastic and most important reform made in Indian government in the whole period from 1861 to the achievement of self-government. Its provisions for the central government of India remained in force, with only slight changes, from 1919 to 1946. It is the only one of these acts whose "secret" legislative background is no longer a secret. And it is the only one which indicated a desire on the part of the British government to establish in India a responsible government patterned on that in Britain.

The legislative history of the Act of 1919 as generally known is simple enough. It runs as follows. In August 1917 the Secretary of State for India, Edwin S. Montagu, issued a statement which read: "The policy of H.M. Government, with which the Government of India are in complete accord, is that of the increasing association of Indians in every branch of the administration and the gradual development of self-government institutions with a view to the progressive realization of responsible government in India as an integral part of the British Empire." The critical word here is *responsible* government, since the prospect of eventual self-government had been held out to India for years. In accordance with this promise, Montagu visited India and, in cooperation with the Viceroy, Lord Chelmsford, issued the Montagu-Chelmsford Report, indicating the direction of future policy. This report became the basis for the bill of 1918, which, after a certain amount of amendment by Lord Selborne's Joint Select Committee, came into force as the Government of India Act of 1919.

The secret history of this Act is somewhat different, and begins in Canada in 1909, when Lionel Curtis accepted from his friend William

Marris the idea that responsible government on the British pattern should be extended to India. Two years later, Curtis formed a study group of six or eight persons within the London Round Table Group. We do not know for certain who were the members of the study group, but apparently it included Curtis, Kerr, Fisher, and probably Brand. To these were added three officials of the India Office. These included Malcolm Seton (Sir Malcolm after 1919), who was secretary to the Judicial Department of the India Office and joined Curtis's group about 1913; and Sir William Duke, who was Lieutenant Governor of Bengal in 1911-1912, senior member of the council of the Governor of Bengal in 1912-1914, and a member of the Council of India in London after 1914. At this last date he joined the Curtis group. Both of these men were important figures in the India Office later, Sir William as Permanent Under Secretary from 1920 to his death in 1924, and Sir Malcolm as Assistant Under Secretary (1919-1924) and Deputy Under Secretary (1924-1933). Sir Malcolm wrote the biographical sketch of Sir William in the *Dictionary of National Biography,* and also wrote the volume on *The India Office* in the Whitehall Series (1926). The third member from this same source was Sir Lionel Abrahams, Assistant Under Secretary in the India Office.

The Curtis study group was not an official committee, although some persons (both at the time and since) have believed it was. Among these persons would appear to be Lord Chelmsford, for in debate in the House of Lords in November 1927 he said:

> I came home from India in January 1916 for six weeks before I went out again as Viceroy, and, when I got home, I found that there was a Committee in existence at the India Office, which was considering on what lines future constitutional development might take place. That Committee, before my return in the middle of March gave me a pamphlet containing in broad outline the views which were held with regard to future constitutional development. When I reached India I showed this pamphlet to my Council and also to my noble friend, Lord Meston, who was then Lieutenant Governor of the United Provinces. It contained, what is now known as the diarchic principle. . . . Both the Council and Lord Meston, who was then Sir James Meston, reported adversely on the proposals for constitutional development contained in that pamphlet.

Lord Chelmsford then goes on to say that Austen Chamberlain combated their objections with the argument that the Indians must acquire experience in self-government, so, after the announcement to this effect was made publicly in August 1917, the officials in India accepted dyarchy.

If Lord Chelmsford believed that the pamphlet was an official document from a committee in the India Office, he was in error. The other side of the story was revealed by Lionel Curtis in 1920 in his book

Dyarchy. According to Curtis, the study group was originally formed to help him write the chapter on India in the planned second volume of *The Commonwealth of Nations*. It set as its task "to enquire how self-government could be introduced and peacefully extended to India." The group met once a fortnight in London and soon decided on the dyarchy principle. This principle, as any reader of Curtis's writings knows, was basic in Curtis's political thought and was the foundation on which he hoped to build a federated Empire. According to Curtis, the study group asked itself: "Could not provincial electorates through legislatures and ministers of their own be made clearly responsible for certain functions of government to begin with, leaving all others in the hands of executives responsible as at present to the Government of India and the Secretary of State? Indian electorates, legislatures, and executives would thus be given a field for the exercise of genuine responsibility. From time to time fresh powers could be transferred from the old governments as the new elective authorities developed and proved their capacity for assuming them." From this point of view, Curtis asked Duke to draw up such "a plan of Devolution" for Bengal. This plan was printed by the group, circulated, and criticized in typical Milner Group fashion. Then the whole group went to Oxford for three days and met to discuss it in the old Bursary of Trinity College. It was then rewritten. "No one was satisfied." It was decided to circulate it for further criticism among the Round Table Groups throughout the world, but Lord Chelmsford wrote from New South Wales and asked for a copy. Apparently realizing that he was to be the next Viceroy of India, the group sent a copy to him and none to the Round Table Groups, "lest the public get hold of it and embarrass him." It is clear that Chelmsford was committed to a program of reform along these or similar lines before he went out as Viceroy. This was revealed in debate in the House of Lords by Lord Crewe on 12 December 1919.

After Chelmsford went to India in March 1916, a new, revised version of the study group's plan was drawn up and sent to him in May 1916. Another copy was sent to Canada to catch up with Curtis, who had already left for India by way of Canada, Australia, and New Zealand. This itinerary was undoubtedly followed by Curtis in order to consult with members of the Group in various countries, especially with Brand in Canada. On his arrival in India, Curtis wrote back to Kerr in London:

> The factor which impressed me most in Canada, New Zealand, and Australia was the rooted aversion these peoples have to any scheme which meant their sharing in the Government of India. . . . To these young democratic communities the principle of self-government is the breath of

their nostrils. It is almost a religion. They feel as if there were something inherently wrong in one people ruling another. It is the same feeling as that which makes the Americans dislike governing the Philippines and decline to restore order in Mexico. My first impressions on this subject were stongly confirmed on my recent visit to these Dominions. I scarcely recall one of the numerous meetings I addressed at which I was not asked why India was not given self-government and what steps were being taken in that direction.

Apparently this experience strengthened Curtis's idea that India must be given responsible government. He probably felt that by giving India what it and the Dominions wanted for India, both would be bound in loyalty more closely to Britain. In this same letter to Kerr, Curtis said, in obvious reference to the Round Table Group:

> Our task then is to bring home to the public in the United Kingdom and the Dominions how India differs from a country like Great Britain on the one hand and from Central Africa on the other, and how that difference is now reflected in the character of its government. We must outline clearly the problems which arise from the contact of East and West and the disaster which awaits a failure to supply their adequate solution by realizing and expressing the principle of Government for which we stand. We must then go on to suggest a treatment of India in the general work of Imperial reconstruction in harmony with the facts adduced in the foregoing chapters. And all this must be done with the closest attention to its effects upon educated opinion here. We must do our best to make Indian Nationalists realize the truth that like South Africa all their hopes and aspirations are dependent on the maintenance of the British Commonwealth and their permanent membership therein.

This letter, written on 13 November 1916, was addressed to Philip Kerr but was intended for all the members of the Group. Sir Valentine Chirol corrected the draft, and copies were made available for Meston and Marris. Then Curtis had a thousand copies printed and sent to Kerr for distribution. In some way, the extremist Indian nationalists obtained a copy of the letter and published a distorted version of it. They claimed that a powerful and secret group organized about *The Round Table* had sent Curtis to India to spy out the nationalist plans in order to obstruct them. Certain sentences from the letter were torn from their context to prove this argument. Among these was the reference to Central Africa, which was presented to the Indian people as a statement that they were as uncivilized and as incapable of self-government as Central Africans. As a result of the fears created by this rumor, the Indian National Congress and the Moslem League formed their one and only formal alliance in the shape of the famous Lucknow Compact of 29 December 1916. The Curtis letter was not the only factor behind the Lucknow agreement, but it was certainly very influential. Curtis was present at the Congress meeting and was horrified at the version of his letter which was circulating. Accordingly, he published the correct version with an extensive commentary, under the title *Letters to the People of India* (1917). In this he said categorically that he believed: "(1) That it is the duty of those who govern the whole British Commonwealth to do anything in their power to enable Indians to govern themselves as soon as possible. (2) That Indians must also come to share in the government of the British Commonwealth as a whole." There can be no doubt that Curtis was sincere in this and that his view reflected, perhaps in an extreme form, the views of a large and influential group in Great Britain. The failure of this group to persuade the Indian nationalists that they were sincere is one of the great disasters of the century, although the fault is not entirely theirs and must be shared by others, including Gandhi.

In the first few months of 1917, Curtis consulted groups of Indians and individual British (chiefly of the Milner Group) regarding the form which the new constitution would take. The first public use of the word "dyarchy" was in an open letter of 6 April 1917, which he wrote to Bhupendra Nath Basu, one of the authors of the Lucknow Compact, to demonstrate how dyarchy would function in the United Provinces. In writing this letter, Curtis consulted with Valentine Chirol and Malcolm Hailey. He then wrote an outline, "The Structure of Indian Government," which was revised by Meston and printed. This was submitted to many persons for comment. He then organized a meeting of Indians and British at Lord Sinha's house in Darjeeling and, after considerable discussion, drew up a twelve-point program, which was signed by sixty-four Europeans and ninety Indians. This was sent to Chelmsford and to Montagu.

In the meantime, in London, preparations were being made to issue the historic declaration of 20 August 1917, which promised "responsible" government to India. There can be no doubt that the Milner Group was the chief factor in issuing that declaration. Curtis, in *Dyarchy*, says: "For the purpose of the private enquiry above described the principle of that pronouncement was assumed in 1915." It is perfectly clear that Montagu (Secretary of State in succession to Austen Chamberlain from June 1917) did not draw up the declaration. He drew up a statement, but the India Office substituted for it one which had been drawn up much earlier, when Chamberlain was still Secretary of State. Lord Ronaldshay (Lord Zetland), in the third volume of his *Life of Curzon*, prints both drafts and claims that the one which was finally issued was drawn up by Curzon. Sir Stanley Reed, who was editor of *The Times of India* from 1907 to 1923, declared at a meeting of the Royal Institute of International Affiars in 1926 that the declaration was drawn up by Milner and Curzon. It is clear that someone other than Curzon had a hand in it, and the strongest probability would be Milner, who was with Curzon in the War Cabinet at the time. The fact is that Curzon could not have drawn it up alone unless he was unbelievably careless, because, after it was published, he was horrified when the promise of "progressive realization of responsible government in India" was pointed out to him.

Montagu went to India in November 1917, taking Sir William Duke with him. Curtis, who had been moving about India as the guest of Stanley Reed, Chirol, Chelmsford, Meston, Marris, and others, was invited to participate in the Montagu-Chelmsford conferences on several occasions. Others who were frequently consulted were Hailey, Meston, Duke, and Chirol. The Montagu-Chelmsford Report was written by Sir William Marris of Milner's Kindergarten after Curtis had returned to England. Curtis wrote in *Dyarchy* in 1920: "It was afterwards suggested in the press that I had actually drafted the report. My prompt denial has not prevented a further complaint from many quarters that Lord Chelmsford and Mr. Montagu were unduly influenced by an irresponsible tourist. . . . With the exception of Lord Chelmsford himself I was possibly the only person in India with first-hand knowledge of responsible government as applied in the Dominions to the institutions of provinces. Whether my knowledge of India entitled me to advance my views is more open to question. Of this the reader can judge for himself. But in any case the interviews were unsought by me." Thus Curtis does not deny the accusation that he was chiefly responsible for dyarchy. It was believed at the time by persons in a position to know that he was, and these persons were both for and against the plan. On the latter side, we might quote Lord Ampthill, who, as a former acting Viceroy, as private secretary to Joseph Chamberlain, as Governor of Madras, and as brother-in-law of Samuel Hoare, was in a position to know what was going on. Lord Ampthill declared in the House of Lords in 1919: "The incredible fact is that, but for the chance visit to India of a globe-trotting doctrinaire, with a positive mania for constitution-mongering, nobody in the world would ever have thought of so peculiar a notion as Dyarchy. And yet the Joint Committee tells us in an airy manner that no better plan can be conceived."

The Joint Committee's favorable report on the Dyarchy Bill was probably not unconnected with the fact that five out of fourteen members were from the Cecil Bloc or Milner Group, that the chairman had in his day presided over meetings of the Round Table Groups and was regarded by them as their second leader, and that the Joint Committee spent most of its time hearing witnesses who were close to the Milner Group. The committee heard Lord Meston longer than any other witness (almost four days), spent a day with Curtis on the stand,

and questioned, among others, Feetham, Duke, Thomas Holland (Fellow of All Souls from 1875 to his death in 1926), Michael Sadler (a close friend of Milner's and practically a member of the Group), and Stanley Reed. In the House of Commons the burden of debate on the bill was supported by Montagu, Sir Henry Craik, H. A. L. Fisher, W. G. A. Ormsby-Gore, and Thomas J. Bennett (an old journalist colleague of Lord Salisbury and principal owner of *The Times of India* from 1892). Montagu and Craik both referred to Lionel Curtis. The former said: "It is suggested in some quarters that this bill arose spontaneously in the minds of the Viceroy and myself without previous inquiry or consideration, under the influence of Mr. Lionel Curtis. I have never yet been able to understand that you approach the merits of any discussion by vain efforts to approximate to its authorship. I do not even now understand that India or the Empire owes anything more or less than a great debt of gratitude to the patriotic and devoted services Mr. Curtis has given to the consideration of this problem."

Sir Henry Craik later said: "I am glad to join in the compliment paid to our mutual friend, Mr. Lionel Curtis, who belongs to a very active, and a very important body of young men, whom I should be the last to criticize. I am proud to know him, and to pay that respect to him due from age to youth. He and others of the company of the Round Table have been doing good work, and part of that good work has been done in India."

Mr. Fisher had nothing to say about Lionel Curtis but had considerable to say about the bill and the Montagu-Chelmsford Report. He said: "There is nothing in this Bill which is not contained in that Report. That Report is not only a very able and eloquent State Paper, but it is also one of the greatest State Papers which have been produced in Anglo-Indian history, and it is an open-minded candid State Paper, a State Paper which does not ignore or gloss over the points of criticism which have since been elaborated in the voluminous documents which have been submitted to us." He added, a moment later: "This is a great Bill."[2] *The Round Table*, which also approved of the bill, as might be imagined, referred to Fisher's speech in its issue of September 1919 and called him "so high an authority." The editor of that issue was Lionel Curtis.

In the House of Lords there was less enthusiasm. Chief criticism centered on two basic points, both of which originated with Curtis: (1) the principle of dyarchy — that is, that government could be separated into two classes of activities under different regimes; and (2) the effort to give India "responsible" government rather than merely "self-government" — that is, the effort to extend to India a form of government patterned on Britain's. Both of these principles were criticized vigorously, especially by members of the Cecil Bloc, including Lord Midleton, Lord Lansdowne, Lord Selborne, Lord Salisbury, and others. Support for the bill came chiefly from Lord Curzon (Leader in the Upper House) and Lord Islington (Under Secretary in the India Office).

As a result of this extensive criticism, the bill was revised considerably in the Joint Committee but emerged with its main outlines unchanged and became law in December 1919. These main outlines, especially the two principles of "dyarchy" and "responsibility," were, as we have said, highly charged with Curtis's own connotations. These became fainter as time passed, both because of developments in India and because Curtis from 1919 on became increasingly remote from Indian affairs. The refusal of the Indian National Congress under Gandhi's leadership to cooperate in carrying on the government under the Act of 1919 persuaded the other members of the Group (and perhaps Curtis himself) that it was not possible to apply responsible government on the British model to India. This point of view, which had been stated so emphatically by members of the Cecil Bloc even before 1900, and which formed the chief argument against the Act of 1919 in the debates in the House of Lords, was accepted by the Milner Group as their own after 1919. Halifax, Grigg, Amery, Coupland, Fisher, and others stated this most emphatically from the early 1920s to the middle 1940s. In 1943 Grigg stated this as a principle in his book *The British Commonwealth* and quoted with approval Amery's statement of 30 March 1943 to the House of Commons, rejecting the British parliamentary system as suitable for India. Amery, at that time Secretary of State for India, had said: "Like wasps buzzing angrily up and down against a window pane when an adjoining window may be wide open, we are all held up, frustrated and irritated by the unrealized and unsuperable barrier of our constitutional prepossessions." Grigg went even further, indeed, so far that we might suspect that he was deprecating the use of parliamentary government in general rather than merely in India. He said:

> It is entirely devoid of flexibility and quite incapable of engendering the essential spirit of compromise in countries where racial and communal divisions present the principal political difficulty. The idea that freedom to be genuine must be accommodated to this pattern is deeply rooted in us, and we must not allow our statesmanship to be imprisoned behind the bars of our own experience. Our insistence in particular on the principle of a common roll of electors voting as one homogeneous electorate has caused reaction in South Africa, rebellion or something much too like it in Kenya, and deadlock in India, because in the different conditions of those countries it must involve the complete and perpetual dominance of a single race or creed.

Unfortunately, as Reginald Coupland has pointed out in his book,

India, a Re-statement (1945), all agreed that the British system of government was unsuited to India, but none made any effort to find an indigenous system that would be suitable. The result was that the Milner Group and their associates relaxed in their efforts to prepare Indians to live under a parliamentary system and finally cut India loose without an indigenous system and only partially prepared to manage a parliamentary system.

This decline in enthusiasm for a parliamentary system in India was well under way by 1921. In the two year-interval from 1919 to 1921, the Group continued as the most important British factor in Indian affairs. Curtis was editor of *The Round Table* in this period and continued to agitate the cause of the Act of 1919. Lord Chelmsford remained a Viceroy in this period. Meston and Hailey were raised to the Viceroy's Executive Council. Sir William Duke became Permanent Under Secretary, and Sir Malcolm Seton became Assistant Under Secretary in the India Office. Sir William Marris was made Home Secretary of the Government of India and Special Reforms Commissioner in charge of setting up the new system. L. F. Rushbrook Williams was given special duty at the Home Department, Government of India, in connection with the reforms. Thus the Milner Group was well placed to put the new law into effect. The effort was largely frustrated by Gandhi's boycott of the elections under the new system. By 1921 the Milner Group had left Indian affairs and shifted its chief interest to other fields. Curtis became one of the chief factors in Irish affairs in 1921; Lord Chelmsford returned home and was raised to a Viscounty in the same year; Meston retired in 1919; Marris became Governor of Assam in 1921; Hailey became Governor of the Punjab in 1924; Duke died in 1924; and Rushbrook Williams became director of the Central Bureau of Information, Government of India, in 1920.

This does not indicate that the Milner Group abandoned all interest in India by 1924 or earlier, but the Group never showed such concentrated interest in the problem of India again. Indeed, the Group never displayed such concentrated interest in any problem either earlier or later, with the single exception of the effort to form the Union of South Africa in 1908-1909.

The decade 1919-1929 was chiefly occupied with efforts to get Gandhi to permit the Indian National Congress to cooperate in the affairs of government, so that its members and other Indians could acquire the necessary experience to allow the progressive realization of self-government. The Congress Party, as we have said, boycotted the elections of 1920 and cooperated in those of 1924 only for the purpose of wrecking them. Nonetheless, the system worked, with the support of moderate groups, and the British extended one right after another in steady succession. Fiscal automony was granted to India in 1921, and

that country at once adopted a protective tariff, to the considerable injury of British textile manufacturing. The superior Civil Services were
opened to Indians in 1924. Indians were admitted to Woolwich and
Sandhurst in the same year, and commissions in the Indian Army were
made available to them.

The appointment of Baron Irwin of the Milner Group to be Viceroy
in 1926 — an appointment in which, according to A. C. Johnson's
biography *Viscount Halifax* (1941), "the influence of Geoffrey Dawson
and other members of *The Times'* editorial staff" may have played a
decisive role — was the chief step in the effort to achieve some real progress under the Act of 1919 before that Act came under the critical examination of another Royal Commission, scheduled for 1929. The new
Viceroy's statement of policy, made in India, 17 July 1926, was, according to the same source, embraced by *The Times* in an editorial
"which showed in no uncertain terms that Irwin's policy was appreciated and underwritten by Printing House Square."

Unfortunately, in the period 1924-1931 the India Office was not in
control of either the Milner Group or Cecil Bloc. For various reasons,
of which this would seem to be the most important, coordination
between the Secretary of State and the Viceroy and between Britain
and the Indian nationalists broke down at the most crucial moments.
The Milner Group, chiefly through *The Times*, participated in this
situation in the period 1926-1929 by praising their man, Lord Irwin,
and adversely criticizing the Secretary of State, Lord Birkenhead.
Relationships between Birkenhead and the Milner (and Cecil) Group
had not been cordial for a long time, and there are various indications
of feuding from at least 1925. We may recall that in April 1925 a
secret, or at least unofficial, "committee" of Milner Group and Cecil
Bloc members had nominated Lord Milner for the post of Chancellor of
Oxford University. Lord Birkenhead had objected both to the candidate and to the procedure. In regard to the candidate, he would have
preferred Asquith. In regard to the procedure, he demanded to know
by what authority this "committee" took upon itself the task of naming
a chancellor to a university of which he (Lord Birkenhead) had been
High Steward since 1922. This protest, as usual when Englishmen of
this social level are deeply moved, took the form of a letter to *The
Times*. It received a tart answer in a letter, written in the third person,
in which he was informed that this committee had existed before the
World War, and that, when it was reconstituted at the end of the war,
Mr. F. E. Smith had been invited to be a member of it but had not seen
fit even to acknowledge the invitation.

The bad relationship between the Milner Group and Lord
Birkenhead was not the result of such episodes as this but rather, it
would seem, based on a personal antipathy engendered by the

character of Lord Birkenhead and especially by his indiscreet and undiplomatic social life and political activity. Nonetheless, Lord Birkenhead was a man of unquestioned vigor and ability and a man of considerable political influence from the day in 1906 when he had won a parliamentary seat for the Conservatives in the face of a great Liberal tidal wave. As a result, he had obtained the post of Secretary of State for India in November 1924 at the same time that Leopold Amery went to the Colonial Office. The episode regarding the Milner candidacy to the Oxford Chancellorship occurred six months later and was practically a direct challenge from Birkenhead to Amery, since at that time the latter was Milner's active political lieutenant and one of the chief movers in the effort to make him Chancellor.

Thus, in the period 1926-1929, the Milner Group held the Viceroy's post but did not hold the post of Secretary of State. The relationship between these two posts was such that good government could not be obtained without close cooperation between them. Such cooperation did not exist in this period. As far as the constitutional development was concerned, this lack of cooperation appeared in a tendency on the part of the Secretary of State to continue to seek a solution of the problem along the road marked by the use of a unilateral British investigatory commission, and a tendency on the part of Irwin (and the Milner Group) to seek a solution along the newer road of cooperative discussion with the Indians. These tendencies did not appear as divergent routes until after the Simon Commission had begun its labors, with the result that accumulating evidence that the latter road would be used left that unilateral commission in an unenviable position.

The Government of India Act of 1919 had provided that an investigation should be made of the functioning of the Act after it had been in effect for ten years. The growing unrest of the Indians and their failure to utilize the opportunities of the Act of 1919 persuaded many Englishmen (including most of the Milner Group) that the promised Statutory Commission should begin its work earlier than anticipated and should direct its efforts rather at finding the basis for a new constitutional system than at examining the obvious failure of the system provided in 1919.

The first official hint that the date of the Statutory Commission would be moved up was given by Birkenhead on 30 March 1927, in combination with some rather "arrogant and patronizing" remarks about Indian politics. *The Times,* while criticizing Birkenhead for his additional remarks, took up the suggestion regarding the commission and suggested in its turn "that the ideal body would consist of judicially minded men who were able to agree." This is, of course, exactly what was obtained. The authorized biography *Viscount Halifax*, whence these quotations have been taken, adds at this point: "It is interesting to speculate how far Geoffrey Dawson, the Editor, was again expressing Irwin's thoughts and whether a deliberate *ballon d'essai* was being put up in favor of Sir John Simon."

The Simon Commission was exactly what *The Times* had wanted, a body of "judicially minded men who were able to agree." Its chairman was the most expensive lawyer in England, a member of the Cecil Bloc since he was elected to All Souls in 1897, and in addition a member of the two extraordinary clubs already mentioned, Grillion's and The Club. Although he was technically a Liberal, his associations and inclinations were rather on the Conservative side, and it was no surprise in 1931 when he became a National Liberal and occupied one of the most important seats in the Cabinet, the Foreign Office. From this time on, he was closely associated with the policies of the Milner Group and, in view of his personal association with the leaders of the Group in All Souls, may well be regarded as a member of the Group. As chairman of the Statutory Commission, he used his legal talents to the full to draw up a report on which all members of the commission could agree, and it is no small example of his abilities that he was able to get an unanimous agreement on a program which in outline, if not in all its details, was just what the Milner Group wanted.

Of the six other members of the Commission, two were Labourite (Clement Attlee and Vernon Hartshorn). The others were Unionist or Conservative. Viscount Burnham of Eton and Balliol (1884) had been a Unionist supporter of the Cecil Bloc in Commons from 1885 to 1906, and his father had been made baronet and baron by Lord Salisbury. His own title of Viscount came from Lloyd George in 1919.

The fifth member of the Commission, Donald Palmer Howard, Baron Strathcona and Mount Royal, of Eton and Trinity College, Cambridge, had no special claim to fame except that he had been a Unionist M.P. in 1922-1926.

The sixth member, Edward Cecil Cadogan of Eton and Balliol (1904), was the sixth son of Earl Cadogan and thus the older brother of Sir Alexander Cadogan, British delegate to the United Nations. Their father, Earl Cadogan, grandnephew of the first Duke of Wellington, had been Lord Privy Seal in Lord Salisbury's second government and Lord Lieutenant of Ireland in Salisbury's third government. Edward, who was knighted in 1939, had no special claim to fame except that he was a Unionist M.P. from 1922 to 1935 and was Chairman of the House of Commons under the National Government of 1931-1935.

The seventh member, George R. Lane-Fox (Baron Bingley since 1933) of Eton and New College, was a Unionist M.P. from 1906 to 1931 and Secretary of Mines from 1922 to 1928. He is a brother-in-law and lifelong friend of Lord Halifax, having married the Honourable Mary Wood in 1903.

The most extraordinary fact about the Simon Commission was the lack of qualification possessed by its members. Except for the undoubted advantages of education at Eton and Oxford, the members had no obvious claims to membership on any committee considering Indian affairs. Indeed, not one of the eight members had had any previous contact with this subject. Nevertheless, the commission produced an enormous two-volume report which stands as a monumental source book for the study of Indian problems in this period. When, to the lack of qualifications of its members, we add the fact that the commission was almost completely boycotted by Indians and obtained its chief contact with the natives by listening to their monotonous chants of "Simon, go back," it seems more than a miracle that such a valuable report could have emerged from their investigations. The explanation is to be found in the fact that they received full cooperation from the staff of the Government of India, including members of the Milner Group.

It is clear that by the end of 1928 the Milner Group, as a result of the strong Indian opposition to the Simon Commission, the internal struggle within that commission between Simon and Burnham (because of the latter's refusal to go as far as the former desired in the direction of concessions to the Indians), and their inability to obtain cooperation from the Secretary of State (as revealed in the steady criticism of Birkenhead in *The Times*), had decided to abandon the commission method of procedure in favor of a round-table method of procedure. It is not surprising that the Round Table Groups should prefer a round-table method of procedure even in regard to Indian affairs, where many of the participants would have relatively little experience in the typical British procedure of agreement through conference. To the Milner Group, the round-table method was not only preferable in itself but was made absolutely necessary by the widespread Indian criticism of the Simon Commission for its exclusively British personnel. This restriction had been adopted originally on the grounds that only a purely British and purely parliamentary commission could commit Parliament in some degree to acceptance of the recommendations of the commission — at least, this was the defense of the restricted membership made to the Indians by the Viceroy on 8 November 1927. In place of this argument, the Milner Group now advanced a somewhat more typical idea, namely, that only Indian participation on a direct and equal basis could commit Indians to any plans for the future of India. By customary Milner Group reasoning, they decided that the responsibility placed on Indians by making them participate in the formulation of plans would moderate the extremism of their demands and bind them to participate in the execution of these plans after they were enacted into law. This basic idea—that if you have faith in people, they will prove worthy of that faith, or, expressed in somewhat more concrete terms, that if you give dissatisfied people voluntarily more than they expect and, above all, before they really expect to get it, they will not abuse the gift but will be sobered simultaneously by the weight of responsibility and the sweetness of gratitude—was an underlying assumption of the Milner Group's activities from 1901 to the present. Its validity was defended (when proof was demanded) by a historical example—that is, by contrasting the lack of generosity in Britain's treatment of the American Colonies in 1774 with the generosity in her treatment of the Canadian Colonies in 1839. The contrast between the "Intolerable Acts" and the Durham Report was one of the basic ideas at the back of the minds of all the important members of the Milner Group. In many of those minds, however, this assumption was not based on political history at all but had a more profound and largely unconscious basis in the teachings of Christ and the Sermon on the Mount. This was especially true of Lionel Curtis, John Dove, Lord Lothian, and Lord Halifax. Unless this idea is recognized, it is not possible to see the underlying unity behind the actions of the Group toward the Boers in 1901-1910, toward India in 1919 and 1935, and toward Hitler in 1934-1939.

These ideas as a justification of concessions to India are to be found in Milner Group discussions of the Indian problem at all periods, especially just before the Act of 1919. A decade later they were still exerting their influence. They will be found, for example, in *The Round Table* articles on India in September 1930 and March 1931. The earlier advocated the use of the round-table method but warned that it must be based on complete equality for the Indian members. It continued: "Indians should share equally with Great Britain the responsibility for reaching or failing to reach an agreement as to what the next step in Indian constitutional development should be. It is no longer a question, as we see it, of Great Britain listening to Indian representatives and then deciding for herself what the next Indian constitution should be. . . . The core of the *round table* idea is that representative Britons and representative Indians should endeavour to reach an agreement, on the understanding that if they can reach an agreement, each will loyally carry it through to completion, as was the case with Ireland in 1922." As seen by the Milner Group, Britain's responsibility was

her obligation to help Indians to take maximum responsibility for India's government on their own shoulders, and to insist on their doing so, not only because it is the right thing in itself, but because it is the most certain antidote to the real danger of anarchy which threatens India unless Indians do learn to carry responsibility for government at a very early date. There is less risk in going too fast in agreement and cooperation with political India than in going at a more moderate pace without its agreement and cooperation. Indeed, in our view, the most successful foundation for the Round Table Conference would be that Great Britain should ask the Indian delegates to table agreed proposals and then do her utmost to accept them and place on Indian shoulders the responsibility for carrying them into effect.

It is very doubtful if the Milner Group could have substituted the round-table method for the commission method in quite so abrupt a fashion as it did, had not a Labour government come to office early in 1929. As a result, the difficult Lord Birkenhead was replaced as Secretary of State by the much more cooperative Mr. Wedgewood Benn (Viscount Stansgate since 1941). The greater degree of cooperation which the Milner Group received from Benn than from Birkenhead may be explained by the fact that their hopes for India were not far distant from those held in certain circles of the Labour Party. It may also be explained by the fact that Wedgewood Benn was considerably closer, in a social sense, to the Milner Group than was Birkenhead. Benn had been a Liberal M.P. from 1906 to 1927; his brother Sir Ernest Benn, the publisher, had been close to the Milner Group in the Ministry of Munitions in 1916-1917 and in the Ministry of Reconstruction in 1917-1918; and his nephew John, oldest son of Sir Ernest, married the oldest daughter of Maurice Hankey in 1929. Whatever the cause, or combination of causes, Lord Irwin's suggestion that the round-table method be adopted was accepted by the Labour government. The suggestion was made when the Viceroy returned to London in June 1929, months before the Simon Report was drafted and a year before it was published. With this suggestion Lord Irwin combined another, that the government formally announce that its goal for India was "Dominion status." The plan leaked out, probably because the Labour government had to consult with the Liberal Party, on which its majority depended. The Liberals (Lord Reading and Lloyd George) advised against the announcement, but Irwin was instructed to make it on his return to India in October. Lord Birkenhead heard of the plan and wrote a vigorous letter of protest to *The Times*. When Geoffrey Dawson refused to publish it, it appeared in the *Daily Telegraph*, thus repeating the experience of Lord Lansdowne's even more famous letter of 1917.

Lord Irwin's announcement of the Round Table Conference and of the goal of Dominion status, made in India on 31 October 1929, brought a storm of protest in England. It was rejected by Lord Reading

and Lloyd George for the Liberals and by Lord Birkenhead and
Stanley Baldwin for the Conservatives. It is highly unlikely that the
Milner Group were much disturbed by this storm. The reason is that
the members of the Group had already decided that "Dominion status"
had two meanings — one meaning for Englishmen, and a second, rather
different, meaning for Indians. As Lord Irwin wrote in a private
memorandum in November 1929:

> To the English conception, Dominion Status now connotes, as indeed the
> word itself implies, an *achieved* constitutional position of complete free-
> dom and immunity from interference by His Majesty's Government in
> London. . . . The Indian seems generally to mean something different.
> . . . The underlying element in much of Indian political thought seems to
> have been the desire that, by free conference between Great Britain and
> India, a constitution should be fashioned which may contain within itself
> the seed of full Dominion Status, growing naturally to its full develop-
> ment in accordance with the particular circumstances of India, without
> the necessity — the implications of which the Indian mind resents — of
> further periodic enquiries by way of Commission. What is to the English-
> man an accomplished process is to the Indian rather a *declaration of
> right*, from which future and complete enjoyment of Dominion privilege
> will spring.[3]

This distinction, without any reference to Lord Irwin (whose
memorandum was not published until 1941), was also made in the
September 1930 issue of *The Round Table*. On this basis, for the sake of
appeasement of India, the Milner Group was willing to promise India
"Dominion status" in the Indian meaning of the expression and allow
the English who misunderstood to cool off gradually as they saw that
the development was not the one they had feared. Indeed, to the
Milner Group, it probably appeared that the greater the rage in Britain, the greater the appeasement in India.

Accordingly, the first session of the Round Table Conference was
called for November 1930. It marked an innovation not only because of
the status of equality and responsibility which it placed on the Indians,
but also because, for the first time, it tried to settle the problem of the
Indian States within the same framework as it settled the constitutional
problem of British India. This was a revolutionary effort, and its
degree of success was very largely due to the preparatory work of Lord
Irwin, acting on the advice of Malcolm Hailey.

The Indian States had remained as backward, feudalistic, and ab-
solutist enclaves, within the territorial extent of British India and
bound to the British Raj by individual treaties and agreements. As
might be expected from the Milner Group, the solution which they proposed was federation. They hoped that devolution in British India
would secure a degree of provincial autonomy that would make it

possible to bind the provinces and the Indian States within the same federal structure and with similar local autonomy. However, the Group knew that the Indian States could not easily be federated with British India until their systems of government were raised to some approximation of the same level. For this reason, and to win the Princes over to federation, Lord Irwin had a large number of personal consultations with the Princes in 1927 and 1928. At some of these he lectured the Princes on the principles of good government in a fashion which came straight from the basic ideology of the Milner Group. The memorandum which he presented to them, dated 14 June 1927 and published in Johnson's biography, *Viscount Halifax*, could have been written by the Kindergarten. This can be seen in its definitions of the function of government, its emphasis on the reign of law, its advocacy of devolution, its homily on the duty of princes, its separation of responsibility in government from democracy in government, and its treatment of democracy as an accidental rather than an essential characteristic of good government.

The value of this preparatory work appeared at the first Round Table Conference, where, contrary to all expectations, the Indian Princes accepted federation. The optimism resulting from this agreement was, to a considerable degree, dissipated, however, by the refusal of Gandhi's party to participate in the conference unless India were granted full and immediate Dominion status. Refusal of these terms resulted in an outburst of political activity which made it necessary for Irwin to find jails capable of holding sixty thousand Indian agitators at one time.

The view that the Round Table Conference represented a complete repudiation of the Simon Commission's approach to the Indian problem was assiduously propagated by the Milner Group in order to prevent Indian animosity against the latter from being carried over against the former. But the differences were in detail, since in main outline both reflected the Group's faith in federation, devolution, responsibility, and minority rights. The chief recommendations of the Simon Commission were three in number: (1) to create a federation of British India and the Indian States by using the provinces of the former as federative units with the latter; (2) to modify the central government by making the Legislative Assembly a federal organization but otherwise leave the center unchanged; (3) to end dyarchy in the provinces by making Indians responsible for all provincial activities. It also advocated separation of Burma from India.

These were also the chief conclusions of the various Round Table Conferences and of the government's White Papers of December 1931 (Cmd. 3972) and of March 1933 (Cmd. 4268). The former was presented to Parliament and resulted in a debate and vote of confidence on the government's policy in India as stated in it. The attack was led by Winston Churchill in the Commons and by Lords Lloyd, Salisbury, Midleton, and Sumner in the House of Lords. None of these except Churchill openly attacked the government's policy, the others contenting themselves with advising delay in its execution. The government was defended by Samuel Hoare, John Simon, and Stanley Baldwin in the Commons and by Lords Lothian, Irwin, Zetland, Dufferin, and Hailsham, as well as Archbishop Lang, in the Lords. Lord Lothian, in opening the debate, said that while visiting in India in 1912 he had written an article for an English review saying that the Indian Nationalist movement "was essentially healthy, for it was a movement for political virtue and self-respect," although the Indian Civil Servant with whom he was staying said that Indian Nationalism was sedition. Lord Lothian implied that he had not changed his opinion twenty years later. In the Lower House the question came to a vote, which the government easily carried by 369 to 43. In the majority were Leopold Amery, John J. Astor, John Buchan, Austen Chamberlain, Viscount Cranborne, Samuel Hoare, W. G. A. Ormsby-Gore, Lord Eustace Percy, John Simon, and D. B. Somervell. In the minority were Churchill, George Balfour, and Viscount Wolmer.

Practically the same persons appeared on the same sides in the discussion regarding the White Paper of 1933. This document, which embodied the government's suggestions for a bill on Indian constitutional reform, was defended by various members of the Milner Group outside of Parliament, and anonymously in *The Round Table*. John Buchan wrote a prefece to John Thompson's *India: The White Paper* (1933), in which he defended the extension of responsible government to India, saying, "We cannot exclude her from sharing in what we ourselves regard as the best." Samuel Hoare defended it in a letter to his constituents at Chelsea. Malcolm Hailey defended it before the Royal Empire Society Summer School at Oxford, in a speech afterwards published in *The Asiatic Review*. Hailey had resigned as Governor of the United Provinces in India in order to return to England to help the government put through its bill. During the long period required to accomplish this, Samuel Hoare, who as Secretary of State for India was the official government spokesman on the subject, had Hailey constantly with him as his chief adviser and support. It was this support that permitted Hoare, whose knowledge of India was definitely limited, to conduct his astounding campaign for the Act of 1935.

The White Paper of 1933 was presented to a Joint Select Committee of both Houses. It was publicly stated as a natural action on the part of the government that this committee be packed with supporters of the bill. For this reason Churchill, George Balfour, and Lord Wolmer refused to serve on it, although Josiah Wedgwood, a Labour Member who opposed the bill, asked to be put on the committee because it was packed.

The Joint Select Committee, as we have seen, had thirty-two members, of whom at least twelve were from the Cecil Bloc and Milner Group and supported the bill. Four were from the inner circles of the Milner Group. The chief witnesses were Sir Samuel Hoare; who gave testimony for twenty days; Sir Michael O'Dwyer, who gave testimony for four days; and Winston Churchill, who gave testimony for three days. The chief witness was thus Hoare, who answered 5594 questions from the committee. At all times Hoare had Malcolm Hailey at his side for advice.

The fashion in which the government conducted the Joint Select Committee aroused a good deal of unfavorable comment. Lord Rankeillour in the House of Lords criticized this, especially the fashion in which Hoare used his position to push his point of view and to influence the evidence which the committee received from other witnesses. He concluded: "This Committee was not a judicial body, and its conclusions are vitiated thereby. You may say that on their merits they have produced a good or a bad Report, but what you cannot say is that the Report is the judicial finding of unbiased or impartial minds." As a result of such complaints, the House of Commons Committee on Privilege investigated the conduct of the Joint Select Committee. It found that Hoare's actions toward witnesses and in regard to documentary evidence could be brought within the scope of the Standing Orders of the House if a distinction were made between judicial committees and nonjudicial committees and between witnesses giving facts and giving opinions. These distinctions made it possible to acquit Sir Samuel of any violation of privilege, but aroused such criticism that a Select Committee on Witnesses was formed to examine the rules for dealing with witnesses. In its report, on 4 June 1935, this Select Committee rejected the validity of the distinctions between judicial and nonjudicial and between fact and opinion made by the Committee on Privilege, and recommended that the Standing Rules be amended to forbid any tampering with documents that had been received by a committee. The final result was a formal acquittal, but a moral condemnation, of Hoare's actions in regard to the Joint Select Committee on the Government of India.

The report of the Joint Select Committee was accepted by nineteen out of its thirty-two members. Nine voted against it (five Conservative and four Labour Members). A motion to accept the report and ask the government to proceed to draw up a bill based on it was introduced in the House of Lords by the President of the Board of Education, Lord Halifax (Lord Irwin), on 12 December 1934, in a typical Milner Group speech. He said: "As I read it, the whole of our British and Imperial experience shouts at us the warning that representative government without responsibility, once political consciousness has been aroused, is apt to be a source of great weakness and, not impossibly, great danger. We had not learned that lesson, let me remind the House, in the eighteenth century, and we paid very dearly for it. We learned it some sixty years later and, by having learned it, we transformed the face and history of Canada." Lord Salisbury once again advised delay, and attacked the idea that parliamentary government could work in India or indeed had worked anywhere outside the British Commonwealth. Lord Snell, speaking for the Labour opposition, objected to the lack of protection against economic exploitation for the Indian masses, the omission of any promise of Dominion status for India, the weighing of the franchise too heavily on the side of the landlords and too lightly on the side of women or of laborers, the provisions for a second chamber, and the use of indirect election for the first chamber. Lord Lothian answered both speakers, supporting only one criticism, that against indirect election to the central assembly. He made the significant statement that he did not fear to turn India over to the Congress Party of Gandhi because (1) "though I disagree with almost everything that they say in public and most of their political programme, I have a sneaking sympathy with the emotion which lies underneath them . . . the aspiration of young impetuous India anxious to take responsibility on its own shoulders"; and (2) "because I believe that the one political lesson, which has more often been realized in the British Commonwealth of Nations than anywhere else in the world, is that the one corrective of political extremism is to put responsibility upon the extremists, and, by these proposals, that is exactly what we are doing." These are typical Milner Group reasons.

In the debate, Halifax was supported by Archbishop Lang and Lords Zetland, Linlithgow, Midleton, Hardinge of Penshurst, Lytton, and Reading. Lord Salisbury was supported by Lords Phillimore, Rankeillour, Ampthill, and Lloyd. In the division, Salisbury's motion for delay was beaten by 239 to 62. In addition to the lords mentioned, the majority included Lords Dufferin, Linlithgow, Cranbrook, Cobham, Cecil of Chelwood, Goschen, Hampden, Elton, Lugard, Meston, and Wemyss, while the minority included Lords Birkenhead, Westminster, Carnock, Islington, and Leconfield. It is clear that the Milner Group voted completely with the majority, while the Cecil Bloc was split.

The bill was introduced in the House of Commons on 6 February 1935 by Sir Samuel Hoare. As was to be expected, his argument was based on the lessons to be derived from the error of 1774 and the success of 1839 in North America. The government's actions, he declared, were based on "plain, good intentions." He was mildly criticized from the left by Attlee and Sir Herbert Samuel; supported by Sir Arthur Steel-Maitland, Sir Edward Grigg, and others; and then subjected to a long-sustained barrage from Winston Churchill. Churchill had already revealed his opinion of the bill over the BBC when he said, on 29 January 1935, that it was "a monstrous monument of sham built by the pygmies." He continued his attack in a similar vein, with the result that almost every government speaker felt the need to caution him that his intemperance was hurting his own cause. From our point of view, his most interesting statement, and one which was not contradicted, said: "I have watched this story from its very unfolding, and what has struck me more than anything else about it has been the amazingly small number of people who have managed to carry matters to their present lamentable pitch. You could almost count them on the fingers of one hand. I have also been struck by the prodigious power which this group of individuals have been able to exert and relay, to use a mechanical term, through the vast machinery of party, of Parliament, and of patronage, both here and in the East. It is tragical that they should have been able to mislead the loyalties and use the assets of the Empire to its own undoing. I compliment them on their skill, and I compliment them also on their disciples. Their chorus is exceedingly well drilled." This statement was answered by Lord Eustace Percy, who quoted Lord Hugh Cecil on "profitable mendacity." This led to an argument, in which both sides appealed to the Speaker. Order was restored when Lord Eustace said of Churchill, "I would never impute to him . . . any intention of making a charge which he did not believe himself."

It is quite clear that Churchill believed his charge and was referring to what we have called the Milner Group, although he would not have known it under that name, nor would he have realized its extreme ramifications. He was merely referring to the extensive influence of that close group of associates which included Hoare, Hailey, Curtis, Lothian, Dawson, Amery, Grigg, and Halifax.

After four days of debate on the second reading, the opposition amendment was rejected by 404-133, and the bill passed to the committee stage. In the majority were Amery, Buchan, Grigg, Hoare, Ormsby-Gore, Simon, Sir Donald Somervell, and Steel-Maitland. The minority consisted of three ill-assorted groups: the followers of Churchill, the leaders of the Labour Party, and a fragment of the Cecil Bloc with a few others.

The Government of India Act of 1935 was the longest bill ever submitted to Parliament, and it underwent the longest debate in history (over forty days in Commons). In general, the government let the opposition talk itself out and then crushed it on each division. In the third reading, Churchill made his final speech in a tone of baneful warning regarding the future of India. He criticized the methods of pressure used by Hoare and said that in ten years' time the Secretary of State would be haunted by what had been done, and it could be said of him,

> "God save thee, ancient Mariner,
> From the fiends that plague thee thus.
> Why look'st thou so?" With my cross-bow,
> I shot the Albatross.

These somber warnings were answered by Leopold Amery, who opened his rejoinder with the words, "Here endeth the last chapter of the Book of the Prophet Jeremiah."

In the House of Lords the bill was taken through its various stages by Lord Zetland (who replaced Hoare as Secretary of State for India in June 1935), and the final speech for the government was from Halifax (recently made Secretary of State for War). The Act received the Royal Assent on 1 August 1935.

The Act never went into effect completely, and by 1939 the Milner Group was considering abandoning it in favor of complete self-government for India. The portions of the Act of 1935 dealing with the central government fell to the ground when the refusal of the Princes of the Indian States to accept the Act made a federal solution impossible. The provincial portion began to function in 1937, but with great difficulty because of the extremist agitation from the Congress Party. This party obtained almost half of the seats in the eleven provinces and had a clear majority in six provinces. The provincial governments, started in 1937, worked fairly well, and the emergency powers of the central governments, which continued on the 1919 model, were used only twice in over two years. When the war began, the Congress Party ordered its ministries to resign. Since the Congress Party members in the legislatures would not support non-Congress ministries, the decree powers of the Provincial Governors had to be used in those provinces with a Congress majority. In 1945 six out of the eleven provinces had responsible government.

From 1939 on, constitutional progress in India was blocked by a double stalemate: (1) the refusal of the Congress Party to cooperate in government unless the British abandoned India completely, something which could not be done while the Japanese were invading Burma; and (2) the growing refusal of the Moslem League to cooperate with the Congress Party on any basis except partition of India and complete autonomy for the areas with Moslem majorities. The Milner Group, and the British government generally, by 1940 had given up all hope of any successful settlement except complete self-government for India, but it could not give up to untried hands complete control of defense policy during the war. At the same time, the Milner Group generally supported Moslem demands because of its usual emphasis on minority rights.

During this period the Milner Group remained predominant in Indian affairs, although the Viceroy (Lord Linlithgow) was not a member of the Group. The Secretary of State for India, however, was Leopold Amery for the whole period 1940-1945. A number of efforts were made to reach agreement with the Congress Party, but the completely unrealistic attitude of the party's leaders, especially Gandhi, made this impossible. In 1941, H. V. Hodson, by that time one of the most important members of the Milner Group, was made Reforms Commissioner for India. The following year the most important effort to break the Indian stalemate was made. This was the Cripps Mission, whose chief adviser was Sir Reginald Coupland, another member of the inner circle of the Milner Group. As a result of the failure of this mission and of the refusal of the Indians to believe in the sincerity of the British (a skepticism that was completely without basis), the situation dragged on until after the War. The election of 1945, which drove the Conservative Party from office, also removed the Milner Group from its positions of influence. The subsequent events, including complete freedom for India and the division of the country into two Dominions within the British Commonwealth, were controlled by new hands, but the previous actions of the Milner Group had so committed the situation that these new hands had no possibility (nor, indeed, desire) to turn the Indian problem into new paths. There can be little doubt that with the Milner Group still in control the events of 1945-1948 in respect to India would have differed only in details.

The history of British relations with India in the twentieth century was disastrous. In this history the Milner Group played a major role. To be sure, the materials with which they had to work were intractable and they had inconvenient obstacles at home (like the diehards within the Conservative Party), but these problems were made worse by the misconceptions about India and about human beings held by the Milner Group. The bases on which they built their policy were fine — indeed, too fine. These bases were idealistic, almost utopian, to a degree which made it impossible for them to grow and function and made it highly likely that forces of ignorance and barbarism would be released, with results exactly contrary to the desires of the Milner Group. On the basis of love of liberty, human rights, minority guarantees, and self-responsibility, the Milner Group took actions that broke down the lines of external authority in Indian society faster than any lines of internal self-discipline were being created. It is said that the road to perdition is paved with good intentions. The road to the Indian tragedy of 1947-1948 was also paved with good intentions, and those paving blocks were manufactured and laid down by the Milner Group. The same good intentions contributed largely to the dissolution of the British Empire, the race wars of South Africa, and the unleashing of the horrors of 1939-1945 on the world.

To be sure, in India as elsewhere, the Milner Group ran into bad luck for which they were not responsible. The chief case of this in India was the Amritsar Massacre of 1919, which was probably the chief reason for Gandhi's refusal to cooperate in carrying out the constitutional reforms of that same year. But the Milner Group's policies were self-inconsistent and were unrealistic. For example, they continually insisted that the parliamentary system was not fitted to Indian conditions, yet they made no real effort to find a more adaptive political system, and every time they gave India a further dose of self-government, it was always another dose of the parliamentary system. But, clinging to their beliefs, they loaded down this system with special devices which hampered it from functioning as a parliamentary system should. The irony of this whole procedure rests in the fact that the minority of agitators in India who wanted self-government wanted it on the parliamentary pattern and regarded every special device and every statement from Britain that it was not adapted to Indian conditions as an indication of the insincerity in the British desire to grant self-government to India.

A second error arises from the Milner Group's lack of enthusiasm for democracy. Democracy, as a form of government, involves two parts: (1) majority rule and (2) minority rights. Because of the Group's lack of faith in democracy, they held no brief for the first of these but devoted all their efforts toward achieving the second. The result was to make the minority uncompromising, at the same time that they diminished the majority's faith in their own sincerity. In India the result was to make the Moslem League almost completely obstructionist and make the Congress Party almost completely suspicious. The whole policy encouraged extremists and discouraged moderates. This appears at its worst in the systems of communal representation and communal electorates established in India by Britain. The Milner Group knew these were bad, but felt that they were a practical necessity in order to preserve minority rights. In this they were not only wrong, as proved by history, but were sacrificing principle to expediency in a way that can never be permitted by a group whose actions claim to be so largely dictated by principle. To do this weakens the faith of others in the group's principles.

The Group made another error in their constant tendency to accept the outcry of a small minority of Europeanized agitators as the voice of India. The masses of the Indian people were probably in favor of British rule, for very practical reasons. The British gave these masses good government through the Indian Civil Service and other services, but they made little effort to reach them on any human, intellectual, or ideological level. The "color line" was drawn — not between British and Indians but between British and the masses, for the educated upper-class Indians were treated as equals in the majority of cases. The existence of the color line did not bother the masses of the people, but when it hit one of the educated minority, he forgot the more numerous group of cases where it had not been applied to him, became anti-British and began to flood the uneducated masses with a deluge of anti-British propaganda. This could have been avoided to a great extent by training the British Civil Servants to practice racial toleration toward all classes, by increasing the proportion of financial expenditure on elementary education while reducing that on higher education, by using the increased literacy of the masses of the people to impress on them the good they derived from British rule and to remove those grosser superstitions and social customs which justified the color line to so many English. All of these except the last were in accordance with Milner Group ideas. The members of the Group objected to the personal intolerance of the British in India, and regretted the disproportionate share of educational expenditure which went to higher education (see the speech in Parliament of Ormsby-Gore, 11 December 1934), but they continued to educate a small minority, most of whom became anti-British agitators, and left the masses of the people exposed to the agitations of that minority. On principle, the Group would not interfere with the superstitions and grosser social customs of the masses of the people, on the grounds that to do so would be to interfere with religious freedom. Yet Britain had abolished suttee, child marriage, and thuggery, which were also religious in foundation. If the British could have reduced cow-worship, and especially the number of cows, to moderate proportions, they would have conferred on India a blessing greater than the abolition of suttee, child marriage, and thuggery together, would have removed the chief source of animosity between Hindu and Moslem, and would have raised the standard of living of the Indian people to a degree that would have more than paid for a system of elementary education.

If all of these things had been done, the agitation for independence could have been delayed long enough to build up an electorate capable of working a parliamentary system. Then the parliamentary system, which educated Indians wanted, could have been extended to them without the undemocratic devices and animadversions against it which usually accompanied any effort to introduce it on the part of the British.

12

Foreign Policy, 1919-1940

ANY EFFORT to write an account of the influence exercised by the Milner Group in foreign affairs in the period between the two World Wars would require a complete rewriting of the history of that period. This cannot be done within the limits of a single chapter, and it will not be attempted. Instead, an effort will be made to point out the chief ideas of the Milner Group in this field, the chief methods by which they were able to make those ideas prevail, and a few significant examples of how these methods worked in practice.

The political power of the Milner Group in the period 1919-1939 grew quite steadily. It can be measured by the number of ministerial portfolios held by members of the Group. In the first period, 1919-1924, they generally held about one-fifth of the Cabinet posts. For example, the Cabinet that resigned in January 1924 had nineteen members; four were of the Milner Group, only one from the inner circle. These four were Leopold Amery, Edward Wood, Samuel Hoare, and Lord Robert Cecil. In addition, in the same period other members of the Group were in the government in one position or another. Among these were Milner, Austen Chamberlain, H. A. L. Fisher, Lord Ernle, Lord Astor, Sir Arthur Steel-Maitland, and W. G. A. Ormsby-Gore. Also, relatives of these, such as Lord Onslow (brother-in-law of Lord Halifax), Captain Lane-Fox (brother-in-law of Lord Halifax), and Lord Greenwood (brother-in-law of Amery), were in the government.

In this period the influence of the Milner Group was exercised in two vitally significant political acts. In the first case, the Milner Group appears to have played an important role behind the scenes in persuading the King to ask Baldwin rather than Curzon to be Prime Minister in 1923. Harold Nicolson, in *Curzon: The Last Phase* (1934), says that Balfour, Amery, and Walter Long intervened with the King to oppose Curzon, and "the cumulative effect of these representations was to reverse the previous decision." Of the three names mentioned by

Nicolson, two were of the Cecil Bloc, while the third was Milner's closest associate. If Amery did intervene, he undoubtedly did so as the representative of Milner, and if Milner opposed Curzon to this extent through Amery, he was in a position to bring other powerful influences to bear on His Majesty through Lord Esher as well as through Brand's brother, Viscount Hampden, a lord-in-waiting to the King, or more directly through Milner's son-in-law, Captain Alexander Hardinge, a private secretary to the King. In any case, Milner exercised a very powerful influence on Baldwin during the period of his first government, and it was on Milner's advice that Baldwin waged the General Election of 1924 on the issue of protection. The election manifesto issued by the party and advocating a tariff was written by Milner in consultation with Arthur Steel-Maitland.

In the period 1924-1929 the Milner Group usually held about a third of the seats in the Cabinet (seven out of twenty-one in the government formed in November 1924). These proportions were also held in the period 1935-1940, with a somewhat smaller ratio in the period 1931-1935. In the Cabinet that was formed in the fall of 1931, the Milner Group exercised a peculiar influence. The Labour Party under Ramsay MacDonald was in office with a minority government from 1929 to September 1931. Toward the end of this period, the Labour government experienced increasing difficulty because the deflationary policy of the Bank of England and the outflow of gold from the country were simultaneously intensifying the depression, increasing unemployment and public discontent, and jeopardizing the gold standard. In fact, the Bank of England's policy made it almost impossible for the Labour Party to govern. Without informing his Cabinet, Ramsay MacDonald entered upon negotiations with Baldwin and King George, as a result of which MacDonald became Prime Minister of a new government, supported by Conservative votes in Parliament. The obvious purpose of this intrigue was to split the Labour Party and place the administration back in Conservative hands.

In this intrigue the Milner Group apparently played an important, if secret, role. That they were in a position to play such a role is clear. We have mentioned the pressure which the bankers were putting on the Labour government in the period 1929-1931. The Milner Group were clearly in a position to influence this pressure. E. R. Peacock (Parkin's old associate) was at the time a director of the Bank of England and a director of Baring Brothers; Robert Brand, Thomas Henry Brand, and Adam Marris (son of Sir William Marris) were all at Lazard and Brothers; Robert Brand was also a director of Lloyd's Bank; Lord Selborne was a director of Lloyd's Bank; Lord Lugard was a director of Barclay's Bank; Major Astor was a director of Hambros Bank; and Lord Goschen was a director of the Westminster Bank.

We have already indicated the ability of the Milner Group to influence the King in respect to the choice of Baldwin as Prime Minister in 1923. By 1931 this power was even greater. Thus the Milner Group was in a position to play a role in the intrigue of 1931. That they may have done so is to be found in the fact that two of the important figures in this intrigue within the Labour Party were ever after closely associated with the Milner Group. These two were Malcolm MacDonald and Godfrey Elton.

Malcolm MacDonald, son and intimate associate of Ramsay MacDonald, clearly played an important role in the intrigue of 1931. He was rewarded with a position in the new government and has never been out of office since. These offices included Parliamentary Under Secretary in the Dominions Office (1931-1935), Secretary of State for the Dominions (1935-1938 and 1938-1939), Secretary of State for the Colonies (1935-and 1938-1940), Minister of Health (1940-1941), United Kingdom High Commissioner in Canada (1941-1946), Governor-General of Malaya and British South-East Asia (since 1946). Since all of these offices but one (Minister of Health) were traditionally in the sphere of the Milner Group, and since Malcolm MacDonald during this period was closely associated with the Group in its other activities, such as Chatham House and the unofficial British Commonwealth relations conferences, Malcolm MacDonald should probably be regarded as a member of the Group from about 1932 onward.

Godfrey Elton (Lord Elton since 1934), of Rugby and Balliol, was a Fellow of Queen's College, Oxford, from 1919, as well as lecturer on Modern History at Oxford. In this role Elton came in contact with Malcolm MacDonald, who was an undergraduate at Queen's in the period 1920-1925. Through this connection, Elton ran for Parliament on the Labour Party ticket in 1924 and again in 1929, both times without success. He was more successful in establishing himself as an intellectual leader of the Labour Party, capping this by publishing in 1931 a study of the early days of the party. As a close associate of the MacDonald family, he supported the intrigue of 1931 and played a part in it. For this he was expelled from the party and became honorary political secretary of the new National Labour Committee and editor of its *News-Letter* (1932-1938). He was made a baron in 1934, was on the Ullswater Committee on the Future of Broadcasting the following year, and in 1939 succeeded Lord Lothian as Secretary to the Rhodes Trustees. By his close association with the MacDonald family, he became the obvious choice to write the "official" life of J. R. (Ramsay) MacDonald, the first volume of which was published in 1939. In 1945 he published a history of the British Empire called *Imperial Commonwealth*.

After the election of 1935, the Milner Group took a substantial part in the government, with possession of seven places in a Cabinet of twenty-one seats. By the beginning of September of 1939, they had only five out of twenty-three, the decrease being caused, as we shall see, by the attrition within the Group on the question of appeasement. In the War Cabinet formed at the outbreak of the war, they had four out of nine seats. In this whole period from 1935 to 1940, the following members of the Group were associated with the government as officers of state: Halifax, Simon, Malcolm MacDonald, Zetland, Ormsby-Gore, Hoare, Somervell, Lothian, Hankey, Grigg, Salter, and Amery.

It would appear that the Milner Group increased its influence on the government until about 1938. We have already indicated the great power which they exercised in the period 1915-1919. This influence, while great, was neither decisive nor preponderant. At the time, the Milner Group was sharing influence with at least two other groups and was, perhaps, the least powerful of the three. It surely was less powerful than the Cecil Bloc, even as late as 1929, and was less powerful, perhaps, than the rather isolated figure of Lloyd George as late as 1922. These relative degrees of power on the whole do not amount to very much, because the three that we have mentioned generally agreed on policy. When they disagreed, the views of the Milner Group did not usually prevail. There were two reasons for this. Both the Cecil Bloc and Lloyd George were susceptible to pressure from the British electorate and from the allies of Britain. The Milner Group, as a nonelected group, could afford to be disdainful of the British electorate and of French opinion, but the persons actually responsible for the government, like Lloyd George, Balfour, and others, could not be so casual. As a consequence, the Milner Group were bitterly disappointed over the peace treaty with Germany and over the Covenant of the League of Nations. This may seem impossible when we realize how much the Group contributed to both of these. For they did contribute a great deal, chiefly because of the fact that the responsible statesmen generally accepted the opinion of the experts on the terms of the treaty, especially the territorial terms. There is only one case where the delegates overruled a committee of experts that was unanimous, and that was the case of the Polish Corridor, where the experts were more severe with Germany than the final agreement. The experts, thus, were of very great importance, and among the experts the Milner Group had an important place, as we have seen. It would thus seem that the Milner Group's disappointment with the peace settlement was largely criticism of their own handiwork. To a considerable extent this is true. The explanation lies in the fact that much of what they did as experts was done on instructions from the responsible delegates and the fact that the Group ever after had a tendency to focus their eyes on the few blemishes of the settlement, to the complete neglect of the much larger body of acceptable decisions. Except for this, the Group could have no justification for their dissatisfaction except as self-criticism. When the original draft of the Treaty of Versailles was presented to the Germans on 7 May 1919, the defeated delegates were aghast at its severity. They drew up a detailed criticism of 443 pages. The answer to this protest, making a few minor changes in the treaty but allowing the major provisions to stand, was drafted by an interallied committee of five, of which Philip Kerr was the British member. The changes that were made as concessions to the Germans were made under pressure from Lloyd George, who was himself under pressure from the Milner Group. This appears clearly from the minutes of the Council of Four at the Peace Conference. The first organized drive to revise the draft of the treaty in the direction of leniency was made by Lloyd George at a meeting of the Council of Four on 2 June 1919. The Prime Minister said he had been consulting with his delegation and with the Cabinet. He specifically mentioned George Barnes ("the only Labour representative in his Cabinet"), the South African delegation (who "were also refusing to sign the present Treaty"), Mr. Fisher ("whose views carried great weight"), Austen Chamberlain, Lord Robert Cecil, and both the Archbishops. Except for Barnes and the Archbishops, all of these were close to the Milner Group. The reference to H. A. L. Fisher is especially significant, for Fisher's views could "carry great weight" only insofar as he was a member of the Milner Group. The reference to the South African delegation meant Smuts, for Botha was prepared to sign, no matter what he felt about the treaty, in order to win for his country official recognition as a Dominion of equal status with Britain. Smuts, on the other hand, refused to sign from the beginning and, as late as 23 June 1919, reiterated his refusal (according to Mrs. Millen's biography of Smuts).

Lloyd George's objections to the treaty as presented in the Council of Four on 2 June were those which soon became the trademark of the Milner Group. In addition to criticisms of the territorial clauses on the Polish frontier and a demand for a plebiscite in Upper Silesia, the chief objections were aimed at reparations and the occupation of the Rhineland. On the former point, Lloyd George's advisers "thought that more had been asked for than Germany could pay." On the latter point, which "was the main British concern," his advisers were insistent. "They urged that when the German Army was reduced to a strength of 100,000 men it was ridiculous to maintain an army of occupation of 200,000 men on the Rhine. They represented that it was only a method of quartering the French Army on Germany and making Germany pay the cost. It had been pointed out that Germany would not constitute a danger to France for 30 years or even 50 years; certainly not in 15 years. . . . The advice of the British military authorities was that two years was the utmost limit of time for the occupation."

To these complaints, Clemenceau had replied that "in England the view seemed to prevail that the easiest way to finish the war was by making concessions. In France the contrary view was held that it was best to act firmly. The French people, unfortunately, knew the Germans very intimately, and they believed that the more concessions we made, the more the Germans would demand. . . . He recognized that Germany was not an immediate menace to France. But Germany would sign the Treaty with every intention of not carrying it out. Evasions would be made first on one point and then on another. The whole Treaty would go by the board if there were not some guarantees such as were provided by the occupation."[1]

Under such circumstances as these, it seems rather graceless for the Milner Group to have started at once, as it did, a campaign of recrimination against the treaty. Philip Kerr was from 1905 to his death in 1940 at the very center of the Milner Group. His violent Germanophobia in 1908-1918, and his evident familiarity with the character of the Germans and with the kind of treaty which they would have imposed on Britain had the roles been reversed, should have made the Treaty of Versailles very acceptable to him and his companions, or, if not, unacceptable on grounds of excessive leniency. Instead, Kerr, Brand, Curtis, and the whole inner core of the Milner Group began a campaign to undermine the treaty, the League of Nations, and the whole peace settlement. Those who are familiar with the activities of the "Cliveden Set" in the 1930s have generally felt that the appeasement policy associated with that group was a manifestation of the period after 1934 only. This is quite mistaken. The Milner Group, which was the reality behind the phantom-like Cliveden Set, began their program of appeasement and revision of the settlement as early as 1919. Why did they do this?

To answer this question, we must fall back on the statements of the members of the Group, general impressions of their psychological outlook, and even a certain amount of conjecture. The best statement of what the Group found objectionable in the peace of 1919 will be found in a brilliant book of Zimmern's called *Europe in Convalescence* (1922). More concrete criticism, especially in regard to the Covenant of the League, will be found in *The Round Table*. And the general mental outlook of the Group in 1919 will be found in Harold Nicolson's famous book *Peace-Making*. Nicolson, although on close personal relationships with most of the inner core of the Milner Group, was not a member of the Group himself, but his psychology in 1918-1920 was similar to that of the members of the inner core.

In general, the members of this inner core took the propagandist slogans of 1914-1918 as a truthful picture of the situation. I have indicated how the Group had worked out a theory of history that saw the whole past in terms of a long struggle between the forces of evil and the forces of righteousness. The latter they defined at various times as "the rule of law" (a la Dicey), as "the subordination of each to the welfare of all," as "democracy," etc. They accepted Wilson's identification of his war aims with his war slogans ("a world safe for democracy," "a war to end wars," "a war to end Prussianism," "self-determination," etc.) as meaning what they meant by "the rule of law." They accepted his Fourteen Points (except "freedom of the seas") as implementation of these aims. Moreover, the Milner Group, and apparently Wilson, made an assumption which had a valid basis but which could be very dangerous if carried out carelessly. This was the assumption that the Germans were divided into two groups, "Prussian autocrats" and "good Germans." They assumed that, if the former group were removed from positions of power and influence, and magnanimous concessions were made to the latter, Germany could be won over on a permanent basis from "Asiatic despotism" to "Western civilization." In its main outlines, the thesis was valid. But difficulties were numerous.

In the first place, it is not possible to distinguish between "good" Germans and "bad" Germans by any objective criterion. The distinction certainly could not be based on who was in public office in 1914-1918. In fact, the overwhelming mass of Germans — almost all the middle classes, except a few intellectuals and very religious persons; a considerable portion of the aristocratic class (at least half); and certain segments of the working class (about one-fifth) — were "bad" Germans in the sense in which the Milner Group used that expression. In their saner moments, the Group knew this. In December 1918, Curtis wrote in *The Round Table* on this subject as follows: "No one class, but the nation itself was involved in the sin. There were Socialists who licked their lips over Brest-Litovsk. All but a mere remnant, and those largely in prison or exile, accepted or justified the creed of despotism so long as it promised them the mastery of the world. The German People consented to be slaves in their own house as the price of enslaving mankind." If these words had been printed and posted on the walls of All Souls, of Chatham House, of New College, of *The Times* office in Printing House Square, and of *The Round Table* office at 175 Piccadilly, there need never have been a Second World War with Germany. But these words were not remembered by the Group. Instead, they assumed that the "bad" Germans were the small group that was removed from office in 1918 with the Kaiser. They did not see that the Kaiser was merely a kind of facade for four other groups: The Prussian Officers' Corps, the Junker landlords, the governmental bureaucracy (especially the administrators of police and justice), and the great industrialists. They did not see that these four had been able to save themselves in 1918 by jettisoning the Kaiser, who had become a liability. They did not see that these four were left in their positions of influence, with their power practically intact — indeed, in many ways with their power greater than ever, since the new "democratic" politicians like Ebert, Scheidemann, and Noske were much more subservient to the four groups than the old imperial authorities had ever been. General Gröner gave orders to Ebert over his direct telephone line from Kassel in a tone and with a directness that he would never have used to an imperial chancellor. In a word, there was no revolution in Germany in 1918. The Milner Group did not see this, because they did not want to see it. Not that they were not warned. Brigadier General John H. Morgan, who was almost a member of the Group and who was on the Interallied Military Commission of Control in Germany in 1919-1923, persistently warned the government and the Group of the continued existence and growing power of the German Officers' Corps and of the unreformed character of the German people. As a graduate of Balliol and the University of Berlin (1897-1905), a leader-writer on *The Manchester Guardian* (1904-1905), a Liberal candidate for Parliament with Amery in 1910, an assistant adjutant general with the military section of the British delegation to the Peace Conference of 1919, the British member on the Prisoners of War Commission (1919), legal editor of *The Encyclopedia Britannica* (14th edition), contributor to *The Times*, reader in constitutional law to the Inns of Court (1926-1936), Professor of Constitutional Law at the University of London, Rhodes Lecturer at London (1927-1932), counsel to the Indian Chamber of Princes (1934-1937), counsel to the Indian State of Gwalior, Tagore Professor at Calcutta (1939) — as all of these things, and thus close to many members of the Group, General Morgan issued warnings about Germany that should have been heeded by the Group. They were not. No more attention was paid to them than was paid to the somewhat similar warnings coming from Professor Zimmern. And the general, with less courage than the professor, or perhaps with more of that peculiar group loyalty which pervades his social class in England, kept his warnings secret and private for years. Only in October 1924 did he come out in public with an article in the *Quarterly Review* on the subject, and only in 1945 did he find a wider platform in a published book (*Assize of Arms*), but in neither did he name the persons who were suppressing the warnings in his official reports from the Military Commission.

In a similar fashion, the Milner Group knew that the industrialists, the Junkers, the police, and the judges were cooperating with the reactionaries to suppress all democratic and enlightened elements in Germany and to help all the forces of "despotism" and "sin" (to use Curtis's words). The Group refused to recognize these facts. For this, there were two reasons. One, for which Brand was chiefly responsible, was based on certain economic assumptions. Among these, the chief was the belief that "disorder" and social unrest could be avoided only if prosperity were restored to Germany as soon as possible. By "disorder," Brand meant such activities as were associated with Trotsky in Russia, Béla Kun in Hungary, and the Spartacists or Kurt Eisner in Germany. To Brand, as an orthodox international banker, prosperity could be obtained only by an economic system under the control of the old established industrialists and bankers. This is perfectly clear from Brand's articles in *The Round Table*, reprinted in his book, *War and National Finance* (1921). Moreover, Brand felt confident that the old economic groups could reestablish prosperity quickly only if they were given concessions in respect to Germany's international financial position by lightening the weight of reparations on Germany and by advancing credit to Germany, chiefly from the United States. This point of view was not Brand's alone. It dominated the minds of all international bankers from Thomas Lamont to Montague Norman and from 1918 to at least 1931. The importance of Brand, from out point of view, lies in the fact that, as "the economic expert" of the Milner Group and one of the leaders of the Group, he brought this point of view into the Group and was able to direct the great influence of the Group in this direction.[2]

Blindness to the real situation in Germany was also encouraged from another point of view. This was associated with Philip Kerr. Roughly, this point of view advocated a British foreign policy based on the old balance-of-power system. Under that old system, which Britain had followed since 1500, Britain should support the second strongest power on the Continent against the strongest power, to prevent the latter from obtaining supremacy on the Continent. For one brief moment in 1918, the Group toyed with the idea of abandoning this traditional policy; for one brief moment they felt that if Europe were given self-determination and parliamentary governments, Britain could permit some kind of federated or at least cooperative Europe without danger to Britain. The moment soon passed. The League of Nations, which had been regarded by the Group as the seed whence a united Europe might grow, became nothing more than a propaganda machine, as soon as the Group resumed its belief in the balance of power. Curtis, who in December 1918 wrote in *The Round Table*: "That the balance of power has outlived its time by a century and that the world has remained a prey to wars, was due to the unnatural alienation of the British and American Commonwealths" — Curtis, who wrote this in

1918, four years later (9 January 1923) vigorously defended the idea of balance of power against the criticism of Professor A. F. Pollard at a meeting of the RIIA.

This change in point of view was based on several factors. In the first place, the Group, by their practical experience at Paris in 1919, found that it was not possible to apply either self-determination or the parliamentary form of government to Europe. As a result of this experience, they listened with more respect to the Cecil Bloc, which always insisted that these, especially the latter, were intimately associated with the British outlook, way of life, and social traditions, and were not articles of export. This issue was always the chief bone of contention between the Group and the Bloc in regard to India. In India, where their own influence as pedagogues was important, the Group did not accept the Bloc's arguments completely, but in Europe, where the Group's influence was remote and indirect, the Group was more receptive.

In the second place, the Group at Paris became alienated from the French because of the latter's insistence on force as the chief basis of social and political life, especially the French insistence on a permanent mobilization of force to keep Germany down and on an international police force with autonomous power as a part of the League of Nations. The Group, although they frequently quoted Admiral Mahan's kind words about force in social life, did not really like force and shrank from its use, believing, as might be expected from their Christian background, that force could not avail against moral issues, that force corrupts those who use it, and that the real basis of social and political life was custom and tradition. At Paris the Group found that they were living in a different world from the French. They suddenly saw not only that they did not have the same outlook as their former allies, but that these allies embraced the "despotic" and "militaristic" outlook against which the late war had been waged. At once, the Group began to think that the influence which they had been mobilizing against Prussian despotism since 1907 could best be mobilized, now that Prussianism was dead, against French militarism and Bolshevism. And what better ally against these two enemies in the West and the East than the newly baptized Germany? Thus, almost without realizing it, the Group fell back into the old balance-of-power pattern. Their aim became the double one of keeping Germany in the fold of redeemed sinners by concessions, and of using this revived and purified Germany against Russia and France.[3]

In the third place, the Group in 1918 had been willing to toy with the idea of an integrated Europe because, in 1918, they believed that a permanent system of cooperation between Britain and the United States was a possible outcome of the war. This was the lifelong dream of Rhodes, of Milner, of Lothian, of Curtis. For that they would have sacrificed anything within reason. When it became clear in 1920 that the United States had no intention of underwriting Britain and instead would revert to her prewar isolationism, the bitterness of disappoint-ment in the Milner Group were beyond bounds. Forever after, they blamed the evils of Europe, the double-dealing of British policy, and the whole train of errors from 1919 to 1940 on the American reversion to isolationism. It should be clearly understood that by American reversion to isolationism the Milner Group did not mean the American rejection of the League of Nations. Frequently they said that they did mean this, that the disaster of 1939-1940 became inevitable when the Senate rejected the League of Nations in 1920. This is completely un-true, both as a statement of historical fact and as a statement of the Group's attitude toward that rejection at the time. As we shall see in a moment, the Group approved of the Senate's rejection of the League of Nations, because the reasons for that rejection agreed completely with the Group's own opinion about the League. The only change in the Group's opinion, as a result of the Senate's rejection of the League, oc-curred in respect to the Group's opinion regarding the League itself. Previously they had disliked the League; now they hated it — except as a propaganda agency. The proofs of these statements will appear in a moment.

The change in the Group's attitude toward Germany began even before the war ended. We have indicated how the Group rallied to give a public testimonial of faith in Lord Milner in October 1918, when he became the target of public criticism because of what was regarded by the public as a conciliatory speech toward Germany. The Group ob-jected violently to the anti-German tone in which Lloyd George con-ducted his electoral campaign in the "khaki election" of December 1918. *The Round Table* in March 1919 spoke of Lloyd George and "the odious character of his election campaign." Zimmern, after a devastating criticism of Lloyd George's conduct in the election, wrote: "He erred, not, like the English people, out of ignorance but deliber-ately, out of cowardice and lack of faith." In the preface to the same volume (*Europe in Convalescence*) he wrote: "Since December, 1918, when we elected a Parliament pledged to violate a solemn agreement made but five weeks earlier, we stand shamed, dishonoured, and, above all, distrusted before mankind." The agreement to which Zimmern referred was the so-called Pre-Armistice Agreement of 5 November 1918, made with the Germans, by which, if they accepted an armistice, the Allies agreed to make peace on the basis of the Four-teen Points. It was the thesis of the Milner Group that the election of 1918 and the Treaty of Versailles as finally signed violated this Pre-Armistice Agreement. As a result, the Group at once embarked on its campaign for revision of the treaty, a campaign whose first aim, apparently, was to create a guilty conscience in regard to the treaty in Britain and the United States. Zimmern's book, Brand's book of the previous year, and all the articles of *The Round Table* were but ammunition in this campaign. However, Zimmern had no illusions about the Germans, and his attack on the treaty was based solely on the need to redeem British honor. As soon as it became clear to him that the Group was going beyond this motive and was trying to give concessions to the Germans without any attempt to purge Germany of its vicious elements and without any guarantee that those concessions would not be used against everything the Group held dear, he left the inner circle of the Group and moved to the second circle. He was not convinced that Germany could be redeemed by concessions made blindly to Germany as a whole, or that Germany should be built up against France and Russia. He made his position clear in a brilliant and courageous speech at Oxford in May 1925, a speech in which he denounced the steady sabotage of the League of Nations. It is not an accident that the most intelligent member of the Group was the first member to break publicly with the policy of appeasement.

The Milner Group thus regarded the Treaty of Versailles as too severe, as purely temporary, and as subject to revision almost at once. When *The Round Table* examined the treaty in its issue of June 1919, it said, in substance: "The punishment of Germany was just, for no one can believe in any sudden change of heart in that country, but the treaty is too severe. The spirit of the Pre-Armistice Commitments was violated, and, in detail after detail, Germany was treated unjustly, although there is broad justice in the settlement as a whole. Specifically the reparations are too severe, and Germany's neighbors should have been forced to disarm also, as promised in Wilson's Fourth Point. No demand should have been made for William II as a war criminal. If he is a menace, he should be put on an island without trial, like Napoleon. Our policy must be magnanimous, for our war was with the German government, not with the German people." Even earlier, in December 1918, *The Round Table* said: "It would seem desirable that the treaties should not be long term, still less perpetual, instruments. Perpetual treaties are indeed a lien upon national sovereignty and a standing contradiction of the principle of the democratic control of foreign policy.
. . . It would establish a salutory precedent if the network of treaties signed as a result of the war were valid for a period of ten years only."
In March 1920, *The Round Table* said: "Like the Peace Conference, the Covenant of the League of Nations aimed too high and too far. Six months ago we looked to it to furnish the means for peaceful revision of the terms of the peace, where revision might be required. Now we have to realize that national sentiment sets closer limits to international ac-

tion than we were willing then to recognize." The same article then goes on to speak of the rejection of the treaty by the United States Senate. It defends this action and criticizes Wilson severely, saying: "The truth of the matter is that the American Senate has expressed the real sentiment of all nations with hard-headed truthfulness. . . . The Senate has put into words what has already been demonstrated in Europe by the logic of events — namely that the Peace of Versailles attempted too much, and the Covenant which guarantees it implies a capacity for united action between the Allies which the facts do not warrant. The whole Treaty was, in fact, framed to meet the same impractical desire which we have already noted in the reparation terms — the desire to mete out ideal justice and to build an ideal world."

Nowhere is the whole point of view of the Milner Group better stated than in a speech of General Smuts to the South African Luncheon Club in London, 23 October 1923. After violent criticism of the reparations as too large and an attack on the French efforts to enforce these clauses, he called for a meeting "of principals" to settle the problem. He then pointed out that a continuation of existing methods would lead to the danger of German disintegration, "a first-class and irreparable disaster. . . . It would mean immediate economic chaos, and it would open up the possibility of future political dangers to which I need not here refer. Germany is both economically and politically necessary to Central Europe." He advocated applying to Germany "the benevolent policy which this country adopted toward France after the Napoleonic War. . . . And if, as I hope she will do, Germany makes a last appeal . . . I trust this great Empire will not hesitate for a moment to respond to that appeal and to use all its diplomatic power and influence to support her, and to prevent a calamity which would be infinitely more dangerous to Europe and the world than was the downfall of Russia six or seven years ago." Having thus lined Britain up in diplomatic opposition to France, Smuts continued with advice against applying generosity to the latter country on the question of French war debts, warning that this would only encourage "French militarism."

> Do not let us from mistaken motives of generosity lend our aid to the further militarization of the European continent. People here are already beginning to be seriously alarmed about French armaments on land and in the air. In addition to these armaments, the French government have also lent large sums to the smaller European States around Germany, mainly with a view to feeding their ravenous military appetites. There is a serious danger lest a policy of excessive generosity on our part, or on the part of America, may simply have the effect of enabling France still more effectively to subsidize and foster militarism on the Continent. . . . If things continue on the present lines, this country may soon have to start rearming herself in sheer self-defence.

This speech of Smuts covers so adequately the point of view of the Milner Group in the early period of appeasement that no further quotations are necessary. No real change occurred in the point of view of the Group from 1920 to 1938, not even as a result of the death of democratic hopes in Germany at the hands of the Nazis. From Smuts's speech of October 1923 before the South African Luncheon Club to Smuts's speech of November 1934 before the RIIA, much water flowed in the river of international affairs, but the ideas of the Milner Group remained rigid and, it may be added, erroneous. Just as the speech of 1923 may be taken as the culmination of the revisionist sentiment of the Group in the first five years of peace, so the speech of 1934 may be taken as the initiation of the appeasement sentiment of the Group in the last five years of peace. The speeches could almost be interchanged. We may call one revisionist and the other appeasing, but the point of view, the purpose, the method is the same. These speeches will be mentioned again later.

The aim of the Milner Group through the period from 1920 to 1938 was the same: to maintain the balance of power in Europe by building up Germany against France and Russia; to increase Britain's weight in that balance by aligning with her the Dominions and the United States; to refuse any commitments (especially any commitments through the League of Nations, and above all any commitments to aid France) beyond those existing in 1919; to keep British freedom of action; to drive Germany eastward against Russia if either or both of these two powers became a threat to the peace of Western Europe.

The sabotage of the peace settlement by the Milner Group can be seen best in respect to reparations and the League of Nations. In regard to the former, their argument appeared on two fronts: in the first place, the reparations were too large because they were a dishonorable violation of the Pre-Armistice Agreement; and, in the second place, any demand for immediate or heavy payments in reparation would ruin Germany's international credit and her domestic economic system, to the jeopardy of all reparation payments immediately and of all social order in Central Europe in the long run.

The argument against reparations as a violation of the Pre-Armistice Agreement can be found in the volumes of Zimmern and Brand already mentioned. Both concentrated their objections on the inclusion of pension payments by the victors to their own soldiers in the total reparation bill given to the Germans. This was, of course, an obvious violation of the Pre-Armistice Agreement, which bound the Germans to pay only for damage to civilian property. Strangely enough, it was a member of the Group, Jan Smuts, who was responsible for the inclusion of the objectionable items, although he put them in not as a member of the Group, but as a South African politician. This fact alone should have prevented him from making his speech of October 1923. However, love of consistency has never prevented Smuts from making a speech.

From 1921 onward, the Milner Group and the British government (if the two policies are distinguishable) did all they could to lighten the reparations burden on Germany and to prevent France from using force to collect reparations. The influence of the Milner Group on the government in this field may perhaps be indicated by the identity of the two policies. It might also be pointed out that a member of the Group, Arthur (now Sir Arthur) Salter, was general secretary of the Reparations Commission from 1920 to 1922. Brand was financial adviser to the chairman of the Supreme Economic Council (Lord Robert Cecil) in 1919; he was vice-president of the Brussels Conference of 1920; and he was the financial representative of South Africa at the Genoa Conference of 1922 (named by Smuts). He was also a member of the International Committee of Experts on the Stabilization of the German Mark in 1922. Hankey was British secretary at the Genoa Conference of 1922 and at the London Reparations Conference of 1924. He was general secretary of the Hague Conference of 1929-1930 (which worked out the detailed application of the Young Plan) and of the Lausanne Conference (which ended reparations).

On the two great plans to settle the reparations problem, the Dawes Plan of 1924 and the Young Plan of 1929, the chief influence was that of J. P. Morgan and Company, but the Milner Group had half of the British delegation on the former committee. The British members of the Dawes Committee were two in number: Sir Robert Molesworth (now Lord) Kindersley, and Sir Josiah (later Lord) Stamp. The former was chairman of the board of directors of Lazard Brothers and Company. Of this firm, Brand was a partner and managing director for many years. The instigation for the formation of this committee came chiefly from the parliamentary agitations of H. A. L. Fisher and John Simon in the early months of 1923.

The Milner Group was outraged at the efforts of France to compel Germany to pay reparations. Indeed, they were outraged at the whole policy of France: reparations, the French alliances in Eastern Europe, the disarmament of Germany, French "militarism," the French desire for an alliance with Britain, and the French desire for a long-term occupation of the Rhineland. These six things were listed in *The Round Table* of March 1922 as "the Poincaré system." The journal then continued: "The Poincaré system, indeed, is hopeless. It leads inevitably to fresh war, for it is incredible that a powerful and spirited people like the Germans will be content to remain forever meekly obeying every flourish of Marshal Foch's sword." Earlier, the reader was informed: "The system is impracticable. It assumes that the interests of Poland

and the Little Entente are the same as those of France. . . . It forgets that the peoples of Europe cannot balance their budgets and recover prosperity unless they cut down their expenditures on armaments to a minimum. . . . It ignores the certainty that British opinion can no more tolerate a French military hegemony over Europe than it could a German or Napoleonic, with its menace to freedom and democracy everywhere."

When the French, in January 1923, occupied the Ruhr in an effort to force Germany to pay reparations, the rage of the Milner Group almost broke its bounds. In private, and in the anonymity of *The Round Table*, they threatened economic and diplomatic retaliation, although in public speeches, such as in Parliament, they were more cautious. However, even in public Fisher, Simon, and Smuts permitted their real feelings to become visible.

In the March 1923 issue *The Round Table* suggested that the reparations crisis and the Ruhr stalemate could be met by the appointment of a committee of experts (including Americans) to report on Germany's capacity to pay reparations. It announced that H. A. L. Fisher would move an amendment to the address to this effect in Parliament. This amendment was moved by Fisher on 19 February 1923, before *The Round Table* in question appeared, in the following terms:

> That this House do humbly represent to your Majesty that, inasmuch as the future peace of Europe cannot be safeguarded nor the recovery of reparations be promoted by the operations of the French and Belgian Governments in the Ruhr, it is urgently necessary to seek effective securities against aggression by international guarantees under the League of Nations, and to invite the Council of the League without delay to appoint a Commission of Experts to report upon the capacity of Germany to pay reparations and upon the best method of effecting such payments, and that, in view of the recent indication of willingness on the part of the Government of the United States of America to participate in a Conference to this end, the British representatives on the Council of the League should be instructed to urge that an invitation be extended to the American government to appoint experts to serve upon the Commission.

This motion had, of course, no chance whatever of passing, and Fisher had no expectation that it would. It was merely a propaganda device. Two statements in it are noteworthy. One was the emphasis on American participation, which was to be expected from the Milner Group. But more important than this was the thinly veiled threat to France contained in the words "it is urgently necessary to seek effective securities against aggression by international guarantees." This clause referred to French aggression and was the seed from which emerged, three years later, the Locarno Pacts. There were also some significant phrases, or slips of the tongue, in the speech which Fisher made in support of his motion. For example, he used the word "we" in a way that apparently referred to the Milner Group; and he spoke of "liquidation of the penal clauses of the Treaty of Versailles" as if that were the purpose of the committee he was seeking. He said: "We are anxious to get the amount of the reparation payment settled by an impartial tribunal. We propose that it should be remitted to the League of Nations. . . . But I admit that I have always had a considerable hesitation in asking the League of Nations to undertake the liquidation of the penal clauses of the Treaty of Versailles. . . . It is an integral part of this Amendment that the Americans should be brought in." Lord Robert Cecil objected to the amendment on the ground that its passage would constitute a censure of the government and force it to resign. John Simon then spoke in support of the motion. He said that France would never agree to any reparations figure, because she did not want the reparations clauses fulfilled, since that would make necessary the evacuation of the Rhineland. France went into the Ruhr, he said, not to collect reparations, but to cripple Germany; France was spending immense sums of money on military occupation and armaments but still was failing to pay either the principal or interest on her debt to Britain.

When put to a vote, the motion was defeated, 305 to 196. In the majority were Ormsby-Gore, Edward Wood, Amery, three Cecils (Robert, Evelyn, and Hugh), two Astors (John and Nancy), Samuel Hoare, Eustace Percy, and Lord Wolmer. In the minority were Fisher, Simon, and Arthur Salter.

By March, Fisher and Simon were more threatening to France. On the sixth of that month, Fisher said in the House of Commons: "I can only suggest this, that the Government make it clear to France, Germany, and the whole world that they regard this present issue between France and Germany, not as an issue affecting two nations, but as an issue affecting the peace and prosperity of the whole world. We should keep before ourselves steadily the idea of an international solution. We should work for it with all our power, and we should make it clear to France that an attempt to effect a separate solution of this question could not be considered otherwise than as an unfriendly act." Exactly a week later, John Simon, in a parliamentary maneuver, made a motion to cut the appropriation bill for the Foreign Office by £100 and seized the opportunity to make a violent attack on the actions of France. He was answered by Eustace Percy, who in turn was answered by Fisher.

In this way the Group tried to keep the issue before the minds of the British public and to prepare the way for the Dawes settlement. *The Round Table*, appealing to a somewhat different public, kept up a similar barrage. In the June 1923 issue, and again in September, it condemned the occupation of the Ruhr. In the former it suggested a three-part program as follows: (1) find out what Germany can pay, by an expert committee's investigation; (2) leave Germany free to work and produce, *by an immediate evacuation of the Rhineland* [!! my italics]; and (3) protect France and Germany from each other [another hint about the future Locarno Pacts]. This program, according to *The Round Table*, should be imposed on France with the threat that if France did not accept it, Britain would withdraw from the Rhineland and Reparations Commissions and formally terminate the Entente. It concluded: "*The Round Table* has not hesitated in recent months to suggest that [British] neutrality . . . was an attitude inconsistent either with the honour or the interests of the British Commonwealth." *The Round Table* even went so far as to say that the inflation in Germany was caused by the burden of reparations. In the September 1923 issue it said (probably by the pen of Brand): "In the last two years it is not inflation which has brought down the mark; the printing presses have been engaged in a vain attempt to follow the depreciation of the currency. That depreciation has been a direct consequence of the world's judgment that the Allied claims for reparation were incapable of being met. It will continue until that judgment, or in other words, those claims are revised."

In October 1923, Smuts, who was in London for the Imperial Conference and was in close contact with the Group, made speeches in which he compared the French occupation of the Ruhr with the German attack on Belgium in 1914 and said that Britain "may soon have to start rearming herself in sheer self-defence" against French militarism. John Dove, writing to Brand in a private letter, found an additional argument against France in the fact that her policy was injuring democracy in Germany. He wrote:

> It seems to me that the most disastrous effect of Poincaré's policy would be the final collapse of democracy in Germany, the risk of which has been pointed out in *The Round Table*. The irony of the whole situation is that if the Junkers should capture the Reich again, the same old antagonisms will revive and we shall find ourselves willy-nilly, lined up again with France to avert a danger which French action has again called into being. . . . Even if Smuts follows up his fine speech, the situation may have changed so much before the Imperial Conference is over that people who think like him and us may find ourselves baffled. . . . I doubt if we shall again have as good a chance of getting a peaceful democracy set up in Germany.

After the Dawes Plan went into force, the Milner Group's policies continued to be followed by the British government. The "policy of fulfillment" pursued by Germany under Stresemann was close to the heart of the Group. In fact, there is a certain amount of evidence that the Group was in a position to reach Stresemann and advise him to follow this policy. This was done through Smuts and Lord D'Abernon.

There is little doubt that the Locarno Pacts were designed in the Milner Group and were first brought into public notice by Stresemann, at the suggestion of Lord D'Abernon.

Immediately after Smuts made his speech against France in October 1923, he got in touch with Stresemann, presumably in connection with the South African Mandate in South-West Africa. Smuts himself told the story to Mrs. Millen, his authorized biographer, in these words:

> I was in touch with them [the Germans] in London over questions concerning German South-West. They had sent a man over from their Foreign Office to see me.[4] I can't say the Germans have behaved very well about German South-West, but that is another matter. Well, naturally, my speech meant something to this fellow. The English were hating the Ruhr business; it was turning them from France to Germany, the whole English-speaking world was hating it. Curzon, in particular, was hating it. Yet very little was being done to express all this feeling. I took it upon myself to express the feeling. I acted, you understand, unofficially. I consulted no one. But I could see my action would not be abhorrent to the Government—would, in fact, be a relief to them. When the German from the Foreign Office came to me full of what this sort of attitude would mean to Stresemann I told him I was speaking only for myself. "But you can see," I said, "that the people here approve of my speech. If my personal advice is any use to you, I would recommend the Germans to give up their policy of non-cooperation, to rely on the goodwill of the world and make a sincere advance towards the better understanding which I am sure can be brought about." I got in touch with Stresemann. Our correspondence followed those lines. You will remember that Stresemann's policy ended in the Dawes Plan and the Pact of Locarno and that he got the Nobel Peace for this work!"

In this connection it is worthy of note that the German Chancellor, at a Cabinet meeting on 12 November 1923, quoted Smuts by name as the author of what he (Stresemann) considered the proper road out of the crisis.

Lord D'Abernon was not a member of the Milner Group. He was, however, a member of the Cecil Bloc's second generation and had been, at one time, a rather casual member of "The Souls." This, it will be recalled, was the country-house set in which George Curzon, Arthur Balfour, Alfred Lyttelton, St. John Brodrick, and the Tennant sisters were the chief figures. Born Edgar Vincent, he was made Baron D'Abernon in 1914 by Asquith who was also a member of "The Souls" and married Margot Tennant in 1894. D'Abernon joined the Coldstream Guards in 1877 after graduating from Eton, but within a few years was helping Lord Salisbury to unravel the aftereffects of the Congress of Berlin. By 1880 he was private secretary to Lord Edmond Fitzmaurice, brother of Lord Lansdowne and Commissioner for European Turkey. The following year he was assistant to the British Commissioner for Evacuation of the Territory ceded to Greece by Turkey. In 1882 he was the British, Belgian, and Dutch representative on the Council of the Ottoman Public Debt, and soon became president of that Council. From 1883 to 1889 he was financial adviser to the Egyptian government and from 1889 to 1897 was governor of the Imperial Ottoman Bank in Constantinople. In Salisbury's third administration he was a Conservative M.P. for Exeter (1899-1906). The next few years were devoted to private affairs in international banking circles close to Milner. In 1920 he was the British civilian member of the "Weygand mission to Warsaw." This mission undoubtedly had an important influence on his thinking. As a chief figure in Salisbury's efforts to bolster up the Ottoman Empire against Russia, D'Abernon had always been anti-Russian. In this respect, his background was like Curzon's. As a result of the Warsaw mission, D'Abernon's anti-Russian feeling was modified to an anti-Bolshevik one of much greater intensity. To him the obvious solution seemed to be to build up Germany as a military bulwark against the Soviet Union. He said as much in a letter of 11 August 1920 to Sir Maurice Hankey. This letter, printed by D'Abernon in his book on the Battle of Warsaw (*The Eighteenth Decisive Battle of the World*, published 1931), suggests that "a good bargain might be made with the German military leaders in cooperating against the Soviet." Shortly afterwards, D'Abernon was made British Ambassador at Berlin. At the time, it was widely rumored and never denied that he had been appointed primarily to obtain some settlement of the reparations problem, it being felt that his wide experience in international public finance would qualify him for this work. This may have been so, but his prejudices likewise qualified him for only one solution to the problem, the one desired by the Germans.[5]

In reaching this solution, D'Abernon acted as the intermediary among Stresemann, the German Chancellor;• Curzon, the Foreign Secretary; and, apparently, Kindersley, Brand's associate at Lazard Brothers. According to Harold Nicolson in his book *Curzon: The Last Phase* (1934), "The initial credit for what proved the ultimate solution belongs, in all probability, to Lord D'Abernon — one of the most acute and broad-minded diplomatists which this country has ever possessed." In the events leading up to Curzon's famous note to France of 11 August 1923, the note which contended that the Ruhr occupation could not be justified under the Treaty of Versailles, D'Abernon played an important role both in London and in Berlin. In his *Diary of an Ambassador*, D'Abernon merely listed the notes between Curzon and France and added: "Throughout this controversy Lord D'Abernon had been consulted."

During his term as Ambassador in Berlin, D'Abernon's policy was identical with that of the Milner Group, except for the shading that he was more anti-Soviet and less anti-French and was more impetuous in his desire to tear up the Treaty of Versailles in favor of Germany. This last distinction rested on the fact that D'Abernon was ready to appease Germany regardless of whether it were democratic or not; indeed, he did not regard democracy as either necessary or good for Germany. The Milner Group, until 1929, was still in favor of a democratic Germany, because they realized better than D'Abernon the danger to civilization from an undemocratic Germany. It took the world depression and its resulting social unrest to bring the Milner Group around to the view which D'Abernon held as early as 1920, that appeasement to an undemocratic Germany could be used as a weapon against "social disorder."

Brigadier General J. H. Morgan, whom we have already quoted, makes perfectly clear that D'Abernon was one of the chief obstacles in the path of the Interallied Commission's efforts to force Germany to disarm. In 1920, when von Seeckt, Commander of the German Army, sought modifications of the disarmament rules which would have permitted large-scale evasion of their provisions, General Morgan found it impossible to get his dissenting reports accepted in London. He wrote in *Assize of Arms:* "At the eleventh hour I managed to get my reports on the implications of von Seeckt's plan brought to the direct notice of Mr. Lloyd George through the agency of my friend Philip Kerr who, after reading these reports, advised the Prime Minister to reject von Seeckt's proposals. Rejected they were at the Conference of Spa in July 1920, as we shall see, but von Seeckt refused to accept defeat and fell back on a second move." When, in 1921, General Morgan became "gravely disturbed" at the evasions of German disarmament, he wrote a memorandum on the subject. It was suppressed by Lord D'Abernon. Morgan added in his book: "I was not altogether surprised. Lord D'Abernon was the apostle of appeasement." In January 1923, this "apostle of appeasement" forced the British delegation on the Disarmament Commission to stop all inspection operations in Germany. They were never resumed, although the Commission remained in Germany for four more years, and the French could do nothing without the British members.[6]

Throughout 1923 and 1924, D'Abernon put pressure on both the German and the British governments to pursue a policy on the reparations question which was identical with that which Smuts was advocating at the same time and in the same quarters. He put pressure on the British government to follow this policy on the grounds that any different policy would lead to Stresemann's fall from office. This would result in a very dangerous situation, according to D'Abernon (and

Stresemann), where Germany might fall into the control of either the extreme left or the extreme right. For example, a minute of a German Cabinet meeting of 2 November 1923, found by Eric Sutton among Stresemann's papers and published by him, said in part: "To the English Ambassador, who made some rather anxious enquiries, Stresemann stated that the maintenance of the state of siege was absolutely essential in view of the risk of a *Putsch* both from the Left and from the Right. He would use all his efforts to preserve the unity of the Reich. . . . Lord D'Abernon replied that his view, which was shared in influential quarters in London, was that Stresemann was the only man who could steer the German ship of State through the present troubled waters." Among the quarters in London which shared this view, we find the Milner Group.

The settlement which emerged from the crisis, the Dawes Plan and the evacuation of the Ruhr, was exactly what the Milner Group wanted. From that point on to the banking crisis of 1931, their satisfaction continued. In the years 1929-1931 they clearly had no direct influence on affairs, chiefly because a Labour government was in office in London, but their earlier activities had so predetermined the situation that it continued to develop in the direction they wished. After the banking crisis of 1931, the whole structure of international finance with which the Group had been so closely associated disappeared and, after a brief period of doubt, was replaced by a rapid growth of monopolistic national capitalism. This was accepted by the Milner Group with hardly a break in stride. Hichens had been deeply involved in monopolistic heavy industry for a quarter of a century in 1932. Milner had advocated a system of "national capitalism" with "industrial self-regulation" behind tariff walls even earlier. Amery and others had accepted much of this as a method, although they did not necessarily embrace Milner's rather socialistic goals. As a result, in the period 1931-1933, the Milner Group willingly liquidated reparations, war debts, and the whole structure of international capitalism, and embraced protection and cartels instead.

Parallel with their destruction of reparations, and in a much more direct fashion, the Milner Group destroyed collective security through the League of Nations. The Group never intended that the League of Nations should be used to achieve collective security. They never intended that sanctions, either military or economic, should be used to force any aggressive power to keep the peace or to enforce any political decision which might be reached by international agreement. This must be understood at the beginning. *The Milner Group never intended that the League should be used as an instrument of collective security or that sanctions should be used as an instrument by the*

League. From the beginning, they expected only two things from the League: (1) that it could be used as a center for international cooperation in international administration in nonpolitical matters, and (2) that it could be used as a center for consultation in political matters. In regard to the first point, the Group regarded the League as a center for such activities as those previously exercised through the International Postal Union. In all such activities as this, each state would retain full sovereignty and would cooperate only on a completely voluntary basis in fields of social importance. In regard to the second point (political questions), no member of the Group had any intention of any state yielding any sliver of its full sovereignty to the League. The League was merely an agreement, like any treaty, by which each state bound itself to confer together in a crisis and not make war within three months of the submission of the question to consultation. The whole purpose of the League was to delay action in a crisis by requiring this period for consultation. There was no restriction on action after the three months. There was some doubt, within the Group, as to whether sanctions could be used to compel a state to observe the three months' delay. Most of the members of the Group said "no" to this question. A few said that economic sanctions could be used. Robert Cecil, at the beginning, at least, felt that political sanctions might be used to compel a state to keep the peace for the three months, but by 1922 every member of the Group had abandoned both political and economic sanctions for enforcing the three months' delay. There never was within the Group any intention at any time to use sanctions for any other purpose, such as keeping peace after the three-month period.

This, then, was the point of view of the Milner Group in 1919, as in 1939. Unfortunately, in the process of drawing up the Covenant of the League in 1919, certain phrases or implications were introduced into the document, under pressure from France, from Woodrow Wilson, and from other groups in Britain, which could be taken to indicate that the League might have been intended to be used as a real instrument of collective security, that it might have involved some minute limitation of state sovereignty, that sanctions might under certain circumstances be used to protect the peace. As soon as these implications became clear, the Group's ardor for the League began to evaporate. When the United States refused to join the League, this dwindling ardor turned to hatred. Nevertheless, the Group did not abandon the League at this point. On the contrary, they tightened their grip on it — in order to prevent any "foolish" persons from using the vague implications of the Covenant in an effort to make the League an instrument of collective security. The Group were determined that if any such effort as this were made, they would prevent it and, if necessary, destroy the League to prevent it. Only they would insist, in such a case, that the League was destroyed not by them but by the persons who tried to use it as an instrument of collective security.

All of this may sound extreme. Unfortunately, it is not extreme. That this was what the Group did to the League is established beyond doubt in history. That the Group intended to do this is equally beyond dispute. The evidence is conclusive.

The British ideas on the League and the British drafts of the Covenant were formed by four men, all close to the Milner Group. They were Lord Robert Cecil, General Smuts, Lord Phillimore, and Alfred Zimmern. For drafting documents they frequently used Cecil Hurst, a close associate, but not a member, of the Group. Hurst (Sir Cecil since 1920) was assistant legal adviser to the Foreign Office in 1902-1918, legal adviser in 1918-1929, a judge on the Permanent Court of International Justice at The Hague in 1929-1946, and Chairman of the United Nations War Crimes Commission in 1943-1944. He was the man responsible for the verbal form of Articles 10-16 (the sanction articles) of the Covenant of the League of Nations, for the Articles of Agreement with Ireland in 1921, and for the wording of the Locarno Pact in 1925. He frequently worked closely with the Milner Group. For example, in 1921 he was instrumental in making an agreement by which the British Yearbook of International Law, of which he was editor, was affiliated with the Royal Institute of International Affairs. At the time, he and Curtis were working together on the Irish agreement.

As early as 1916, Lord Robert Cecil was trying to persuade the Cabinet to support a League of Nations. This resulted in the appointment of the Phillimore Committee, which drew up the first British draft for the Covenant. As a result, in 1918-1919 Lord Robert became the chief government spokesman for a League of Nations and the presumed author of the second British draft. The real author of this second draft was Alfred Zimmern. Cecil and Zimmern were both dubious of any organization that would restrict state sovereignty. On 12 November 1918, the day after the armistice, Lord Robert made a speech at Birmingham on the type of League he expected. That speech shows clearly that he had little faith in the possibility of disarmament and none in international justice or military sanctions to preserve the peace. The sovereignty of each state was left intact. As W. E. Rappard (director of the Graduate School of International Studies at Geneva) wrote in *International Conciliation* in June 1927, "He [Lord Cecil] was very sceptical about the possibility of submitting vital international questions to the judgment of courts of law and 'confessed to the gravest doubts' as to the practicability of enforcing the decrees of such courts by any 'form of international force.' On the other hand, he firmly believed in the efficacy of economic pressure as a means of coercing a country bent on aggression in violation of its pacific agreements." It might be remarked in passing that the belief that economic sanctions could be used without a backing of military force, or the possibility of needing such backing, is the one sure sign of a novice in foreign politics, and Robert Cecil could never be called a novice in such matters. In the speech itself he said:

> The most important step we can now take is to devise machinery which, in case of international dispute, will, at the least, delay the outbreak of war, and secure full and open discussion of the causes of the quarrel. For that purpose . . . all that would be necessary would be a treaty binding the signatories never to wage war themselves or permit others to wage war till a formal conference of nations had been held to enquire into, and, if possible, decide the dispute. It is probably true, at least in theory, that decisions would be difficult to obtain, for the decisions of such a conference, like all other international proceedings, would have to be unanimous to be binding. But since the important thing is to secure delay and open discussion, that is to say, time to enable public opinion to act and information to instruct it, this is not a serious objection to the proposal. Indeed, from one point of view, it is an advantage, since it avoids any interference with national sovereignty except the interposition of a delay in seeking redress by force of arms. This is the essential thing. . . . To that extent, and to that extent only, international coercion would be necessary.

This speech of Cecil's was approved by *The Round Table* and accepted as its own point of view in the issue of December 1918. At the same time, through Smuts, the Milner Group published another statement of its views. This pamphlet, called *The League of Nations, a Practical Suggestion*, was released in December 1918, after having been read in manuscript and criticized by the inner circle, especially Curtis. This statement devoted most of its effort to the use of mandates for captured German colonies. For preserving the peace, it had considerable faith in compulsory arbitration and hoped to combine this with widespread disarmament.

The Group's own statement on this subject appeared in the December 1918 issue of *The Round Table* in an article called "Windows of Freedom," written by Curtis. He pointed out that British seapower had twice saved civilization and any proposal that it should be used in the future only at the request of the League of Nations must be emphatically rejected. The League would consist of fallible human beings, and England could never yield her decision to them. He continued: "Her own existence and that of the world's freedom are inseparably connected. . . . To yield it without a blow is to yield the whole citadel in which the forces that make for human freedom are entrenched; to covenant to yield it is to bargain a betrayal of the world in

advance. . . . [The League must not be a world government.] If the
burden of a world government is placed on it it will fall with a crash."
He pointed out it could be a world government only if it represented
peoples and not states, and if it had the power to tax those peoples. It
should simply be an interstate conference of the world.

> The Peace Conference . . . cannot hope to produce a written constitution
> for the globe or a genuine government of mankind. What it can do is
> establish a permanent annual conference between foreign ministers them-
> selves, with a permanent secretariat, in which, as at the Peace Conference
> itself, all questions at issue between States can be discussed and, if pos-
> sible, settled by agreement. Such a conference cannot itself govern the
> world, still less those portions of mankind who cannot yet govern them-
> selves. But it can act as a symbol and organ of the human conscience,
> however imperfect, to which real governments of existing states can be
> made answerable for facts which concern the world at large."

In another article in the same issue of *The Round Table* ("Some Principles and Problems of the Settlement," December 1918), similar ideas
were expressed even more explicitly by Zimmern. He stated that the
League of Nations should be called the League of States, or th'
Interstate Conference, for sovereign states would be its units, and ᶨ
would make not laws but contracts. "The League of Nations, in fact, s
far from invalidating or diminishing national sovereignty, shou'
strengthen and increase it. . . . The work before the coming age is n
to supersede the existing States but to moralize them. . . . Membershi.
must be restricted to those states where authority is based upon the
consent of the people over whom it is exercised . . . the reign of law. . . .
It can reasonably be demanded that no States should be admitted
which do not make such a consummation one of the deliberate aims of
their policy." Under this idea, *The Round Table* excluded by name
from the new League, Liberia, Mexico, "and above all Russia." "The
League," it continued, "will not simply be a League of States, it will be
a League of Commonwealths." As its hopes in the League dwindled,
The Round Table became less exclusive, and, in June 1919, it declared,
"without Germany or Russia the League of Nations will be dangerously
incomplete."

In the March 1919 issue, *The Round Table* described in detail the
kind of League it wanted—"a common clearing house for non-
contentious business." Its whole basis was to be "public opinion," and
its organization was to be that of "an assembly point of bureaucrats of
various countries" about an international secretariat and various
organizations like the International Postal Union or the International
Institute of Agriculture.

> Every great department of government in each country whose activities

touch those of similar departments in other countries should have its recognized delegates on a permanent international commission charged with the study of the sphere of international relations in question and with the duty of making recommendations to their various Governments. . . . Across the street, as it were, from these permanent Bureaux, at the capital of the League, there should be another central permanent Bureau . . . an International secretariat. . . . They must not be national ambassadors, but civil servants under the sole direction of a non-national chancellor; and the aim of the whole organization . . . must be to evolve a practical international sense, a sense of common service.

This plan regarded the Council of the League as the successor of the Supreme War Council, made up of premiers and foreign ministers, and the instrument for dealing with political questions in a purely consultative way. Accordingly, the Council would consist only of the Great Powers.

These plans for the Covenant of the League of Nations were rudely shattered at the Peace Conference when the French demanded that the new organization be a "Super-state" with its own army and powers of action. The British were horrified, but with the help of the Americans were able to shelve this suggestion. However, to satisfy the demand from their own delegations as well as the French, they spread a camouflage of sham world government over the structure they had planned. This was done by Cecil Hurst. Hurst visited David Hunter Miller, the American legal expert, one night and persuaded him to replace the vital clauses 10 to 16 with drafts drawn up by Hurst. These drafts were deliberately drawn with loopholes so that no aggressor need ever be driven to the point where sanctions would have to be applied. This was done by presenting alternative paths of action leading toward sanctions, some of them leading to economic sanctions, but one path, which could be freely chosen by the aggressor, always available, leading to a loophole where no collective action would be possible. The whole procedure was concealed beneath a veil of legalistic terminology so that the Covenant could be presented to the public as a watertight document, but Britain could always escape from the necessity to apply sanctions through a loophole.

In spite of this, the Milner Group were very dissatisfied. They tried simultaneously to do three things: (1) to persuade public opinion that the League was a wonderful instrument of international cooperation designed to keep the peace; (2) to criticize the Covenant for the "traces of a sham world-government" which had been thrown over it; and (3) to reassure themselves and the ruling groups in England, the Dominions, and the United States that the League was not "a world-state." All of this took a good deal of neat footwork, or, more accurately, nimble tongues and neat pen work. More doubletalk and doublewriting were emitted by the Milner Group on this subject in the two decades 1919-1939 than was issued by any other group on this subject in the period.

Among themselves the Group did not conceal their disappointment with the Covenant because it went too far. In the June 1919 issue of *The Round Table* they said reassuringly: "The document is not the Constitution of a Super-state, but, as its title explains, a solemn agreement between Sovereign States which consent to limit their complete freedom of action on certain points. . . . The League must continue to depend on the free consent, in the last resort, of its component States; this assumption is evident in nearly every article of the Covenant, of which the ultimate and most effective sanction must be the public opinion of the civilized world. If the nations of the future are in the main selfish, grasping, and bellicose, no instrument or machinery will restrain them." But in the same issue we read the complaint: "In the Imperial Conference Sir Wilfrid Laurier was never tired of saying, 'This is not a Government, but a conference of Governments with Governments.' It is a pity that there was no one in Paris to keep on saying this. For the Covenant is still marked by the traces of sham government."

By the March 1920 issue, the full bitterness of the Group on this last point became evident. It said: "The League has failed to secure the adhesion of one of its most important members, The United States, and is very unlikely to secure it. . . . This situation presents a very serious problem for the British Empire. We have not only undertaken great obligations under the League which we must now both in honesty and in self-regard revise, *but we have looked to the League to provide us with the machinery for United British action in foreign affairs.*" (my italics; this is the cat coming out of the bag). The article continued with criticism of Wilson, and praise of the Republican Senate's refusal to swallow the League as it stood. It then said:

> The vital weakness of the Treaty and the Covenant became more clear than ever in the months succeeding the signature at Versailles. A settlement based on ideal principles and poetic justice can be permanently applied and maintained only by a world government to which all nations will subordinate their private interests. . . . It demands, not only that they should sacrifice their private interests to this world-interest, but also that they should be prepared to enforce the claims of world-interest even in matters where their own interests are in no wise engaged. It demands, in fact, that they should subordinate their national sovereignty to an international code and an international ideal. The reservations of the American Senate . . . point the practical difficulties of this ideal with simple force. All the reservations . . . are affirmations of the sovereign right of the American people to make their own policy without interference from an International League. . . . None of these reservations, it

should be noted, contravenes the general aims of the League; but they are, one and all, directed to ensure that no action is taken in pursuit of those aims except with the consent and approval of the Congress. . . . There is nothing peculiar in this attitude. It is merely, we repeat, the broad reflex of an attitude already taken up by all the European Allies in questions where their national interests are affected, and also by the British Dominions in their relations with the British Government. It gives us a statement in plain English, of the limitations to the ideal of international action which none of the other Allies will, in practice, dispute. So far, therefore, from destroying the League of Nations, the American reservations have rendered it the great service of pointing clearly to the flaws which at present neutralize its worth.

Among these flaws, in the opinion of the Milner Group, was the fact that their plan to use the League of Nations as a method of tying the Dominions more closely to the United Kingdom had failed and, instead, the Covenant

gave the Dominions the grounds, or rather the excuse, to avoid closer union with the United Kingdom. . . . It had been found in Paris that in order to preserve its unity the British delegation must meet frequently as a delegation to discuss its policy before meeting the representatives of foreign nations in conference. How was this unity of action to be maintained after the signature of peace without committing the Dominion Governments to some new constitutional organization within the Commonwealth? And if some new constitutional organization were to be devised for this purpose, how could it fail to limit in some way the full national independent status which the Dominion Governments had just achieved by their recognition as individual members of the League of Nations? The answer to these questions was found in cooperation within the League, which was to serve, not only as the link between the British Empire and foreign Powers, but as the link also between the constituent nations of the British Empire itself. Imbued with this idea, the Dominion statesmen accepted obligations to foreign Powers under the Covenant of the League more binding than any obligations which they would undertake to their kindred nations within the British Empire. In other words, they mortgaged their freedom of action to a league of foreign States in order to avoid the possibility of mortgaging it to the British Government. It hardly required the reservations of the American Senate to demonstrate the illusory character of this arrangement. . . . The British Dominions have made no such reservations with regard to the Covenant, and they are therefore bound by the obligations which have been rejected by the United States. Canada, Australia, South Africa, and New Zealand are, in fact, bound by stronger written obligations to Poland and Czechoslovakia, than to the British Isles. . . . It is almost needless to observe that none of the democracies of the British Empire has grasped the extent of its obligations to the League of Nations or would hesitate to repudiate them at once, if put to the test. If England were threatened by invasion, the other British domocracies would mobilize at once for her support; but though they have a written obligation to Poland, which they have never dreamed of giving to England, they would not in practice mobilise a single man to defend the integrity of the Corridor to Danzig or any other Polish territorial interest. . . . This is a dangerous and equivocal situation. . . . It is time that our democracies reviewed and corrected it with the clearness of vision and candour of statement displayed by the much-abused Senate of the United States. . . . To what course of action do these conclusions point? They point in the first place to revision of our obligations under the League. We are at present pledged to guarantees of territorial arrangements in Europe which may be challenged at any time by forces too powerful for diplomatic control, and it is becoming evident that in no part of the Empire would public opinion sanction our active interference in the local disputes which may ensue. The Polish Corridor to Danzig is a case in point. . . . Our proper course is to revise and restate our position towards the League in accordance with these facts. . . . First, we wish to do our utmost to guarantee peace, liberty, and law throughout the world without committing ourselves to quixotic obligations to foreign States. Second, we wish to assist and develop the simple mechanism of international dealing embodied in the League without mortgaging our freedom of action and judgment under an international Covenant. Our policy toward the League should, therefore, be revised on the following guiding lines: 1. We should state definitely that our action within the League will be governed solely by our own judgment of every situation as it arises, and we must undertake no general obligations which we may not be able or willing, when the test comes, to discharge. 2. We must in no case commit ourselves to responsibilities which we cannot discharge to the full with our own resources, independent of assistance from any foreign power. 3. We must definitely renounce the idea that the League may normally enforce its opinions by military or economic pressure on the recalcitrant States. It exists to bring principals together for open discussion of international difficulties, to extend and develop the mechanisms and habit of international cooperation, and to establish an atmosphere in which international controversies may be settled with fairness and goodwill. . . . With the less ambitious objects defined above it will sooner or later secure the whole-hearted support of American opinion. . . . The influence of the League of Nations upon British Imperial relations has for the moment been misleading and dangerous. . . . It is only a question of time before this situation leads to an incident of some kind which will provoke the bitterest recrimination and controversy. . .

In the leading article of the September 1920 issue, *The Round Table* took up the same problem and repeated many of its arguments. It blamed Wilson for corrupting the Covenant into "a pseudo world-government" by adding sham decorations to a fundamentally different structure based on consultation of sovereign states. Instead of the Covenant, it concluded, we should have merely continued the Supreme Council, which was working so well at Spa.

In spite of this complete disillusionment with the League, the Milner Group still continued to keep a firm grip on as much of it as Britain could control. In the first hundred sessions of the Council of the League of Nations (1920-1938), thirty different persons sat as delegates for Britain. Omitting the four who sat for Labour governments, we have twenty-six. Of these, seven were from the Milner Group; seven others were present at only one session and are of little significance. The others were almost all from the Cecil Bloc close to the Milner Group. The following list indicates the distribution.

NAME	SESSIONS AS DELEGATE
Anthony Eden	39
Sir John Simon	22
Sir Austen Chamberlain	20
Arthur Balfour	16
Lord Robert Cecil	15
Sir Alexander Cadogan	12
E. H. Carr	8
H. A. L. Fisher	7
Sir William Malkin	7
Viscount Cranborne	5
Lord Curzon	3
Lord Londonderry	3
Leopold Amery	2
Edward Wood (Lord Halifax)	2
Cecil Hurst	2
Sir Edward H. Young	2
Lord Cushendun	2
Lord Onslow	2
Gilbert Murray	1
Sir Rennell Rodd	1
Six others	1 each

At the annual meetings of the Assembly of the League, a somewhat similar situation existed. The delegations had from three to eight members, with about half of the number being from the Milner Group, except when members of the Labour Party were present. H. A. L. Fisher was a delegate in 1920, 1921, and 1922; Mrs. Alfred Lyttelton was one in 1923, 1926, 1927, 1928, and 1931; Lord Astor was one in 1931, 1936, and 1938; Cecil Hurst was one in 1924, 1926, 1927, and 1928; Gilbert Murray was one in 1924; Lord Halifax was one in 1923 and 1936; Ormsby-Gore was one in 1933; Lord Robert Cecil was one in 1923, 1926, 1929, 1930, 1931, and 1932; E. H. Carr was one in 1933 and 1934; etc. The Milner Group control was most complete at the crucial Twelfth Assembly (1931), when the delegation of five members consisted of Lord Robert Cecil, Lord Lytton, Lord Astor, Arthur

Salter, and Mrs. Lyttelton. In addition, the Group frequently had other members attached to the delegations as secretaries or substitutes. Among these were E. H. Carr, A. L. Smith, and R. M. Makins. Moreover, the Group frequently had members on the delegations from the Dominions. The South African delegation in 1920 had Robert Cecil; in 1921 it had Robert Cecil and Gilbert Murray; in 1923 it had Smuts and Gilbert Murray. The Australian delegation had Sir John Latham in 1926, while the Canadian delegation had Vincent Massey ten years later. The Indian delegation had L. F. Rushbrook Williams in 1925.

The Milner Group was also influential in the Secretariat of the League. Sir Eric Drummond (now sixteenth Earl of Perth), who had been Balfour's private secretary from 1916 to 1919, was Secretary-General to the League from 1919 to 1933, when he resigned to become British Ambassador in Rome. Not a member of the Group, he was nevertheless close to it. Harold Butler, of the Group and of All Souls, was deputy director and director of the International Labor Office in the period 1920-1938. Arthur Salter, of the Group and All Souls, was director of the Economic and Financial Section of the League in 1919-1920 and again in 1922-1931. B. H. Sumner, of the Group and All Souls (now Warden), was on the staff of the ILO in 1920-1922. R. M. Makins, of the Group and All Souls, was assistant adviser and adviser on League of Nations affairs to the Foreign Office in 1937-1939.

To build up public opinion in favor of the League of Nations, the Milner Group formed an organization known as the League of Nations Union. In this organization the most active figures were Lord Robert Cecil, Gilbert Murray, the present Lord Esher, Mrs. Lyttelton, and Wilson Harris. Lord Cecil was president from 1923 to 1945; Professor Murray was chairman from 1923 to 1938 and co-president from 1938 to 1945; Wilson Harris was its parliamentary secretary and editor of its paper, *Headway*, for many years. Among others, C. A. Macartney, of All Souls and the RIIA, was head of the Intelligence Department from 1928 to 1936. Harris and Macartney were late additions to the Group, the former becoming a member of the inner circle about 1922, while the latter became a member of the outer circle in the late 1920s, probably as a result of his association with the *Encyclopedia Britannica* as an expert on Central Europe. Wilson Harris was one of the most intimate associates of Lionel Curtis, Philip Kerr, and other members of the inner core in the 1920s, and this association became closer, if possible, in the 1930s. A graduate of Cambridge University in 1906, he served for many years in various capacities with the *Daily News*. Since 1932 he has been editor of *The Spectator*, and since 1945 he has been a Member of Parliament from Cambridge University. He was one of the most ardent advocates of appeasement in the period 1935-1939, especially in the meetings at Chatham House. In this connection, it might be mentioned that he was a member of the council of the RIIA in 1924-1927. He has written books on Woodrow Wilson, the peace settlement, the League of Nations, disarmament, etc. His most recent work is a biography of J. A. Spender, onetime editor of the *Westminster Gazette* (1896-1922), which he and his brother founded in 1893 in collaboration with Edmund Garrett and Edward Cook, when all four left the *Pall Mall Gazette* after its purchase by Waldorf Astor.

The ability of the Milner Group to mobilize public opinion in regard to the League of Nations is almost beyond belief. It was not a simple task, since they were simultaneously trying to do two things: on the one hand, seeking to build up popular opinion in favor of the League so that its work could be done more effectively; and, at the same time, seeking to prevent influential people from using the League as an instrument of world government before popular opinion was ready for a world government. In general, *The Round Table* and *The Times* were used for the latter purpose, while the League of Nations Union and a strange assortment of outlets, such as Chatham House, Toynbee Hall, extension courses at Oxford, adult-education courses in London, *International Conciliation* in the United States, the Institute of Politics at Williamstown, the Institute of Intellectual Cooperation at Paris, the Geneva School of International Studies and the Graduate Institute of International Studies at Geneva, and the various branches of the Carnegie Endowment for International Peace, were used for the former purpose. The Milner Group did not control all of these. Their influence was strong in all of them, and, since the influence of J. P. Morgan and Company was also strong in most of them and since Morgan and the Group were pursuing a parallel policy on this issue, the Group were usually able to utilize the resources of these various organizations when they wished.

As examples of this, we might point out that Curtis and Kerr each gave a series of lectures at the Institute of Politics, Williamstown, in 1922. Selections from these, along with an article from the September 1922 issue of *The Round Table*, were published in *International Conciliation* for February 1923. Kerr and Lord Birkenhead spoke at the Institute in 1923; Sir Arthur Willert, a close associate if not a member of the Group, spoke at the Institute of Politics in 1927. Sir Arthur was always close to the Group. He was a member of the staff of *The Times* from 1906 to 1921, chiefly as head of the Washington office; he was in the Foreign Office as head of the News Department from 1921 to 1935, was on the United Kingdom delegation to the League of Nations in 1929-1934, was an important figure in the Ministry of Information (a

Milner Group fief) in 1939-1945, and wrote a book called *The Empire and the World* in collaboration with H. V. Hodson and B. K. Long of the Kindergarten.

Other associates of the Group who spoke at the Institute of Politics at Williamstown were Lord Eustace Percy, who spoke on wartime shipping problems in 1929, and Lord Meston, who spoke on Indian nationalism in 1930.[7]

The relationship between the Milner Group and the valuable little monthly publication called *International Conciliation* was exercised indirectly through the parallel group in America, which had been organized by the associates of J. P. Morgan and Company before the First World War, and which made its most intimate connections with the Milner Group at the Peace Conference of 1919. We have already mentioned this American group in connection with the Council on Foreign Relations and the Institute of Pacific Relations. Through this connection, many of the activities and propaganda effusions of the Milner Group were made available to a wide public in America. We have already mentioned the February 1923 issue of *International Conciliation*, which was monopolized by the Group. A few other examples might be mentioned. Both of General Smuts's important speeches, that of 23 October 1923 and that of 13 November 1934, were reproduced in *International Conciliation*. So too was an article on "The League and Minorities" by Wilson Harris. This was in the September 1926 issue. A *Times* editorial of 22 November 1926 on "The Empire as It Is" was reprinted in March 1927; another of 14 July 1934 is in the September issue of the same year; a third of 12 July 1935 is in the issue of September 1935. Brand's report on Germany's Foreign Creditors' Standstill Agreements is in the May issue of 1932; while a long article from the same pen on "The Gold Problem" appears in the October 1937 issue. This article was originally published, over a period of three days, in *The Times* in June 1937. An article on Russia from *The Round Table* was reprinted in December 1929. Lord Lothian's speeches of 25 October 1939 and of 11 December 1940 were both printed in the issues of *International Conciliation* immediately following their delivery. An article by Lothian called "League or No League," first published in *The Observer* in August 1936, was reprinted in the periodical under consideration in December 1936. An article by Lord Cecil on disarmament, another by Clarence Streit (one of the few American members of the Group) on the League of Nations, and a third by Stephen King-Hall on the Mediterranean problem were published in December 1932, February 1934, and January 1938 respectively. A speech of John Simon's appears in the issue of May 1935; one of Samuel Hoare's is in the September issue of the same year; another by Samuel Hoare is in the issue of November 1935. Needless to say, the activities of the Institute of Pacific Relations, of the Imperial Conferences, of the League of Nations, and of the various international meetings devoted to reparations and disarmament were adequately reflected in the pages of *International Conciliation.*

The deep dislike which the Milner Group felt for the Treaty of Versailles and the League of Nations was shared by the French, but for quite opposite reasons. The French felt insecure in the face of Germany because they realized that France had beaten Germany in 1918 only because of the happy fact that she had Russia, Great Britain, Italy, and the United States to help her. From 1919 onward, France had no guarantee that in any future attack by Germany she would have any such assistance. To be sure, the French knew that Britain must come to the aid of France if there was any danger of Germany defeating France. The Milner Group knew this too. But France wanted some arrangement by which Britain would be alongside France from the first moment of a German attack, since the French had no assurance that they could withstand a German onslaught alone, even for a brief period. Moreover, if they could, the French were afraid that the opening onslaught would deliver to the Germans control of the most productive part of France as captured territory. This is what had happened in 1914. To avoid this, the French sought in vain one alternative after another: (a) to detach from Germany, or, at least, to occupy for an extended period, the Rhineland area of Germany (this would put the Ruhr, the most vital industrial area of Germany, within striking distance of French forces); (b) to get a British-American, or at least a British, guarantee of French territory; (c) to get a "League of Nations with teeth," that is, one with its own police forces and powers to act automatically against an aggressor. All of these were blocked by the English and Americans at the Peace Conference in 1919. The French sought substitutes. Of these, the only one they obtained was a system of alliances with new states, like Poland, Czechoslovakia, and the enlarged Rumania, on the east of Germany. All of these states were of limited power, and the French had little faith in the effectiveness of their assistance. Accordingly, the French continued to seek their other aims: to extend the fifteen years' occupation of the Rhineland into a longer or even an indefinite period; to get some kind of British guarantee; to strengthen the League of Nations by "plugging the gaps in the Covenant"; to use the leverage of reparations and disarmament as provided in the Treaty of Versailles to keep Germany down, to wreck her economically, or even to occupy the Ruhr. All of these efforts were blocked by the machinations of the Milner Group. At the moment, we shall refer only to the efforts to "plug the gaps in the Covenant."

These "gaps," as we have indicated, were put in by Cecil Hurst and were exactly to the taste of the Milner Group. The chief efforts of the French and their allies on the Continent to "plug the gaps" were the Draft Treaty of Mutual Assistance (1923) and the Geneva Protocol (1924). What the Milner Group thought of both of these can be gathered from the following extracts from *The Round Table*'s denunciation of the Protocol. In the December 1924 issue, in an article entitled "The British Commonwealth, the Protocol, and the League," we find the following: "What is to be the British answer to this invitation to reenter the stormy field of internal European politics? Can the British Commonwealth afford to become permanently bound up with the internal political structure of Europe? And will it promote the peace and stability of Europe or the world that Europe should attempt to solve its problems on the basis of a permanent British guarantee? The answer in our judgment to both these questions must be an emphatic, No." Then, after repeating its contention that the only purpose of the Covenant was to secure delay in a crisis for consultation, it continued:

> The idea that all nations ought to consult how they are to deal with States which precipitate war without allowing any period for enquiry and mediation is the real heart of the League of Nations, and, if the British Commonwealth wants to prevent a recurrence of the Great War, it must be willing to recognize that it has a vital interest in working out with other nations the best manner of giving effect to this fundamental idea. . . . Decisions as to the rights and wrongs of international disputes, and of what common action the nations should take when they are called together to deal with such an outlaw, must be left to be determined in the light of the circumstances of the time. . . . The view of *The Round Table* is that the British Commonwealth should make it perfectly clear . . . that it will accept no further obligations than this and that the Covenant of the League must be amended to establish beyond question that no authority, neither the Council nor any arbitral body it may appoint, has any power to render a binding decision or to order a war, except with the consent of the members themselves.

The bitterness of the Group's feelings against France at the time appears in the same article a couple of pages later when it asked: "Or is the proposal implicit in the Protocol merely one for transferring to the shoulders of Great Britain, which alone is paying her debts, some part of the cost of maintaining that preponderance which now rests upon the European States which profit most by it. . . . It is sheer rubbish to suggest that France needs military guarantees for security. . . . What France really wants is a guarantee that the allies will maintain a perpetual preponderance over Germany. This we can never give her, for in the long run it makes not for peace but for war."

In another article in the same issue, the Protocol was analyzed and denounced. The final conclusion was: "It is our firm conviction that no alternative is acceptable which fails to provide for the free exercise by the Parliaments and peoples of the Empire of their judgment as to how to deal with any disturbance of the peace, or any threat of such disturbance, on its merits as it arises. That has been the guiding principle throughout the political history of the British peoples. The methods of the Protocol belong to another world, and, if for no other reason, they should be rejected."

The Protocol was officially rejected by Austen Chamberlain at a session of the Council of the League of Nations in March 1925. John Dove, Lionel Curtis, Philip Kerr, and Wilson Harris went to Geneva to be present at the meeting. After the deed was done, they went to visit Prague and Berlin, and ended by meeting Lady Astor in Paris. From Geneva and Paris, John Dove wrote to Brand letters which Brand later published in his edition of *The Letters of John Dove.*

One of the reasons given by Austen Chamberlain in 1925 for rejecting the Geneva Protocol was the opposition of the Dominions. That the Milner Group was able to affect Dominion opinion on this subject is clear. They could use men like Massey and Glazebrook in Canada, Bavin and Eggleston in Australia, Downie Stewart and Allen in New Zealand, Smuts and Duncan in South Africa.

More important than the Milner Group's ability to influence opinion in the Dominions was its ability to influence decisions in London. In much of this latter field, Lord Esher undoubtedly played an important role. It is perfectly clear that Lord Esher disliked collective security, and for the same reasons as *The Round Table.* This can be seen in his published *Journals and Letters.* For example, on 18 February 1919, in a letter to Hankey, he wrote: "I fervently believe that the happiness and welfare of the human race is more closely concerned in the evolution of English democracy and of our Imperial Commonwealth than in the growth of any international League." On 7 December 1919, in another letter to Hankey, he wrote: "You say that my letter was critical and not constructive. So it was. But the ground must be cleared of debris first. I assume that this is done. We will forget the high ideals and the fourteen points for the moment. We will be eminently practical. So here goes. Do not let us bother about a League of Nations. It may come slowly or not at all. What step forward, if any, can we take? We can get a League of Empire." Shortly afterwards, writing to his heir, the present Viscount Esher, he called the League "a paper hoop." The importance of this can be seen if we realize that Lord Esher was the most important factor on the Committee of Imperial Defence, and this committee was one of the chief forces determining British foreign policy in this period. In fact, no less an authority than Lord Robert Cecil has said that the Geneva Protocol was rejected on the advice of the Committee of Imperial Defence and that he accepted that decision only when he was promised a new project which subsequently became the Locarno Pacts.[8]

The rejection of the Protocol by Britain was regarded subsequently by real supporters of the League as the turning point in its career. There was an outburst of public sentiment against this selfish and cold-blooded action. Zimmern, who knew more than he revealed, went to Oxford in May 1925 and made a brilliant speech against those who were sabotaging the League. He did not identify them, but clearly indicated their existence, and, as the cruelest blow of all, attributed their actions to a failure of intelligence.

As a result of this feeling, which was widespread throughout the world, the Group determined to give the world the appearance of a guarantee to France. This was done in the Locarno Pacts, the most complicated and most deceitful international agreement made between the Treaty of Versailles and the Munich Pact. We cannot discuss them in detail here, but must content ourselves with pointing out that in appearance, and in the publicity campaign which accompanied their formation, the Locarno agreements guaranteed the frontier of Germany with France and Belgium with the power of these three states plus Britain and Italy. In reality the agreements gave France nothing, while they gave Britain a veto over French fulfillment of her alliances with Poland and the Little Entente. The French accepted these deceptive documents for reasons of internal politics: obviously, any French government which could make the French people believe that it had been able to secure a British guarantee of France's eastern frontier could expect the gratitude of the French people to be reflected at the polls. The fundamental shrewdness and realism of the French, however, made it difficult to conceal from them the trap that lay in the Locarno agreements. This trap consisted of several interlocking factors. In the first place, the agreements did not guarantee the German frontier and the demilitarized condition of the Rhineland against German actions, but against the actions of either Germany or France. This, at one stroke, gave Britain the legal grounds for opposing France if she tried any repetition of the military occupation of the Ruhr, and, above all, gave Britain the right to oppose any French action against Germany in support of her allies to the east of Germany. This meant that if Germany moved east against Czechoslovakia, Poland, and, eventually, Russia, and if France attacked Germany's western frontier in support of Czechoslovakia or Poland, as her alliances bound her to do, Great Britain, Belgium, and Italy might be bound by the Locarno Pacts to come to the aid of Germany. To be sure, the same agreement might bind these three powers to oppose Germany if she drove westward against France, but the Milner Group did not object to this for several reasons. In the first place, if Germany attacked France directly, Britain would have to come to the help of France whether bound by treaty or not. The old balance-of-power principle made that clear. In the second place, Cecil Hurst, the old master of legalistic doubletalk, drew up the Locarno Pacts with the same kind of loopholes which he had put in the crucial articles of the Covenant. As a result, if Germany did violate the Locarno Pacts against France, Britain could, if she desired, escape the necessity of fulfilling her guarantee by slipping through one of Hurst's loopholes. As a matter of fact, when Hitler did violate the Locarno agreements by remilitarizing the Rhineland in March 1936, the Milner Group and their friends did not even try to evade their obligation by slipping through a loophole, but simply dishonored their agreement.

This event of March 1936, by which Hitler remilitarized the Rhineland, was the most crucial event in the whole history of appeasement. So long as the territory west of the Rhine and a strip fifty kilometers wide on the east bank of the river were demilitarized, as provided in the Treaty of Versailles and the Locarno Pacts, Hitler would never have dared to move against Austria, Czechoslovakia, and Poland. He would not have dared because, with western Germany unfortified and denuded of German soldiers, France could have easily driven into the Ruhr industrial area and crippled Germany so that it would be impossible to go eastward. And by this date, certain members of the Milner Group and of the British Conservative government had reached the fantastic idea that they could kill two birds with one stone by setting Germany and Russia against one another in Eastern Europe. In this way they felt that the two enemies would stalemate one another, or that Germany would become satisfied with the oil of Rumania and the wheat of the Ukraine. It never occurred to anyone in a responsible position that Germany and Russia might make common cause, even temporarily, against the West. Even less did it occur to them that Russia might beat Germany and thus open all Central Europe to Bolshevism.

This idea of bringing Germany into a collision with Russia was not to be found, so far as the evidence shows, among any members of the inner circle of the Milner Group. Rather it was to be found among the personal associates of Neville Chamberlain, including several members of the second circle of the Milner Group. The two policies followed parallel courses until March 1939. After that date the Milner Group's disintegration became very evident, and part of it took the form of the movement of several persons (like Hoare and Simon) from the second circle of the Milner Group to the inner circle of the new group rotating around Chamberlain. This process was concealed by the fact that this new group was following, in public at least, the policy desired by the

Milner Group; their own policy, which was really the continuation of appeasement for another year after March 1939, was necessarily secret, so that the contrast between the Chamberlain group and the inner circle of the Milner Group in the period after March 1939 was not as obvious as it might have been.

In order to carry out this plan of allowing Germany to drive eastward against Russia, it was necessary to do three things: (1) to liquidate all the countries standing between Germany and Russia; (2) to prevent France from honoring her alliances with these countries; and (3) to hoodwink the English people into accepting this as a necessary, indeed, the only solution to the international problem. The Chamberlain group were so successful in all three of these things that they came within an ace of succeeding, and failed only because of the obstinacy of the Poles, the unseemly haste of Hitler, and the fact that at the eleventh hour the Milner Group realized the implications of their policy and tried to reverse it.

The program of appeasement can be divided into three stages: the first from 1920 to 1934, the second from 1934 to 1937, and the third from 1937 to 1940. The story of the first period we have almost completed, except for the evacuation of the Rhineland in 1930, five years ahead of the date set in the Treaty of Versailles. It would be too complicated a story to narrate here the methods by which France was persuaded to yield on this point. It is enough to point out that France was persuaded to withdraw her troops in 1930 rather than 1935 as a result of what she believed to be concessions made to her in the Young Plan. That the Milner Group approved this evacuation goes without saying. We have already mentioned *The Round Table*'s demand of June 1923 that the Rhineland be evacuated. A similar desire will be found in a letter from John Dove to Brand in October 1927.

The second period of appeasement began with Smuts's famous speech of 13 November 1934, delivered before the RIIA. The whole of this significant speech deserves to be quoted here, but we must content ourselves with a few extracts:

> With all the emphasis at my command, I would call a halt to this war talk as mischievous and dangerous war propaganda. The expectation of war tomorrow or in the near future is sheer nonsense, and all those who are conversant with affairs know it. . . . The remedy for this fear complex is . . . bringing it into the open and exposing it to the light of day. . . . And this is exactly the method of the League of Nations . . . it is an open forum for discussion among the nations, it is a round table for the statesmen around which they can ventilate and debate their grievances and viewpoints. . . . There are those who say that this is not enough — that as long as the League remains merely a talking shop or debating society, and is not furnished with "teeth" and proper sanctions, the sense of insecurity

will remain. . . . It is also felt that the inability of the League to guarantee the collective system by means of force, if necessary, is discrediting it and leading to its decay. . . . I cannot visualize the League as a military machine. It was not conceived or built for that purpose, it is not equipped for such functions. And if ever the attempt were made to transform it into a military machine, into a system to carry on war for the purpose of preventing war, I think its fate is sealed. . . . Defection of the United States has largely defeated its main objects. And the joining up of the United States must continue to be the ultimate goal of all true friends of the League and of the cause of peace. A conference of the nations the United States can, and eventually will, join; it can never join an international War Office. Remembering the debates on this point in the League of Nations Commission which drafted the Covenant, I say quite definitely that the very idea of a league of force was negatived there; and the League would be quite false to its fundamental idea and to its great mission . . . if it allowed itself to be turned into something quite different, something just the opposite of its original idea — into a league of force. . . . To endeavor to cast out the Satan of fear by calling in the Beelzebub of militarism, and militarizing the League itself, would be a senseless and indeed fatal proceeding. . . . The removal of the inferiority complex from Germany is just as essential to future peace as the removal of fear from the mind of France; and both are essential to an effective disarmament policy. How can the inferiority complex which is obsessing and, I fear, poisoning the mind and indeed the soul of Germany be removed? There is only one way, and that is to recognize her complete equality of status with her fellows, and to do so frankly, freely, and unreservedly. That is the only medicine for her disease. . . . While one understands and sympathizes with French fears, one cannot but feel for Germany in the position of inferiority in which she still remains sixteen years after the conclusion of the War. The continuance of her Versailles status is becoming an offense to the conscience of Europe and a danger to future peace. . . . There is no place in international law for second-rate nations, and least of all should Germany be kept in that position. . . . Fair play, sportsmanship — indeed, every standard of private and public life — calls for frank revision of the position. Indeed, ordinary prudence makes it imperative. Let us break those bonds and set the captive, obsessed, soul free in a decent human way. And Europe will reap a rich reward in tranquillity, security, and returning prosperity. . . . I would say that to me the future policy and association of our great British Commonwealth lie more with the United States than with any other group in the world. If ever there comes a parting of the ways, if ever in the crisis of the future we are called upon to make a choice, *that*, it seems to me, should be the company we should prefer to walk with and march with to the unknown future. . . . Nobody can forecast the outcome of the stormy era of history on which we are probably entering.

At the time that Smuts made this significant speech, the Milner Group had already indicated to Hitler officially that Britain was prepared to give Germany arms equality. France had greeted the arrival to power of Hitler by desperate efforts to form an "Eastern Locarno" against Germany. Sir John Simon, who was Foreign Secretary from September 1931 to June 1935, repudiated these efforts on 13 July 1934 in a speech which was approved by *The Times* the following day. He warned the French that Britain would not approve any effort "to build up one combination against another," would refuse to assume any new obligations herself, would insist that Russia join the League of Nations before she become a party to any multilateral settlement, and insisted on arms equality for Germany. On the same day, Austen Chamberlain laid the groundwork for the German remilitarization of the Rhineland by a speech in which he insisted that the Locarno agreements did not bind Britain to use troops. He clearly indicated how Britain, by her veto power in the Council of the League, could prevent a League request to provide troops to enforce Locarno, and added that such a request would not be binding on Britain, even if voted, since "there was no automatic obligation under the Government to send our Army to any frontier."

In a debate in the House of Lords on 5 December 1934, Lord Cecil contradicted Smuts's statement that "the idea of a League of force was negatived" in 1918 and restated his own views that force should be available to compel the observance of the three months' moratorium between the settlement of a question by the Council and the outbreak of war. He said: "The thing which we were most anxious to secure against a renewal of a great war was that there should be collective action to prevent a sudden outbreak of war. It was never part of the Covenant system that force should be used in order to compel some particular settlement of a dispute. That, we thought, was going beyond what public opinion of the world would support; but we did think we could go so far as to say: 'You are not to resort to war until every other means for bringing about a settlement has been exhausted.' " This was merely a restatement of the point of view that Lord Cecil had held since 1918. It did not constitute collective security, as the expression was used by the world in general. Yet this use of the words "collective security" to mean the enforcement of a three months' moratorium before issuing a declaration of war — this weaker meaning — was being weakened even further by the Milner Group. This was made perfectly clear in a speech by Lord Lothian (Philip Kerr) immediately after Lord Cecil. On this day the latter parted from the Milner Group program of appeasement; more than ten years after Zimmern's, this defection is of less significance than the earlier one because Lord Cecil did not see clearly what was being done and he had never been, apparently, a member of the inner circle of the Group, although he had attended meetings of the inner circle in the period after 1910.[9]

Lord Lothian's speech of 5 December 1934 in the House of Lords is, at first glance, a defense of collective security, but a second look shows clearly that by "collective security" the speaker meant appeasement. He contrasts collective security with power diplomacy and, having excluded all use of force under the former expression, goes on to interpret it to mean peaceful change without war. In the context of events, this could only mean appeasement of Germany. He said: "In international affairs, unless changes are made in time, war becomes inevitable. . . . If the collective system is to be successful, it must contain two elements. On the one hand, it must be able to bring about by pacific means alterations in the international structure, and, on the other hand, it must be strong enough to restrain Powers who seek to take the law into their own hands either by war or by power diplomacy, from being successful in their efforts." This was nothing but the appeasement program of Chamberlain and Halifax — that concessions should be made to Germany to strengthen her on the Continent and in Eastern Europe, while Britain should remain strong enough on the sea and in the air to prevent Hitler from using war to obtain these concessions. The fear of Hitler's using war was based not so much on a dislike of force (neither Lothian nor Halifax was a pacifist in that sense) but on the realization that if Hitler made war against Austria, Czechoslovakia, or Poland, public opinion in France and England might force their governments to declare war in spite of their desire to yield these areas to Germany. This, of course, is what finally happened.

Hitler was given ample assurance by the Milner Group, both within and without the government, that Britain would not oppose his efforts "to achieve arms equality." Four days before Germany officially denounced the disarmament clauses of the Treaty of Versailles, Leopold Amery made a slashing attack on collective security, comparing "the League which exists" and "the league of make-believe, a cloud cuckoo land, dreams of a millennium which we were not likely to reach for many a long year to come; a league which was to maintain peace by going to war whenever peace was disturbed. That sort of thing, if it could exist, would be a danger to peace; it would be employed to extend war rather than to put an end to it. But dangerous or not, it did not exist, and to pretend that it did exist was sheer stupidity."

Four days later, Hitler announced Germany's rearmament, and ten days after that, Britain condoned the act by sending Sir John Simon on a state visit to Berlin. When France tried to counterbalance Germany's rearmament by bringing the Soviet Union into her eastern alliance system in May 1935, the British counteracted this by making the Anglo-

German Naval Agreement of 18 June 1935. This agreement, concluded by Simon, allowed Germany to build up to 35 percent of the size of the British Navy (and up to 100 percent in submarines). This was a deadly stab in the back to France, for it gave Germany a navy considerably larger than the French in the important categories of ships (capital ships and aircraft carriers) in the North Sea, because France was bound by treaty in these categories to only 33 percent of Britain's; and France, in addition, had a worldwide empire to protect and the unfriendly Italian Navy off her Mediterranean coast. This agreement put the French Atlantic coast so completely at the mercy of the German Navy that France became completely dependent on the British fleet for protection in this area. Obviously, this protection would not be given unless France in a crisis renounced her eastern allies. As if this were not enough, Britain in March 1936 accepted the German remilitarization of the Rhineland and in August 1936 began the farcical nonintervention agreement in Spain, which put another unfriendly government on France's remaining land frontier. Under such pressure, it was clear that France would not honor her alliances with the Czechs, the Poles, or the Russians, if they came due.

In these actions of March 1935 and March 1936, Hitler was running no risk, for the government and the Milner Group had assured him beforehand that it would accept his actions. This was done both in public and in private, chiefly in the House of Commons and in the articles of *The Times*. Within the Cabinet, Halifax, Simon, and Hoare resisted the effort to form any alignment against Germany. The authorized biographer of Halifax wrote in reference to Halifax's attitude in 1935 and 1936:

"Was England to allow herself to be drawn into war because France had alliances in Eastern Europe? Was she to give Mussolini a free pass to Addis Ababa merely to prevent Hitler marching to Vienna?" Questions similar to these were undoubtedly posed by Halifax in Cabinet. His own friends, in particular Lothian and Geoffrey Dawson of *The Times*, had for some time been promoting Anglo-German fellowship with rather more fervour than the Foreign Office. In January 1935 Lothian had a long conversation with Hitler, and Hitler was reputed to have proposed an alliance between England, Germany, and the United States which would in effect give Germany a free hand on the Continent, in return for which he had promised not to make Germany "a world power" or to attempt to compete with the British Navy. *The Times* consistently opposed the Eastern Locarno and backed Hitler's non-aggression alternative. Two days before the Berlin talks, for instance, it advocated that they should include territorial changes, and in particular the question of Memel; while on the day they began [March 1935] its leading article suggested that if Herr Hitler can persuade his British visitors, and through them the rest of the world, that his enlarged army is really designed to give them equality of status and equality of negotiation with other countries, and is not to be trained for aggressive purposes, then Europe may be on the threshold of an era in which changes can be made without the use of force, and a potential aggressor may be deterred by the certain prospect of having to face overwhelming opposition! How far *The Times* and Lothian were arguing and negotiating on the Government's behalf is still not clear, but that Halifax was intimately acquainted with the trend of this argument is probable.

It goes without saying that the whole inner core of the Group, and their chief publications, such as *The Times* and *The Round Table*, approved the policy of appeasement completely and prodded it along with calculated indiscretions when it was felt necessary to do so. After the remilitarization of the Rhineland, *The Times* cynically called this act "a chance to rebuild." As late as 24 February 1938, in the House of Lords, Lothian defended the same event. He said: "We hear a great deal of the violation by Herr Hitler of the Treaty because he returned his own troops to his own frontier. You hear much less today of the violation by which the French Army, with the acquiescence of this country, crossed the frontier in order to annihilate German industry and in effect produced the present Nazi Party."

In the House of Commons in October 1935, and again on 6 May 1936, Amery systematically attacked the use of force to sustain the League of Nations. On the earlier occasion he said:

> From the very outset there have been two schools of thought about the League and about our obligations under the League. There has been the school, to which I belong and to which for years, I believe, the Government of this country belonged, that regards the League as a great institution, an organization for promoting cooperation and harmony among the nations, for bringing about understanding, a permanent Round Table of the nations in conference . . . provided always that it did not have at the background the threat of coercion. There is another school which thinks that the actual Articles of the Covenant, concocted in the throes of the peace settlement and in that atmosphere of optimism which led us to expect ten million pounds or more in reparations from Germany, constitute a sacrosanct dispensation, that they have introduced a new world order, and would, if they were only loyally adhered to, abolish war for good and all. The Covenant, I admit, as originally drafted, embodied both aspects and it was because the Covenant contained the Clauses that stood for coercion and for definite automatic obligations that the United States . . . repudiated it. From that moment the keystone was taken out of the whole arch of any League of coercion. . . . The League is now undergoing a trial which may well prove disastrous to it. In this matter, as in other matters, it is the letter that killeth. The letter of the Covenant is the one thing which is likely to kill the League of Nations.

Amery then continued with a brief résumé of the efforts to make the League an instrument of coercion, especially the Geneva Protocol. In regard to this, he continued: "The case I wish to put to the House is that the stand taken by His Majesty's Government then and the arguments they used were not arguments merely against the Protocol, but arguments against the whole conception of a League based on economic and military sanctions." He quoted Austen Chamberlain in 1925 and General Smuts in 1934 with approval, and concluded: "I think that we should have got together with France and Italy and devised some scheme by which under a condominium or mandate certain if not all of the non-Amharic provinces of Abyssinia should be transferred to Italian rule. The whole thing could have been done by agreement, and I have no doubt that such agreement would have been ratified at Geneva."

This last statement was more then seven weeks before the Hoare-Laval Plan was made public, and six weeks after its outlines were laid down by Hoare, Eden, and Laval at a secret meeting in Paris (10 September 1935).

In his speech of 6 May 1936, Amery referred back to his October speech and demanded that the Covenant of the League be reformed to prevent sanctions in the future. Once again he quoted Smuts's speech of November 1934 with approval, and demanded "a League which is based not upon coercion but upon conciliation."

Between Amery's two speeches, on 5 February 1936, Sir Arthur Salter, of the Group and All Souls, offered his arguments to support appeasement. He quoted Smuts's speech of 1934 with approval and pointed out the great need for living space and raw materials for Japan, Italy, and Germany. The only solution, he felt, was for Britain to yield to these needs.

> I do not think it matters [he said] if you reintroduce conscription and quadruple or quintuple your Air Force. That will not protect you. I believe that the struggle is destined to come unless we are prepared to agree to a fairer distribution of the world's land surface and of the raw materials which are needed by modern civilized nations. But there is a way out; there is no necessity for a clash. I am sure that time presses and that we cannot postpone a settlement indefinitely. . . . I suggest that the way out is the application of those principles [of Christianity], the deliberate and conscious application of those principles to international affairs by this nation and by the world under the leadership of this nation. . . . Treat other nations as you would desire to be treated by them.

The liquidation of the countries between Germany and Russia could proceed as soon as the Rhineland was fortified, without fear on Germany's part that France would be able to attack her in the west while she was occupied in the east. The chief task of the Milner Group was to see that this devouring process was done no faster than public opinion in Britain could accept, and that the process did not result in any outburst of violence, which the British people would be unlikely to accept. To this double purpose, the British government and the Milner Group made every effort to restrain the use of force by the Germans and to soften up the prospective victims so that they would not resist the process and thus precipitate a war.

The countries marked for liquidation included Austria, Czechoslovakia, and Poland, but did not include Greece and Turkey, since the Group had no intention of allowing Germany to get down onto the Mediterranean "lifeline". Indeed, the purpose of the Hoare-Laval Plan of 1935, which wrecked the collective-security system by seeking to give most of Ethiopia to Italy, was intended to bring an appeased Italy into position alongside England, in order to block any movement of Germany southward rather than eastward. The plan failed because Mussolini decided that he could get more out of England by threats from the side of Germany than from cooperation at the side of England. As a result of this fiasco, the Milner Group lost another important member, Arnold J. Toynbee, who separated himself from the policy of appeasement in a fighting and courageous preface to *The Survey of International Affairs for 1935* (published in 1936). As a result of the public outcry in England, Hoare, the Foreign Secretary, was removed from office and briefly shelved in December 1935. He returned to the Cabinet the following May. Anthony Eden, who replaced him, was not a member of the Milner Group and considerably more to the public taste because of his reputation (largely undeserved) as an upholder of collective security. The Milner Group was in no wise hampered in its policy of appeasement by the presence of Eden in the Foreign Office, and the government as a whole was considerably strengthened. Whenever the Group wanted to do something which Eden's delicate stomach could not swallow, the Foreign Secretary went off for a holiday, and Lord Halifax took over his tasks. Halifax did this, for example, during the first two weeks of August 1936, when the nonintervention policy was established in Spain; he did it again in February 1937, when the capable British Ambassador in Berlin, Sir Eric Phipps, was removed at Ribbentrop's demand and replaced by Sir Nevile Henderson; he did it again at the end of October 1937, when arrangements were made for his visit to Hitler at Berchtesgaden in November; and, finally, Halifax replaced Eden as Foreign Secretary permanently in February 1938, when Eden refused to accept the recognition of the Italian conquest of Ethiopia in return for an Italian promise to withdraw their forces from Spain. In this last case, Halifax was already negotiating with Count Grandi in the Foreign Office before Eden's resignation statement was made. Eden and Halifax were second cousins, both being great-grandsons of Lord Grey of the Reform Bill of 1832, and Halifax's daughter in 1936 married the half-brother of

Mrs. Anthony Eden. Halifax and Eden were combined in the Foreign Office in order that the former could counterbalance the "youthful impetuosities" of the latter, since these might jeopardize appeasement but were regarded as necessary stage-settings to satisfy the collective-security yearnings of public opinion in England. These yearnings were made evident in the famous "Peace Ballot" of the League of Nations Union, a maneuver put through by Lord Cecil as a countermove to the Group's slow undermining of collective security. This countermove, which was regarded with extreme distaste by Lothian and others of the inner circle, resulted, among other things, in an excessively polite crossing of swords by Cecil and Lothian in the House of Lords on 16 March 1938.

During the period in which Halifax acted as a brake on Eden, he held the sinecure Cabinet posts of Lord Privy Seal and Lord President of the Council (1935-1938). He had been added to the Cabinet, after his return from India in 1931, as President of the Board of Education, but devoted most of his time from 1931 to 1935 in helping Simon and Hoare put through the Government of India Act of 1935. In October 1933, the same group of Conservative members of Convocation who had made Lord Milner Chancellor of Oxford University in 1925 selected Lord Irwin (Halifax), for the same position, in succession to the late Lord Grey of Fallodon. He spent almost the whole month of June 1934 in the active functions of this position, especially in drawing up the list of recipients of honorary degrees. This list is very significant. Among sixteen recipients of the Doctorate of Civil Law, we find the following five names: Samuel Hoare, Maurice Hankey, W. G. S. Adams, John Buchan, and Geoffrey Dawson.

We have indicated that Halifax's influence on foreign policy was increasingly important in the years 1934-1937. It was he who defended Hoare in the House of Lords in December 1935, saying: "I have never been one of those . . . who have thought that it was any part in this dispute of the League to try to stop a war in Africa by starting a war in Europe. It was Halifax who went with Eden to Paris in March 1936 to the discussions of the Locarno Powers regarding the remilitarization of the Rhineland. That his task at this meeting was to act as a brake on Eden's relatively large respect for the sanctity of international obligations is admitted by Lord Halifax's authorized biographer. It was Halifax, as we have seen, who inaugurated the nonintervention policy in Spain in August 1936. And it was Halifax who opened the third and last stage of appeasement in November 1937 by his visit to Hitler in Berchtesgaden.

It is probable that the groundwork for Halifax's visit to Hitler had been laid by the earlier visits of Lords Lothian and Londonderry to the same host, but our knowledge of these earlier events is too scanty to be certain. Of Halifax's visit, the story is now clear, as a result of the publication of the German Foreign Office memorandum on the subject and Keith Feiling's publication of some of the letters from Neville Chamberlain to his sister. The visit was arranged by Halifax himself, early in November 1937, at a time when he was Acting Foreign Secretary, Eden being absent in Brussels at a meeting of signers of the Nine-Power Pacific Treaty of 1922. As a result, Halifax had a long conversation with Hitler on 19 November 1937 in which, whatever may have been Halifax's intention, Hitler's government became convinced of three things: (a) that Britain regarded Germany as the chief bulwark against communism in Europe; (b) that Britain was prepared to join a Four Power agreement of France, Germany, Italy, and herself; and (c) that Britain was prepared to allow Germany to liquidate Austria, Czechoslovakia, and Poland if this could be done without provoking a war into which the British Government, however unwillingly, would be dragged in opposition to Germany. The German Foreign Ministry memorandum on this conversation makes it perfectly clear that the Germans did not misunderstand Halifax except, possibly, on the last point. There they failed to see that if Germany made war, the British Government would be forced into the war against Germany by public opinion in England. The German diplomatic agents in London, especially the Ambassador, Dirksen, saw this clearly, but the Government in Berlin listened only to the blind and conceited ignorance of Ribbentrop. As dictators themselves, unfamiliar with the British social or constitutional systems, the German rulers assumed that the willingness of the British Government to accept the liquidation of Austria, Czechoslovakia, and Poland implied that the British Government would never go to war to prevent this liquidation. They did not see that the British Government might have to declare war to stay in office if public opinion in Britain were sufficiently aroused. The British Government saw this difficulty and as a last resort were prepared *to declare war* but not *to wage war* on Germany. This distinction was not clear to the Germans and was not accepted by the inner core of the Milner Group. It was, however, accepted by the other elements in the government, like Chamberlain himself, and by much of the second circle of the Milner Group, including Simon, Hoare, and probably Halifax. It was this which resulted in the "phony war" from September 1939 to April 1940.

The memorandum on Halifax's interview, quoting the Englishman in the third person, says in part:[10]

In spite of these difficulties [British public opinion, the English Church, and the Labour Party] he and other members of the British Government were fully aware that the Führer had not only achieved a great deal inside

Germany herself, but that, by destroying Communism in his country, he had barred its road to Western Europe, and that Germany therefore could rightly be regarded as a bulwark of the West against Bolshevism. . . . After the ground had been prepared by an Anglo-German understanding, the four Great West-European Powers must jointly lay the foundation for lasting peace in Europe. Under no conditions should any of the four Powers remain outside this cooperation, or else there would be no end to the present unstable situation. . . . Britons were realists and were perhaps more than others convinced that the errors of the Versailles dictate must be rectified. Britain always exercised her influence in this realistic sense in the past. He pointed to Britain's role with regard to the evacuation of the Rhineland ahead of the fixed time, the settlement of the reparations problem, and the reoccupation of the Rhineland. . . . He therefore wanted to know the Führer's attitude toward the League of Nations, as well as toward disarmament. All other questions could be characterized as relating to changes in the European order, changes that sooner or later would probably take place To these questions belonged Danzig, Austria, and Czechoslovakia. England was only interested that any alterations should be effected by peaceful evolution, so as to avoid methods which might cause far-reaching disturbances, which were not desired either by the Fuhrer or by other countries. . . . Only one country, Soviet Russia, stood to gain from a general conflict. All others were at heart in favour of the consolidation of peace.

That this attitude was not Halifax's personal argument but the point of view of the government (and of the Milner Group) is perfectly clear. On arrival, Halifax assured the Germans that the purposes of his visit had been discussed and accepted by the Foreign Secretary (Eden) and the Prime Minister. On 26 November 1937, one week after Halifax's conversation with Hitler, Chamberlain wrote to his sister that he hoped to satisfy German colonial demands by giving them the Belgian Congo and Angola in place of Tanganyika. He then added: "I don't see why we shouldn't say to Germany, 'Give us satisfactory assurances that you won't use force to deal with the Austrians and Czechoslovakians, and we will give you similar assurances that we won't use force to prevent the changes you want if you can get them by peaceful means.' "[11]

It might be noted that when John W. Wheeler-Bennett, of Chatham House and the Milner Group, wrote his book on *Munich: Prologue to Tragedy*, published in 1948, he relegated the last quotation to a footnote and suppressed the references to the Belgian Congo and Angola. This, however, was an essential part of the appeasement program of the Chamberlain group. On 3 March 1938, the British Ambassador in Berlin, Nevile Henderson, one of the Chamberlain group, tried to persuade Hitler to begin negotiations to carry out this plan but did not succeed. He repeated Lord Halifax's statement that changes in Europe were acceptable to Britain if accomplished without "the free play of forces," and stated that he personally "had often expressed himself in favour of the Anschluss." In the colonial field, he tried to interest Hitler in an area in Africa between the 5th parallel and the Zambezi River, but the Führer insisted that his interest was restricted to restoration of Germany's 1914 colonies in Africa.

At the famous interview between Hitler and Schuschnigg in February 1938, Hitler told the Austrian that Lord Halifax agreed "with everything he [Hitler] did with respect to Austria and the Sudeten Germans." This was reported in a "rush and strictly confidential" message of 16 February 1938 from the American Consul General in Vienna to Secretary of State Hull, a document released to the American press on 18 December 1948. Chamberlain and others made it perfectly clear, both in public and in private, that Britain would not act to prevent German occupation of Austria or Czechoslovakia. On 21 February 1938, during the Austrian crisis, John Simon said in the House of Commons, "Great Britain has never given special guarantees regarding Austrian independence." Six days later, Chamberlain said: "We must not try to delude small nations into thinking that they will be protected by the League against aggression and acting accordingly when we know that nothing of the kind can be expected." Five days after the seizure of Austria on 12 March 1938, the Soviet Union sent Britain a proposal for an international conference to stop aggression. The suggestion was rejected at once, and, on 20 March 1938, Chamberlain wrote to his sister: "I have therefore abandoned any idea of giving guarantees to Czechoslovakia or to the French in connection with her obligation to that country."

When Daladier, the French Premier, came to London at the end of April 1938 to seek support for Czechoslovakia, Chamberlain refused and apparently, if we can believe Feiling, put pressure on the French to compel the Czechoslovaks to make an agreement with Hitler. On 1 May, Chamberlain wrote to his sister in this connection: "Fortunately the papers have had no hint of how near we came to a break over Czechoslovakia."

In a long report of 10 July 1938, Ambassador Dirksen wrote to Ribbentrop as follows:

> In England the Chamberlain-Halifax Cabinet is at the helm and the first and most essential plank of its platform was and is agreement with the totalitarian States. . . . This government displays with regard to Germany the maximum understanding that could be displayed by any of the likely combinations of British politicians. It possesses the inner-political strength to carry out this task. It has come nearer to understanding the most essential points of the major demands advanced by Germany, with respect to excluding the Soviet Union from the decision of the destinies of Europe, the League of Nations likewise, and the advisability of bilateral negotia-

278 / THE ANGLO-AMERICAN ESTABLISHMENT

tions and treaties. It is displaying increasing understanding of Germany's demands in the Sudeten German question. It would be prepared to make great sacrifices to meet Germany's other just demands — on the *one* condition that it is endeavoured to achieve these ends by peaceful means. If Germany should resort to military means to achieve these ends, England would without the slightest doubt go to war on the side of France.

This point of view was quite acceptable to the Milner Group. In the leading article for December 1937, *The Round Table* examined the German question at some length. In regard to the colonial problem, it contrasted two points of view, giving greater emphasis to "those who now feel that it was a mistake to have deprived Germany of all her colonies in 1918, and that Great Britain should contribute her share towards finding a colonial area — say, in central west Africa — which could be transferred to Germany under mandate. But they, too, make it a condition that colonial revision should be part of a final all-round settlement with Germany, and that the colonies should not be used as leverage for fresh demands or as strategic bases." Later it said: "A majority would regard the abandonment of France's eastern alliances as a price well worth paying for lasting peace and the return of Germany to the League." It welcomed German rearmament, since this would force revision of the evil Treaty of Versailles. In this connection, the same article said: "The pressure of rearmament and the events of the last few years have at least had this effect, that the refusal of those who have benefited most by the peace settlement to consider any kind of change is rapidly disappearing; for forcible changes which they have been unable to prevent have already taken place, and further changes will certainly follow, especially in eastern Europe, unless they are prepared to fight a very formidable war to prevent them." The article rejected such a war on the grounds that its "outcome is uncertain" and it "would entail objectionable domestic disasters." In adding up the balance of military forces in such a war, the article significantly omitted all mention of Czechoslovakia, whose forces at that time were considerably stronger than Germany's. It placed the French Army at two-thirds the size of Germany's (which was untrue) and Britain at no more than two or three divisions. The point of view of *The Round Table* was not identical with that of the Chamberlain group (which intersected, through common members, with the second circle of the Milner Group). *The Round Table*, speaking for the inner circle of the Milner Group, was not nearly so anti-Russian as the Chamberlain group. Accordingly, it never regarded a collision between Nazi Germany and the Soviet Union as a practical solution of Europe's problems. It did accept the idea of a four-power pact to exclude Russia from Europe, but it was not willing to allow Germany to expand eastward as she wished. The

Milner Group's misunderstanding of the Nazi system and of Germany itself was so great that they envisioned a stable situation in which Europe was dominated by a four-power pact, with Soviet Russia on one side and an Oceanic bloc of the British Commonwealth and the United States on the other. The Group insisted on rapid British rearmament and the building up of the Oceanic System because they had a lower opinion of Britain's own powers than did the Chamberlain group (this idea was derived from Milner) and they were not prepared to allow Germany to go eastward indefinitely in the hope she would be satisfied by a war with Russia. As we shall see, the policies of the Milner Group and the Chamberlain group went jointly forward, with slight shifts of emphasis, until March 1939, when the Group began to disintegrate.

In the same article of December 1937 *The Round Table* said that the democracies must

> make clear the point at which they are prepared to risk war rather than retreat. . . . During the last year or two *The Round Table* has criticized the popular dogma of "collective security" on two main grounds: that it meant fighting to maintain an out-of-date settlement, and that security depended, not merely on public opinion but on ability to bring effective military superiority to bear at the critical point. On the other hand, *The Round Table* is resolutely in favour of adequate defensive armaments and of a vigorous and if necessary defiant foreign policy at those points where we are sure that . . . we can bring superior power effectively to bear. And for this purpose we consider that the nations of the Commonwealth should not only act together themselves, but should also work in the closest cooperation with all the democracies, especially the United States.

In February 1938, Lord Lothian, "leader" of the Group, spoke in the House of Lords in support of appeasement. This extraordinary speech was delivered in defense of the retiring of Sir Robert Vansittart. Sir Robert, as Permanent Under Secretary in the Foreign Office from 1930 to 1938, was a constant thorn in the side of the appeasers. The opening of the third stage of appeasement at the end of 1937 made it necessary to get rid of him and his objections to their policy. Accordingly, he was "promoted" to the newly created post of Chief Diplomatic Adviser, and the Under Secretaryship was given to Sir Alexander Cadogan of the Cecil Bloc. This action led to a debate in February 1938. Lord Lothian intervened to insist that Sir Robert's new role would not be parallel to that of the new Under Secretary but was restricted to advising only on "matters specifically referred to him by the Secretary of State, and he is no longer responsible for the day to day work of the Office." From this point, Lothian launched into a long attack on the League of Nations, followed by a defense of Germany. In regard to the former, he expressed satisfaction that the most dangerous aspect of the League of Nations — namely, the interpretation which has habitually been put upon it by the League of Nations Union in this country — is pretty well dead. . . . It seems to me that that [interpretation] is inevitably going to turn the League of Nations itself not into an instrument for maintaining peace but into an instrument for making war. That was not the original concept of the League at all. The original concept of the League definitely left the way open for alteration after six months' examination even if it meant war. . . . I think the League of Nations now, at last, is going to have a chance of recovery, for the reason that this particular interpretation, which has been its besetting sin, the one thing which has led to its failure from the beginning, is now dead. . . . Therefore I am more hopeful of the League today than I have been for a good long time, because it has ceased to be an instrument to try to perpetuate the status quo.

When Lothian turned to the problem of Germany, his arguments became even more ridiculous. "The fundamental problem of the world today is still the problem of Germany. . . . Why is Germany the issue? In my view the fundamental reason is that at no time in the years after 1919 has the rest of the world been willing to concede any substantial justice or reasonable understanding to Germany, either when she was a Republic or since she has become a Totalitarian State." There followed a long attack on the war guilt thesis as applied to 1914, or even to 1870. This thesis Lothian called "propaganda," and from this false propaganda he traced all the cruel treatment given Germany since 1919. He disapproved of the Nazi Government's methods inside Germany, but added: "I do not think there is any doubt that modern Germany is the result of the policy of the United States, whom I cannot absolve from responsibility, of ourselves, and of France; and in this matter the responsibility of the United States and ourselves is more than that of France for defaulting on the obligation to give France some security so that she could allow Germany to recover."

It seems impossible that this could be the same man who was calling for the extirpation of "Prussianism" in 1908-1918 and who was to call for the same crusade as Ambassador in Washington in 1940.

In this same speech Lothian laid down what might be called the Milner Group solution to this German problem, 1938 model:

There is only one solution to this problem. You have got to combine collective justice with collective security. You have got to give remedies to those nations which are entitled to them. . . . You have got to be willing to concede to them — and one of them is Germany — alterations in the status quo and you have also got to incur obligations with other like-minded nations to resist changes which go beyond what impartial justice regards as fair. . . . When we are willing to admit that we are ourselves largely responsible for the tragedy that confronts us, for the fact that Germany is the center of the world problem, and are willing to concede to Germany what a fair-minded and impartial authority would say was a fair solution of her problem, and if, in addition to that, we are willing to say, "We will meet aggression to secure more than this with the only means in which it can be met," then I consider there is hope for the world.

The fallacy in all of this rests on the fact that every concession to Germany made her stronger, with no guarantee that she ever would stop; and if, after years of concessions, she refused to stop, she might be too strong to be compelled to do so. The Milner Group thesis was based not only on ignorance but also on logical deficiencies. The program of the Chamberlain group was at least more consistent, since it involved no effort to stop Germany at any point but aimed to solve the German problem by driving it into Russia. Such an "immoral" solution could not be acceptable to the Milner Group, so they should have had sense enough to stop Germany while she was weak.

Shortly after this speech, on 24 February 1938, Lothian intervened in the debate on Eden's resignation to reject Eden's point of view and defend Chamberlain's. He rejected the idea that Britain should commit herself to support Czechoslovakia against Germany and criticized the President of Czechoslovakia for his failure to make concessions to Republican Germany. He then repeated his speech of the week before, the chief addition being a defense of the German remilitarization of the Rhineland in March 1936.

Four days after the seizure of Austria, Lothian again advised against any new pledges to anyone and demanded rearmament and national service. In regard to rearmament he said: "Unpreparedness and the belief that you are unwilling to accept that challenge or that you do not mean what you say, does contribute to war. That will remain to be a condition of the world until the nations are willing in some way to pool their sovereignty in a common federation."

All of these ideas of Lothian's were explictly restated by him in a speech at Chatham House on 24 March 1938. He refuted the "war-guilt thesis," condemned the Versailles settlement as "a very stiff Peace Treaty," insisted on revision, blamed all the disasters of Europe on America's withdrawal from the League in 1920, called the Hitler government a temporary "unnatural pathological state" solely caused by the stiff treaty and the failure to revise it, defended the remilitarization of the Rhineland and the seizure of Austria, condemned Czechoslovakia as "almost the only racially heterogeneous State left in Europe," praised "nonintervention" in Spain, praised Chamberlain's statement of the same day refusing to promise support to Czechoslovakia, and demanded "national service" as insurance that Hitler would not continue to use force after he obtained what he deserved in justice.

These arguments of Lothian's were all supported by the Group in other ways. *The Round Table* in its leading articles of March 1938, September 1938, and March 1939 demanded "national service." In the leading article of June 1938 it repeated all Lothian's arguments in somewhat different words. These arguments could be summed up in the slogan "appeasement and rearmament." Then it added:

> Until the nations can be brought to the two principles of collective security already described, the best security for peace is that the world should be divided into zones within each of which one of the great armed Powers, or a group of them, is clearly preponderant, and in which therefore other Powers do not seek to interfere. Then there may be peace for a time. The peace of the 19th century rested on the fact that the supremacy of the British Navy kept the whole oceanic area free from general war. . . . The vital question now arises whether in that same zone, to which France and Scandinavia must be added, it is not possible, despite the immense armaments of central Europe, Russia, and the Far East, for the democracies to create security, stability, and peace in which liberal institutions can survive. The oceanic zone in fact constitutes the one part of the world in which it is possible today to realise the ideals of the League of Nations.

From this point onward (early 1938), the Milner Group increasingly emphasized the necessity for building up this Oceanic bloc. In England the basic propaganda work was done through *The Round Table* and Lionel Curtis, while in the United States it was done through the Rhodes Scholarship organization, especially through Clarence Streit and Frank Aydelotte. In England, Curtis wrote a series of books and articles advocating a new federal organization built around the English-speaking countries. The chief work of this nature was his *Civitas Dei*, which appeared in three volumes in 1934-1937. A one-volume edition was issued in 1938, with the title *The Commonwealth of God*. The first two volumes of this work are nothing more than a rehash and expansion of the older work *The Commonwealth of Nations* (1916). By a superficial and frequently erroneous rewriting of world history, the author sought to review the evolution of the "commonwealth" idea and to show that all of history leads to its fulfillment and achievement in federation. Ultimately, this federation will be worldwide, but en route it must pass through stages, of which the chief is federation of the English-speaking peoples. Writing early in 1937, he advocated that the League of Nations be destroyed by the mass resignation of the British democracies. These should then take the initiative in forming a new league, also at Geneva, which would have no power to enforce anything but would merely form a kind of international conference. Since it would be foolish to expect any federation to evolve from any such organization as this, a parallel, but quite separate, effort should be made to create an international commonwealth, based on the example of the United States in 1788. This international commonwealth would differ from the League of Nations in that its members would yield up part of their sovereignty, and the central organization would function directly on individuals and not merely on states. This international commonwealth would be formed, at first, only of those states that have evolved furthest in the direction of obtaining a commonwealth form of government for themselves. It will be recalled that this restriction on membership was what Curtis had originally advocated for the League of Nations in *The Round Table* of December 1918. According to Curtis, the movement toward the Commonwealth of God can begin by the union of any two national commonwealths, no matter how small. He suggested New Zealand and Australia, or these two and Great Britain. Then the international commonwealth could be expanded to include India, Egypt, Holland, Belgium, Scandinavia, France, Canada, the United States, and Ireland. That the chief obstacle to this union was to be found in men's minds was perfectly clear to Curtis. To overcome this obstacle, he put his faith in propaganda, and the chief instruments of that propaganda, he said, must be the churches and the universities. He said nothing about the Milner Group, but, considering Curtis's position in this Group and that Lothian and others agreed with him, it is not surprising that the chief source of this propaganda is to be found in those agencies controlled by the Group.[12]

In the United States, the chief source of this propaganda was the organization known as Union Now, which was an offshoot of the Rhodes Scholarship network. The publicized originator of the idea was Clarence Streit, Rhodes Scholar at Oxford in 1920 and League of Nations correspondent of *The New York Times* in 1929-1938. Mr. Streit's plan, which was very similar to Curtis's, except that it included fifteen countries to begin with, was first made public at a series of three lectures at Swarthmore College in February 1939. Almost simultaneously his book, *Union Now*, was launched and received wide publicity. Before we look at that, we might mention that at the time the president of Swarthmore College was Frank Aydelotte, the most important member of the Milner Group in the United States since the death of George Louis Beer. Dr. Aydelotte was one of the original Rhodes Scholars, attending Brasenose in 1905-1907. He was president of Swarthmore from 1921 to 1940; has been American secretary to the Rhodes Trustees since 1918; has been president of the Association of American Rhodes Scholars since 1930; has been a trustee of the Carnegie Foundation since 1922; and was a member of the Council on Foreign Relations for many years. In 1937, along with three other members of the Milner Group, he received from Oxford (and Lord Halifax) the honorary degree of Doctor of Civil Law. The other three recipients who were members of the Group were Brand, Ormsby-Gore, and Sir Herbert Baker, the famous architect.

As soon as Streit's book was published, it was hailed by Lord Lothian in an interview with the press. Shortly afterwards, Lothian gave it a favorable review in the *Christian Science Monitor* of 6 May 1939. The book was distributed to educational institutions in various places by the Carnegie Foundation and was greeted in the June 1939 issue of *The Round Table* as "the only way." This article said: "There is, indeed, no other cure. . . . In *The Commonwealth of God* Mr. Lionel Curtis showed how history and religion pointed down the same path. It is one of the great merits of Mr. Streit's book that he translates the general theme into a concrete plan, which he presents, not for the indefinite hereafter, but for our own generation, *now*." In the September 1939 issue, in an article headed "Union: Oceanic or Continental," *The Round Table* contrasted Streit's plan with that for European union offered by Count Coudenhove-Kalergi and gave the arguments for both.

While all this was going on, the remorseless wheels of appeasement were grinding out of existence one country after another. The fatal loss was Czechoslovakia. This disaster was engineered by Chamberlain with the full cooperation of the Milner Group. The details do not concern us here, but it should be mentioned that the dispute arose over the position of the Sudeten Germans *within* the Czechoslovak state, and as late as 15 September 1938 was still being expressed in those terms. Up to that day, Hitler had made no demand to annex the Sudeten area, although on 12 September he had for the first time asked for "self-determination" for the Sudetens. Konrad Henlein, Hitler's agent in Czechoslovakia and leader of the Sudeten Germans, expressed no desire "to go back to the Reich" until after 12 September. Who, then, first demanded frontier rectification in favor of Germany? Chamberlain did so privately on 10 May 1938, and the Milner Group did so publicly on 7 September 1938. The Chamberlain suggestion was made by one of those "calculated indiscretions" of which he was so fond, at an "off-the-record" meeting with certain Canadian and American newspaper reporters at a luncheon arranged by Lady Astor and held at her London house. On this occasion Chamberlain spoke of his plans for a four-power pact to exclude Russia from Europe and the possibility of frontier revisions in favor of Germany to settle the Sudeten issue. When the news leaked out, as it was bound to do, Chamberlain was questioned in Commons by Geoffrey Mander on 20 June but refused to answer, calling his questioner a troublemaker. This answer was criticized by Sir Archibald Sinclair the following day, but he received no better treatment. Lady Astor, however, interjected, "I would like to say that there is not a word of truth in it." By 27 June, however, she had a change of heart and stated: "I never had any intention of denying that the Prime Minister had attended a luncheon at my house. The Prime Minister did so attend, the object being to enable some American journalists who had not previously met him to do so privately and informally, and thus to make his acquaintance."

The second suggestion for revision of frontiers also had an Astor flavor, since it appeared as a leading article in *The Times* on 7 September 1938. The outraged cries of protest from all sides which greeted this suggestion made it clear that further softening up of the British public was urgently necessary before it would be safe to hand over Czechoslovakia to Hitler. This was done in the war-scare of September 15-28 in London. That this war-scare was fraudulent and that Lord Halifax was deeply involved in its creation is now clear. All the evidence cannot be given here. There is no evidence whatever that the Chamberlain government intended to fight over Czechoslovakia unless this was the only alternative to falling from office. Even at the height of the crisis, when all ways out without war seemed closed (27 September), Chamberlain showed what he thought of the case by telling the British people over the BBC that the issue was "a quarrel in a far-away country between people of whom we know nothing."

To frighten the British people, the British government circulated stories about the strength of the German Army and Air Force which were greatly exaggerated; they implied that Germany would use poison gas at once and from the air, although this was quite untrue; they distributed gas masks and madly built trenches in London parks, although the former were needless and the latter worthless. On 23 September, the British advised the Czechoslovakian government to mobilize, although they had previously forbidden it. This was done to increase the crisis in London, and the fact that Göring's air force allowed it to go through without attack indicates his belief that Germany did not need to fight. In fact, Göring told the French Ambassador on 12 September that he had positive assurance that Britain would not fight. As early as 1 September 1938, Sir Horace Wilson, Chamberlain's alter ego, told the German chargé d'affaires in London, Theodor Kordt, "If we two, Great Britain and Germany, come to agreement regarding the settlement of the Czech problem, we shall simply brush aside the resistance that France or Czechoslovakia herself may offer to the decision."

The fraudulent nature of the Munich crisis appears throughout its history. We might mention the following: (1) the suspicious fashion in which the Runciman Mission was sent to Czechoslovakia, immediately after Hitler's aide, Captain Wiedemann, visited Halifax at the latter's home (not the Foreign Office) on 18 July 1938, and with the statement, which was untrue, that it was being sent at the desire of the Czechoslovaks;[13] (2) the fact that Runciman in Czechoslovakia spent most of his time with the Sudetens and put pressure on the government to make one concession after another to Henlein, when it was perfectly clear that Henlein did not want a settlement; (3) the fact that Runciman wrote to Hitler on 2 September that he would have a plan for a settlement by 15 September; (4) the fact that this Runciman plan was practically the same as the Munich settlement finally adopted; (5) the fact that Chamberlain made the war-scare over the Godesberg proposals and, after making a settlement at Munich, made no effort to enforce those provisions by which Munich differed from Godesberg, but on the contrary allowed the Germans to take what they wished in Czechoslovakia as they wished; (6) the fact that the government did all it could to exclude Russia from the settlement, although Russia was allied to both Czechoslovakia and France; (7) the fact that the government and the French government tried to spread the belief that Russia would not honor these commitments, although all the evidence indicated that she would; (8) the fact that Chamberlain had a tête-à-tête conference with Hitler at Berchtesgaden on 15 September, which lasted for three hours, and at which only Hitler's private interpreter was present as a third party, and that this was repeated at Godesberg on 23 September; (9) the fact that the Czechoslovaks were forced to yield to Chamberlain's settlement under pressure of ultimatums from both France and Britain, a fact that was concealed from the British people by omitting a crucial document from the White Paper of 28 September 1938 (Cmd. 5847).

Two additional points, concerned with the degree of German armaments and the position of the anti-Hitler resistance within Germany, require further elucidation. For years before June 1938, the government had insisted that British rearming was progressing in a satisfactory fashion. Churchill and others had questioned this and had produced figures on German rearmament to prove that Britain's own progress in this field was inadequate. These figures were denied by the government, and their own accomplishments were defended. In 1937 and in 1938, Churchill had clashed with Baldwin and Chamberlain on this issue. As late as March 1938, Chamberlain said that British armaments were such as to make her an "almost terrifying power . . . on the opinion of the world." But as the year went on, the government adopted a quite different attitude. In order to persuade public opinion that it was necessary to yield to Germany, the Government pretended that its armaments were quite inadequate in comparison with Germany." We now know, thanks to the captured papers of the German Ministry of War, that this was a gross exaggeration. These papers were studied by Major General C. F. Robinson of the United States Army, and analyzed in a report which he submitted to the Secretary of War in October 1947. This document, entitled *Foreign Logistical Organiza-*

tions and Methods, shows that all of the accepted estimates of German rearmament in the period 1933-1939 were gross exaggerations. From 1936 to the outbreak of war, German aircraft production was not raised, but averaged 425 planes a month. Her tank production was low and *even in 1939* was less than Britain's. In the first 9 months of 1939, Germany produced only 50 tanks a month; in the last 4 months of 1939, in wartime, Germany produced 247 "tanks and self-propelled guns," compared to a British production of 314 tanks in the same period. At the time of the Munich crisis, Germany had 35 infantry and 4 motorized divisions, none of them fully manned or equipped. This was no more than Czechoslovakia had alone. Moreover, the Czech Army was better trained, had far better equipment, and had better morale and better fortifications. As an example of this point, we might mention that the Czech tank was of 38 tons, while the Germans, before 1938, had no tank over 10 tons. During 1938 they brought into production the Mark III tank of less than 20 tons, and in 1939 brought into production the Mark IV of 23 tons. Up to September 1939, the German Army had obtained only 300 tanks of the Mark III and Mark IV types together. Most of these were delivered during 1939. In comparison, the Germans captured in Czechoslovakia, in March 1939, 469 of the superior Czech tanks. At the same time they captured 1500 planes (of which 500 were first-line), 43,000 machineguns, and over 1 million rifles. These figures are comparable with what Germany had at Muni h, and at that time, if the British government had desired, Germany would have been facing France, Britain, and Russia, as well as Czechoslovakia.

It should perhaps be mentioned that up to September 1939 the German Navy had acquired only 53 submarines during the Hitler regime. No economic mobilization for war had been made and no reserve stocks built up. When the war began, in September 1939, Germany had ammunition for 6 weeks, and the air force had bombs for 3 months at the rate of expenditure experienced during the Polish campaign. At that time the Air Force consisted of 1000 bombers and 1050 fighters. In contrast, the British air program of May 1938 planned to provide Britain with a first-line force of 2370 planes; this program was stepped up in 1939. Under it, Britain produced almost 3000 military planes in 1938 and about 8000 in 1939. The German figures for planes produced in these 2 years are 5235 and 8295, but these are figures for all planes produced in the country, including civil as well as military airplanes. As Hanson Baldwin put it, "Up until 1940, at least, Germany's production did not markedly outstrip Britain's." It might also be mentioned that British combat planes were of better quality.

We have no way of knowing if the Chamberlain government knew these facts. It should have known them. At the least, it should not have deluged its own people with untrue stories about German arms. Surprisingly, the British have generally refused to modify these stories, and, in order to perpetuate the fable about the necessity for the Munich surrender, they have continued to repeat the untrue propaganda stories of 1937-1939 regarding German armaments. This is as true of the critics of Munich as of its defenders. Both have adopted the version that Britain yielded to superior and overwhelming force at Munich. They have done this even though this story is untrue and they are in a position to know that it is untrue. For example, Winston Churchill, in his war memoirs, repeats the old stories about German rearmament, although he has been writing two years or more after the Reichswehr archives were captured. For this he was criticized by Hanson Baldwin in *The New York Times* of 9 May 1948. In his recent book, *Munich: Prologue to Tragedy*, J. W. Wheeler-Bennett, the British editor of the captured papers of the German Foreign Ministry, accepts the old propaganda tales of German rearmament as axiomatic, and accordingly does not even discuss the subject. He merely tells his readers: "By the close of 1937 Germany's preparedness for war was complete. The preference for guns rather than for butter had brought forth results. Her rearmament had reached its apogee and could hold that peak level for a certain time. Her economy was geared to a strict regime of rationing and output on a war level." None of this was true, and Mr. Wheeler-Bennett should have examined the evidence. If he had, he would not have been so severe on what he calls Professor Frederick Schumann's "fantastic theory of the 'Pre-Munich Plot.' "[14]

The last piece of evidence which we might mention to support the theory — not of a plot, perhaps, but that the Munich surrender was unnecessary and took place because Chamberlain and his associates wanted to dismember Czechoslovakia — is even more incriminating. As a result of the inadequate rearmament of Germany, a group of conservatives within the regime formed a plot to liquidate Hitler and his close supporters if it appeared that his policy in Czechoslovakia would result in war. This group, chiefly army officers, included men on the highest level of government. In the group were Colonel General Ludwig Beck (Chief of the General Staff), Field Marshal von Witzleben, General Georg Thomas, Carl Friedrich Goerdeler (Mayor of Leipzig in 1930-1936), Ulrich von Hassell (ex-Ambassador to Italy), Johannes Popitz (Prussian Minister of Finance), and Paul Schmidt (Hitler's private interpreter). This group formed a plot to kill Hitler and remove the Nazis from power. The date was set eventually for 28 September 1938. Lord Halifax, on 5 September 1938, was informed of the plot by Theodore Kordt, the German chargé d'affaires in London, whose brother, Erich Kordt, chief of Ribbentrop's office in the Foreign Ministry, was one of the conspirators. The message which Kordt gave to Halifax begged the British government to stand fast with Czechoslovakia in the Sudeten crisis and to make perfectly clear that Britain would go to war if Germany violated Czechoslovakian territory. The plot was canceled at noon on 28 September, when the news reached Berlin that Chamberlain was going to Munich. It was this plot which eventually, after many false starts, reached fruition in the attempt to assassinate Hitler on 20 July 1944.

There can be little doubt that the Milner Group knew of these anti-Nazi plots within Germany. Several of the plotters were former Rhodes Scholars and were in touch with members of the inner circle of the Milner Group in the period up to 1943, if not later. One of the leaders of the anti-Hitler plotters in Germany, Helmuth von Moltke, was probably a member of the Milner Group as well as intellectual leader of the conspirators in Germany. Count von Moltke was the son of the German commander of 1914 and grandnephew of the German commander of 1870. His mother, Dorothy Rose-Innes, was the daughter of Sir James Rose-Innes, whom Milner made Chief Justice of the Transvaal in 1902. Sir James was a supporter of Rhodes and had been Attorney General in Rhodes's ministry in 1890. He was Chief Justice of South Africa in 1914-1927 and was always close to the Milner Group. The von Moltkes were Christian Scientists, and Dorothy, as Countess von Moltke after 1905, was one of the persons who translated Mary Baker Eddy's *Science and Health* into German. The younger Helmuth, son of Dorothy, and Count von Moltke after his father's death in 1938, was openly anti-Nazi and came to England in 1934 to join the English bar. He visited Lionel Curtis, at his mother's suggestion, and "was made a member of the family, rooms in Duke of York Street being put at his disposal, and Kidlington and All Souls thrown open to him at week-ends; the opportunities of contact which these brought with them were exploited to the full. . . . He was often in England until the summer of 1939, and in 1937 visited South Africa and the grandparents there to whom he was deeply attached." This quotation, from *The Round Table* for June 1946, makes perfectly clear to those who can read between the lines that Moltke became a member of the Milner Group. It might be added that Curtis also visited the Rose-Innes family in South Africa while Helmuth was there in 1937.

Von Moltke kept in close contact with both Curtis and Lothian even after the war began in 1939. He was made adviser on international law to the Supreme Command of the German Armed Forces (OKW) in 1939 and retained this position until his arrest in 1944. The intellectual leader of the German Underground, he was the inspiration and addressee of Dorothy Thompson's book *Listen, Hans.* He was the center of a group of plotters called the "Kreisau Circle," named after his estate in Silesia. After his execution by the Nazis in January 1945, his connection with the Milner Group was revealed, to those able to interpret the evidence, in the June 1946 issue of *The Round Table*. This article extolled Moltke and reprinted a number of his letters. The same article, with an additional letter, was published as a pamphlet in Johannesburg in 1947.[15]

Another plotter who appears to be close to the Milner Group was Adam von Trott zu Solz, a Rhodes Scholar who went to the Far East on a mission for the Rhodes Trust in 1936 and was in frequent contact with the Institute of Pacific Relations in the period 1936-1939. He seems to have attended a meeting of the Pacific Council in New York late in 1939, coming from Germany, by way of Gibraltar, after the war began. He remained in contact with the democratic countries until arrested and executed by the Nazis in 1944. It is not without significance that one of the chief projects which the plotters hoped to further in post-Hitler German foreign policy was a "federation of Europe in a commonwealth not unlike the British Empire."[16]

All of this evidence and much more would seem to support the theory of a "Munich plot" — that is, the theory that the British government had no intention or desire to save Czechoslovakia in 1938 and was willing or even eager to see it partitioned by Hitler, and only staged the war scare of September in order to make the British people accept this abuse of honor and sacrifice of Britain's international position. The efforts which the British government made after Munich to conceal the facts of that affair would support this interpretation. The chief question, from our point of view, lies in the degree to which the Milner Group were involved in this "plot." There can be no doubt that the Chamberlain group was the chief factor in the scheme. There is also no doubt that various members of the Milner Group second circle, who were close to the Chamberlain group, were involved. The position of the inner core of the Milner Group is not conclusively established, but there is no evidence that they were not involved and a certain amount of evidence that they were involved.

Among this latter evidence is the fact that the inner core of the Group did not object to or protest against the partition of Czechoslovakia, although they did use the methods by which Hitler had obtained his goal as an argument in support of their pet plan for national service. They prepared the ground for the Munich surrender both in *The Times* and in *The Round Table*. In the June 1938 issue of the latter, we read: "Czechoslovakia is apparently the danger spot of the next few months. It will require high statesmanship on all sides to find a peaceful and stable solution of the minorities problem. The critical question for the next six months is whether the four great Powers represented by the Franco-British entente and the Rome-Berlin axis can make up their minds that they will not go to war with one another and that they must settle outstanding problems by agreement together." In this statement, three implications are of almost equal importance. These are the time limit of "six months," the exclusion of both Czechoslovakia and Russia from the "agreement," and the approval of the four-power pact.

In the September 1938 issue of *The Round Table*, published on the eve of Munich, we are told: "It is one thing to be able, in the end, to win a war. It is a far better thing to be able to prevent a war by a readiness for just dealing combined with resolute strength when injustice is threatened." Here, as always before 1939, *The Round Table* by "justice" meant appeasement of Germany.

After the dreadful deed was done, *The Round Table* had not a word of regret and hardly a kind word for the great sacrifice of the Czechs or for the magnificent demonstration of restraint which they had given the world. In fact, the leading article in the December 1938 issue of *The Round Table* began with a severe criticism of Czechoslovakia for failure to reconcile her minorities, for failure to achieve economic cooperation with her neighbors, and for failure to welcome a Hapsburg restoration. From that point on, the article was honest. While accepting Munich, it regarded it solely as a surrender to German power and rejected the arguments that it was done by negotiation, that it was a question of self-determination or minority rights, or that Munich was any better or more lenient than the Godesberg demands. The following article in the same issue, also on Czechoslovakia, is a tissue of untruths except for the statement that there never was any real Sudeten issue, since the whole thing was a fraudulent creation engineered from Germany. Otherwise the article declares categorically: (1) that Czechoslovakia could not have stood up against Hitler more than two or three weeks; (2) that no opposition of importance to Hitler existed in Germany ("A good deal has been written about the opposition of the military commanders. But in fact it does not and never did exist."); (3) "There is no such thing as a conservative opposition in Germany." In the middle of such statements as these, one ray of sanity shines like a light: in a single sentence, *The Round Table* tossed onto the scrap heap its basic argument in support of appeasement, namely the "injustices of Versailles." The sentence reads: "It is not Versailles but defeat that is the essential German grievance against the western Powers." This sentence should have been printed in gold letters in the Foreign Office in London in 1919 and read daily thereafter.

It is worthy of note that this issue of *The Round Table* discussed the Czech crisis in two articles of twenty-seven pages and had only one sentence on Russia. This sentence spoke of the weakness of Russia, where "a new Tiberius had destroyed the morale and the material efficiency of the Russian Army." However, in a separate article, dealing largely with Soviet-German relations, we find the significant sentences: "The Western democracies appear to be framing their policies on the principle of 'letting Germany go east.'. . . [Russia faces] the fundamental need of preventing a hostile coalition of the great Powers of western Europe."

The final judgment of the Milner Group on the Munich surrender could probably be found in the December 1938 issue of *The Round Table,* where we read the following: "The nation as a whole is acutely aware that Anglo-French predominance, resulting from victory in the great war, is now a matter of history, that the conception of an international society has foundered because the principle of the rule of law was prostituted to perpetuate an impossible inequality. . . . The terms of the Versailles Treaty might have been upheld for some time longer by the consistent use of military power — notably when Germany remilitarized the Rhineland zone — but it was illogical to expect a defeated and humiliated foe to accept inferiority as the immutable concomitant of a nobler world, and it was immoral to try to build the City of God on lopsided foundations."

As late as the March 1939 issue, *The Round Table* point of view remained unchanged. At that time it said: "The policy of appeasement, which Mr. Chamberlain represents and which he brought to what seemed to be its most triumphant moment at Munich, was the only possible policy on which the public opinion of the different nations of the Commonwealth could have been unified. It had already been unanimously approved in general terms at the Imperial Conference of 1937."

The German occupation of Bohemia and Moravia in March 1939 marked the turning point for the Milner Group, *but not for the Chamberlain group.* In the June 1939 issue, the leading article of *The Round Table* was entitled "From Appeasement to Grand Alliance." Without expressing any regrets about the past, which it regarded as embodying the only possible policy, it rejected appeasement in the future. It demanded a "grand alliance" of Poland, Rumania, France, Britain, and others. Only one sentence referred to Russia; it said: "Negotiations to include Soviet Russia in the system are continuing." Most of the article justified the previous policy as inevitable in a world of sovereign states. Until federation abolishes sovereignty and creates a true world government amenable to public opinion, the nations will continue to live in anarchy, whatever their contractual obligations may be; and under conditions of anarchy it is power and not public opinion that counts. . . . The fundamental, though not the only, explanation of the tragic history of the last eight years is to be found in the failure of the English-speaking democracies to realize that they could prevent aggression only by unity and by being strongly armed enough to resist it wherever it was attempted."

This point of view had been expressed earlier, in the House of Lords, by Lothian and Astor. On 12 April 1939, the former said:

> One of Herr Hitler's great advantages has been that, for very long, what he sought a great many people all over the world felt was not unreasonable, whatever they may have thought of his methods. But that justification has completely and absolutely disappeared in the last three months. It began to disappear in my mind at the Godesberg Conference. . . . I think the right answer to the situation is what Mr. Churchill has advocated elsewhere, a grand alliance of all those nations whose interest is paramountly concerned with the maintenance of their own status-quo. But in my view if you are going to do that you have got to have a grand alliance which will function not only in the West of Europe but also in the East. I agree with what my noble friend Lord Snell has just said that in that Eastern alliance Russia may be absolutely vital. . . . Nobody will suspect me of any ideological sympathy with Russia or Communism. I have even less ideological sympathy with Soviet Russia than I had with the Czarist Russia. But in resisting aggression it is power alone that counts.

He then went on to advocate national service and was vigorously supported by Lord Astor, both in regard to this and in regard to the necessity of bringing Russia into the "grand alliance."

From this point onward, the course of the Milner Group was more rigid against Germany. This appeared chiefly as an increased emphasis on rearmament and national service, policies which the Group had been supporting for a long time. Unlike the Chamberlain group, they learned a lesson from the events of 15 March 1939. It would be a mistake, however, to believe that they were determined to resist any further acquisition of territory or economic advantage by Germany. Not at all. They would undoubtedly have been willing to allow frontier rectifications in the Polish Corridor or elsewhere in favor of Germany, if these were accomplished by a real process of negotiation and included areas inhabited by Germans, and if the economic interests of Poland, such as her trade outlet to the Baltic, were protected. In this the Milner Group were still motivated by ideas of fairness and justice and by a desire to avoid a war. The chief changes were two: (1) they now felt, as they (in contrast to Chamberlain's group) had long suspected, that peace could be preserved better by strength than by weakness; and (2) they now felt that Hitler would not stop at any point based only on justice but was seeking world domination. The short-run goal of the Milner Group still remained a Continent dominated by Hitler between an Oceanic Bloc on the west and the Soviet Union on the east. That they assumed such a solution could keep the peace, even on a short-term basis, shows the fundamental naïveté of the Milner Group. The important point is that this view did not prohibit any modification of the Polish frontiers;, not did it require any airtight understanding with the Soviet Union. It did involve an immediate rearming of Britain and a determination to stop Hitler if he moved by force again. Of these three points, the first two were shared with the Chamberlain group; the third was not. The difference rested on the fact that the Chamberlain group hoped to permit Britain to escape from the necessity of fighting Germany by getting Russia to fight Germany. The Chamberlain group did not share the Milner Group's naïve belief in the possibility of three great power blocs standing side by side in peace. Lacking that belief, they preferred a German-Russian war to a British-German war. And, having that preference, they differed from the Milner Group in their willingness to accept the partition of Poland by Germany. The Milner Group would have yielded parts of Poland to Germany if done by fair negotiation. The Chamberlain group was quite prepared to liquidate Poland entirely, if it could be presented to the British people in terms which they would accept without demanding war. Here again appeared the difference we have already mentioned between the Milner Group and Lloyd George in 1918 and between the Group and Baldwin in 1923, namely that the Milner Group tended to neglect the electoral considerations so important to a party politician. In 1939 Chamberlain was primarily interested in building up to a victorious electoral campaign for November, and, as Sir Horace Wilson told German Special Representative Wohl in June, "it was all one to the Government whether the elections were held under the cry 'Be Ready for a Coming War' or under a cry 'A Lasting Understanding with Germany.' "

These distinctions between the point of view of the Milner Group and that of the Chamberlain group are very subtle and have nothing in common with the generally accepted idea of a contrast between appeasement and resistance. There were still appeasers to be found, chiefly in those ranks of the Conservative Party most remote from the Milner Group; British public opinion was quite clearly committed to resistance after March 1939. The two government groups between these, with the Chamberlain group closer to the former and the Milner Group closer to the latter. It is a complete error to say, as most students of the period have said, that before 15 March the government was solidly appeasement and afterwards solidly resistant. The Chamberlain group, after 17 March 1939, was just as partial to appeasement as before, perhaps more so, but it had to adopt a pretense of resistance to satisfy public opinion and keep a way open to wage the November election on either side of the issue. The Milner Group was anti-appeasement after March, but in a limited way that did not involve any commitment to defend the territorial integrity of Poland or to ally with Russia.

This complicated situation is made more so by the fact that the Milner Group itself was disintegrating. Some members, chiefly in the second circle, like Hoare or Simon, continued as wholehearted, if secret, appeasers and became closer to Chamberlain. Halifax, who did not have to run for office, could speak his mind more honestly and probably had a more honest mind. He was closer to the Milner Group, although he continued to cooperate so closely with Chamberlain that he undoubtedly lost the prime minister's post in May 1940 as a result. Amery, closer than Halifax to the inner core of the Group, was also more of a resister and by the middle of 1939 was finished with appeasement. Lothian was in a position between Halifax and Amery.

The point of view of the inner core can be found, as usual, in the pages of *The Round Table*. In the issue of September 1939, the leading article confessed that Hitler's aim was mastery of the world. It continued: "In this light, any further accretion of German strength — for instance through control of Danzig, which is the key to subjection of all Poland — appears as a retreat from the ramparts of the British Commonwealth itself. Perhaps our slowness to realize these facts, or at least to act accordingly in building an impregnable defence against aggression in earlier years, accounts for our present troubles." For the Milner Group, this constitutes a magnificent confession of culpability.

In the December 1939 issue of *The Round Table*, the whole tone has reverted to that of 1911-1918. Gone is the idea that modern Germany was the creation of the United States and Britain or that Nazism was merely a temporary and insignificant aberration resulting from Versailles. Instead the issue is "Commonwealth or Weltreich?" Nazism "is only Prussianism in more brutal shape." It quotes Lord Lothian's speech of 25 October 1939, made in New York, that "The establishment of a true reign of law between nations is the only remedy for war." And we are told once again that such a reign of law must be sought in federation. In the same issue, the whole of Lothian's speech was reprinted as a "document." In the March 1940 issue, *The Round Table* harked back even further than 1914. It quoted an extensive passage from Pericles's funeral oration in a leading article entitled "The Issue," and added: "That also is our creed, but it is not Hitler's."

The same point of view of the Group is reflected in other places. On 16 March 1939, in the Commons, when Chamberlain was still defending the appeasement policy and refusing to criticize Germany's policy of aggression, Lady Astor cried out to him, "Will the Prime Minister lose no time in letting the German Government know with what horror the whole of this country regards Germany's action?"

The Prime Minister did not answer, but a Conservative Member, Major Vyvyan Adams, hurled at the lady the remark, "You caused it yourself."

Major Adams was not a man to be lightly dismissed. A graduate of Haileybury and Cambridge, past president of the Cambridge Union, member of the Inner Temple Bar, an executive of the League of Nations Union, and a vice-president of Lord Davies's New Commonwealth Society, he was not a man who did not know what was going on. He subsequently published two books against appeasement under the pseudomyn "Watchman."

Most of the members of the inner core of the Group who took any public stand on these issues refused to rake over the dead embers of past policy and devoted themselves to a program of preparedness and national service. The names of Amery, Grigg, Lothian, and *The Times* became inseparably associated with the campaign for conscription, which ultimately resulted in the National Service Act of 26 April 1939. The more aloof and more conciliatory point of view of Halifax can be seen in his speech of 9 June in the House of Lords and the famous speech of 29 June before the Royal Institute of International Affairs. The lingering overtones of appeasement in the former resulted in a spirited attack by Lord Davies, while Arthur Salter, who had earlier been plumping for a Ministry of All the Talents with Halifax as Premier, by the middle of the year was begging him, at All Souls, to meet Stalin face to face in order to get an alliance.[17]

The events of 1939 do not require our extended attention here, although they have never yet been narrated in any adequate fashion. The German seizure of Bohemia and Moravia was not much of a surprise to either the Milner or Chamberlain groups; both accepted it, but the former tried to use it as a propaganda device to help get conscription, while the latter soon discovered that, whatever their real thoughts, they must publicly condemn it in order to satisfy the outraged moral feelings of the British electorate. It is this which explains the change in tone between Chamberlain's speech of 15 March in Commons and his speech of 17 March in Birmingham. The former was what he thought; the latter was what he thought the voters wanted.

The unilateral guarantee to Poland given by Chamberlain on 31 March 1939 was also a reflection of what he believed the voters wanted. He had no intention of ever fulfilling the guarantee if it could possibly be evaded and, for this reason, refused the Polish requests for a small rearmament loan and to open immediate staff discussions to implement the guarantee. The Milner Group, less susceptible to public opinion, did not want the guarantee to Poland at all. As a result, the guarantee was worded to cover Polish "independence" and not her "territorial integrity." This was interpreted by the leading article of *The Times* for 1 April to leave the way open to territorial revision without revoking the guarantee. This interpretation was accepted by Chamberlain in Commons on 3 April. Apparently the government believed that it was making no real commitment because, if war broke out in eastern Europe, British public opinion would force the government to declare war on Germany, no matter what the government itself wanted, and regardless whether the guarantee existed or not. On the other hand, a guarantee to Poland might deter Hitler from precipitating a war and give the government time to persuade the Polish government to yield the Corridor to Germany. If the Poles could not be persuaded, or if Germany marched, the fat was in the fire anyway; if the Poles could be persuaded to yield, the guarantee was so worded that Britain could not act under it to prevent such yielding. This was to block any possibility that British public opinion might refuse to accept a Polish Munich. That this line of thought was not far distant from British government circles is indicated by a Reuters news dispatch released on the same day that Chamberlain gave the guarantee to Poland. This dispatch indicated that, under cover of the guarantee, Britian would put pressure on Poland to make substantial concessions to Hitler through negotiations. According to Hugh Dalton, Labour M.P., speaking in Commons on 3 April, this dispatch was inspired by the government and was issued through either the Foreign Office, Sir Horace Wilson, John Simon, or Samuel Hoare. Three of these four were of the Milner Group, the fourth being the personal agent of Chamberlain. Dalton's charge was not denied by any government spokesman, Hoare contenting himself with a request to Dalton "to justify that statement." Another M.P. of Churchill's group suggested that Geoffrey Dawson was the source, but Dalton rejected this.

It is quite clear that neither the Chamberlain group nor the Milner Group wanted an alliance with the Soviet Union to stop Hitler in 1939, and that the negotiations were not sincere or vigorously pursued. The Milner Group was not so opposed to such an agreement as the Chamberlain group. Both were committed to the four-power pact. In the case of the Chamberlain group, this pact could easily have developed into an anti-Russian alliance, but in the case of the Milner Group it was regarded merely as a link between the Oceanic Bloc and a Germanic Mitteleuropa. Both groups hated and despised the Soviet Union, but the Milner Group did not fear it as the Chamberlain group did. This fear was based on the Marxist threat to the British economic system, and the Milner Group was not wedded nearly as closely to that system as Chamberlain and his friends. The Toynbee-Milner tradition, however weak it had become by 1939, was enough to prevent the two groups from seeing eye to eye on this issue.

The efforts of the Chamberlain group to continue the policy of appeasement by making economic and other concessions to Germany and their efforts to get Hitler to agree to a four-power pact form one of the most shameful episodes in the history of recent British diplomacy.

These negotiations were chiefly conducted through Sir Horace Wilson and consisted chiefly of offers of colonial bribes and other concessions to Germany. These offers were either rejected or ignored by the Nazis.

One of these offers revolved around a semi-official economic agreement under which British and German industrialists would form cartel agreements in all fields to fix prices of their products and divide up the world's market. The Milner Group apparently objected to this on the grounds that it was aimed, or could be aimed, at the United States. Nevertheless, the agreements continued; a master agreement, negotiated at Dusseldorf between representatives of British and German industry, was signed in London on 16 March 1939. A British government mission to Berlin to help Germany exploit the newly acquired areas of eastern Europe was postponed the same day because of the strength of public feeling against Germany. As soon as this had died down, secret efforts were made through R. S. Hudson, secretary to the Department of Overseas Trade, to negotiate with Helmuth Wohlthat, Reich Commissioner for the Four Year Plan, who was in London to negotiate an international whaling agreement. Although Wholthat had no powers, he listened to Hudson and later to Sir Horace Wilson, but refused to discuss the matter with Chamberlain. Wilson offered: (1) a nonaggression pact with Germany; (2) a delimitation of spheres among the Great Powers; (3) colonial concessions in Africa along the lines previously mentioned; (4) an economic agreement. These conversations, reported to Berlin by Ambassador Dirksen in a dispatch of 21 July 1939, would have involved giving Germany a free hand in eastern Europe and bringing her into collision with Russia. One sentence of Dirksen's says: "Sir Horace Wilson definitely told Herr Wohlthat that the conclusion of a non-aggression pact would enable Britian to rid herself of her commitments vis-a-vis Poland." In another report, three days later, Dirksen said: "Public opinion is so inflamed, and the warmongers and intriguers are so much in the ascendancy, that if these plans of negotiations with Germany were to become public they would immediately be torpedoed by Churchill and other incendiaries with the cry 'No second Munich!' "

The truth of this statement was seen when news of the Hudson-Wohlthat conversations did leak out and resulted in a violent controversy in the House of Commons, in which the Speaker of the House repeatedly broke off the debate to protect the government. According to Press Adviser Hesse in the German Embassy in London, the leak was made by the French Embassy to force a break in the negotiations. The negotiations, however, were already bogging down because of the refusal of the Germans to become very interested in them. Hitler and Ribbentrop by this time despised the British so thoroughly that they paid no attention to them at all, and the German Ambassador in

London found it impossible to reach Ribbentrop, his official superior, either by dispatch or personally. Chamberlain, however, in his eagerness to make economic concessions to Germany, gave to Hitler £6 million in Czechoslovak gold in the Bank of England, and kept Lord Runciman busy training to be chief economic negotiator in the great agreement which he envisaged. On 29 July 1939, Kordt, the German charge d'affaires in London, had a long talk with Charles Roden Buxton, brother of the Labour Peer Lord Noel-Buxton, about the terms of this agreement, which was to be patterned on the agreement of 1907 between Britain and Russia. Buxton insisted that his visit was quite unofficial, but Kordt was inclined to believe that his visit was a feeler from the Chamberlain group. In view of the close parallel between Buxton's views and Chamberlain's, this seems very likely. This was corroborated when Sir Horace Wilson repeated these views in a highly secret conversation with Dirksen at Wilson's home from 4 to 6 p.m. on 3 August 1939. Dirksen's minute of the same day shows that Wilson's aims had not changed. He wanted a four-power pact, a free hand for Germany in eastern Europe, a colonial agreement, an economic agreement, etc. The memorandum reads, in part: "After recapitulating his conversation with Wohlthat, Sir Horace Wilson expatiated at length on the great risk Chamberlain would incur by starting confidential negotiations with the German Government. If anything about them were to leak out there would be a grand scandal, and Chamberlain would probably be forced to resign." Dirksen did not see how any binding agreement could be reached under conditions such as this; "for example, owing to Hudson's indiscretion, another visit of Herr Wohlthat to London was out of the question." To this, Wilson suggested that "the two emissaries could meet in Switzerland or elsewhere." The political portions of this conversation were largely repeated in an interview that Dirksen had with Lord Halifax on 9 August 1939.[18]

It was not possible to conceal these activities completely from the public, and, indeed, government spokesmen referred to them occasionally in trial balloons. On 3 May, Chamberlain suggested an Anglo-German nonaggression pact, although only five days earlier Hitler had denounced the Anglo-German naval agreement of 1935 and the Polish-German nonaggression pact of 1934. As late as 28 August, Sir Nevile Henderson offered Germany a British *alliance* if she were successful in direct negotiations with the Poles.[19] This, however, was a personal statement and probably went further than Halifax would have been willing to go by 1939. Halifax apparently had little faith in Chamberlain's ability to obtain any settlement with the Germans. If, by means of another Munich, he could have obtained a German-Polish settlement that would satisfy Germany and avoid war, he would have taken it. It was the hope of such an agreement that prevented him from making any real agreement with Russia, for it was, apparently, the expectation of the British government that if the Germans could get the Polish Corridor by negotiation, they could then drive into Russia across the Baltic States. For this reason, in the negotiations with Russia, Halifax refused any multilateral pact against aggression, any guarantee of the Baltic States, or any tripartite guarantee of Poland. Instead, he sought to get nothing more than a unilateral Russian guarantee to Poland to match the British guarantee to the same country. This was much too dangerous for Russia to swallow, since it would leave her with a commitment which could lead to war and with no promise of British aid to her if she were attacked directly, after a Polish settlement, or indirectly across the Baltic States. Only after the German Soviet Nonaggression Pact of 21 August 1939 did Halifax implement the unilateral guarantee to Poland with a more formal mutual assistance pact between Britain and Poland. This was done to warn Hitler that an attack on Poland would bring Britain into the war under pressure of British public opinion. Hitler, as usual, paid no attention to Britain. Even after the German attack on Poland, the British government was reluctant to fulfill this pact and spent almost three days asking the Germans to return to negotiation. Even after the British were forced to declare war on Germany, they made no effort to fight, contenting themselves with dropping leaflets on Germany. We now know that the German generals had moved so much of their forces to the east that they were gravely worried at the effects which might follow an Allied attack on western Germany or even an aerial bombing of the Ruhr.

In these events of 1939, the Milner Group took little part. They must have known of the negotiations with Germany and probably did not disapprove of them, but they had little faith in them and by the early summer of 1939 were probably convinced that war with Germany was inevitable in the long run. In this view Halifax probably shared, but other former members of the Group, such as Hoare and Simon, by now were completely in the Chamberlain group and can no longer be regarded as members of the Milner Group. From June 1939 to May 1940, the fissure between the Milner Group and the Chamberlain government became wider.

From the outbreak of war, the Milner Group were determined to fight the war against Germany; the Chamberlain group, on the other hand, were very reluctant to fight Germany, preferring to combine a declared but unfought war with Germany with a fought but undeclared war with Russia. The excuse for this last arose from the Russian pressure on Finland for bases to resist a future German attack. The Russian attack on Finland began on the last day of November 1939; by 27 December, the British and French were putting pressure on Sweden to join them in action to support the Finns. In these notes, which have been published by the Swedish Foreign Ministry, the Western Powers stated that they intended to send men, equipment, and money to Finland. By February 1940, the Western Powers had plans for a force of 30,000 to 40,000 men for Finland and were putting pressure on Sweden to allow passage for this force across Scandinavia. By 2 March 1940, the British had a force of 100,000 men ready and informed the Swedish and Norwegian governments that "the force with its full equipment is available and could sail at short notice." They invited the Scandinavian countries to receive Allied missions to make all the necessary preparations for the transit. The note to Norway, in an additional passage, said that forces would be sent to the Norwegian ports within four days of receiving permission, and the transit itself could begin on 20 March. On 12 March the Allies sent to the Scandinavian countries a formal request for right of transit. It was refused. Before anything further could be done, Finland collapsed and made peace with Russia. On 5 April, Halifax sent a very threatening note to the Scandinavian countries. It said in part:

> . . . considering, in consultation with the French Government, the circumstances attending the termination of the war between the Union of Soviet Socialist Republics and Finland and the attitude adopted by the Swedish Government at that time . . . they feel therefore that the time has come to notify the Swedish Government frankly of certain vital interests and requirements which the Allied Governments intend to assert and defend by whatever measure they may think necessary. The vital interests and the requirements which the Allied Governments wish to bring to the notice of the Swedish Government are the following: (a) The Allied Governments cannot acquiesce in any further attack on Finland by either the Soviet or German Governments. In the event therefore, of such an attack taking place, any refusal by the Swedish Government to facilitate the efforts of the Allied Governments to come to the assistance of Finland in whatever manner they may think fit, and still more any attempt to prevent such assistance would be considered by the Allied Governments as endangering their vital interests. . . . (c) Any attempt by the Soviet Government to obtain from Norway a footing on the Atlantic seaboard would be contrary to the vital interests of the Allied Governments."

The Swedish Foreign Minister expressed his government's astonishment at this note and its determination to decide such questions for itself and to preserve Sweden's neutrality in the future as it had been preserved in the past.[20]

It is not clear what was the attitude of the Milner Group toward this effort to open active hostilities against the Soviet Union while remaining technically in a state of war with Germany. Halifax was still at the Foreign Office and apparently actively concerned in this project. *The Times* was wholeheartedly in favor of the plan. On 5 March, for example, it said of the Finnish war: "It is becoming clearer every day that this war is no side issue. Finland is defending more than the cause of liberty and more than her own soil. . . . Our own cause is being buttressed by her resistance to the evil of tryanny. . . . Our interest is clear and there is a moral issue involved as well as the material. The whole sentiment of this country demands that Finland should not be allowed to fall."

The Round Table, in the only issue which appeared during the Finnish troubles, had a propagandist article on "The Civilization of Finland." It called Finland "one of the most democratic nations, on any definition, in all Europe." The rest of the article was a paean of praise for the kind and magnanimous conduct of the Finnish government in every crisis of its history from 1917, but nothing was said about the Finnish war, nor was there any mention of Allied aid.

During this period the Milner Group became increasingly impatient with the Chamberlain group. This was clear from the June 1940 issue of *The Round Table*, which criticized the Cabinet reshuffle of April as evoking "almost universal derision." It also criticized Chamberlain's failure to include able members of his own party in the Cabinet. This may have been a reference to Amery's continued exclusion. The article said: "This lack of imagination and courage could be seen in almost every aspect of the Chamberlain Government's conduct of the war." It excluded Simon and Hoare as possible prime ministers, on the ground that they were too close to Chamberlain. It was probably thinking of Halifax as prime minister, but, when the time came, others thought him, also, to be too closely associated with appeasement. On the crucial day, 8 May 1940, the Group was badly split. In fact, on the division that preceded Chamberlain's resignation, Lady Astor voted against the government, while her brother-in-law, John Jacob Astor, voted with the government. The debate was one of the most bitter in recent history and reached its high point when Amery cried out to the Government benches the words of Cromwell: "You have sat too long here for any good you have been doing. Depart, I say, and let us have done with you. In the name of God, go!" In the ensuing division, the whips were on with a vengeance, but the government's majority was only 81, more than a hundred Conservatives abstaining from voting. Most of the Milner Group members, since they held offices in the government, had to vote with it. Of the inner core, only Amery and Lady Astor broke away. In the majority, still supporting Chamberlain, were J. J. Astor, Grigg, Hoare, Malcolm MacDonald, Salter, Simon, and Somervell. But the fight had been too bitter. Chamberlain was replaced by Churchill, and Amery came to office (as Secretary of State for India). Once again the Milner Group and the government were united on the issues. Both, from 8 May 1940, had only one aim: to win the war with Germany.

13

The Second World War,
1939-1945

THE MILNER GROUP played a considerable role in the Second World War, not scattered throughout the various agencies associated with the great struggle, but concentrated in four or five chief fiefs. Among these were: (1) the Research and Intelligence Department of the Foreign Office; (2) the British Embassy in Washington; (3) the Ministry of Information; and (4) those agencies concerned with economic mobilization and economic reconstruction. Considering the age of most of the inner core of the Milner Group during the Second World War (the youngest, Lothian, was 57 in 1939; Hichens was 65; Brand was 61; Dawson was 65; and Curtis was 67), they accomplished a great deal. Unable, in most cases, to serve themselves, except in an advisory capacity, they filled their chief fiefs with their younger associates. In most cases, these were recruited from All Souls, but occasionally they were obtained elsewhere.

We have already indicated how the Research and Press Department of Chatham House was made into the Research and Intelligence Department of the Foreign Office, at first unofficially and then officially. This was dominated by Lionel Curtis and Arnold Toynbee, the latter as director of the department for the whole period 1939-1946. Others who were associated with this activity were B. H. Sumner (Warden of All Souls), C. A. Macartney, A. E. Zimmern, J. W. Wheeler-Bennett, and most of the paid staff from Chatham House. Zimmern was deputy director in 1943-1945, and Wheeler-Bennett was deputy director in 1945.

Of even greater significance was the gathering of Milner Group members and their recruits in Washington. The Group had based most of their foreign policy since 1920 on the hope of "closer union" with the United States, and they realized that American intervention in the war was absolutely essential to insure a British victory. Accordingly, more than a dozen members of the Group were in Washington during the war, seeking to carry on this policy.

Lord Lothian was named Ambassador to the United States as soon as the war began. It was felt that his long acquaintance with the country and the personal connections built up during almost fifteen years as Rhodes Secretary more than counteracted his intimate relationship with the notorious Cliveden Set, especially as this latter relationship was unknown to most Americans. On Lothian's unexpected and lamented death in December 1940, the position in Washington was considered to be of such crucial importance that Lord Halifax was shifted to the vacant post from the Foreign Office. He retained his position in the War Cabinet. Thus the post at Washington was raised to a position which no foreign legation had ever had before. Lord Halifax continued to hold the post until 1946, a year after the war was actually finished. During most of the period, he was surrounded by members of the Milner Group, chiefly Fellows of All Souls, so that it was almost impossible to turn around in the British Embassy without running into a member of that select academic circle. The most important of these were Lord Brand, Harold Butler, and Arthur Salter.

Lord Brand was in America from March 1941 to May 1946, as head of the British Food Mission for three years and as representative of the British Treasury for two years. He was also chairman of the British Supply Council in North America in 1942 and again in 1945-1946. He did not resign his position as managing director of Lazard Brothers until May 1944. Closely associated with Brand was his protégé, Adam D. Marris, son of Sir William Marris of the Kindergarten, who was employed at Lazard Brothers from 1929 to the outbreak of war, then spent a brief period in the Ministry of Economic Warfare in London. In 1940 he came to the Embassy in Washington, originally as First Secretary, later as Counsellor. After the war he was, for six months, secretary general of the Emergency Economic Committee for Europe. In February 1946 he returned to Lazard Brothers.

Harold Butler (Sir Harold since 1946) came to Washington in 1942 with the rank of minister. He stayed for four years, being chiefly concerned with public relations. Sir Arthur Salter, who married a Washington lady in 1940, came to America in 1941 as head of the British Merchant Shipping Mission. He stayed until UNRRA was set up early in 1944, when he joined the new organization as Senior Deputy Director General. A year later he joined the Cabinet as Chancellor for the Duchy of Lancaster. Sir Arthur was well qualified as a shipping expert, having been engaged intermittently in government shipping problems since he left Brasenose College in 1904. His close personal relations with Lord Halifax went back to an even earlier period, when they both were students at Oxford.

Among the lesser persons who came to Washington during the war, we should mention four members of All Souls: I. Berlin, J. G. Foster,

R. M. Makins, and J. H. A. Sparrow. Isaiah Berlin, one of the newer recruits to the Milner Group, made his way into this select circle by winning a Fellowship to All Souls in 1932, the year after he graduated from Corpus Christi. Through this connection, he became a close friend of Mr. and Mrs. H. A. L. Fisher and has been a Fellow and Tutor of New College since 1938. In 1941 he came to New York to work with J. W. Wheeler-Bennett in the Ministry of Information's American branch but stayed for no more than a year. In 1942 he became First Secretary in the Embassy in Washington, a position but recently vacated by Adam Marris. After the war he went for a brief period of four months to a similar post in the British Embassy in Moscow. In 1949 he came to Harvard University as visiting lecturer on Russia.

John Galway Foster is another recent recruit to the Milner Group and, like Berlin, won his entry by way of All Souls (1924). He is also a graduate of New College and from 1935 to 1939 was lecturer in Private International Law at Oxford. In 1939 he went to the Embassy in Washington as First Secretary and stayed for almost five years. In 1944 he was commissioned a brigadier on special service and the following year gained considerable prestige by winning a Conservative seat in Parliament in the face of the Labour tidal wave. He is still a Fellow of All Souls, after twenty-five years, and this fact alone would indicate he has a position as an important member of the Group.

Roger Mellor Makins, son of a Conservative M.P., was elected a Fellow of All Souls immediately after graduation from Christ Church in 1925. He joined the diplomatic service in 1928 and spent time in London, Washington, and (briefly) Oslo in the next nine years. In 1937 he became assistant adviser on League of Nations affairs to the Foreign Office. He was secretary to the British delegation to the Evian Conference on Refugees from Germany in 1938 and became secretary to the Intergovernmental Committee on Refugees set up at that meeting. In 1939 he returned to the Foreign Office as adviser on League of Nations Affairs but soon became a First Secretary; he was adviser to the British delegation at the New York meeting of the International Labour Conference in 1941 and the following year joined the staff of the Resident Minister in West Africa. When the Allied Headquarters in the Mediterranean area was set up in 1943, he joined the staff of the Resident British Minister with that unit. At the end of the war, in 1945, he went to the Embassy in Washington with the rank of Minister. In this post he had the inestimable advantage that his wife, whom he married in 1934, was the daughter of the late Dwight F. Davis, Secretary of War in the Hoover Administration. During this period Makins played an important role at various international organizations. He was the United Kingdom representative on the Interim Commission for Food and Agriculture of the United Nations in 1945; he was adviser to the United Kingdom delegation to the first FAO Conference at Quebec the same year; he was a delegate to the Atlantic City meeting of UNRRA in the following year. In 1947 he left Washington to become Assistant Under Secretary of State in the Foreign Office in London.

Another important member of All Souls who appeared briefly in Washington during the war was John H. A. Sparrow. Graduated from Winchester School and New College by 1927, he became an Eldon Law Scholar and a Fellow of All Souls in 1929. He is still a Fellow of the latter after twenty years. Commissioned in the Coldstream Guards in 1940, he was in Washington on a confidential military mission during most of 1940 and was attached to the War Office from 1942 to the end of the war.

Certain other members of the Group were to be found in the United States during the period under discussion. We have already mentioned the services rendered to the Ministry of Information by J. W. Wheeler-Bennett in New York from 1939 to 1944. Robert J. Stopford was Financial Counsellor to the British Embassy in 1940-1943. We should also mention that F. W. Eggleston, chief Australian member of the Group, was Australian Minister in Washington from 1944 to 1946. And the story of the Milner Group's activities in Washington would not be complete without at least mentioning Percy E. Corbett.

Percy Corbett of Prince Edward Island, Canada, took a M.A. degree at McGill University in 1915 and went to Balliol as a Rhodes Scholar. He was a Fellow of All Souls in 1920-1928 and a member of the staff of the League of Nations in 1920-1924. He was Professor of Roman Law at McGill University from 1924 to 1937 and had been Professor of Government and Jurisprudence and chairman of the Department of Political Science at Yale since 1944. He has always been close to the Milner Group, participating in many of their Canadian activities, such as the Canadian Royal Institute of International Affairs, the unofficial British Commonwealth relations conferences, and the Institute of Pacific Relations. He was chairman of the Pacific Council of the last organization in 1942. During the war he spent much of his time in the United States, especially in Washington, engaged in lobbying activities for the British Embassy, chiefly in Rhodes Scholarship and academic circles but also in government agencies. Since the war ended, he has obtained, by his position at Yale, a place of considerable influence, especially since Yale began, in 1948, to publish its new quarterly review called *World Politics*. On this review, Professor Corbett is one of the more influential members. At present he must be numbered among the three most important Canadian members of the Milner Group, the other two being Vincent Massey and George Parkin Glazebrook.

In view of the emphasis which the Milner Group has always placed on publicity and the need to control the chief avenues by which the general public obtains information on public affairs, it is not surprising to find that the Ministry of Information was one of the fiefs of the Group from its establishment in 1939.

At the outbreak of war, H. A. L. Fisher had been Governor of the BBC for four years. It was probably as a result of this connection that L. F. Rushbrook Williams, whom we have already mentioned in connection with Indian affairs and as a member of All Souls since 1914, became Eastern Service Director of the BBC. He was later adviser on Middle East affairs to the Ministry of Information but left this, in 1944, to become an editor of *The Times*. Edward Griggs, now Lord Altrincham, was Parliamentary Secretary to the Ministry of Information from its creation to the Cabinet revision of 1940, when he shifted to the War Office. J. W. Wheeler-Bennett and Isaiah Berlin were with the New York office of the Ministry of Information, as we have seen, the former throughout the war and the latter in 1941-1942. H. V. Hodson, Fellow of All Souls and probably the most important of the newer recruits to the Milner Group, was Director of the Empire Division of the Ministry of Information from its creation in 1939 until he went to India as Reforms Commissioner in 1941-1942. And finally, Cyril John Radcliffe (Sir Cyril after 1944), a graduate of New College in 1922 and a Fellow of All Souls for fifteen years (1922-1937), son-in-law of Lord Charnwood since 1939, was in the Ministry of Information for the whole period of the war, more than four years of it as Director General of the whole organization.[1]

In addition to these three great fiefs (the Research and Intelligence Department of the Foreign Office, the Embassy in Washington, and the Ministry of Information), the Milner Group exercised considerable influence in those branches of the administration concerned with emergency economic regulations, although here the highest positions were reserved to those members of the Cecil Bloc closest to the Milner Group. Oliver Lyttelton, whose mother was a member of the Group, was Controller of Non-Ferrous Metals in 1939-1940, was President of the Board of Trade in 1940-1941, and was Minister of Production in 1942-1945. Lord Wolmer (Lord Selborne since 1942) was Director of Cement in the Ministry of Works in 1940-1942 and Minister of Economic Warfare in 1942-1945. In this connection, it should be mentioned that the Milner Group had developed certain economic interests in non-ferrous metals and in cement in the period of the 1920s and 1930s. The former developed both from their interest in colonial mines, which were the source of the ores, and from their control of electrical utilities, which supplied much of the power needed to reduce these ores. The center of these interests was to be found, on the one hand, in the Rhodes Trust and the economic holdings of the associates of Milner and Rhodes like R. S. Holland, Abe Bailey, P. L. Gell, etc., and, on the other hand, in the utility interests of Lazard Brothers and of the Hoare family. The ramifications of these interests are too complicated, and too well concealed, to be described in any detail here, but we might point out that Lord Milner was a director of Rio Tinto, that Dougal Malcolm was a director of Nchanga Consolidated Copper Mines, that Samuel Hoare was a director of Birmingham Aluminum Casting Company until he took public office, that the Hoare family had extensive holdings in Associated Tin Mines of Nigeria, in British-American Tin Corporation, in London Tin Corporation, etc.; that R. S. Holland was an Anglo-Spanish Construction Company, on British Copper Manufacturers, and on the British Metal Corporation; that Lyttelton Gell was a director of Huelva Copper and of the Zinc Corporation; that Oliver Lyttelton was managing director of the British Metal Corporation and a director of Metallgesellschaft, the German light-metals monopoly. The chief member of the Group in the cement industry was Lord Meston, who was placed on many important corporations after his return from India, including the Associated Portland Cement Manufacturers and the British Portland Cement Manufacturers. The third Lord Selborne was chairman of the Cement Makers' Federation from 1934 to 1940, resigning to take charge of the government's cement-regulation program.

In lesser posts in these activities, we might mention the following. Charles R. S. Harris, whom we have already mentioned as an associate of Brand, a Fellow of All Souls for fifteen years, a leader-writer on *The Times* for ten years, the authority on Duns Scotus who wrote a book on Germany's foreign indebtedness for Chatham House, was in the Ministry of Economic Warfare in 1939-1940. He then spent two years in Iceland for the Foreign Office, and three years with the War Office, ending up in 1944-1945 as a member of the Allied Control Commission for Italy. H. V. Hodson was principal assistant secretary and later head of the Non-Munitions Division of the Ministry of Production from his return from India to the end of the war (1942-1945). Douglas P. T. Jay, a graduate of New College in 1930 and a Fellow of All Souls in the next seven years, was on the staff of *The Times* and *The Economist* in the period 1929-1937 and was city editor of *The Daily Herald* in 1937-1941. He was assistant secretary to the Ministry of Supply in 1941-1943 and principal assistant secretary to the Board of Trade in 1943-1945. After the Labour government came to power in the summer of 1945, he was personal assistant to the Prime Minister (Clement Attlee) until he became a Labour M.P. in 1946. Richard Pares, son of the famous authority on Russia, the late Sir Bernard Pares, and son-in-law of the famous historian Sir Maurice Powicke, was a Fellow of All Souls for twenty-one years after he graduated from Balliol in 1924. He was a lecturer at New College for eleven years, 1929-1940 and then was with the Board of Trade for the duration of the war, 1940-1945. Since the war, he has been Professor of History at Edinburgh. During most of the war his father, Sir Bernard Pares, lectured in the United States as a pro-Russian propagandist in the pay of the Ministry of Information. We have already mentioned the brief period in which Adam Marris worked for the Ministry of Economic Warfare in 1939-1940.

As the war went on, the Milner Group shifted their attention increasingly to the subject of postwar planning and reconstruction. Much of this was conducted through Chatham House. When the war began, Toynbee wrote a letter to the Council of the RIIA, in which he said: "If we get through the present crisis and are given a further chance to try and put the world in order, we shall then feel a need to take a broader and deeper view of our problems than we were inclined to take after the War of 1914-1918. . . . I believe this possibility has been in Mr. Lionel Curtis's mind since the time when he first conceived the idea of the Institute; his *Civitas Dei* and my *Study of History* are two reconnaissances of this historical background to the study of comtemporary international affairs."[2] At the end of 1942 the Group founded a quarterly journal devoted to reconstruction. It was founded technically under the auspices of the London School of Economics, but the editor was G. N. Clark, a member of All Souls since 1912 and Chichele Professor of Economic History from 1931 to 1943. The title of this journal was *Agenda*, and its editorial offices were in Chatham House. These tentative plans to dominate the postwar reconstruction efforts received a rude jolt in August 1945, when the General Election removed the Conservative government from power and brought to office a Labour government. The influence of the Group in Labour circles has always been rather slight.

Since this blow, the Milner Group has been in eclipse, and it is not clear what has been happening.[3] Its control of *The Times*, of *The Round Table*, of Chatham House, of the Rhodes Trust, of All Souls, and of Oxford generally has continued but has been used without centralized purpose or conviction. Most of the original members of the Group have retired from active affairs; the newer recruits have not the experience or the intellectual conviction, or the social contacts, which allowed the older members to wield such great power. The disasters into which the Group directed British policy in the years before 1940 are not such as to allow their prestige to continue undiminished. In imperial affairs, their policies have been largely a failure, with Ireland gone, India divided and going, Burma drifting away, and even South Africa more distant than at any time since 1910. In foreign policy their actions almost destroyed western civilization, or at least the European center of it. *The Times* has lost its influence; *The Round Table* seems lifeless. Far worse than this, those parts of Oxford where the Group's influence was strongest have suffered a disastrous decline. The Montague Burton Professorship of International Relations, to which Professor Zimmern and later Professor Woodward brought such great talents, was given in 1948 to a middle-aged spinster, daughter of Sir James Headlam-Morley, with one published work to her credit. The Chichele Professorship of International Law and Diplomacy, held with distinction for twenty-five years by Professor James L. Brierley, was filled in 1947 by a common-law lawyer, a specialist in the law of real property, who, by his own confession, is largely ignorant of international law and whose sole published work, written with the collaboration of a specialist on equity, is a treatise on the *Law of Mortgages*. These appointments, which gave a shock to academic circles in the United States, do not allow an outside observer to feel any great optimism for the future either of the Milner Group or of the great institutions which it has influenced. It would seem that the great idealistic adventure which began with Toynbee and Milner in 1875 had slowly ground its way to a finish of bitterness and ashes.

Appendix:
A Tentative Roster of
the Milner Group

THE FOLLOWING LISTS are tentative in the sense that they are incomplete and erroneous. The errors are more likely in the attribution of persons to one circle of the Group rather than another, and are less likely in the attribution to the Group of persons who are not members at all. For the names given I have sufficient evidence to convince me that they are members of the Group, although I would not in many cases feel competent to insist that the persons concerned knew that they were members of a secret group. The evidence on which this list is based is derived from documentary evidence, from private information, and from circumstantial evidence.

Persons are listed in each group on the basis of general impression rather than exact demarcation, because the distinction between the two is rather vague and varies from time to time. For example, I know for a fact that Sir Alfred Zimmern and Lord Cecil of Chelwood attended meetings of the inner circle in the period before 1920, but I have attributed them to the outer circle because this appears to be the more accurate designation for the long period since 1920.

Within each list I have placed the names of the various individuals in order of chronology and of importance. In some cases where I suspected a person of being a member without having any very convincing evidence, I have enclosed the name in brackets.

A. The Society of the Elect

Cecil John Rhodes
Nathan Rothschild, Baron Rothschild
Sir Harry Johnston
William T. Stead
Reginald Brett, Viscount Esher
Alfred Milner, Viscount Milner

B. F. Hawksley
Thomas Brassey, Lord Brassey
Edmund Garrett
[Sir Edward Cook]
Alfred Beit
Sir Abe Bailey
Albert Grey, Earl Grey
Archibald Primrose, Earl of Rosebery
Arthur James Balfour
Sir George R. Parkin
Philip Lyttelton Gell
Sir Henry Birchenough
Sir Reginald Sothern Holland
Arthur Lionel Smith
Herbert A. L. Fisher
William Waldegrave Palmer, Earl of Selborne
[Sir Alfred Lyttelton]
Sir Patrick Duncan
Robert Henry Brand, Baron Brand
Philip Kerr, Marquess of Lothian
Lionel Curtis
Geoffrey Dawson
Edward Grigg, Baron Altrincham
Jan C. Smuts
Leopold Amery
Waldorf Astor, Viscount Astor
Nancy Astor, Lady Astor

B. The Association of Helpers

1. The Inner Circle

Sir Patrick Duncan
Robert Henry Brand, Baron Brand
Philip Kerr, Marquess of Lothian
Lionel Curtis
William L. Hichens
Geoffrey Dawson
Edward Grigg, Baron Altrincham
Herbert A. L. Fisher
Leopold Amery
Richard Feetham
Hugh A. Wyndham
Sir Dougal Malcolm

Basil Williams
Basil Kellett Long
Sir Abe Bailey
Jan C. Smuts
Sir William Marris
James S. Meston, Baron Meston
Malcolm Hailey, Baron Hailey
Flora Shaw, Lady Lugard
Sir Reginald Coupland
Waldorf Astor, Viscount Astor
Nancy Astor, Lady Astor
Maurice Hankey, Baron Hankey
Arnold J. Toynbee
Laurence F. Rushbrook Williams
Henry Vincent Hodson
Vincent Todd Harlow

2. The Outer Circle

John Buchan, Baron Tweedsmuir
Sir Fabian Ware
Sir Alfred Zimmern
Gilbert Murray
Robert Cecil, Viscount Cecil of Chelwood
Sir James W. Headlam-Morley
Frederick J. N. Thesiger, Viscount Chelmsford
Sir Valentine Chirol
Edward F. L. Wood, Earl of Halifax
Sir [James] Arthur Salter
Sir Arthur H. D. R. Steel-Maitland
William G. A. Ormsby-Gore, Baron Harlech
Dame Edith Lyttelton, Mrs. Alfred Lyttelton
Frederick Lugard, Baron Lugard
Sir [Leander] Starr Jameson
Henry W. C. Davis
John A. Simon, Viscount Simon
Samuel J. G. Hoare, Viscount Templewood
Maurice P. A. Hankey, Baron Hankey
Wilson Harris
[Francis Clarke]
William G. S. Adams
[William K. Hancock]
Ernest L. Woodward
Sir Harold Butler

Kenneth N. Bell
Sir Donald B. Somervell
Sir Maurice L. Gwyer
Charles R. S. Harris
Sir Edward R. Peacock
Sir Cyril J. Radcliffe
John W. Wheeler-Bennett
Robert J. Stopford
Robert M. Barrington-Ward
[Kenneth C. Wheare]
Edward H. Carr
Malcolm MacDonald
Godfrey Elton, Baron Elton
Sir Neill Malcolm
Freeman Freeman-Thomas, Viscount Willingdon
Isaiah Berlin
Roger M. Makins
Sir Arthur Willert
Ivison S. Macadam

3. Members in other countries

a. Canada

Arthur J. Glazebrook
Sir George Parkin
Vincent Massey
George P. de T. Glazebrook
Percy Corbett
[Sir Joseph Flavelle]

b. United States

George Louis Beer
Frank Aydelotte
Jerome Greene
[Clarence Steit]

c. South Africa

Jan C. Smuts
Sir Patrick Duncan
Sir Abe Bailey
Basil K. Long
Richard Feetham
[Sir James Rose-Innes]

d. Australia

Sir Thomas Bavin
Sir Frederic Eggleston
[Dudley D. Braham]

e. New Zealand

Sir James Allen
William Downie Stewart
Arthur R. Atkinson

f. Germany

Helmuth James von Moltke
Adam von Trott zu Solz

Notes

Chapter 1

[1]The sources of this information and a more detailed examination of the organization and personnel of the Rhodes secret society will be found in Chapter 3 below.

[2]On Parkin, see the biography (1929) started by Sir John Willison and finished by Parkin's son-in-law, William L. Grant. Also see the sketches of both Parkin and Milner in the *Dictionary of National Biography*. The debate in the Oxford Union which first brought Parkin to Milner's attention is mentioned in Herbert Asquith's (Lord Oxford and Asquith) *Memories and Reflections* (2 vols., Boston, 1928), I, 26.

[3]The ideas for social service work among the poor and certain other ideas held by Toynbee and Milner were derived from the teachings of John Ruskin, who first came to Oxford as a professor during their undergraduate days. The two young men became ardent disciples of Ruskin and were members of his road-building group in the summer of 1870. The standard biography of Ruskin was written by a protege of Milner's, Edward Cook. The same man edited the complete collection of Ruskin's works in thirty-eight volumes. See Lord Oxford and Asquith, *Memories and Reflections* (2 vols., Boston, 1928), I, 48. Cook's sketch in the *Dictionary of National Biography* was written by Asquith's intimate friend and biographer, J. A. Spender.

[4]The quotation is from Cecil Headlam, ed., *The Milner Papers* (2 vols., London, 1931-1933), I, 15. There exists no biography of Milner, and all of the works concerned with his career have been written by members of the Milner Group and conceal more than they reveal. The most important general sketches of his life are the sketch in the *Dictionary of National Biography*, the obituary in *The Times* (May 1925), and the obituary in *The Round Table* (June 1925, XV, 427-430). His own point of view must be sought in his speeches and essays. Of these, the chief collections are *The Nation and the Empire* (Boston, 1913) and *Questions of the Hour* (London, 1923). Unfortunately, the speeches after 1913 and all the essays which appeared in periodicals are still uncollected. This neglect of one of the most important figures of the twentieth century is probably deliberate, part of the policy of secrecy practiced by the Milner Group.

Chapter 2

[1]A. C. Johnson, *Viscount Halifax* (New York, 1941), 54. Inasmuch as Lord Halifax assisted the author of this biography and gave to him previously unpublished material to insert in it, we are justified in considering this an "authorized" biography and giving its statements considerable weight. The author is aware of the existence of the Milner Group and attributes much of Lord Halifax's spectacular career to his connection with the Group.

[2]H. H. Henson, *Retrospect of an Unimportant Life* (2 vols., London, 1942-1943), II, 66.

[3]C. Hobhouse, *Oxford as It Was and as It Is Today* (London, 1939), 18.

[4]On the role of Charles Hardinge in foreign policy, see A. L. Kennedy, "Lord Hardinge of Penshurst," in *The Quarterly Review* (January 1945), CCLXXXIII, 97-104, and Charles Hardinge, 1st Baron Hardinge of Penshurst, *Old Diplomacy; Reminiscences* (London, 1947). Although not mentioned again in this work, A. L. Kennedy appears to be a member of the Milner Group.

[5]Lord Ernle, *Whippingham to Westminster* (London, 1938), 248.

[6]Lionel Curtis, *Dyarchy* (Oxford, 1920), 54.

[7]Another exception was "Bron" Lucas (Auberon Herbert, Lord Lucas and Dingwall), son of Auberon Herbert, the brother of Lord Carnavon. "Bron" went from Balliol to South Africa as a *Times* correspondent in the Boer War and lost a leg from overzealous devotion to the task. A close friend of John Buchan and Raymond Asquith, he became a Liberal M.P. through the latter's influence but had to go to the Upper House in 1905, when he inherited two titles from his mother's brother. He was subsequently private secretary to Haldane (1908), Under Secretary for War (1908-1911), Under Secretary for the Colonies (1911), Parliamentary Secretary to the Board of Agriculture (1911-1914), and President of the Board of Agriculture (1914-1915). He thus became a member of the Cabinet while only thirty-eight years old. He resigned to join the Royal Flying Corps and was killed in 1916, about the same time as Raymond Asquith. Both of these, had they lived, would probably have become members of the Milner Group. Asquith was already a Fellow of All Souls (1901-1916). On "Bron" Lucas, see the autobiographies of Lords Asquith and Tweedsmuir and the article in the memorial volume to Balliol's dead in the First World War.

[8]On these clubs, see Lord Oxford and Asquith, *Memories and Reflections* (2 vols., Boston, 1928), I, 311-325.

[9]The chief published references to the existence of the Milner Group from the pens of members will be found in the obituary notes on deceased members in *The Round Table* and in the sketches in the *Dictionary of National Biography*. In the former, see the notes on Milner, Hickens, Lord Lothian, A. J. Glazebrook, Sir Thomas Bavin, Sir Patrick Duncan, Sir Abe Bailey, etc. See also the references in the published works of Lionel Curtis, John Buchan (Lord Tweedsmuir), John Dove, etc. Quotations to this effect from John Buchan and from Lord Asquith will be found at the end of Chapter 3 below. The best published reference to the Milner Group is in M. S. Geen, *The Making of the Union of South Africa* (London, 1946), 150-152. The best account originating in the Group itself is in the article "Twenty-five Years" in *The Round Table* for September 1935, XV, 653-659.

Chapter 3

[1]This section is based on W. T. Stead, *The Last Will and Testament of Cecil John Rhodes* (London, 1902); Sir Francis Wylie's three articles in the *American Oxonian* (April 1944), XXXI, 65-69; (July 1944), XXXI, 129-138; and (January 1945), XXXII, 1-11; F. Aydelotte, *The American Rhodes Scholars* (Princeton, 1946); and the biographies and memoirs of the men mentioned.

[2]No such claim is made by Sir Francis Wylie, from whose articles Dr. Aydelotte derived most of the material for his first chapter. Sir Francis merely mentions the secret society in connection with the early wills and then drops the whole subject.

[3]W. T. Stead, *The Last Will and Testament of Cecil John Rhodes* (London, 1902), 110-111. The statement of 1896 to Brett is in *Journals and Letters of Reginald, Viscount Esher* (4 vols., London, 1934-1938), I, 197.

[4]Dr. Aydelotte quotes at length from a letter which Rhodes sent to Stead in 1891, but he does not quote the statements which Stead made about it when he published it in 1902. In this letter he spoke about the project of federal union with the United States and said, "The only feasible [way] to carry this idea out is a secret one (society) gradually absorbing the wealth of the world to be devoted to such an object." At the end of this document Stead wrote: "Mr. Rhodes has never to my knowledge said a word nor has he ever written a syllable, that justifies the suggestion that he surrendered the aspirations which were expressed in this letter of 1891. So far from this being the case, in the long discussions which took place between us in the last years of his life, he reaffirmed as emphatically as at first his unshaken conviction as to the dream — if you like to call it so — a vision, which had ever been the guiding star of his life." See W. T. Stead, *The Last Will and Testament of Cecil John Rhodes* (London, 1902), 73-77.

[5]Sir John Willison, *Sir George Parkin* (London, 1929), 234.

[6]This paragraph and the two preceding it are from Sir Frederick Whyte, *The Life of W. T. Stead* (2 vols., Boston, 1925), 270-272 and 39.

[7]See *Journals and Letters of Reginald, Viscount Esher* (4 vols., London, 1938), I, 149-150. It should be noted that the excision in the entry for 3 February marked by three points (. . .) was made by Lord Esher's son when he edited the journals for publication.

[8]See F. Whyte, *Life of W. T. Stead* (2 vols., Boston, 1925), 199-212.

[9]No mention of the secret society is to be found in either Sir Harry Johnston, *The Story of My Life* (London, 1923), or in Alex. Johnston, *Life and Letters of Sir Harry Johnston* (London, 1929). The former work does contain an account of Johnston's break with Rhodes on page 497. More details are on pages 145-148 of the later work, including a record of Rhodes's saying, "I will smash you, Johnston, for this." Johnston was convinced that it was a result of this enmity that Milner rather than he was chosen to be High Commissioner of South Africa in 1897. See pages 338-339.

[10]Rhodes's reason for eliminating him (given in the January 1901 codicil to his will) was "on account of the extraordinary eccentricity of Mr. Stead, though having always a great respect for him, but feeling the objects of my Will would be embarrassed by his views." Milner's reasons (given in the "Stead Memorial"

number of *The Review of Reviews*, May 1912) were his "lack of balance," which was "his Achilles heel." See also the letter of 12 April 1902 from Edmund Garrett to Stead, quoted below, from F. Whyte, *The Life of W. T. Stead* (2 vols., Boston, 1925), 211.

[11]The quotation is from the sketch of Lord Esher in the *Dictionary of National Biography*. The other quotations from Brett are from *The Journals and Letters of Reginald, Viscount Esher* (4 vols., London, 1934-1938).

[12]E. T. Cook, *Edmund Garrett* (London, 1909), 158. The excision in this letter marked by three points (. . .) was made by Cook. Cook was a protege of Milner's, found in New College, invited to contribute to the *Pall Mall Gazette* in 1881, and added to the staff as an editor in August 1883, when Milner was acting as editor-in-chief, during the absence of Morley and Stead. See F. Whyte, *The Life of W. T. Stead* (2 vols., Boston, 1925), I, 94. Cook remained close to Milner for many years. On 4 October 1899 Lord Esher wrote to his son a letter in which he said: "Cook is the Editor of the *Daily News* and is in close touch with Milner and his friends" — *Journals and Letters of Reginald, Viscount Esher* (4 vols., London, 1938), I, 240.

[13]F. Whyte, *Life of W. T. Stead* (2 vols., Boston, 1925), 211. The quotation in the next paragraph is from the same place.

[14]As an example of this and an example of the way in which the secret society functioned in the early period, see the following passage from the *Journals and Letters of Reginald, Viscount Esher* (4 vols., London, 1938), under the date 21 November 1892: "I went to London on Friday and called on Rhodes. He had asked me to do so. . . . Rhodes asked for the Government carriage of his telegraph poles and 200 Sikhs at Blantyre. Then he will make the telegraph. He would like a gunboat on Tanganyika. I stayed there to lunch. Then saw Rosebery. He was in good spirits." From Sir Harry Johnston's autobiography, it is clear that the 200 Sikhs were for him.

[15]S. G. Millen, *Rhodes* (London, 1934), 341-342.

[16]In the House of Commons, Maguire was a supporter of Parnell, acting on orders from Rhodes, who had given £10,000 to Parnell's cause in 1888. Rhodes's own explanation of why he supported Parnell is a typical Milner Group statement. He said that he gave the money "since in Mr. Parnell's cause. . . . I believe he's the key to the Federal System, on the basis of perfect Home Rule in every part of the Empire." This quotation is from S. G. Millin, *Rhodes* (London, 1934), 112, and is based on W. T. Stead, *The Last Will and Testament of Cecil John Rhodes* (London, 1902).

[17]The first quotation is from Edmund Garrett, "Milner and Rhodes," in *The Empire and the Century* (London, 1905), 478. According to *The Times* obituary of Milner, 14 May 1925, Rhodes repeated these sentiments in different words on his deathbed, 26 March 1902. The statement to Stead will be found in W. T. Stead, *The Last Will and Testament of Cecil John Rhodes* (London, 1902), 108.

[18]See Cecil Headlam, ed., *The Milner Papers, 1897-1905* (2 vols., London, 1931-1933), II, 412-413; the unpublished material is at New College, Oxford, in Milner Papers, XXXVIII, ii, 200.

Chapter 4

[1]The obituary of Patrick Duncan in *The Round Table* (September 1943), XXXIII, 303-305, reads in part: "Duncan became the *doyen* of the band of

brothers, Milner's young men, who were nicknamed . . . 'The Kindergarten,' then in the first flush of youthful enthusiasm. It is a fast ageing and dwindling band now; but it has played a part in the Union of South Africa colonies, and it is responsible for the foundation and conduct of *The Round Table*. For forty years and more, so far as the vicissitudes of life have allowed, it has kept together; and always, while looking up to Lord Milner and to his successor in South Africa, the late Lord Selborne, as its political Chief, has revered Patrick Duncan as the Captain of the band." According to R. H. Brand, ed., *The Letters of John Dove* (London, 1938), Duncan was coming to England to the meetings of the Group as late as 1932.

²The above list of eighteen names does not contain all the members of the Kindergarten. A complete list would include: (1) Harry Wilson (Sir Harry after 1908), who was a "Seeley lecturer" with Parkin in the 1890s; was chief private secretary to Joseph Chamberlain in 1895-1897; was legal adviser to the Colonial Office and to Milner in 1897-1901; was Secretary and Colonial Secretary to the Orange River Colony in 1901-1907; was a member of the Intercolonial Council and of the Railway Committee in 1903-1907. (2) E. B. Sargant, who organized the school system of South Africa for Milner in 1900-1904 and was Director of Education for both the Transvaal and the Orange River Colony in 1902-1904; he wrote a chapter for *The Empire and the Century* in 1905. (3) Gerard Craig Sellar, who died in 1929, and on whom no information is available. There was a Craig-Sellar Fellowship in his honor at Balliol in 1946. (4) Oscar Ferris Watkins, a Bible Clerk at All Souls at the end of the nineteenth century, received a M.A. from this college in 1910; he was in the South African Constabulary in 1902-1904; was in the Transvaal Civil Service in 1904-1907; was in the East African Protectorate Service and the E.A. Civil Service from 1908, being a District Commissioner in 1914, Acting Chief Native Commissioner in 1920-1927, a member of the Legislative Council in 1920-1922, Deputy Chief Native Commissioner of Kenya in 1921-1927; he was Director of Military Labour under Smuts in German East Africa in 1914-1918. (5) Percy Girouard (later Sir Percy) was chairman of the Egyptian Railway Board in 1898-1899; was Director of Railways in the Boer War in 1899-1902; was Commissioner of Railways and Head of the Central South African Railways in 1902-1904; was High Commissioner of Northern Nigeria in 1907-1908 and Governor in 1908-1909; was Governor of the East African Protectorate in 1909-1912; was director of Armstrong, Whitworth and Company in 1912-1915; and was Director General of Munitions Supply in 1914-1915. He was fired by Lloyd George for inefficiency in 1915.

³Douglas Malcolm's sister in 1907 married Neill Malcolm (since 1919 Major General Sir Neill Malcolm), who was a regular army officer from 1889 to his retirement in 1924. He was on the British Military Mission to Berlin in 1919-1921; Commanding General in Malaya, 1921-1924; a founder of the RIIA, of which he was chairman from 1926 (succeeding Lord Meston) to 1935 (succeeded by Lord Astor). He was High Commissioner for German Refugees in 1936-1938, with R. M. Makins (member of All Souls and the Milner Group and later British Minister in Washington) as his chief British subordinate. He is president of the British North Borneo Company, of which Dougal Malcolm is vice-president.

Ian Malcolm (Sir Ian since 1919), a brother of Neill Malcolm, was an attaché at Berlin, Paris, and Petersburg in 1891-1896; and M.P. in 1895-1906 and again 1910-1919; assistant private secretary to Lord Salisbury (1895-1900); parliamentary private secretary to the Chief Secretary for Ireland (George Wyndham) in 1901-1903; Secretary to the Union Defence League, organized by

Walter Long, in 1906-1910; a Red Cross officer in Europe and North America (1914-1917); on Balfour's mission to the United States in 1917; private secretary to Balfour during the Peace Conference (1919); and British representative on the Board of Directors of the Suez Canal Company. He wrote Walter Long's biography in the *Dictionary of National Biography*.

[4]See W. B. Worsfold, *The Reconstruction of the New Colonies under Lord Milner* (2 vols., London, 1913), II, 207-222 and 302-419.

[5]The last quotation is from *Dyarchy* (Oxford, 1920), liii. The other are from *The Problem of the Commonwealth* (London, 1915), 18, and 200-219.

[6]Fisher was one of the most important members of the Milner Group, a fact which would never be gathered from the recent biography written by David Ogg, *Herbert Fisher, 1865-1940* (London, 1947). He was associated with members of the Group, or persons close to it all his life. At New College in the period 1884-1888, he was a student of W. L. Courtney, whose widow, Dame Janet Courtney, was later close to the Group. He became a Fellow of New College in 1888, along with Gilbert Murray, also a member of the Group. His pupils at New College included Curtis, Kerr, Brand, Malcolm, and Hichens in the first few years of teaching; the invitation to South Africa in 1908 came through Curtis; his articles on the trip were published in *The Times*. He sailed to India in 1913 with Herbert Baker of the Group (Rhodes's architect). He refused the post of Chief Secretary for Ireland in 1918, so it was given to Amery's brother-in-law; he refused the post of Assistant Secretary of State for Foreign Affairs in December 1918, when Robert Cecil resigned. He played a certain role in drafting the Montagu-Chelmsford Report of 1919 and the Government of Ireland Bill of 1921, and piloted the latter through Commons. He refused the post of Ambassador to Washington in 1919. Nevertheless, he did not see eye to eye with the inner core of the Group on either religion or protection, since he was an atheist and a free-trader to the end. His book on Christian Science almost caused a break with some members of the Group.

[7]H. H. Henson, *Memoirs of Sir William Anson* (Oxford, 1920), 212.

[8]Cecil Headlam, ed., *The Milner Papers, 1897-1905* (2 vols., London, 1931-1933), II, 501.

[9]R. H. Brand, *The Union of South Africa* (Oxford, 1909), 39.

[10]Smuts was frequently used by the Milner Group to enunciate its policies in public (as, for example, in his speeches of 15 May 1917 and 13 November 1934). The fact that he was speaking for the Milner Group was generally recognized by the upper classes in England, was largely ignored by the masses in England, and was virtually unknown to Americans. Lord Davies assumed this as beyond the need of proof in an article which he published in *The Nineteenth Century* in January 1935. He was attacking the Milner Group's belief that British defense could be based on the Dominions and the United States and especially on its efforts to reduce the League of Nations to a simple debating society. He pointed out the need for an international police force, then asked, "Will the Dominions and the United States volunteer as special constables? And, if they refuse, does it mean that Great Britain is precluded from doing so? The reply of *The Round Table* is 'yes,' and the most recent exposition of its policy is contained in the speech delivered by General Smuts at the dinner given in his honor by the Royal Institute of International Affairs on November 13"— *The Nineteenth Century* (January 1935), CXVII, 51.

Smuts's way in imperial affairs was much smoothed by the high opinion which Lord Esher held of him; see, for example, *The Journals and Letters of Reginald Viscount Esher* (4 vols., London, 1938), IV, 101, 224, and 254.

[11]Lord Oxford and Asquith, *Memories and Reflections 1852-1927* (2 vols.,

Boston, 1928), I, 213-214. Asquith was a member of the Cecil Bloc and of "The Souls." He was a lifelong friend of both Balfour and Milner. It was the former who persuaded Asquith to write his memoirs, after talking the matter over privately with Margot Asquith one evening while Asquith himself was at Grillions. When Asquith married Margot Tennant in 1894, the witnesses who signed the marriage certificates were A. J. Balfour, W. E. Gladstone, Lord Rosebery, Charles Tennant, H. J. Tennant, and R. B. Haldane. Asquith's friendship with Milner went back to their undergraduate days. In his autobiography Asquith wrote (pp. 210-211): "We sat together at the Scholar's table in Hall for three years. We then formed a close friendship, and were for many years on intimate terms and in almost constant contact with one another. . . . At Oxford we both took an active part at the Union in upholding the unfashionable Liberal cause. . . . In my early married days [1877-1885] he used often to come to my house at Hampstead for a frugal Sunday supper when we talked over political and literary matters, for the most part in general agreement." For Milner's relationship with Margot Tennant before her marriage to Asquith in 1894, see her second fling at autobiography, *More or Less about Myself* (London, 1932). On 22 April 1908, W. T. Stead wrote to Lord Esher that Mrs. Asquith had three portraits over her bed: Rosebery, Balfour, and Milner. See *The Journals and Letters of Reginald, Viscount Esher* (4 vols., London, 1938), II, 304.

Chapter 5

[1]*The Times*'s obituary on Milner (14 May 1925), obviously written by a person who knew the situation well (probably either Dawson or Amery), said; "He would never in any circumstances have accepted office again. . . . That he always disliked it, assumed it with reluctance, and laid it down with infinite relief, is a fact about which in his case there was never the smallest affectation." It will be recalled that Milner had refused the Colonial Secretaryship in 1903; about six years later, according to *The Times* obituary, he refused a Unionist offer of a Cabinet post in the next Conservative government, unless the party would pledge itself to establish compulsory military training. This it would not do. It is worth recalling that another initiate, Lord Esher, shared Milner's fondness for compulsory military training, as well as his reluctance to hold public office.

[2]E. Garrett, *The Empire and the Century* (London, 1905), 481. Eight years later, in 1913, in the introduction to a collection of his speeches called *The Nation and the Empire* (Boston, 1913), Milner said almost the same thing. Milner's distaste for party politics was shared by Lord Esher and Lord Grey to such an extent as to become a chief motivating force in their lives. See H. Begbie, *Albert, Fourth Earl Grey* (London, 1918), especially p. 52, and *The Journals and Letters of Reginald, Viscount Esher* (4 vols., London, 1938), *passim*.

[3]Letter of Milner to Congdon, 23 November 1904, in Cecil Headlam, ed., *The Milner Papers* (2 vols., London, 1931-1933), II, 506.

[4]Cecil Headlam, ed., *The Milner Papers* (2 vols., London, 1931-1933), I, 267 and 288; II, 505. Milner's antipathy for party politics was generally shared by the inner circle of the Milner Group. The future Lord Lothian, writing in *The Round Table*, August 1911, was very critical of party politics and used the same arguments against it as Milner. He wrote: "At any moment a party numbering among its numbers all the people best qualified to manage foreign

affairs may be cast from office, for reasons which have nothing to do with their conduct of these matters. . . . If the people of Great Britain manage to keep at the head of the great Imperial offices of State, men who will command the confidence of the Dominions, and who pursue steadfastly a . . . successful policy, and if the people of the Dominions are tolerant and far-sighted enough to accept such a policy as their own, the present arrangement may last. Does history give us any reason for expecting that the domestic party system will produce so great a combination of good fortune and good management?" (*The Round Table*, I, 414-418).

In the introduction to *The Nation and the Empire*, written in 1913, Milner expressed himself in a similar vein.

[5]Marquess of Crewe, *Lord Rosebery* (2 vols., London, 1931), 615.

[6]See John, Viscount Morley, *Recollections* (2 vols., New York, 1917), II.

[7]The fact that a small "secret" group controlled the nominations for Chancellor of Oxford was widely recognized in Britain, but not frequently mentioned publicly. In May 1925 the Earl of Birkenhead wrote a letter to *The Times* to protest against this usurpation by a nonofficial group and was answered, in *The Times*, by a letter which stated that, when the group was formed after the interruption of the First World War, he had been invited to join it but had never acknowledged the invitation! Milner's nomination was made by a group that met in New College, under the chairmanship of H. A. L. Fisher, on 5 May 1925. There were about thirty present, including Fisher, Lord Astor, Lord Ernle, Steel-Maitland, Pember, Wilkinson, Brand, Lucas, M. G. Glazebrook, Sir Herbert Warren (classmate and friend of Milner's), Archbishop Davidson, Cyril Bailey, etc. The same group, according to Lord Halifax's biographer, nominated Lord Halifax to the Chancellorship in 1933.

[8]The editors were assisted in the work of producing the two volumes by Margaret Toynbee. The influence of the Milner Group can be discerned in the list of acknowledgments in the preface to Weaver's volume. Among eighteen names listed may be found those of Cyril Bailey (Fellow of Balliol, 1902-1939, and member of the Ministry of Munitions, 1915-1918); C. R. M. F. Cruttwell (member of All Souls and the Round Table Group, Principal of Hertford College since 1930); Geoffrey Dawson, H. A. L. Fisher; and Ernest Swinton (Fellow of All Souls, 1925-1939). Apparently these persons decided what names should be included in the *Dictionary*.

Chapter 6

[1]The Milner Group's control over these lectures appears as much from the list of presiding officers as from the list of lecturers, thus:

PRESIDENT	SPEAKER	TITLE
A. D. Steel-Maitland	Michael Sadler	The Universities and the War
Lord Bryce	Charles Lucas	The Empire and Democracy
Lord Milner	A. L. Smith	The People and the Duties of Empire
Lord Selborne	H. A. L. Fisher	Imperial Administration
Earl St. Aldwyn	Philip Kerr	The Commonwealth and the Empire
Lord Sumner	G. R. Parkin	The Duty of the Empire in the World

[2]Buckle came to *The Times* staff in 1880 because of his All Souls connection, being recommended by Sir William Anson, according to the official *History of*

The Times. He was apparently selected to be the future editor from the beginning, since he was given a specially created position as "confidential assistant" to the editor, at a salary "decidedly higher than an Oxford graduate with a good degree could reasonably hope to gain in a few years in any of the regular professions." See *The History of The Times* (4 vols., London, 1935), II, 529. Buckle may have been the link between Lord Salisbury and *The Times*, since they could easily meet at All Souls. Obviously *The History of the Times*, which devotes a full volume of 862 pages to the period of Buckle's editorship, does not tell the full story on Buckle, since he rarely appears on the scene as an actor and would seem, from the *History*, to have been ignorant of most of what was happening in his offices (the Rhodes-Jameson connection, for example). This is difficult to believe.

The *History of The Times* is unsatisfactory on other grounds as well. For example, it is not possible from this work to construct a complete record of who held various staff positions. We are told, for example, that Flora Shaw became head of the Colonial Department in 1890, but that ends that department as far as the volume is concerned. There is considerable material on Miss Shaw, especially in the chapters on the Transvaal, but we never find out who was her successor, or when she left the staff, or if (as appears likely) the Colonial Department was a creation for her occupancy only and did not survive her (undated) withdrawal from the staff; similarly the exact dates and positions of men like Amery and Grigg are not clear.

[3]*The History of The Times* (4 vols., London, 1935), III, 755.

[4]There were others, but they are not of primary, or even secondary importance in the Milner Group. We might mention Aubrey L. Kennedy (son of Sir John Kennedy of the diplomatic service), who was on *The Times* staff from 1910 to 1942, in military intelligence in 1914-1919, diplomatic correspondent for the BBC in 1942-1945, and an influential member of Chatham House since 1919.

[5]E. Moberly Bell, *Flora Shaw* (London, 1947), 115.

[6]At the suggestion of the British Foreign Office, copies of these articles were circulated in America and in Europe. See E. Moberly Bell, *Flora Shaw* (London, 1947), 228.

[7]*The History of The Times* (4 vols., London, 1935), III, 212, 214.

[8]All quotations are from *The History of The Times* (4 vols., London, 1935), III, chapters 7 and 9.

[9]See E. T. Cook, *Edmund Garrett* (London, 1909), 118-119. The difference of opinion between Stead and the others can be traced in F. Whyte, *The Life of W. T. Stead* (2 vols., Boston, 1925), Ch. 21.

The failure of the plotters in Johannesburg to revolt so haunted the plotters elsewhere that they salved their wounds by fantasy. Stead wrote this fantasy for *The Review of Reviews* annual of January 1897, and consulted with Garrett, who had similar plans for the Christmas 1896 number of the *Cape Times*. In Stead's story, the Jameson fiasco was to be turned into a smashing success by a heroic South African editor, who, when all appeared lost, would rush to Johannesburg, stir up the revolt, and save the day. Garrett, who was to be the original model for the hero, wrote back: "A suggestion which will help to keep us distinct, give you a much grander theme, and do something for C.J.R. which no one has yet dared—I went nearer to 'Cecil Rhodes' Dream' but that was a hint only: viz. Make world see what he was driving at and what would have come if all had come off and if Johannesburg had played up. . . . As to making *me* the hero. No. . . . But he must be not only me but you also, and A. Milner, and a few more rolled into one; and he must do what I dreamed of doing but time and space prevented." For the name of this hero Garrett suggested combining the three names into "Milner Garsted" or "Milstead." Ultimately, Stead made the hero a woman. The new model was probably Flora Shaw. The story appeared with the title "The History of a Mystery." See F. Whyte, *The Life of W. T. Stead*, 94-95

[10]Even after the view of the majority prevailed, Stead refused to yield and published his version of a proper defense in *The Scandal of the South African Committee* (London, 1899). It was Stead's belief that preparation for "a raid" was a patriotic act which, if confessed, would have won public acclaim rather than condemnation.

[11]On this see *Journals and Letters of Reginald, Viscount Esher*, (4 vols., London, 1938), I, 196-202.

[12]*The History of The Times* (4 vols., London, 1935), III, 244. It is clear from Miss Moberly Bell's biography of *Flora Shaw* (183-188) that Buckle knew this fact at least by 24 May 1897, although Miss Shaw had previously written him a letter stating explicitly (probably for the record) that she had been acting without either Buckle's or Bell's knowledge. The night before Miss Shaw testified before the Select Committee, Buckle sent her a detailed letter of instruction on how to answer the committee's questions.

[13]W. S. Blunt, *My Diaries* (London, 1932), 226.

[14]See *The History of The Times* (4 vols., London, 1935), III, 315-316.

Chapter 7

[1]L. Curtis, *Dyarchy* (Oxford, 1920), 41.

There can be no doubt that the original inspiration for the Round Table movement was to be found in anti-German feeling. In fact, there are some indications that this was the primary motive and that the stated purpose of working for imperial federation was, to some extent at least, a mask. *The Round Table*, in 1940, in its obituary of Abe Bailey (September 1940, XXX, 743-746), attributes its foundation to this cause as follows: "German ambitions to destroy and supplant the British Commonwealth were manifest to those who had eyes to see. . . . [These asked] 'Can not all the Dominions be brought to realise the common danger that confronts them as much as it confronts Great Britain and think out in mutual discussion the means of uniting all the force and resolution of the Empire in its defense?' To the solution of this question the founders of the Closer Union Societies resolved to apply a similar procedure. Round Table Groups were established in all the British Dominions to study the problem." A similar cause for the founding appeared in *The Round Table* as recently as the issue of September 1948.

[2]The original leader of the Round Table Groups in New Zealand was apparently James Allen (Sir James after 1917), who had been educated in England, at Clifton School and Cambridge University, and was an M.P. in New Zealand from 1887 to 1920. He was Minister of Defense (1912-1920), Minister of Finance and Education (1912-1915), and Minister of Finance (1919-1920), before he became in 1920, New Zealand's High Commissioner in London. He was a member of the Royal Institute of International Affairs.

In the Round Table Group for New Zealand, Allen was soon supplemented and eventually succeeded by William Downie-Stewart as the most important member. Stewart was at the time Mayor of Dunedin (1913) but soon began a twenty-one-year period as an M.P. (1914-1935). He was also Minister of Customs (1921-1928); Minister of Internal Affairs (1921-1924); Minister of Industries and Commerce (1923-1926); Attorney General (1926); Minister of Finance (1926-1928, 1931-1933); Acting Prime Minister (1926); New Zealand delegate to the Ottawa Conference (1932); Vice-Chancellor of Otago University; prominent businessman, and president of the New Zealand Institute of International Affairs (1935-   ). According to Dove's letters, he attended a Milner Group discussion meeting at Lord Lothian's country house in October 1932.

[3]The chief leaders in Australia were Thomas Bavin (Sir Thomas after 1933) and Frederic W. Eggleston (Sir Frederic since 1941). The former, who died in 1941 (see obituary in *The Round Table* for December 1941), was a barrister in New South Wales from 1897; Professor of Law and Modern History at the University of Tasmania (1900-1901); private secretary to the first Prime Minister of Australia, Sir Edmund Barton, in 1901-1904; Secretary and Chief Law Officer of Australia in 1907; lt. commander in naval intelligence in 1916-1918; an Australian M.P. in 1919-1935; held many cabinet posts in New South Wales from 1922 to 1930, ending as Premier (1927-1930). He finished his career as a judge of the Supreme Court in 1935-1941. He was one of the original members of the Round Table Group in Australia, a regular contributor to *The Round Table*, and an important member of the Australian Institute of International Affairs.

Eggleston was a barrister from 1897; a member, correspondent, and chief agent in Australia for *The Round Table* from 1911; a member of the Legislative Assembly of Australia, (1920-1927); Minister for Railways, (1924-1926); chairman of the Commonwealth Grants Commission, (1934-1941); Minister of China (1941-1944) and to the United States (1944-1946). He was one of the founders and chief officers of the Australian Institute of International Affairs and its representative on the council of the Institute of Pacific Relations.

[4]Glazebrook, although virtually unknown, was a very important figure in Canadian life, especially in financial and imperialist circles, up to his death in 1940. For many years he had a practical monopoly in foreign exchange transactions in Toronto, through his firm, Glazebrook and Cronyn (founded 1900). Like most members of the Milner Group, he was interested in adult education, workers' education, and university management. He promoted all of these in Toronto, lecturing himself to the Workers' Educational Association, and at the University of Toronto where he was assistant Professor of Banking and Finance (1926-1937). He was the chief adviser of leading bankers of Canada, and of London and New York bankers on Canadian matters. *The Round Table* says of him: "Through his friendship with Lord Milner and others he had at one time a wide acquaintance among the prominent figures in British public life, and it is well-known to his intimates that on numerous occasions British ministers, anxious to secure reliable information about certain Canadian affairs through unofficial channels, had recourse of Glazebrook. . . . By precept and example he exercised an immense influence for good upon the characters and outlook of a number of young Canadians who had the privilege of his society and knew him as 'The Sage.' Some of them, who have come to high place in the life of the Dominion, will not be slow to acknowledge the value of the inspiration and enlightenment which they derived from him. Continually he preached the doctrine to his young friends that it was their duty, if fortune had placed them in comfortable circumstances, to give some of their time to the intelligent study of public affairs and to the service of the community, and he awakened in not a few minds for the first time the idea that there were better goals in life than the making of money. It is true that the Round Table Groups which he organized with such enthusiasm have now faded into oblivion, but many of their members did not lose the zest for an intelligent study of politics which Glazebrook had im-

planted in them, and after the last war they proved keen supporters of the Canadian Institute of International Affairs as an agency for continuing the political education which Glazebrook had begun."

[5]That Curtis consulted with Lord Chelmsford on the planned reforms before Lord Chelmsford went to India in 1916 was revealed in the House of Lords by Lord Crewe on 12 December 1919, and by Curtis in his book *Dyarchy* (Oxford, 1920), xxvii.

[6]*Dyarchy* (Oxford, 1920), 74.

[7]See R. H. Brand, ed., *Letters of John Dove* (London, 1938), 115-116.

[8]See R. H. Brand, ed., *Letters of John Dove* (London, 1938), 326, 340.

[9]Some of Milner's Canadian speeches in 1908 and in 1912 will be found in *The Nation and the Empire* (Boston, 1913). Kerr's speech at Toronto on 30 July 1912 was published by Glazebrook in June 1917 as an aid to the war effort. It bore on the cover the inscription "The Round Table in Canada." Curtis's speech, so far as I can determine, is unpublished.

[10]See R. L. Schuyler, "The Rise of Anti-Imperialism in England," in *The Political Science Quarterly* (September 1928 and December 1921); O. D. Skelton, *Life and Times of Sir Alexander Tilloch Galt* (Toronto, 1920), 440; and C. A. Bodelson, *Studies in Mid-Victorian Imperialism* (Copenhagen, 1924), 104.

[11]All of these papers will be found in *The Proceedings of the Royal Colonial Institute*, VI, 36-85; XII, 346-391; and XI, 90-132.

[12]The ideas expressed by Lionel Curtis were really Milner's ideas. This was publicly admitted by Milner in a speech before a conference of British and Dominion parliamentarians called together by the Empire Parliamentary Association, 28 July 1916. At this meeting "Milner expressed complete agreement with the general argument of Mr. Curtis, making lengthy quotations from his book, and also accepted the main lines of his plan for Imperial Federation. The resulting discussion showed that not a single Dominion Member present agreed either with Mr. Curtis or Lord Milner." H. D. Hall, *The British Commonwealth of Nations* (London, 1920), 166. The whole argument of Curtis's book was expressed briefly by Milner in 1913 in the Introduction to *The Nation and the Empire*.

[13]Milner's two letters were in Cecil Headlam, ed., *The Milner Papers* (2 vols., London, 1931-1933), I, 159-160 and 267; On Edward Wood's role, see A. C. Johnson, *Viscount Halifax* (New York, 1941), 88-95. The project for devolution, on a geographic basis for political matters and on a functional basis for economic matters, was advocated by *The Round Table* in an article entitled "Some problems in democracy and reconstruction" in the issue of September 1917. The former type was accepted by Curtis as a method for solving the Irish problem and as a method which might well have been used in solving the Scottish problem in 1707. He wrote: "The continued existence in Edinburgh and London of provincial executives and legislatures, entrusted respectively with interests which were strictly Scottish and strictly English, was not incompatible with the policy of merging Scots and Englishmen in a common state. The possibility of distinguishing local from general interests had not as yet been realized." Again, he wrote: "If ever it should prove expedient to unburden the Parliament of the United Kingdom by delegating to the inhabitants of England, Ireland, Scotland, and Wales the management of their own provincial affairs, and the condition of Ireland should prove no bar to such a measure, the Irish problem will once for all have been closed" — *The Commonwealth of Nations* (London, 1916), 295,518.

[14]R. H. Brand, ed., *Letters of John Dove* (London, 1938), 321.

[15]"The Financial and Economic Future" in *The Round Table* (December 1918), IX, 114-134. The quotation is from pages 121-123.

[16]*The Commonwealth of Nations* (London, 1916), 8. This emphasis on duty to the community is to be found throughout the Milner Group. See, for example, Lord Grey's violent retort to a Canadian (who tried to belittle A. J. Glazebrook because he made no real effort to accumulate wealth) in *The Round Table* obituary of Glazebrook (March 1941 issue). The same idea was advocated by Hichens and Milner to settle the problems of management and labor within the industrial system. In a speech at Swanwick in 1919, the former said: "The industrial problem is primarily a moral one. . . . If we have rights, we also have duties. . . . In the industrial world our duty clearly is to regard our work as the Service which we render to the rest of the community, and it is obvious that we should give, not grudgingly or of necessity but in full measure" (*The Round Table*, December 1940, XXXI, 11). Milner's views are in *Questions of the Hour* (London, 1923).

[17]In the August 1911 issue of *The Round Table* the future Lord Lothian wrote: "There are at present two codes of international morality—the British or Anglo-Saxon and the continental or German. Both cannot prevail. If the British Empire is not strong enough to be a real influence for fair dealing between nations, the reactionary standards of the German bureaucracy will triumph, and it will then only be a question of time before the British Empire itself is victimized by an international 'hold-up' on the lines of the Agadir incident. Unless the British peoples are strong enough to make it impossible for backward rivals to attack them with any prospect of success, they will have to accept the political standards of the aggressive military powers" (*The Round Table*, August 1911, I, 422-423). What a disaster for the world that Lord Lothian, in March 1936, was not able to take to heart his own words written twenty-five years earlier!

[18]As a matter of fact, one American Rhodes Scholar was a Negro; the experiment was not a success, not because of any objections by the English, but because of the objections of other American Rhodes Scholars.

[19]L. Curtis, *Dyarchy* (Oxford, 1920), liii-liv.

[20]*The Commonwealth of Nations* (London, 1916), 16, 24.

[21]*The Commonwealth of Nations* (London, 1916), 181. See also *The Problems of the Commonwealth* (London, 1915), 18-19.

[22]The quotations from Curtis will be found in *The Commonwealth of Nations* (London, 1916), 181 and 176; also *The Problem of the Commonwealth* (London, 1915), 18-19; the quotation from Dove is in a long letter to Brand, dated 9 September 1919, in *Letters of John Dove*, edited by R. H. Brand (London, 1938), 96-106; Philip Kerr's statement will be found in L. Curtis, *Dyarchy* (Oxford, 1920), 73. See also Kerr's speech at King's College in 1915, published in *The Empire and the Future* (London, 1916); he attacks jingo-imperialism, racial superiority, and national conceit as "Prussian heresy" and adds: "That the spirit of Prussia has brooded over this land is proved by the shortest examination of the history of Ireland." He then attacks the Little Englanders and economic or commercial imperialism, giving shocking examples of their effects on native lives and cultures. He concludes: "The one thing you cannot do, if you are a human being, is to do nothing. Civilization cannot stand on one side and see native tribes destroyed by so-called civilized looters and marauders, or as the result of the free introduction of firearms, drink, and other instruments of vice. He decides that Britain, by following a middle ground, has "created not an Empire but a Commonwealth" and defines the latter as a community activated by the spirit "Love thy neighbor as thyself." (*The Empire and the Future*, 70-86). George R. Parkin expresses similar ideas in the same volume on pp. 95-97. Kerr

had expressed somewhat similar sentiments in a speech before the Canadian Round Table in Toronto, 30 July 1912. This was published by Glazebrook as a pamphlet (Toronto, 1917).

²³The quotations from A. L. Smith are from *The Empire and the Future* (London, 1916), 29-30.

Chapter 8

¹The success of the Group in getting the foreign policy they wanted under a Liberal government may be explained by the pressure from without through *The Times* and the assistance from within through Asquith, Grey, and Haldane, and through the less obvious but no less important work of persons like Sir Eyre Crowe and above all Lord Esher.

²During this period Lord Esher played a vital but still mysterious role in the government. He was a strong supporter of Milner and his Group and was an influential adviser of Lloyd George. On 12 November 1917, he had a long walk with his protege, Hankey, in Paris and "urged the vital importance of sending Milner as Ambassador, Minister-Plenipotentiary, call him what you will. Henry Wilson cannot stand alone." Later the same day he spoke to Lloyd George: "I urged most strongly that he should send Milner here, on the ground that he would give stability where there is none and that his presence would ensure Henry Wilson getting 'information.' This I urged specially in view of the future as of the present. Otherwise we might one day find the Italian position reproduced in France. He finds Milner almost indispensable, but he will seriously think of the proposal." Milner was sent to Paris, as Esher wished, four months later. On 2 February 1918, Esher had another conversation, in which Lloyd George spoke of putting Milner in Derby's place at the War Office. The change was made two months later. (*Journals and Letters of Reginald, Viscount Esher* [4 vols., London, 1938], 158-159 and 178.)

³Zimmern was unquestionably one of the better minds in the Milner Group, and his ideas were frequently closer to Milner's than those of others of the inner circle. Although Zimmern agreed with the others in 1919 about the severity of the treaty, his reasons were quite different and do credit to both his integrity and his intelligence. He objected to the severity of the treaty because it was a breach of the pre-armistice commitments to the Germans; at the same time he wanted a continuation of the alliance that had won the war and a strong League of Nations, because he had no illusions about converting the Germans to peaceful ways in the near future. The inner circle of the Milner Group were against a severe treaty or a strong League or an alliance with France because they believed that Germany could be converted to the British way of thinking and acting and because they wanted to rebuild Germany as a weapon in a balance-of-power system against "Russian bolshevism" and "French militarism." Part II of *Europe in Convalescence* (New York, 1922) remains to this day the most brilliant summary available on what went wrong in 1919.

Chapter 9

¹ In June 1908, in a speech to the Royal Colonial Institute, Milner said: "Anything like imperial federation — the effective union of the self-governing

states—is not, indeed, as some think, a dream, but is certainly at present little more than an aspiration" (Milner, *The Nation and the Empire* [Boston, 1913], 293). In 1891 Sir Charles Tupper said: "Most people have come to the conclusion stated by Lord Rosebery at the Mansion House, that a Parliamentary Federation, if practicable, is so remote that during the coming century it is not likely to make any very great advance." In 1899, Rosebery said: "Imperial Federation in any form is an impossible dream." See H. D. Hall, *The British Commonwealth of Nations* (London, 1920), 70-71. In October 1905, Joseph Chamberlain said: "You cannot approach closer union by that means." Philip Kerr in 1911 spoke of federation as "the ill-considered proposals of the Imperial Federation League" (*The Round Table*, August 1911, I, 374). By this last date, only Lionel Curtis, of the Milner Group, had much faith in the possibility of federation. This is why his name alone was affixed, as editor, to the two volumes published by the Group in 1916.

² On the secret group of 1903-1905, see H. D. Hall, *The British Commonwealth of Nations* (London, 1920). The group was clearly made up of members of the Cecil Bloc and Milner Group. On its report, see the *Proceedings* of the Royal Colonial Institute for 1905, appendix; W. B. Worsfold, *The Empire on the Anvil* (London, 1916); and R. Jebb, *The Imperial Conference* (London, 1911), Vol. II. Lyttleton's dispatch is Cond. 2785 of 1905. Kerr's remark is in *The Round Table* (August 1911), I, 410.

³ This opinion of the important role played by Milner in the period 1916-1921 undoubtedly originated from Geoffrey Dawson, but it was shared by all the members of the Kindergarten. It is stated in different words by Basil Williams in *The Dictionary of National Biography* and by John Buchan in his autobiography, *Pilgrim's Way* (Boston, 1940).

⁴ On the reaction to the speeches of Smuts and Halifax, see J. G. Allen, *Editorial Opinion in the Contemporary British Commonwealth and Empire* (Boulder, Colorado, 1946).

⁵ On this whole section, see "George Louis Beer" in *The Round Table* (September 1920), X, 933-935; G. L. Beer, *African Questions at the Peace Conference* (New York, 1923), 424-425; H. D. Hall, *Mandates, Dependencies, and Trusteeship* (Washington, 1948); U.S. State Department, *Foreign Relations of the United States. Paris Peace Conference 1919*, VI, 727-729. That Kerr wrote Article 22 is revealed in H. V. Temperley, *History of the Peace Conference*, VI, 501. That Curtis wrote "Windows of Freedom" and showed it to Smuts before he wrote his memorandum was revealed by Curtis in a private communication to Professor Quincy Wright, according to Q. Wright, *Mandates under the League of Nations* (Chicago, 1930), 22-23, note 53a.

⁶ W. K. Hancock, *Survey of British Commonwealth Affairs* (3 vols., London, 1940-1942), I, 125.

⁷ S. G. Millen, *General Smuts* (2 vols., London, 1936), II, 321.

Chapter 10

¹ Robert Jemmett Stopford (1895-) was a banker in London from 1921 to 1928. He was private secretary to the chairman of the Simon Commission in 1928-1930, a member of the "Standstill Committee" on German Foreign Debts, a member of the Runciman Commission to Czechoslovakia in 1938, Liaison Officer for Refugees with the Czechoslovakian government in 1938-1939, Financial Counsellor at the British Embassy in Washington in 1943-1945.

Chapter 11

[1]See *Journals and Letters of Reginald, Viscount Esher* (4 vols., London, 1938), II, 56, and III, 8.

[2]According to David Ogg, *Herbert Fisher, 1865-1940* (London, 1947), 96, Fisher, "helped Mr. Montagu in drafting the Montagu-Chelmsford Report."

[3]This memorandum was published, with Lord Halifax's permission, in A. C. Johnson, *Viscount Halifax* (New York, 1941).

Chapter 12

[1] See the minutes of the Council of Four, as recorded by Sir Maurice Hankey, in U.S. Department of State, *Papers Relating to the Foreign Relations of the United States. The Paris Peace Conference*, (Washington, D.C., 1946), VI, 138-160.

[2] In *Europe in Convalescence* (New York, 1922), Alfred Zimmern wrote of October 1918 as follows: "Europe, 'from the Rhine to the Volga' to quote from a memorandum written at the time, was in solution. It was not a question now of autocratic against popular government; it was a question of government against anarchy. From one moment to the next every responsible student of public affairs, outside the ranks of the professional revolutionaries, however red his previous affiliations may have been, was turned perforce into a Conservative. The one urgent question was to get Europe back to work" (80).

In *The Round Table* for December 1918 (91-92) a writer (probably Curtis) stated: "Modern civilization is at grips with two great dangers, the danger of organized militarism . . . and the more insidious, because more pervasive danger of anarchy and class conflict. . . . As militarism breeds anarchy, so anarchy in its turn breeds militarism. Both are antagonistic to civilization."

In *The Round Table* for June 1919, Brand wrote: "It is out of any surplus on her foreign balance of trade that Germany can alone — apart from any immediately available assets — pay an indemnity. Why should Germany be able to do the miracle that France and Italy cannot do, and not only balance her trade, but have great surpluses in addition to pay over to her enemies? . . . If, as soon as peace is declared, Germany is given assistance and credit, she can pay us something, and should pay all she can. But what she can pay in the next five years must be, we repeat, limited. If, on the other hand, we take away from her all her liquid assets, and all her working capital, if furthermore, she is bound in future to make yearly payments to an amount which will in any reasonable human expectation exceed her capacity, then no one outside of a lunatic asylum will lend her money or credit, and she will not recover sufficiently to pay anything" — *War and National Finance* (London, 1921), 193.

[3] The attitude of the Group toward "French militarism" can be found in many places. Among others, see Smuts's speech of October 1923, quoted below. This attitude was not shared by Professor Zimmern, whose understanding of Europe in general and of France in particular was much more profound than that of other members of the Group. In *Europe in Convalescence* (158-161) he wrote: "A declaration of British readiness to sign the Guarantee Treaty would be the best possible answer to French, and it may be added also to Belgian, fears. . . . He little knows either the French peasant or the French townsman who thinks that aggression, whether open or concealed, against Germany need

ever be feared from their country. . . . France feels that the same willfully un-comprehending British policy, the same aggravatingly self-righteous professions of rectitude, pursue her in the East, from Danzig to Upper Silesia, as on the Western frontier of her hereditary foe; and in her nervous exasperation she puts herself ever more in the wrong with her impeccably cool-headed neighbor."

The Group's attitude toward Bolshevism was clearly stated is an article in *The Round Table* for March 1919: "Bolshevism is a tyranny — a revolutionary tyr-anny if you will — which is the complete abnegation of democracy and of all freedom of thought and action. Based on force and terroristic violence, it is simply following out the same philosophy which was preached by Nietzsche and Haeckel, and which for the past twenty-five years has glorified the might of force as the final justification of all existence. . . . In its present form Bolshevism must either spread or die. It certainly cannot remain stationary. And at the present moment, it stands as a very real menace to the peace of Europe and to any successful establishment of a League of Nations. *This is the real problem which the Allied delegates in Paris have now to face.*" (The italics are mine.)

⁴ The German emissary, whose name Smuts does not mention, was Walter de Haas, Ministerialdirektor in the Foreign Ministry in Berlin.

⁵ When the Labour government was in power in 1924 and the Dawes settle-ment of reparations was an accomplished fact, Stresemann was so afraid that D'Abernon would be replaced as British Ambassador in Berlin that he wrote a letter to Lord Parmoor (father of Stafford Cripps, Lord President in the Labour Cabinet, and delegate at the time to the League of Nations), asking that D'Aber-non be continued in his post as Ambassador. This letter, dated 16 September 1924, was answered by Lord Parmoor on 18 September from Geneva. He said, in part: "I think that in the first instance Lord D'Abernon was persuaded to go to Berlin especially in relation to financial and economic difficulties, but perhaps he may be persuaded to stay on, and finish the good work he has begun. In any case your letter is sure to be fully considered by our Foreign Minister, who is also our Prime Minister." See E. Sutton, *Gustav Stresemann: His Diaries, Letters, and Papers* (New York, 1935), I, 451-454.

⁶ This paragraph is largely based on J. H. Morgan, *Assize of Arms* (London, 1945), especially 199, 42, and 268. It is worthy of note that H. A. L. Fisher con-sulted with both Lord D'Abernon and General Morgan on his visit to Germany in 1923 and came away accepting the ideas of the former. Furthermore, when Gilbert Murray went to Geneva in 1924 as League delegate from South Africa, Fisher wrote him instructions to this effect. See D. Ogg, *Herbert Fisher* (Lon-don, 1947), 115-117.

⁷ On this organization, see Institute of Politics, Williams College, *The In-stitute of Politics at Williamstown: Its First Decade* (Williamstown, Mass., 1931).

⁸ Viscount Cecil of Chelwood, *The Great Experiment* (London, 1941), 166. The quotations from Lord Esher's *Journals and Letters* (4 vols., London, 1938) are in Vol. IV, 227, 250, and 272.

⁹ Viscount Cecil of Chelwood, *The Great Experiment* (London, 1941), 250.

¹⁰ The whole memorandum and other valuable documents of this period will be found in USSR, Ministry of Foreign Affairs, *Documents and Materials Relating to the Eve of the Second World War* (5 vols., 1948-1949), Vol. I, *November 1937-1938. From the Archives of the German Ministry of Foreign Af-fairs*, 13-45. The authenticity of these documents was challenged by an "un-named spokesman" for the British Foreign Office when they were first issued, but I am informed by the highest American authority on the captured German

documents that the ones published by the Russians are completely authentic.

[11] Keith Feiling, *Life of Neville Chamberlain* (London, 1941), 333. The author is a Fellow of All Souls, close to the Milner Group, and wrote his book on the basis of the late Prime Minister's papers, which were made available by the family.

[12] See Lionel Curtis, *Civitas Dei; The Commonwealth of God* (London, 1938), 914-930.

[13] Robert J. Stopford, a close associate of the Milner Group whom we have already mentioned on several occasions, went to Czechoslovakia with Runciman as a technical adviser. See J. W. Wheeler-Bennett, *Munich: Prologue to Tragedy* (New York, 1948), 79, n.l.

[14] The reference to Professor Schumann is in J. W. Wheeler-Bennett, *Munich* (New York, 1948), 436, n.l. If Mr. Wheeler-Bennett had placed a little more credence in the "pre-Munich plot," many of the facts which he cannot explain would be easily fitted into the picture. Among them we might point out the mystifying (to Mr. Wheeler-Bennett) fact that Lord Runciman's report of 16 September went further than either Hitler or Henlein in demanding sacrifices from the Czechs (see *Munich*, p. 112). Or again he would not have had to make such an about-face as that between page 96 and page 97 of the book. On page 96, *The Times*'s demand of 7 September was similar to the views of Mr. Chamberlain, as expressed at Lady Astor's on 10 May, and "Geoffrey Dawson was a personal friend of Lord Halifax." But on page 97, "The thoughtless irresponsibility of *The Times* did not voice at that moment the views of His Majesty's Government. If Mr. Wheeler-Bennett had added to his picture a few additional facts, such as a more accurate version of German rearmaments, Runciman's letter of 2 September to Hitler, etc., he would have found it even more difficult to make his picture of Munich stand up.

[15] *Count Helmuth James von Moltke, a German of the Resistance* (Johannesburg, 1947). See also Allen W. Dulles, *Germany's Underground (New York,* 1947), 85-90. The additional letter added to the Johannesburg publication was written by von Moltke to his wife just before his death. Curtis's name is mentioned in it.

[16] On this whole movement, see Hans Rothfels, *The German Opposition to Hitler* (Hinsdale, Illinois, 1948), and F. L. Ford, "The Twentieth of July in the History of the German Resistance" in The *American Historical Review* (July 1946), LI, 609-626. On Kordt's message to Lord Halifax, see Rothfels, 58-63.

[17] A. C. Johnson, *Viscount Halifax* (New York, 1941), 531.

[18] USSR Ministry of Foreign Affairs, *Documents and Materials Relating to the Eve of the Second World War. II Dirksen Papers (1938-1939)* (Moscow, 1948), 126-131.

[19] *British Blue Book*, Cmd. 6106.

[20] All documents on these negotiations will be found in a Swedish Foreign Ministry White Paper, *Forspelet till det tyska angreppet pa Danmark och Norge den 9 April 1940* (Stockholm 1947).

Chapter 13

[1] On the Ministry of Information during the war, see Great Britain, Central Office of Information, *First Annual Report, 1947-1948*. This is Cmd. 7567.

[2] This extract is printed in the *Report of the Council of the Royal Institute of International Affairs* for 1938-1939.

[3] The last important public act of the Milner Group was the drawing of the Italo-Yugoslav boundary in 1946. The British Delegate on the Boundary Commission was C. H. Waldock, now a Chichele Professor and Fellow of All Souls, assisted by R. J. Stopford.

Index